MUSLIM IDENTITY, PRINT CULTURE AND THE DRAVIDIAN FACTOR IN TAMIL NADU

Muslim Identity, Print Culture and the Dravidian Factor in Tamil Nadu

J.B.P. MORE

Orient Longman

ORIENT LONGMAN PRIVATE LIMITED

Registered Office
3-6-752 Himayatnagar, Hyderabad 500 029 (A.P.), India
e-mail: hyd2_orlongco@sancharnet.in

Other Offices
Bangalore, Bhopal, Bhubaneshwar, Chennai, Ernakulam, Guwahati, Hyderabad, Jaipur, Kolkata, Lucknow, Mumbai, New Delhi, Patna

First Published 2004

ISBN 81 250 2632 0

Typeset by
Scribe Consultants
New Delhi

Printed in India at
Baba Barkha Nath Printers
New Delhi

Published by
Orient Longman Private Limited
1/24 Asaf Ali Road
New Delhi 110 002
e-mail: olldel@del6.vsnl.net.in

Contents

Acknowledgements

I dedicate this book to the memory of the late Professor Denys Lombard, Director of the Ecole Française d'Extrême Orient, Paris. He was always a great source of encouragement and reposed full confidence in me to undertake this work. He even went to the extent of arranging some modest financial assistance through the Ecole Française d'Extrême Orient, which helped me to some extent to complete this project in France against all odds. It is really unfortunate that he is no more to see this work published.

Professor Francis Robinson, Vice Principal of Royal Holloway and Bedford College, University of London, and President of the Royal Asiatic Society, England, was another great source of encouragement and inspiration. In fact, it was only after reading a copy of his paper titled, 'Technology and Religious Change: Islam and the Impact of Print', which he was kind enough to send me a few years ago, did the idea of writing this book take root.

My special thanks to Professor K.S. Mathew, former Head of the Department of History, Pondicherry University, Dr Sankaralingam, Director, Rosa Muthiah Research Library, Chennai, Dr B. Ram of the Indian Council of Historical Research, Delhi, Dr M.S.S. Pandian of the Madras Institute of Development Studies, Mrs Nalini Prasad, India Office Library, London, late Dr Françoise l'Hernault, Director, Ecole Française d'Extrême Orient, Pondicherry, Dr F. Grimal of the Institut d'Indologie, Pondicherry, Mrs Mohammad, INALCO Library, Paris the late Janab K.M. Sherrif, Tamil Muslim poet, the late Professor Muhammad Yusuf Kokan of Chennai, Janab Syed Mohammad 'Hasan', Chennai, Janab Saluddin, the Kazi of Chennai, Captain Ameer Ali of Ramnad, Professor S.M.M. Mohamadali, Chennai, and Janab Jainulabidin of Kottakuppam, who were extremely helpful in locating material and tendering advice and encouragement. I also thank the staff of the various libraries, archives, and institutions in France, India, and Britain for their help in the preparation of this book.

This work would not have materialised without the patience and cooperation of my wife, Leena, who is also my worst critic, in all respects. My special thanks is also due to Dr Nandini Rao, Orient Longman Pvt. Ltd., for her abiding interest in the publication of this work.

I have paid a good deal of attention to writing this book in the most unbiased and unprejudiced manner. It is for the reader to judge if I have succeeded in this venture or not.

J.B.P. MORE

Abbreviations

AIML	All India Muslim League
ANIL	Al Nasruthul Islam Library
BNP	Bibliothèque Nationale de Paris
DK	Dravida Kazhagam
DMK	Dravida Munnetra Kazhagam
EFEO	Ecole Française d'Extrême Orient
FR	Fortnightly Reports
GO	Government Order
INALCO	Institut National de Langues et Civilisations Orientales
IOL	Indian Office Library
MP	Madras Publications (Catalogue)
MSB	Madras State Bibliography
NMML	Nehru Memorial Museum Library
NNPR	Native Newspaper Reports
RMRL	Rosa Muthiah Research Library
TNA	Tamil Nadu Archives

Introduction

Scholars claim that there are different ways and methods of understanding the realities of any particular society. Anthropologists, ethnologists, and sociologists all attempt to study and understand societies, in accordance with their respective academic and social backgrounds. But a complete understanding of any given society or community is impossible without taking its historical background into consideration. It is here that the historian's role in unravelling the realities of a society or community becomes indispensable. This is an arduous task which requires great care, attention, and honesty. Besides, it requires an approach which is unbiased and unprejudiced. Thus the task of a historian is one of great responsibility. The writing of this book has been motivated by such a sense of responsibility.

Man and society are not only the products of evolution, but also of thousands of years of conditioning on the economic, social, environmental, cultural, and religious planes. Hence the study of any given man, society, or community is the study of their evolution and conditioning and are the central concerns of sociology and anthropology. The degree and ways of evolution and conditioning may vary, but the process is the same whether it is among the pygmies of Africa or among the societies of western Europe or East Asia.

This historical fact, which is as irrefutable as Newton's law of gravity, has to be fully understood and accepted. This will guard us from the fallacy of thinking that in the course of the present study we are going to touch upon some new hitherto unknown human reality peculiar to the Tamil Muslims, which lies outside the framework of the twin processes of evolution and conditioning.

Therefore, my intention, in the course of the following pages, is to delve into the understanding of the Tamil Muslim realities and society, within the framework of their historical evolution and conditionings, with a special emphasis on the nineteenth and the first two decades of the twentieth centuries. As my study focusses on the period before 1920, it could not rely upon only oral evidence of some Tamil Muslims to understand the various facets of Tamil Muslim society. Consequently, I have had to rely more on written records and other material.

The earliest written records available about the Tamil Muslims are the accounts left by travellers and adventurers such as Marco Polo, Abdullah Wassaf, Duarte Barbosa, and Vasco da Gama. There also exist references to Arabs and Muslims in Tamil literature. It appears that from the seventeenth and eighteenth centuries onwards the Tamil-speaking Muslims themselves had begun to produce their own literature. This literature can be classified as the Tamil Muslim literature or the Islamic Tamil literature.

The thoughts and feelings of anyone or any community are best expressed in the mother tongue, therefore, the literature produced in Tamil by the Tamil Muslims, apart from the accounts left by travellers and colonisers is a vital means to understand them as a community. The anthropologist or sociologist who does not take into account this historical dimension can only portray a truncated view of the community or society of his study.

The understanding of the Tamil Muslims as a community, will be based on a survey of the entire gamut of printed or lithographed books, booklets, pamphlets, and tracts of Tamil Muslim authorship published up to 1920. The findings of the survey will help determine the identity of the Muslims. The survey itself will consist of two distinct parts viz., the literary works produced by the Tamil Muslims before 1835 and the works produced after 1835, when printing became popular. But, before focussing on the survey, it is important to have first an idea of the origin of the Tamil Muslims. Therefore, the first part of this book is devoted to determining this origin, and in this context it surveys Tamil Muslim literature later in the book.

A good number of the Tamil Muslim works, printed or lithographed in Tamil or Arabic characters or sometimes in both, are found in the India Office Library, London. Many of the works found here appear to be well preserved and are in good condition, though some others are in very bad shape and decaying, for want of funds to restore them, and some are either missing entirely from the racks or have been misplaced. But, on the whole the India Office Library collection of Tamil Muslim books remains, to this day, one of the greatest, if not the greatest single collection of Tamil Muslim works in the world. Many of these books have been enumerated in two catalogues, one published in 1909 and the other in 1931.[1]

Some Tamil Muslim works of this period are also found in the recently established Rosa Muthiah Research Library of Madras, the Al Nusrathul Islam Library, Tamilnadu, in the Ecole Française d'Extrême Orient of Paris and Pondicherry and the Institut National de Langues et Civilisations Orientales, of Paris.

In the Appendix, I have reproduced a catalogue of not only those Tamil Muslim works that can be located in Britain, or France, or in India, but also of some of those books that I have not been able to locate. The latter may still exist in the hands of some private collectors in Tamil Nadu or may have ceased to exist at all.

Most of such works have been listed in the Quarterly List of Publications of the Madras Presidency, from 1867. But even these quarterly lists are not complete, because all the Tamil Muslim books published during this period were invariably not registered. The Quarterly List of Publications contains only those books which were brought in for registration. But there were many other books which were never registered and therefore never appeared in the Quarterly List of Publications. As a result the exact number of unregistered Tamil Muslim publications can never be known. Nevertheless, it is my opinion that the holdings of the various libraries cited above and the Quarterly List of Publications of the Madras Presidency should have the bulk or the great majority of the Tamil Muslim works and publications. As for the Tamil Muslim publications before 1867, John Murdoch's *Classified Catalogue of Tamil Printed Books with Introductory Notes* is an important source.[2] It should also be noted that many of the original publications have been re-edited and published several times.

Apart from these, there are some other sources, in both English and Tamil, which contain additional material regarding Tamil Muslim publications. The *Madras State Bibliography*, published by the Madras government is one such source in English, which I have utilised to a certain extent.

I have not made use of the catalogue and lists of Tamil Muslim works published in Tamil, mainly because they are sketchy and incomplete. Some of them are: *Islamiya Tamizh Nul Attavanai*, published in 1978, *Islamiya Tamizh Ilakiyyangal*, published in 1990, *Meygnana Sindu*, published also in 1990. In these publications, the reader may find references to some other printed material, which have not been included in the survey and study. Most of these works are of a religious nature. But, the studies on Tamil Muslim literary works by Tamil Muslim scholars such as R.P.M. Kani, M.M. Uvais of Ceylon, J.M. Saali, and M. Mustafa, as listed in the bibliography have been used to the extent that they throw light on the rational understanding of Tamil Muslim literature and society.

At this juncture, I would like to draw the attention of the reader to the fact that the foremost objective while surveying Tamil Muslim literature was as much to enumerate nearly every book or pamphlet of Tamil Muslim origin up to 1920, as to portray their historical evolution through their own literature. For this purpose, I have prepared a list of Tamil Muslim printed works up to 1920 (see Appendix) and divided it subject-wise and year-wise into ten distinct sections. A simple perusal of these sections will throw enough light on the Tamil Muslims' predominant literary penchants. The Appendix in itself is highly self-revealing and portrays the mind-set of the Tamil Muslims during the period under study, in the most convincing and reasonable manner.

This survey and study, based on various sources, attempts to unravel, understand, and interpret the preoccupations and concerns, the hopes and longings, the worries and joys, the religious leanings and the changes therein, and, above all, the frame of mind and psychological disposition of the Tamil Muslims. In short, it is an attempt to determine the identity of the Tamil Muslims, who happened to live in a predominantly Hindu society.

Generally, the great Muslim scholars of northern India and Pakistan such as M. Mujeeb, Ahmad Aziz, Mushirul Hasan, and I.H. Qureshi, in their studies of the Muslims of India have either paid scant attention to the Dravidian-language-speaking Muslims of south India, especially Tamil Nadu, or have marginalised them to a great extent. This is probably because these groups are located outside the sphere of the Persianised Urdu culture and history. But, the fact is that these Muslims exist, and even constitute a majority among the Muslims in south India. Hence, it becomes necessary to study them more closely and to give due recognition to their existence.

The French sociologist Louis Dumont, in his *Homo Hierarchicus* had devoted just about seven pages to the sociological understanding of all the Muslims of India.[3] He hardly refers to the Tamil-speaking Muslim groups of the south, viz., the Marakkayars, the Lebbais and the Rawthers, in spite of having done a lot of fieldwork and research in Tamil Nadu. On the basis of some very limited information on the Muslims of the United Provinces, he tends to make far-flung generalisations about the Muslims of India, regarding them as a homogeneous lot He asserts without any justification that the 'psychological dispositions' of 'each' Muslim has something of the Hindu in him. Further, he suggests that non-Islamic Hindu values underly

Islamic values.[4] One is at a loss to understand how Louis Dumont locates the non-Islamic values under the Islamic values.

Many scholars in India and abroad, were influenced by Dumont either because they had nothing original to contribute, or because they found Dumont's position reasonable, or because Dumont provided an easy solution to the understanding of Indian Muslims, which could be adapted to their particular research without much difficulty. Further, some scholars, tend to write voluminous books and sometimes incomprehensible essays full of sociological and anthropological jargon and wild generalisations without an adequate working knowledge of Indian languages and the literature in the Indian languages, on grounds of their being irrelevant to understanding the realities of Indian society.[5] They tend to rely heavily on local informers and translators who are liable to misinform and mislead the scholar.

For instance, on the basis of some stray ethnographic research on some 6,656 Muslim bangle-makers of Nepal, one scholar concluded in a sweeping generalisation that Hinduism remains the substratum of most of the life-cycle ceremonies of all the converted Muslims of the whole of northern India.[6]

This book does not adopt such a slapdash attitude; rather, it relies largely on the literature produced by the Tamil Muslims themselves, who are also the object of its study. It is with this intention that I have compiled a list of Tamil Muslim printed works, as one may find in the Appendix, and classified them subject-wise in order to ascertain the various interests and characteristics of the Muslims.

Apart from relying on the accounts left by travellers, adventurers, etc., the best way to study the past of any community, as done in this book, is to rely on the literature produced by the members of that community during the period of study. It is on this ground that I examine the validity of the Dumontian assertions about the Muslims, among other things.

Recently, Imtiaz Ahmad, an Indian sociologist from Delhi, advanced a theory about the Muslims of India, which appears to be a variant of the Dumontian one. He asserted that the

Islamic traditions and the indigenous custom-oriented traditions have blended to such an extent that they have become complementary and integral parts of a single, common religious system.[7] He further asserts that the intruding Islamic traditions might well have converted all the indigenous mores and religious traditions to that of Islam, but the latter were so well established and integrated in the life of the people that the attempt could only have been made at the cost of Islam itself.[8] Thus Imtiaz Ahmad attempted to attribute a certain permanency to Indian Muslim life at all levels and at all times.

In order to buttress this theory, he has edited and published three volumes in 1973, 1976, and 1981, which are a collection of essays by different authors on various issues such as social stratification, marriage, and ritual and religion among Muslims in India.[9] This seems to have raised more controversies than it has solved. A closer scrutiny of these volumes would reveal a certain necessity on the part of Muslim intellectuals like Imtiaz Ahmad and those who think like him the world over, to establish that Muslims have a lot of the 'Hindu' in them and that they therefore belong to the Indian or Hindu world and not the breakaway Pakistani or Islamic world.

The historian and Islamicist, Francis Robinson, of the University of London, questioned the validity of Imtiaz Ahmad's views and attributed political motives to them.[10] He vehemently denounced the intellectual background of Ahmad and scholars like Mushirul Hasan.[11]

On the whole according to Francis Robinson, Islam has an identity of its own which should not be mixed or clubbed with that of the Hindu religious systems and traditions. Further, to him any Hindu or syncretic element found among Muslims in India is just a passing phase which will be eventually eliminated by Islam's reformist zeal. Robinson actually maintains:

> We should not be deceived by the fact that in many societies non-Islamic practices have acquired the force of law in Muslim minds. This is often a matter of imperfect knowledge or temporary expedient, although temporary in this sense may

well be several hundred years. Nevertheless, such is the desire to follow the true path, a desire noted by many anthropologists, that, as knowledge of the law had grown more widespread, its provisions have tended to oust false practice. Ideally, then the law stands above society as a pattern of perfection, a standard which all should strive to reach.[12]

Such views were more or less in line with those expressed earlier by the American anthropologist, Clifford Geertz. Actually Robinson dismisses Imtiaz Ahmad's approach to the understanding of Muslims in India as a 'snap shot technique' and prefers a longer view with a historical dimension, in the manner of Geertz.[13]

Both Robinson and Ahmad, have tended to formulate certain judgements about the Muslims of India on the basis of their own experiences of the past or present or both. They have their respective supporters and detractors. Thus, it becomes necessary to ascertain the relevance of the Robinson-Ahmad debate as far as Tamil Muslims are concerned. For this purpose I will take the historical dimension into consideration without at the same time losing sight of the other relevant factors and approaches.

The survey of Tamil Muslim literature and the compilation of a list of printed works by Tamil Muslims would not have been possible in the first place, if the British colonial rulers had not allowed their Indian subjects to take to printing, a modern western technology, in 1835. Though Tamil Muslims as such constituted only about three per cent of the total population of the Tamil country in the nineteenth century, the adoption of print technology by the Tamils in general and the Tamil Muslims in particular had set in motion a sort of revolution in Tamil Muslim literature. Tamil Muslim works produced before the nineteenth century were put to print during the nineteenth and twentieth centuries. Besides, a galaxy of new Tamil Muslim authors, who produced hundreds of works ranging from books to pamphlets and tracts, appeared in the Tamil Muslim literary horizon during this period. All this seems to have been made possible, to a great extent, by the adoption of print technology.

The processes of conditioning, mentioned earlier, vary. They may be natural or artificial, rational or irrational, man-made or revealed, spiritual or material, social or economic, and so on. In fact, these are the factors of conditioning of man and society as such. Just as nature, as in the climatic conditions, influences man and society, so do man-made material objects. This is irrefutable. Though man invented gun powder, yet in its interaction with man the gun powder by itself had set in motion a great revolution in the military and political fields, which, as we know, had and still has enormous implications for the entire society. Gun powder as a technological object has its own dynamics and exerts its own influence on man and society. It conditions them profoundly in various ways, though man may think that he controls it, since it is he who invented it.

Similarly print technology, an invention of man, has its own dynamics and exerts its own influence on society. Thus, in this book, I also address myself to the task of assessing the dynamics of print technology, the reasons for its late adoption by the Tamil Muslims, the extent of its influence in its relationship with Tamil Muslims, and its role as a conditioning factor of man and society. I shall also examine whether print contributed to a change in the identity of Tamil Muslims or whether it simply consolidated their already existing identity. This will constitute the later part of the book.

In this regard, especially while assessing the identity of the Muslims of Tamil Nadu, it is important not to be committed to any idea or ideology. If our minds are committed to or clouded and weighed down by such ideas, we may not be able to clearly assess the identity of the Muslims or the influence of print over them. This is because we will be trying, consciously or unconsciously, to adapt what we observe about the Muslims to our particular ideological commitments or leanings. This is but natural. There is always the risk that sociologists, anthropologists, and even historians may unwittingly fall into this trap.

Take, for instance, a scholar who is committed fully to the ideology of secularism. When such a scholar undertakes a study of the Muslims, Christians, or Hindus of India, there is a great possibility that he may take a position that does not run counter to his ideological commitment. He may avoid an examination of any view that challenges his ideological commitment or intellectual background. He cannot, for example, say that Hindus and Muslims are fundamentally different. Instead, there is a greater possibility that he will argue that Hindus and Muslims are not very different culturally, socially, and even psychologically since the latter assertion will naturally suit his particular ideological commitment. He will always try to sweep the differences under the carpet, consciously or unconsciously, like the politicians committed to secularism have always done. But that has not prevented the birth of Pakistan and further separatist demands on the basis of religion. He may also invent ingenious arguments and draw upon various witnesses to buttress his position. But the credibility of the witnesses needs to be established and they need to be cross-examined.

Similarly a religiously inclined scholar, committed to a particular religion, will invariably hold his religion above anything else and assert that Muslims and Hindus have no common identity. So, it becomes absolutely necessary for a scholar working on the Muslims of India to be fully conscious of his intellectual and ideological background and commitments and the limitations imposed by them on his views, so that they do not cloud his vision. In this work I intend to adopt such an approach, which is not burdened by any sort of prior commitment.

There may be other reasons, primarily political, for Muslim scholars to adopt the position of Imtiaz Ahmad. His approach might have been adopted as a strategy for survival in an overwhelmingly Hindu society. Though it is difficult to identify such scholars, they do exist. Such persons are more visible in the field of politics than in that of academics. Besides, many Hindu intellectuals too might toe the line of Imtiaz Ahmad's, because it may appear to them, from the social and political point of view, that it is better to affirm the Hindu influence over Muslims which makes them belong to the Indian or Hindu world, than to hold that the Muslims are fundamentally different from the Hindus and do not belong to the Indian world but to the Islamic world. Such intellectuals, too, are equally difficult to identify, but they do exist.

We also have the situation, as in the Kashmir Valley, where the Muslims are the overwhelming majority and the Hindu pandits are a negligible minority. Here too, the Hindu intellectuals such as T.N. Madan, have adopted more or less the line of Imtiaz Ahmad.[14] It is politically better for them to affirm that Kashmiri Muslims have a lot of Hindu in them. A claim to the contrary would prove that the Muslims belong to the Pakistani Islamic world.

There is every possibility that Hindu intellectuals working on Kashmir society would have succumbed to such political considerations. Thus politics, as Francis Robinson had indirectly suggested regarding Imtiaz Ahmad, Mushirul Hasan, etc., has the potential to exert its influence on sociological and anthropological studies. In this book, I intend to avoid this eventuality at all costs and set aside all political or even geo-political considerations, which are liable to influence the study directly or indirectly.

But before proceeding further on the lines suggested above, it is absolutely necessary to delve into the origins of the Tamil Muslims and their literature. This will serve as a foundation on which the edifice of Tamil Muslim identity during the printing era will be built.

Notes

1. L.D. Barnett, G.U. Pope, *A Catalogue of the Tamil Books in the Library of the British Museum*, (London, 1909); L.D. Barnett, *A Supplementary Catalogue of the Tamil Books in the Library of the British Musueum*, (London, 1931).
2. John Murdoch, *Classified Catalogue of Tamil Printed Books with Introductory Notes*, (Madras, 1865).
3. Louis Dumont, *Homo Hierarchicus, The Caste System and its Implications*, complete revised edition, (Delhi, 1988), 205–211.

4. Ibid., 211.
5. See for eg., M.L. Reiniche, *Tirouvannamalai, Un Lieu Saint Sivaite du Sud de l'Inde*, 4, (Paris, 1989): 3–4, 196–197. Susan Bayly, Saints, *Goddesses and Kings: Muslims and Christians in South Indian Society, 1700–1900*, (Cambridge, 1989).
6. Marc Gaborieau, 'Life Cycle Ceremonies of Converted Muslims in Nepal and Northern India', in *Islam in Asia*, ed., Yohannan Friedman, 1 (Jerusalem, 1984): 241–262.
7. Imtiaz Ahmad, ed., *Ritual and Religion Among Muslims in India*, (New Delhi, 1981), 15.
8. Ibid.
9. Imtiaz Ahmad, *Family, Kinship and Marriage Among Muslims in India*, (New Delhi, 1976).

   —. *Caste and Social Stratification Among Muslims in India*, (New Delhi, 1978).

   —. *Ritual and Religion among Muslims in India*, (New Delhi, 1981).
10. Francis Robinson, 'Islam and Muslim Society in South Asia' in *Contributions to Indian Sociology*, (1983): 17, 2, 187.
11. Ibid.
12. Ibid., 190–91.
13. Ibid., 186, 190.
14. See for eg., T.N. Madan, 'The Social Construction of Cultural Identities in Rural Kashmir', in *Muslim Communities of South Asia: Culture, Society and Power*, ed., T.N. Madan, enlarged edition, (New Delhi, 1995), 241–287.

PART I

Tamil Muslim Origin and Literature

CHAPTER ONE

Who Were the Tamil Muslims

The Tamil Muslims belonged to the Tamil country of south-east India, which was made up of a great quadrant, a little over 129,500 square kilometres, lying between the sea and the Deccan plateau.[1] Geographically, Tamil Nadu was far removed from the north-western passes and the Gangetic plain. Its evolution, therefore, possessed certain special characteristics. Peninsular or south India in general and Tamil Nadu in particular had always had an independent political existence outside the sphere of the great northern empires of pre-Muslim India. This, though, did not prevent interaction between the north and the south in the intellectual, cultural, and religious fields.

As south India was situated along the maritime trade routes that connected Europe and West Asia with the Indian subcontinent and East Asia, it was but natural that from ancient times its focus was towards the ocean than to the landmass beyond the Vindhya mountains. As a result, ancient Tamil literature is replete with references to foreigners such as the Greeks, Romans, Egyptians, Arabs, and the Chinese. Further, we have accounts left by geographers such as Ptolemy, who appears to have resided in Alexandria during the first half of the second century A.D.

In his work on ancient India, Ptolemy had identified Kanyakumari (Cape Comorin) and the Gulf of Mannar as a centre of pearl fishery. He had also identified 'Korkai', the ancient Tamil port city to the east of Kanyakumari, as an emporium of pearl trade.[2] An Arabic work of the tenth century, *Adja'ib Al-Hind*, refers to a merchant from Alexandria known as Cosmas Indicopleustes, who sailed to south India in the sixth century A.D., before Egypt was Arabised or Islamised.[3]

It appears that Arabs were trading with China even before they were Islamised. South India, Ceylon, and south-east Asia were along their trade routes to China. These Arabs of the pre-Islamic era were probably known as Yavanas, though originally the Yavanas referred to the Greeks and Romans as well. But with the fall of the Roman Empire and the disappearance of Romans and Greeks from international maritime trade, the Arabs and probably also the Persians and Jews, who had fled their homes in West Asia, were frequently referred to as Yavanas. But Pierre Meile asserts that in medieval and modern Tamil, the Arabs or Muslims alone were referred to as Yavanas.[4]

The Islamic political-cum-religious revolution, based on the principle of equality, that swept across Arabia in the seventh century A.D. opened a new chapter in world history. Very soon, great parts of the world stretching from Spain to Arabia and from Arabia to China, Persia, and Sind in the Indian sub-continent, came under the revolutionary sway of Islam. Traders from not only Arabia, but also Egypt, Iraq, and Persia were fully Islamised. It is from this time onwards that Arab and Persian geographers, chroniclers, travellers, and historians became prominent and set their stamp on world intellectual history, a development which was to a large extent emulated by the Europeans a few centuries later.

Among the early Islamised Arab travellers and merchants who sailed to India was Sulaiman al Tajir. In the ninth century, he made several voyages from the Persian Gulf to the Malabar and Coromandel coasts. He referred to the general Indian aversion for wine.[5] But, it was Abu-Zeyed Al Hassan of Siraf, though he had never travelled to India, who modified and completed the work of Sulaiman in the first half of the tenth century, by gathering information from merchants and travellers who had been to India. He has left us a vivid account of certain social and political conditions of southern India and Ceylon. He notes that in the densely populated country called 'Al-Comary', which has been identified as Kanyakumari, the inhabitants went barefoot, abstained from licentiousness and from all sorts of wine, and that 'nothing indecent' was to be seen in this country. When Abu Zeyed uses the words 'nothing indecent', it is quite probable that he would have used it from the Islamic point of view. But, Abu Zeyed mentions the 'Devadasi' custom that was prevalent in the country, where some females were consecrated to the Gods. Such females were allowed to have amorous relationships with foreigners in exchange for money.[6]

Besides, Abu Zeyed notes the extreme licentiousness of the men and women of Ceylon, where even the king's daughter did not hesitate to flirt with a newly arrived Arab merchant, with the full knowledge of the king. On account of such sexual permissiveness, Arab merchants of integrity avoided sending their vessels to Ceylon, specially when there were young men on board.[7]

In the present state of this research, it cannot be ascertained whether such relationships, either with the women of Ceylon, which was not very far from the Tamil coast, or with the Devadasis of the Kanyakumari country resulted in off-spring of mixed Arab-Indian descent, though this is a strong possibility. But as neither Sulaiman nor Abu Zeyed refer to the presence of Muslim communities of mixed descent or otherwise in the Tamil country, it is better not to make any exaggerated assertions at this juncture.

The accounts of contemporaries of Abu Zeyed such as Ibn Khurdadba and the famous Arabian traveller and historian, Al Masudi, have nothing more to add to our knowledge of the Tamil country and the origin of Muslim communities there. But, Ibn Khurdadba points out that in the country of Kumar i.e., Kanyakumari, both fornication and wine-drinking were unlawful.[8]

During the second half of the tenth century, neither did the Persian writer, Al-Istakhri, nor the Baghdadian, Ibn Haukal, shed any light on the Muslims of the Coromandel coast. The great scholar, Abu Raihan Muhammad Ibn Ahmed Alberuni, born at Khwarizm (Khiva) in A.D. 973, came to India along with Mahmud of Ghazni. He too fails to give any detailed account of the Tamil country, but he does mention the pearl-banks of the bay of Ceylon, probably the Gulf of Mannar, and also Rameswaram.[9]

Neither does the ninth century Tamil classic *Tiruvasakam* by Manikkavasagar shed any light on the Muslim communities in the Tamil country. But it does mention the horse trade that was carried on in the Tamil country with the Arabs.[10] Also, the twelfth-century Tamil classic, *Periya Puranam* by the great poet Sekkilar, does not mention the presence of Muslims on the Coromandel coast. Nevertheless, we find ample references in it to ships and merchants, and references to the conservative nature of the then Tamil society.[11] This more or less, confirms the observations of Sulaiman al Tajir, Abu Zeyed and Ibn Khurdadba.

The Venetian traveller, Marco Polo, was in India in the second half of the thirteenth century. His accounts reveal that the most powerful sovereign of the Indian sub-continent of that period was Nasiruddin Mahmud, the Turkish Sultan of Delhi. He notes that though both Sind and Bengal acknowledged his supremacy, no part of south India was under his control. He even makes the significant remark that the hitherto independent kingdoms of southern India were as yet untouched by foreign conquest and the gold accumulated through the ages lay in their temples and treasuries, making them easy prey for the coming invader.[12]

Marco Polo describes the Tamil country (Maabar in Arabic), as a part of the Indian continent and as the finest and noblest in the world. He identifies Sundara Pandya as the principal ruler of Maabar, where pearl fishing and trade existed on an extensive scale.[13] He also identifies the port at Kayal, a great and noble city on the Ramnad coast, under the control of the fabulously wealthy eldest brother of Sundara Pandya. Ships from the Islamised countries of Hormuz, Kis, Dofar and Soer, Aden and the other Arabic countries touched Kayal, carrying merchandise and horses. Foreign merchants, mostly Arabs and Persians, were well received and treated with fairness by the ruler of Kayal.[14]

Horses were eagerly sought by the kings of the Tamil country. More than 10,000 horses seem to have been imported every year. But they did not survive for longer than a year for want of farriers, which the Arabs did not provide and also because they were not handled properly by the Tamils. Thus, the Arabs made enormous profits by selling horses to the Tamils, and the latter spent a great part of their wealth in buying them.[15]

What is notable in the preceding accounts is that though Marco Polo writes about the large numbers of foreign merchants trading at Kayal, he makes no mention of any Tamil-speaking Muslim merchants. Instead, Marco Polo points out that in the Tamil country, there was no killing of bird or beast or any life and for such animal food that they may eat, they delegated the task of butchering animals to the Saracens or 'others' who were not of their own religion.[16]

Saracens in this context could only mean the Muslims. As it seems implausible that the Arab and Persian Muslim merchants of the high seas were butchers for the Tamils, it would not be out of place to assume that during this period, there was a small community of local Muslims in the Ramnad coastal area. Besides, Marco Polo notes that the Saracens of the Tamil country, along with local Christians, used to go on pilgrimages to a little town in Maabar, probably Mylapore, where the body of Saint Thomas the Apostle, was laid to rest. These Saracens, in my opinion, could only be Tamil-speaking Muslim converts, or were of Arab-Tamil descent, who believed that Saint Thomas was a Muslim and a great prophet. Marco Polo notes that such Muslims also went on pilgrimages to Adam's Peak in Ceylon, in the belief that the footprint of Adam was preserved on the peak.[17]

Contrary to the somewhat conservative image of the Tamil

country portrayed by Sulaiman, Abu Zeyed, Ibn Khurdadba, and Sekkilar, Marco Polo assures us that the Pandya king, Sundara Pandya, had at least a thousand wives and concubines, and whenever he saw a beautiful woman, he wanted her for himself. Besides, his brother, who controlled the port city of Kayal, had more than three hundred wives. Marco Polo states that it was considered a great honour in Maabar to have the largest number of wives.[17]

Like Abu Zeyed in the tenth century, Marco Polo mentions the Devadasi custom. But what was most astonishing during this period was that no form or act of lechery or carnal sin was considered sinful by the Tamils. But, he does not fail to point out that a greater number of people abstained from drinking wine, which implied that all did not abstain from it.[18]

This would suggest that the Tamil society, at least the southern part of it, was not as conservative a society as was believed. The king and his vassals along with their numerous wives lived a lavish life. Arab and other merchants at Kayal were shown the greatest regard and their sojourns there were made very comfortable by the Pandya kings. The observations made by Marco Polo does not permit me to affirm that the Arab merchants at Kayal and other places on the coast did not contract any form of alliance, even temporary, with either local dancing girls or of the Devadasi type as Abu Zeyed had observed, or with other Tamil women who need not have been coastal fisherwomen.

The dancing-girl tradition is a very old phenomenon of the Tamil country. There were special quarters for them in cities and port towns. The Tamil epic, *Silapattikaram* by Ilango Adigal, probably dating to the beginning of the Christian era, bears ample testimony to this phenomenon.[19]

It is also possible that the Arab merchants brought women along with them to Kayal and the Tamil coast, from neighbouring Ceylon, where women had a different moral code, as noted earlier, or from other places like the Maldives or the Malabar. Later, in the fourteenth century, the Moroccan traveller, Ibn Battuta, pointed out often in his *Rehla* how it was possible to buy slave girls in various parts of India including Maabar. He himself had bought one from Madurai. He also gives an idea of the temporary *muta* marriages contracted by foreigners to local women.[20] In the fifteenth century, Abd-er-Razzak the Persian traveller, and Nikitine, the Russian traveller, refer to the availability of such slave girls in south India.[21] Arab and Persian merchants, who preceded Ibn Battuta would have in all probability availed of such opportunities to establish families, at least on a temporary basis, on Indian soil.

Abdulla Wassaf of Shiraz, visited India a few years after Marco Polo. He describes it as the most agreeable abode on earth and the most pleasant quarter of the world. He attests to the wealth of the land by asserting that there was never a country to which gold, silver, commodities and curiosities were exported in exchange for only thorns, dregs, pebbles and various aromatic roots. Very much like Marco Polo, Wassaf also refers to the brisk horse trade carried on by the Arabs with Maabar, which he claims, stretched from Kulam (Quilon) on the Malabar coast to Nilawar (Nellore) in the east.[22]

It appears that within the space of about twenty years from about the time when Marco Polo visited Maabar, the influence of Arab merchants had risen to such an extent that the Pandyan king at Madurai seems to have deemed it necessary to have an Arab Muslim, Takiuddin Abdur Rahman, son of Muhammadut Tibi as his deputy (prime) minister and adviser. Kabil (Kayal) and two other cities, 'Fitan' and 'Mali Fitan' were given to him by the Pandya king. Though, all this is not supported by any epigraphical evidence, as pointed out by Krishnaswamy Ayyangar,[23] yet it is quite possible that Takiuddin Abdur Rahman could have wielded great influence in the Pandya court and was the ruler (probably farmer's general) of Kayal and the adjoining regions.

It also appears that during this period, Maliku-l Islam Jamaluddin, brother of Takiuddin was one of the prominent Arab merchants who dealt in horse trading with Maabar.[24] With the death of the Pandya king in the year A.D. 1293, one of his brothers, probably Kales (Kulasekhara) Pandya succeeded him.

But Wassaf claims that Takiuddin continued to be the king's deputy minister or prime minister and probably also retained his control over Kayal and its dependencies. Under Maliku-i-Azam Takiuddin and Maliku-l Islam Jamaluddin, trade flourished in Maabar and was so extensive that the produce of remotest China was carried to the farthest west.[25]

Marco Polo was a keen observer of the then Indian political conditions. He was not at all wrong in his assessment when he claimed that the wealth of southern India was going to be easy prey for the coming invader, for within a few years after his visit, Maabar was invaded by the army of the Sultan of Delhi under Malik Kafur Hazar Dinari, a Hindu convert to Islam, in A.D. 1310. This invasion was a failure as Malik Kafur was obliged to retreat with his army.

It appears from Wassaf's account that Kulasekhara Pandya had two sons, one legitimate known also as Sundara Pandya and another illegitimate, known as Theera (or Vira) Pandya. As the latter was nominated to the throne by Kulasekhara, instead of the legitimate heir, Sundara Pandya killed his father and ascended the throne. But Theera Pandya vanquished him with the help of his army in the middle of A.D. 1310, which obliged Sundara Pandya to take refuge in Delhi under the protection of the Turkish Sultan, Alauddin Khilji. This probably would have been one of the reasons which prompted Alauddin to send his Turkish army under Malik Kafur to subjugate Maabar and Theera Pandya.

Very soon Malik Kafur penetrated Maabar and Madurai with his army and appropriated all the riches there—diamonds, pearls, emeralds, rubies, gold, elephants etc. Amir Khusru, the court-poet of Alauddin Khilji who had accompanied Malik Kafur in his Maabar expeditions refers to some Muslims who had been subjects of the Pandya kings and their joining Malik Kafur's ranks. Khusru writes that Malik Kafur pardoned and accepted them in his ranks as they could recite the 'Kalima', the profession of faith, though they were 'half Hindus' and not so strict in their religious observances.[26] It appears that this characterisation of the Tamil Muslims as 'half Hindus' by

Amir Khusru is a stamp they bear to this day. Many Tamil Muslims complain even today that the Urdu-speaking Muslims of north Indian origin do not consider them at as being on par and dismiss them very much in the manner of Amir Khusru.

Nevertheless, this brings out the fact that local Muslim communities had struck strong roots in the Tamil country by the fourteenth century. Khusru's remark about their being 'half Hindus' can be taken to mean that they were converts to Islam who would not have abandoned their Tamilness in dress, manners, language, etc., though Islam seems to have become central to their lives, given their capacity to recite the Kalima. As Amir Khusru does not mention anything about their Arab ancestry, it could be reasonably concluded that a good number of them were local converts of whom many would have served in the Pandyan army, probably under the influence of Takiuddin or his descendants.

Further, Amir Khusru informs us that Malik Kafur's troops reached 'Fatan' ('pattanam', meaning town or port), which was ruled by a certain Pandya Guru. If this city of 'Fatan' is the same as that pointed out by Wassaf as 'Fitan', then it would appear that 'Fitan' or 'Fatan' and the other cities such as Kayal and Mali Fitan were no more under the control of Takiuddin or his descendants in A.D. 1310. Pandya Guru had many troops comprising both Muslims and Hindus. But, with the arrival of Malik Kafur's army at Fatan, Pandya Guru fled and the local Muslims who were in his service sought protection from the Sultan's army, which was accorded to them promptly as was done earlier.[27]

With the death due to dropsy of Sultan Alauddin Khilji and the death of Malik Kafur, who was decapitated by his foes thirty-five days after Alauddin's death, Sultan Shahid Kutbuddin, son of Alauddin Khilji ascended the throne at Delhi in A.D. 1317. The very next year in 1318, the Turkish Sultan's army, this time under Khusru Khan, marched into Maabar and Madura. Ziauddin Barni tells us that Khusru Khan, a Hindu convert to Islam like Malik Kafur, put to death, Taki Khan, a wealthy merchant of Maabar, and confiscated all his riches. Unlike the

Hindu kings, Taki Khan had not fled from the invading army because he thought he had nothing to fear from an army of Muslims. But Khusru Khan proved him wrong. Taki Khan or Siraj i Taqi was a relative of Takiuddin. It appears that Malik Kafur himself had looted Siraj i Taqi in 1315.[28] Probably, knowing that the Arab merchants were in close collaboration with the Pandyan ruling establishment, Khusru Khan preferred to put Taki to death and take away his wealth. Because we do not have much information on the role played by Arab merchants in the Turkish Sultanate of Madurai, which was established subsequently, it appears that either Khusru Khan eliminated the other Arab merchants in the Pandyan country in a similar manner or they voluntarily withdrew from the region to safer places.

As a result of the invasion of 1318, the Pandya country with Madurai as its capital came under the sway of the Turks where these self-styled Turkish sultans ascended the throne of Madurai. The great Moroccan traveller, Ibn Battuta visited Maabar during this period. He describes Madurai as a big city with spacious streets. He had also noted the extreme cruelty of Sultan Ghiyas-ud-din Damghani, who was then ruling from Madurai. But he does not mention any Arab merchant who wielded influence in the Turkish Sultan's court like Takiuddin did in the Pandya court.

Ibn Battuta also visited the port-city of Pattan or Fattan, probably the same as that pointed out by Wassaf and Amir Khusru.[29] He characterises it as a large and beautiful city on the coast with a wonderful port. There he met Sheik Salih Mohammad of Nishapur (in Khorasan) and thirty other *fakirs* in a beautiful mosque built of stone. But strangely, Ibn Battuta is silent about the existence of Tamil Muslim communities, which, however does not mean that they did not exist at that time.[30]

Ravuttars, Tulukkar, and Sonagars

We have seen that there were Muslims as well as Hindus in the armies of the Pandyas and his vassals. Amir Khusru has often mentioned the Hindu horsemen of south India known as

'Ravuts'.[31] Generally, it seems that in the medieval period, horsemen serving under Hindu kings were known by the term 'Ravut' or 'Ravuta'.[32] It is quite possible that the word 'Ravuta' was retained by Tamil Muslim military men and their descendants in the Pandya country as a title from this period onwards. It is significant to note that the Muslims of Madura and the adjoining regions claim to have been converted by early Muslim Sufis such as Nathar Vali in the Tamil country.[33] Therefore, it is not surprising to note that the traditional homelands of the Ravuttars were in the interior of the south Tamil country.

But in the fourteenth century, with the establishment of a Turkish Sultanate at Madura, which survived for a brief period of about 50 years, the word 'Turukkar' or 'Tulukkar', derived from the original 'Turk' or 'Turki', came into use in the Tamil country to refer to the Muslims. Though, the Tamil Muslims had nothing to do with the Turks, they too were referred to as 'Tulukkars'. In Tamil literature and temple inscriptions too, the word 'Tulukkar' or 'Turukkar' was used extensively from this period onwards.[34] Thus Ravuttar and Tulukkar were the two terms in use to denote Tamil Muslims during this early period of Tamil Muslim existence.

But in Tamil literature, there was a third term which was used simultaneously with the word 'Yavana' to designate the Muslims and Arabs during the medieval period. This term was 'Sonagan' or 'Sonagar'. The word 'Sonagam' actually signifies Arabia in Tamil literature. The commentator of *Pattupatu*, Naccinarkiniyar, uses the word 'Sonagan' wherever the word 'Yavana' occurs.[35] Abdul Rahim actually affirms on the basis of inscriptions that one of the donors of the great temple at Tanjore was one 'Sonagar Savur Paranjodi', an Arab Muslim trader.[36]

Actually 'Sonagan' seems to be the earliest term along with 'Yavana' used to refer to Arab Muslim traders. This term was gradually extended to refer also to Tamil Muslim communities which came into existence later and it continued to exist along with 'Ravuttar' and 'Tulukkar' to denote Tamil Muslims, even to this day.

Marakkayars and Lebbais

In the fifteenth century, the Persian traveller, Abd-er-Razzak writes that the Malabar coast, which includes Calicut, extended up to Kabel (Kayal), situated opposite Serendib (Ceylon).[37] the Venetian traveller, Nicolo Conti was at Kayal in the fifteenth century when it was still a great pearl centre.[38] The maritime historians, Geneviève Bouchon and Denys Lombard report that during this period, Kayal and Kilikarai (near Kayal) traded in, besides pearls, horses also. It seems that horses were exchanged for rice in Hormuz from where they were shipped to ports such as Kayal.[39]

From ancient times, India had always been the cynosure of all eyes attracting Greeks, Romans, Egytians, Chinese, Arabs, Turks, Mongols, etc. It was one of the ironies of history that the great Arab seaman Ahmad Ibn Majid was persuaded by Vasco da Gama, to guide the Portuguese fleet across the ocean from Melindi in East Africa to Calicut on the Malabar coast.[40] This was the beginning of the end of Arab and Muslim navigation and trade in the Indian Ocean region.

Vasco da Gama writes that in the early part of the sixteenth century, Kayal, where pearls were found, was ruled by a powerful Muslim, a subject of the King of Coulam (Quilon).[41] During this time, great Muslim and Hindu merchants who owned a number of ships were found at Pulicate (Pazhaverkadu) in the northern Tamil Coromandel coast.[42]

Duarte Barbosa, who was a Portuguese factor at Cochin in the early sixteenth century, reports that the Moors of Malabar married as many wives as they could support and kept many concubines of low caste (of the Tiyan or Mukkuwa caste) as well. If they had children from these alliances, they made them Moors. He further says that the Moors and Hindu Chettis of Cochin and Quilon possessed many ships and traded with Coromandel, Ceylon, etc. He adds that the port cities of Kayal and Quilicare (Kilakarai) belonged to the King of Quilon and to his vassals and that the land beyond Kayal belonged to the kingdom of Vijayanagar.[43]

Muslim and Hindu natives of Kayal and Kilakarai on the southern Tamil coast traded in pearls, precious stones, and horses, besides rice and cloth which they carried to Malabar.[44] It is significant to note that Barbosa, too, does not talk about Arab traders at Kayal. Instead he mentions Muslim natives. Actually, a wealthy and powerful Muslim resided at Kayal, the same that Vasco da Gama had mentioned, who collected duties levied on pearls and passed judgments and dispensed justice to Muslims without the interference of the king of Coulam, though he was his subject.[45]

Barbosa notes that it was the tradition of the Paravars, the Tamil coastal fishermen, to fish pearls exclusively for the boat-owners every Friday. Generally the boat-owners were Muslims. Besides they also used to fish for a whole week at the end of the season for the Muslim dignitary of Kayal.[46] Thus Barbosa clearly establishes that the Muslims were boat-owners who also wielded immense power and influence in the region. He does not use the terms 'Marakkayars' or 'Lebbais' in his reference to these coastal Muslims.

But this was not the case with the Malabar coastal Muslims. Tomé Pires, who was chosen as the Portuguese ambassador to China, arrived in India in 1511. He refers to a certain Mamale Mercar (Marakkar), a powerful and wealthy merchant of Cannanore. Geneviève Bouchon asserts that 'Marakkar' was frequently employed as a title by the Muslims of Calicut and Cochin, but it was not a title found among the Kolathanad (Cannanore) Muslims. She thinks that Tomé Pires had confused a local term 'Arakkal' with Marakkar.[47] But what she does not seem to realise is that Mamale Marakkar might have been after all a migrant to Cannanore from Cochin. K.S. Mathew, the Indo-Portuguese specialist, from Kerala, had identified a certain Mamale Marakkar in Cochin in 1504.[48] Though, I do not claim that the Cochin 'Mamale Marakkar' is the same as the one from Cannanore, there is every possibility that the latter was a migrant, unless proved otherwise.

In fact, K.S. Mathew and Bouchon, on the basis of Portuguese records, gives us a list of names of Muslim Marakkar traders and seamen of Cochin and Calicut, apart from that of Mamale Marakkar. Some of them were Cherina Marakkar or Cheria Nina (Naina) Marakkar, Nino (Naina) Marakkar, Mitos Marakkar, Chilary Marakkar, Mahomed Marakkar, Pate Marakkar, Icimale Marakkar and Belina Marakkar.[49] The great Indo-Arab historian, Sheik Zainuddin al-Mabri, cites in his sixteenth century work the names of Kunji Ali Marakkar, Ali Ibrahim Marakkar, Kutty Ibrahim Marakkar, and Mohammad Ali Marakkar of Cochin.[50] According to Moplah tradition, the Marakkars were originally marine merchants from Cochin.[51]

As the ruling and military classes of Malabar never went to sea owing to religious reasons, all the merchants and sailors of Malabar, who traded on the sea were Muslims.[52] The merchants of Malabar traded as far as Cambay and Sind and also as far as Pulicat on the Coromandel and Ceylon and the Maldives.[53] K.S. Mathew proves conclusively on the basis of Portuguese sources, that the 'Marakkar' merchants of Cochin had their own factories on the Coromandel coast and that they had actually helped the Portuguese to get commodities from Malacca and other ports of South-East Asia before the Portuguese occupied Malacca in 1511.[54]

These merchants, who frequented the Malabar coast, would have no doubt contracted temporary or even permanent marriage alliances with local Tamil women, as Duarte Barbosa had pointed out in the case of Malabar. The offspring resulting from such alliances would have been brought up as Muslims and would have added to the already existing Tamil Muslim population on the Coromandel coast.

Some Marakkars of Malabar would have, in all probability, settled permanently on the southern Coromandel coast during this period, as they were doing in Ceylon, as reported by Barbosa.[55] Sheikh Zainuddin also reported that the Marakkars of Cochin had sailed to Kayal in their numerous ships laden with goods, when they encountered the Portuguese and had to fight them on sea and on land, which caused heavy losses.[56] It has also to be noted that Kayal was within the realm of the King of

Quilon. Thus, it was but natural, that the Marakkars plied their ships back and forth from Kayal.

It is fairly clear now that the Marakkars of the Malabar coast were present in the southern Coromandel coast. The powerful Muslim of Kayal, who was the subject of the king of Quilon that Duarte Barbosa refers to, would have been in all probability a Marakkar settler from the Malabar coast. It is more than probable that their offspring, born out of their alliances with local women or women brought from other places, would have retained the title 'Marakkar', which in the course of time became Tamilised as 'Marakkayar', meaning seaman or owner of boats. They would have in all probability mixed with the native Muslims in the coastal areas, as was pointed out by Marco Polo. These transitions were taking place in the sixteenth century. Later some of these Marakkayars would have moved further north to Nagore, Nagapattinam, and Porto Novo.

Also, the Ramnad coastal Muslims were conferred with royal honours and titles by the Raja of Ramnad, and the word 'Marakkayar' was incorporated as part of these titles. In the seventeenth century, the Nayaka rulers of the region had vested a leading Muslim trader of the Ramnad coast with the honorific title 'Mudali Pillai Marakkayar' in the form of a copper plate grant, which was found in Kayalpattinam.[57] But, the term 'Marakkayar' was already in use during this period and it was not the invention of the Nayaka ruler. But he chose to honour the Marakkayar trader with the Tamil Hindu title 'Mudali Pillai', along with the trader's own title or name, 'Marakkayar'. The maritime historian, S. Subramanyam has mentioned a certain Marakkayar merchant called Kunju Ali, who traded from Nagore with Burma, in the seventeenth century. Now 'Kunju Ali' is a typical Malayali Muslim name. In fact, O.K. Nambiar attests that 'Kunju' is a term of endearment in Malayalam and is a diminutive prefixed to names to signify affection.[58] Thus, this Kunju Ali Marakkayar should be either a fresh migrant from the Malabar coast or some settler or descendant of settlers, who had moved further north beyond Kayal.

It must also be noted that generally the Marakkayars of

Tamil Nadu, like the Malabar Muslims, belong to the Shafi sect. The non-Marakkayar Muslims of Tamil Nadu belong to the Hanafi sect. This goes to confirm the Malabar origins of the Marakkayars of Tamil Nadu. Moreover, M. Abdul Rahim has pointed out some resemblances in the marriage customs of the Marakkayars of southern Tamil Nadu and the Muslims of the west coast. He specifically singles out the marriage custom of the Marakkayars where the bridegroom goes and lives with the bride in her house. This custom, he affirms prevails among the Muslims of the west coast.[59] Also, the Marakkayars of Tamil Nadu share a set of distinctive Tamil kinship terms for parents and elder siblings with the Muslims of the west coast. All this once again confirms the Malayali origins of the Marakkayars of Tamil Nadu.

During the sixteenth century, the word 'Marakkayar' was becoming well known. It appears that another term, 'Lebbai', was gradually being used in the seventeenth century. W. Francis rightly attributes the term 'Sonagan' to both the Lebbais and Marakkayars. Edgar Thurston applies the word 'Sonagan' to the Lebbais who were sea-fishermen and boatmen, whereas the more prosperous traders were called Marakkayars.[60] It would then seem that the richer among the Sonagars, came to be known as the Marakkayars, while the rest were termed as the Lebbais. But if we take into account, the preceding exposition about the Malayali origins of the Marakkayars of Tamil Nadu, then it would seem that the descendants of Marakkar settlers, who were originally marine merchants on the Malabar coast and therefore economically well-off, came to be known as 'Marakkayars', while the rest were known as 'Lebbais'.

But what is the origin of the term 'Lebbai'? To this day, this remains a mystery. There are some hypotheses regarding its origin. Some believe that it referred to people who had fled Iraq and landed in Tamil Nadu to escape persecution.[61] Another account says that they were descendants of the Arabs who came to India to trade in the eleventh and twelfth centuries. These Arab merchants were persecuted by the Moghuls (or rather I think the Turks), owing to which they were compelled to return to their country, leaving behind their children born of Tamil women.[62]

It should be noted that the Mughal sway over the Tamil country only extended to the late seventeenth century or eighteenth century and there is no recorded instance of Mughal persecution of the Arab merchants during this period. But we have evidence of Turkish invasions of the Tamil country in the fourteenth century and the subsequent establishment of the Sultanate of Madurai by the Turks, which lasted for about 50 years. It is quite possible that Arab traders were persecuted by Turks during this period. We have, for instance, the case of Taki Khan, a wealthy merchant, being put to death by Khusru Khan in 1318. It is quite possible that other Arab merchants were also persecuted or put to death by the Turks during this period. They would have felt obliged to flee the Tamil country at least temporarily, leaving behind their children of mixed descent. We do not have a record of any Arab merchant's association with the Turkish Sultanate. Even though travellers such as Ibn Battuta, were present at Madurai and the Pandya country during this period, he did not note anything concrete about the presence or state of the Arab merchants in the Tamil country during Turkish rule. But, as we have seen, Arab merchants did exist in the Tamil country before the Turkish invasions. Therefore, their sudden disappearance might be attributed to persecution of the Arabs by the Turks, which would have forced many of them to flee, while many others might have been put to death like Taki Khan. This memory seems to have persisted in the minds of the Lebbais Tamil Muslims and Edgar Thurston took care to note it down about a century ago.

As to the origin of the word 'Lebbai', Edgar Thurston writes that as the Lebbais were often oppressed by the others, they cried 'labbek' to them, which means, 'we are your servants'.[63] This simple explanation may be true. It is quite possible that the Lebbais might have cried 'we are your servants', to the oppressive and invading Turks, who were probably mistaken for the Mughals by the Lebbais. This will anyhow remain in the domain of hypothesis, for no clear historical proof seems to be forthcoming.

Nevertheless, it is apparent that the term, 'Lebbai', designating a group of Muslims, is unique to Tamil Nadu. It does not seem to have been in use either in Kerala or in any other part of India. Therefore, its origin cannot be traced outside of Tamil Nadu, i.e., in the rest of the Indian sub-continent. It is probable that it originated outside India.

In the fifteenth century, Muslim traders of the Coromandel coast were present in the various kingdoms of South-East Asia.[64] They seem to have wielded much influence there. The historian, S. Arasaratnam, in his study of trade on the Coromandel coast from 1650 to 1740, has identified a certain 'Lebbai' family, whose members were prominent allies of the Sultan of Johore.[65] He has also referred to another Tamil Muslim merchant, Sidi Lebbai, who controlled the entire tin trade of the kingdom of Perak and had contacts with powerful Tamil Muslim merchants of Porto Novo and Cuddalore.[66] Thus the connection of the Tamil Muslims with South-East Asia was quite old and intimate.

This connection had naturally led to a lot of cultural interaction. Edgar Thurston had noted a century ago that many Tamil Muslims spoke Straits Malay.[67] They had even borrowed some of their cultural features like the use of the Malay blow-gun.[68]

But what is more astonishing is the use of the word 'Lebbai' among the South-East Asian Muslims and the way they use it. They, of course, do not use it to identify a group or clan of Muslims as in Tamil Nadu.

Antoine Cabaton, in his study of Malay and Tcham Muslims in Cambodia bordering Malayasia, has remarked that both the groups have common religious officials who are given certain names according to their office. Thus the name 'Lebbai' is given by both to those who occupy the function of 'religious officiant'.[69] Cabaton adds further that Malays and Tchams attribute the word 'Lebbai' to pious men who conduct the Friday service in the villages.[70] It seems that in the Indo-Chinese peninsula, these 'Lebbais' are known for their piety and are placed in the front ranks in the mosques.[71]

In Malaysia, it appears that the 'Lebbais' were always known to be religious and learned and well-versed in the fundamentals of the teachings of Islam. They also know how to lead a prayer and can chant the right *du'a* (prayer) for the right occasion. In some religious functions, they are often the ones selected to lead the performance of such functions, or to occupy positions of priority during its performance.[72] Even in Indonesia, 'Lebbai' generally signifies a religious officiant.

From the foregoing it is quite clear that in South-East Asia the term 'Lebbai' was never used to identify any Muslim ethnic group or clan. It was actually used to refer to religious officiants or intellectuals, or to those known for their knowledge and piety. In Tamil Nadu though, the term 'Lebbai' was deemed by some as pertaining to religiosity, yet, on the whole it was used to identify a group or clan of Tamil Muslims, who indulged in various occupations as noted by Thurston. Thus, while in South-East Asia the word 'Lebbai' had a very restricted sense and application, in the Tamil country it had a very broad application. As a result, it is almost impossible to affirm that the South-East Asian Muslims had borrowed the word from the Lebbais of Tamil Nadu, who were had close connections with them from the fifteenth century. Moreover, the Lebbais of Tamil Nadu were Hanafites, while the Muslims of South-East Asia were generally Shafiites, which only demonstrates that the former had no role in the spreading of Islam in South-East Asia.

But as the Lebbais of Tamil Nadu were trading with South-East Asia from the fifteenth century, which had resulted in a certain cultural interaction, and as the term 'Lebbai' itself, as noted by Thurston, was of recent origin, (for in the Tamil lexicon this group was known as 'Sonagars', even in the beginning of this century[73]), it would not be out of place to conclude that the term might have been imported from South-East Asia (like the Malay blow-gun) as a sort of prestigious title for the non-Marakkayar Tamil Muslims. The references to Lebbai families and individuals of Tamil descent by Arasaratnam in South-East Asia during 1650–1740, lends some credibility to the possibility of the term 'Lebbai' being imported from there into Tamil Nadu and applied gradually to cover many Tamil Muslims, especially of non-Marakkayar descent.

Unlike the north Indian and the Deccani Muslims and also the Mappilas (moplah) of Kerala, Tamil Muslim sub-divisions were not hierarchically ranked, but were of approximately equal status.[74] Among the north Indian and Deccani Muslims, there seem to exist a sort of hierarchical division between the Ashrafs, who are generally of superior foreign origin, and the Ajlafs, who are inferior indigenous converts to Islam. A similar situation seems to prevail in Kerala where the Tangals of foreign Sayyid origin are considered to be superior to the Arabis, Malabaris, Pusalars, and Ossans of indigenous or mixed origin.[75]

But among Tamil Muslims, such notions of hierarchy based on foreign and Indian origin, which has nothing to do with the Hindu caste hierarchy, are totally absent. This confers on them a distinct identity in the Indian religious landscape, which Louis Dumont and many others have failed to take note of.

Tamil Muslim literature which reflects the life of Tamil Muslims from at least the sixteenth century treats all Muslims and Tamil Muslims on an equal footing. There is nothing in this literature distinguishing the Marakkayars as superior to the other Tamil Muslims. Members from all the three sub-divisions have contributed equally to this literature.

At the beginning of the twentieth century Thurston recorded that the Marakkayars were actually incorporating converts from various classes of Hindus (probably including the untouchables) into their ranks.[76] During the nineteenth century, many Mukkuwa fishermen had converted to Islam in Karikal.[77] They mixed and mingled with the Marakkayars to such an extent that there is no trace of them now. It should also be noted that many Marakkayars have always used the term 'Lebbai' along with their names. This means that the Marakkayars never considered the term 'Lebbai' as inferior or derogatory. The Urdu-speaking Muslims of Tamil Nadu had generally applied the term 'Lebbai' to all Tamil Muslims including the Marakkayars. The Marakkayars never seem to have raised any opposition to it.

Arasaratnam, who himself is a Tamil, maintains that the Tamil Muslim sub-divisions carried equal social status, though there may have been economic disparities between them.[78] M. Abdul Rahim who was also a Tamil Muslim and a professor of history at Tiruchirappalli writes, that names such as Marakkayars and Ravuttars can neither be caste names nor can they refer to classes. These are names which have been assumed by accident. He adds that it is extremely difficult to distinguish one from the other as they merge with one another.[79]

In the light of these facts, it is reasonable to state, as Mattison Mines does, that the sub-divisions among the Tamil Muslims carry approximately equal status and are not hierarchically ranked. They, thus, are fundamentally different from the hierarchical Hindu social order. This being the case, there is no basis to assert, as Louis Dumont does as far as Tamil Muslims are concerned, that beneath the ultimate Islamic values lie the non-Islamic Hindu values and for some scholars as Susan Bayly of Cambridge to invent a hierarchy where there is none.[80]

Notes

1. O.H.K. Spate, A.T.A. Learmouth, B.H. Farmer, *India, Pakistan, Ceylon: The Regions*, (London, 1960), 739.
2. S.M. Sastri ed., *McCrindle's Ancient India as Described by Ptolemy*, XIII, (Calcutta, 1927), 29, 55, 58.
3. Marcel Devie, trans., *Adja'ib Al Hind—Les Mervielles de l'Inde*, (Paris, n.d.).
4. Pierre Miele, 'Les Yavanas dans l'Inde Tamoule' in *Mélanges Asiatiques*, (Paris, 1940–41), 100–101.
5. M. Reinaud, *Relation des Voyages Faits par les Arabes et les Persans dans l'Inde et à la Chine dans le IXe siècle de l'ère Chrètienne*, (Osnabruck, 1988), 51.
6. Ibid., 97, 135.
7. Ibid., 131.
8. H.M. Elliott, 'The Muhammadan Period,' *The History of India as*

Told by its Own Historians, ed., John Dowson, (Allahabad, n.d.), vol. 1, 13.

9. Edward Sachau, *Alberuni's India: An Account of the Religion, Philosophy, Literature, Geography, Chronology, Astronomy, Customs, Laws and Astrology of India About A.D. 1030*, (New Delhi, 1983), 209–210.
10. M. Arunachalam, *An Introduction to the History of Tamil Literature*, (Tiruchitrambalam, 1974), 136–37.
11. Arumuga Navalar Yalpannam, *Cekkilar, Periya Puranam*, (1884), 517, and M. Arunachalam, *An Introduction to the History of Tamil Literature*, 145–146.
12. Colonel Yule, ed. and trans., *The Book of Marco Polo*, (London, 1903), I, 12.
13. Ibid., 331–332.
14. Ibid., 370–371.
15. Ibid., 340.
16. Ibid., 342.
17. Aldo Ricci, trans., *The Travels of Marco Polo*, second edition, (1st edition 1931, London, 1950) 309, 322.
18. Ibid., 301, 328.
19. Ramachandra Dikshitar, *The Silapattikaram*, (1st edition 1939, Tinnevely, 1978).
20. Mahdi Husain, trans., *The Rehla of Ibn Battuta* (*India, Maldive Islands and Ceylon*), (Baroda 1976), 200, 202–203, 225, 230; see also Geneviève Bouchon, *Les Musulmans de Kérala à l'époque de la Découverte Portugaise*, (Mare Luso-Indicum, Genève, 1973), II, 19–20.
21. Charles Malamoud, trans., *Ahkanase Nikitine: Le voyage au delà des Trois Mers*, (Paris, 1982), 42, 44; R.H. Major, ed., *India in the 15th Century*, (New York, n.d.), 29.
22. John Dowson, *History of India* III, 30, 32, 33.
23. Krishnaswami Ayyangar, *South India and Her Muhammadan Invaders*, (New Delhi, 1921), 73.
24. John Dowson, *History of India* III, 33, 52.
25. Ibid., I: 69; III, 35.
26. Amir Khusru, *Khaza'inul Futuh* (Treasures of Victory), trans., M. Habib, (Madras, 1931), 99. John Dowson, *History of India* III, 50–54, 90.
27. John Dowson, *History of India* III, Appendix, 550–551.

28. Ibid., III, 208–211, 219; Peter Jackson, *The Delhi Sultanate: A Political and Military History*, (Cambridge, 1999), 208.
29. Mahdi Hussain, trans., *The Rehla of Ibn Battuta* (*India, Maldive Islands and Ceylon*), (Baroda, 1976), 229.
30. Ibid., 230.
31. Amir Khusru, *The Rehla of Ibn Battuta*, 60; John Dowson, *History of India*, 81.
32. Abdul Rahim, 'Islam in Negapatam', in *Bulletin of the Institute of Traditional Cultures*, (July–December, 1974): 90.
33. K.H. Khan, 'South Indian Mussalmans', *Madras Christian College Magazine*, (Madras, 1912–13): 294; Tara Chand, *Influence of Islam on Indian Culture*, (Allahabad, 1963), 40.
34. A.K. Rifaye, *Tamizhakathil Islamiya Varalaru*, (Tenkasi, 1988), 131–32.
35. Pierre Meile, *Melanges Asiatiques*, 101; Abdul Rahim, *Bulletin*, 86.
36. Abdul Rahim, *Bulletin of the Institute of Traditional Culture*, 87.
37. R.H. Major, 'Narration of the Voyage of Abd-er-Razzak, A.D. 1442', *India in the 15th Century*, 19.
38. R.H. Major, 'The Travels of Nicolo Conti in the East in the Early part of the 15th century', *India in the 15th Century*, 7.
39. G. Bouchon, D. Lombard, 'India and the Indian Ocean in the 15th century', in *India and the Indian Ocean, 1500–1800*, eds. Ashin Das Gupta, M.N. Pearson, (Oxford, 1987).
40. George Hourani, *Arab Sea-faring in the Indian Ocean in Ancient and Early Medieval Times*, (New Jersey, 1951), 83.
41. Arthur Morelet, trans., *Journal de Voyage de Vasco Da Gama*, MDCCCLXIV, 85.
42. M.L. Dames, ed. and trans., *The Book of Duarte Barbosa*, (New Delhi 1989), I, 130; G.P. Badger, ed., *Travels of Ludovico di Varthema, A.D. 1503 to 1508*, (New York, 1964), 195.
43. M.L. Dames, *The Book of Duarte Barbosa* II, 116–125.
44. Ibid., II, 116, 121–123.
45. Ibid., 123–124.
46. Ibid., 124.
47. G. Bouchon, *Regent of the Sea: Cannanore's Responses to Portuguese Expansion, 1507–1528*, trans., Louis Shackley, (Delhi, 1988), 105fn.
48. K.S. Mathew, *Portuguese Trade with India in the 16th Century*, (Delhi, 1983), 210.

49. Ibid., G. Bouchon, *Les Musulmans du Kérala à l'époque de la Découverte Portugaise*, (*Regent of the Sea*), 52–53.
50. M.J. Rowlandson, *Tohfut-ul-Mujahideen, An Historical Work in Arabic Language*, (London, 1833), 120, 126.
51. O.K. Nambiar, *The Kunjalis—Admirals of Calicut*, (Bombay, 1963), 59.
52. Tomé Pires, *The Sumo Oriental*, trans. and ed. Armando Cortesao, (Liechenstein, 1967), I, 82.
53. Ibid.
54. K.S. Mathew, *Portugese Trade with India*, 211.
55. M.L. Dames, *The Book of Duarte Barbosa*, II, 111.
56. M.J. Rowlandson, *Tohfut-ul-Mujahideen*, 140–160; O.K. Nambiar, *The Kunjalis*, 90–93.
57. Interview with Capt. Ameer Ali; Susan Bayly, *Saints, Goddesses and Kings: Muslims and Christians in South Indian Society, 1700–1900*, (Cambridge, 1989), 80; Ali Ameer, *Vallal Seethakathiyin Vazhvum Kaalamum*, (Madras, 1983), 56; K.M. Sheriff, *Vallal Seethakathiyin Varalaru*, (Madras, 1985), 67–68.
58. S. Subramanyan, *Improvising Empire—Portuguese Trade and Settlement in the Bay of Bengal, 1500–1700*, (Delhi, 1990), 91, 221, 226–27; O.K. Nambiar, *The Kunjalis*, 76fn.
59. Abdul Rahim, *Bulletin*, 98; Dennis McGilvray, 'Arabs, Moors and Muslims: Sri Lankan Muslim Ethnicity in Regional Perspective', in *Contributions to Indian Sociology*, (1998), 32, 2, 439, 441, 444.
60. Edgar Thurston, *Castes and Tribes of Southern India*, (Madras, 1909), V, 4.
61. Ibid., IV, 199.
62. Ibid.
63. Ibid.
64. N.J. Ryan, *A History of Malaysia and Singapore*, (Kuala Lumpur, 1976).
65. S. Arasaratnam, *Merchants, Companies and Commerce on the Coromandel Coast, 1650–1740*, (Delhi, 1986), 117–148.
66. B. Andaya, *Perak: The Abode of Grace*, (Kuala Lumpur, 1979), 50.
67. Edgar Thurston, *Castes and Tribes of Southern India*, IV, 201.
68. Ibid., 200.
69. *Encyclopaedia of Islam, 1913–36*, (Leiden, 1987) III, 507.
70. Ibid., fn.
71. Marcel, 'Les Musulmans de l'Indochine française', in *Bulletin d'Ecole Française d'Extrême Orient*, (1941) XLI, 186.

72. S.H. Ali, *Social Stratification in Kampang Bagan—A Study of Class, Status, Conflict and Mobility in a Rural Malay Community*, (Singapore, 1964), 64.
73. Edgar Thurston, *Castes and Tribes of Southern India*, IV, 199–200.
74. Mattison Mines, 'Social Stratification among Muslim Tamils in Tamil Nadu', in *Caste and Social Stratification among Muslims in India*, ed., Imtiaz Ahmad, (Delhi, 1978).
75. Victor D'Souza, 'Status Groups among the Moplahs on the South-West Coast of India', in *Caste and Social Stratification among Muslims in India*, ed., Imtiaz Ahmad, (Delhi, 1978), 45–46.
76. Edgar Thurston, *Castes and Tribes of Southern India*, V, 40.
77. See J.B.P. More, 'Muslim Evolution and Conversions in Karikal, South India', in *Islam and Christian-Muslim Relations*, 4 (Birmingham, June 1993): 1.
78. S. Arasaratnam, *Merchants, Companies and Commerce*, 219.
79. Abdul Rahim, *Bulletin*, 85.
80. See J.B.P. More, 'Review of Susan Bayly's *Saints, Goddesses and Kings: Muslims and Christians in South Indian Society, 1700–1900*', in *Contributions to Indian Sociology*, 1 (New Delhi, 1994): 28.

CHAPTER TWO

Tamil Muslim Literature before 1835

Tamil is one of the oldest languages of the world. It is a classical language. Its literature dates back to at least the Christian era, if not earlier, and is so ancient, abundant, varied, and copious that it can be compared only to Sanskrit, which unfortunately is no more a spoken language.

In the course of its evolution, Tamil literature has been enriched by various currents, both religious and secular. The various branches of Hinduism such as Vaishnavism, Saivism, and Saiva Siddhantism, along with Buddhism and Jainism were the major contributors to this literature.

From the sixteenth century onwards, west European Christian missionaries too contributed to Tamil literature in a big way. The literature that they produced was basically Christian, but they adopted Tamil literary styles and motifs to convey Christian values and stories.

The Arab (and Persian) traders, sailors, and missionaries who had been frequenting southern India wielded great influence in the southern Indian courts, especially in the Pandya and Chera countries. But, they contributed nothing to any literature in Tamil, either Islamic or otherwise. They probably were never interested in Tamil or its literature, either because they were traders and they probably thought it was not their business, or, because they did not think it worthwhile to write in any language other than their own. As a result, even Sheik Zainuddin, the great Indo-Arab historian of Ponnani and the sixteenth century author of the historical work, *Tuhfat al Mujahideen*, seems to have preferred to produce his work in Arabic, rather than Tamil or its derivative Malayalam.

Marco Polo has clearly pointed to the emergence of indigenous Tamil Muslim communities in the Tamil country in the thirteenth century. Since the Arabs, Persians, and later the Turks were not interested in Tamil or their literature, it was left to these Tamil Muslims to develop their own literature. It appears that it took another two to three centuries before some Tamil Muslims could produce literature in Tamil.

Tamil Muslim scholars are conscious of this lacuna. So they keep striving to find some old Tamil Muslim literature, dating back to at least Manikkavasagar's time. Being totally unsuccessful in this venture, some even blame the Portuguese for having wilfully destroyed all their literature produced before the sixteenth century. This is, of course, not based on any historical evidence at all.

Recently, some scholars have claimed that the literary works of the Tamils could be traced to at least the fourteenth century, if not earlier. They cite as proof a small work of eight stanzas called *Palsanthmalai*, probably of the fourteenth century. Whatever be the truth, the work itself contains some interesting details. It actually refers to the Sonagars who praise Allah and also refers to a ruler or *Kazi* or *Kalifa* of the Sonagars who was a great philanthropist.[1]

The author of *Palsanthmalai* is not known. But as no tradition of Tamil Muslim writing before the fourteenth century and even up to at least the sixteenth century has been identified unequivocally, it appears more probable that the author of *Palsanthmalai* was a Hindu. The fact that the eight stanzas hardly contain any Arabic or Persian word, unlike the later

Tamil Muslim works, lends credence to the theory that the author was a Hindu.

The author, moreover, could not be an Arab or Persian or Turk, for there was no tradition of their taking to writing in Tamil and that too more or less chaste Tamil. If the author was a Tamil-speaking Muslim of mixed descent or a local convert, he would not have used the same words as the Hindus to designate the Muslims or Arabs as 'Yavana', 'Sonagar', 'Anjuvannathar'. As the word 'Yavana' has been used along with 'Sonagar', to refer to the Muslims, it definitely cannot refer to the local Tamil Muslims. It also cannot refer to the Muslim invaders of the fourteenth century, who were mostly Turks and not Arabs. As noted earlier, from the fourteenth century itself, these invaders have been rightly identified as 'Turukkars' or 'Tulukkars' in Tamil literature and inscriptions. They should not be confused with the 'Yavanas' and 'Sonagars'.

In the present state of research, it is not possible to affirm unequivocally that Tamil Muslims as a community had emerged before the thirteenth century. Also, it is impossible to affirm that Tamil Muslims in the fourteenth century, were a part of 'Anjuvannam', a trade guild which seems to have originated in the western coast.[2] But, there is evidence to show that Arab, merchants and traders were also members of this trade guild, along with Jews and Christians of the western coast.[3] They alone (and not the Tamil Muslims) can be referred to as 'Yavana' in the *Palsanthmalai*. Thus, the Muslims referred to in *Palsanthmalai* should be Arab merchants or probably officials and vassals of the Pandya kings such as Malik Takiuddin.

It took nearly two centuries from the fourteenth century, for the first genuine Tamil Muslim literary work to emerge. Tamil Muslim scholars concur that this work came to being in 1572. The name of the work was *Aayira Masala Venru Vazhankum Adisaya Puranam*, and its author was Seyku Issaku. He was also known as Vanna Parimala Pulavar. The entire work is in the form of questions and answers and contains a good number of Arabic words. The title itself has the Arabic word, 'masala', which is actually an Arabic literary style, not known in Tamil literature.

The great number of Arabic words used in this literary work testifies that this work was meant for the Tamil-speaking Muslim community and its religious needs and was therefore unintelligible to the Tamil Hindus. It appears to be a conscious attempt to distinguish Tamil Muslim literature from the rest of the Tamil literature.

'Aayira Masala' is actually based on the Quran and the Hadith. It delineates the various Islamic principles and beliefs. It describes heaven and hell, and also some events in Prophet Mohammad's life.

On the whole the work attests to the Islamic and Arabic foundations of Tamil Muslim literature. It is surprising that the very first work in Tamil Muslim literature contains such a plethora of non-Tamil elements. It reveals the vibrant nature of the Tamil Muslim community and its strong grounding not only in Islam but also in Arabic in the late sixteenth century.

The second work attributed to Tamil Muslim authorship in the late sixteenth century is the *Mikurasu Malai*. It is supposed to have been written in 1590. The author is Aali Pulavar. The title contains the Tamilised form of an Arabic word, *Mikurasu* (*Mihraj* in Arabic) and a Tamil word, *malai*, which signifies a Tamil literary style.

This work describes the history of Prophet Mohammad's ascent to heaven, which is considered to be one of the miracles performed by the Prophet. It seems that though Aali Pulavar had made use of several Arabic words in this work, he had taken care to adapt them to the Tamil malai literary style. This thus shows that Arabic words were inevitable in an Islamic Tamil poem. Tamil Muslim poets of those days, like Aali Pulavar, seem to have preferred to borrow Arabic words, rather than replace them with equivalent Tamil words or coin new equivalent Tamil words which would convey the correct meaning of the Arabic words. It is probably because of the difficulty of translating these into Tamil that the early Tamil Muslim poets felt obliged to adopt words of Arabic origin freely in their poems. It might have even been a deliberate strategy adopted by the Tamil Muslim poets to distinguish Tamil Muslim literature from other literature. Whatever it may be, the fundamental Islamic nature of both the *Mikurasu Malai* and *Aayira Masala* is unquestionable.

There were some important Tamil Muslim works probably belonging to the seventeenth century as well. They were the *Thiruneri Neetham*, *Kanakabhisheka Malai*, *Tirumana Katchi*, and *Sackoon Pataippor.*

Thiruneri Neetham was sung by the Sufi master, Pir Mohammad. This work, like *Aayira Masala* is also fashioned in the form of questions and answers. It was written in the Tamil antati style. It is fundamentally an exposition of Islamic values, principles and morals addressed to both men and women. It also deals with property and marriage issues. The last part of the work contains a description of the end of the world, the Last Judgment, heaven and hell.

The author of *Kanakabhisheka Malai* was Kanakavirayar or Seyku Nainar Khan. The song revolves around Prophet Mohammad and his disciples and followers. Some think that the author might have been a Shia Muslim, because of the importance given in the work to Hassan and Hussain.[4] The author uses many Hindu features and forms in his poem, the characters of which are, nevertheless, profoundly Islamic. These Hindu features do not appear to challenge the Islamic principles. They are instead subordinated to them.

Tirumana Katchi is a sort of imaginary work by Sekathi Nainan. It deals with the heavenly life after Judgment Day, when it is believed that Prophet Mohammad's marriage will be celebrated with great pomp and splendour with Asia and Maryam. Some claim that this work may not be the imaginary creation of the poet. Instead it was based on the general Muslim belief, especially Tamil Muslim belief, of a heavenly life after the Last Judgment.

Sackoon Pataippor is believed to have been written towards the end of the seventeenth century. This seems to be a sort of a war ballad in a new Tamil literary style, believed to have been invented by the Tamil Muslims. The ballad describes the war between the Muslims and non-Muslims in Iraq. The non-Muslims headed by Sackoon finally surrender to the Prophet, and convert to Islam. As a result, the Prophet graciously allows Sackoon to continue as the ruler of Iraq.

Other works that may have been created before the end of seventeenth century or during the eighteenth century are: *Yakobu Sithat Patal, Muthu Mozhi Malai*, and *Thirumakkap Pallu*. The first one is a medical work, based on the typically Tamil school of medicine, known as 'Sitha Vaithiyam', which has nothing to do with the Ayurvedic medicine, prevalent all over India.

Yakobu was a convert to Islam. His original name was Rama Thevar, belonging to the Thevar caste. He produced several works both medical and mystical (see Appendix). The use of many Persian words in his works testifies to the fact that they might have been written towards the end of the seventeenth century or during the eighteenth century, when the highly Persianised Urdu-speaking nawabs were ruling large parts of Tamil Nadu.

In one of his works he uses the word 'Lebbaimarkal'. This was probably the first time the word 'Lebbai' seems to have been used in Tamil Muslim literature. We have already seen how the word 'Lebbai' had made its late appearance in Tamil Muslim society and literature. Thus, we can safely conclude that Rama Thevar alias Yakobu Sithar lived during the late seventeenth century.

The date of the work, *Muthu Mozhi Malai* seems very difficult to determine. It is a work of praise of Prophet Mohammad and narrates some important events in his life. The author of this work is not known. But strangely this work, unlike the other ones, does not contain many Arabic words.

Thirumakkap Pallu, whose author also remains unknown, is a work in a Tamil dramatic style known as pallu. It revolves around the city of Mecca and Prophet Mohammad. It praises Allah and the Prophet and Muhaidin Antavar, a Muslim saint. It also recounts some historical events concerning Prophet Mohammad.

In the beginning of the nineteenth century, Umaru Pulavar sang the *Sira Puranam*. It is an elaborate and vivid description of Prophet Mohammad's life. This work is hailed to be the crowning achievement of the entire Tamil Muslim literature. As far as *Sira Puranam* is concerned, David Schulman points out that its 'main sources are undoubtedly drawn from the classical Islamic traditions; the borrowed Tamil or Hindu features merely colour a work in the Muslim mainstream.'[5]

In fact, it seems that wherever Umaru depicts the Tamil Hindu countryside, its people, gods, and customs, he also makes an exposition of true Islamic principles along with it.[6] This shows that the concern of Umaru, the greatest Tamil Muslim poet, was Islam, though, now and then he made use of Tamil Hindu features and forms to drive home the Islamic message among the predominantly non-Islamic Hindu populations.

Sira Puranam is actually made up of *Sira*, an Arabic word and *Purana*, a Sanskrit word, which together means 'Life Story of the Prophet'. Umaru seems to be greatly indebted to Abul Kassim Marakkayar, without whose help he probably could never have sung this song. Some hold that Seyed Abdul Qadir Marakkayar, known popularly as 'Seethakathi' also helped him in this venture. Seethakathi is regarded by Tamil Muslims as the greatest philanthropist in Tamil Muslim history. But, at this juncture, the remark of the Tamil Muslim scholar, R.P.M. Kani is significant. He had said that many false legends on Umaru Pulavar prevailed among the Tamil Muslims at that time.[7]

One very important factor of the *Sira Puranam* is that it contains not only a number of Arabic words, but also a good number of Persian words. Thus, it is possible to suggest that the entire work would have, in all probability, been created during the rule of the Urdu-speaking nawabs of Arcot, who were highly influenced by Persian language and style.

But, for reasons hitherto unknown, Umaru Pulavar was unable to complete his *Sira Puranam*. Prompted by the generosity of another great Tamil Muslim philanthropist, Lebbai Naina Marakkayar, this gap was filled by three other poets who completed the *Sira Puranam* by writing the *Sinna Sira* (Little Sira).[8] After the composition of the *Sinna Sira*, there seems to have been a lull in Tamil Muslim literary activity, which lasted until the beginning of the nineteenth century. The reasons for this are not known. But Tamil Muslim scholars assert that there was a sudden spurt in the literary activity of the Tamil Muslims in the first quarter of the nineteenth century, which resulted in the production of several important Tamil Muslim works. These are: *Raja Nayagam, Kutbu Nayagama, Theen Vilakkam, Thirukaranap Puranam, Kutbu Nayagam Again, Muhaideen Puranam, Thirumani Malai, Iravuculkul Pataippor* and *Puthukusham.*

The first three poetical works were composed by Mohammad Ibrahim alias Vanna Kalanjiya Pulavar, hailing from Madurai Meesal. While *Raja Nayagam* revolves round the illustrious life of Prophet Sulaiman of the Arab lands, *Kutbu Nayagam* narrates the magnanimous life of Saint Mohideen Abdul Qadir Jilani.

Theen Vilakkam on the other hand recounts the life story of Syed Ibrahim Shaheed, who is known to have come from Arabia to Tamil Nadu and worked for the expansion of Islam. He is believed to have fought a war against the Pandya king and died a martyr's death. His tomb is situated at Ervadi in south Tamil Nadu.

Three more works were created by Sekuna Pulavar alias Abdul Qadir Nainar Lebbai Alim Pulavar alias Pulavar Nayagam. These works are: *Kutbu Nayagam, Thirumani Malai, Puthukushsham, Thirukaranap Puranam.*

The *Kutbu Nayagam* also revolves round the personality of Saint Mohideen Abdul Qadir Jilani. *Thirumani Malai,* written in Tamil malai style, relates to the life of Prophet Ibrahim of the Arab lands. *Puthukusham* describes the wars waged by Prophet Mohammad's descendants against Syria (Sham) and the latter's subjugation. It is based on an Arabic work. *Thirukaranap Puranam* narrates the life and miracles of Saint Shaik Abdul Qadir Shahul Hameed of Nagore.

The author of *Muhaideen Puranam* was Badruddin Pulavār. He is believed to have hailed from Ceylon. The work is divided into two parts and recounts the life of Saint Mohideen Abdul Qadir Jilani of the Qadiriyya order. *Iravuculkul Pataippor* was the work of Kunju Musu Lebbai Kazi Alim Pulavar. Its other name is *Salkap Pataippor.* This is a typical Islamic Tamil war song. It appears that the *pataippor* songs are always named after the enemies of Islam.

But, the spurt in literary activity during this period was primarily due to two Tamil Muslim authors, Vanna Kalanjiya Pulavar and Sekuna Pulavar, who had authored seven out of the nine works mentioned. Apart from these works, which are generally considered to be major and important contributions by prominent Tamil Muslim scholars like M.M. Uvais and J.M. Sali, there were also a few other works of lesser importance, written in Tamil, Arabic or Persian style which are attributed to the eighteenth or the beginning of the nineteenth century. They are the *Veda Puranam, Ponnariya Malai, Yusuppu Nabi Kaaviyam, Abushakama Malai, Madinat Antati, Meygnana Satakam, Muhaideen Pillait Tamizh, Nabi Nayagam Pillait Tamizh, Aintu Pataippor, Saithathu Pataippor, Mihraj Nama, Tozhugai Nama.* These works of lesser importance too are not very different from the major works because they too on the whole deal with Islamic themes and principles, the prophets and the saints, the wars waged by Muslims against non-Muslims, and also Islamic mysticism.

The most reliable method to ascertain the exact date of the literary works, both major and minor, consists in examining the original manuscripts on palm leaves, if they are available. It becomes more difficult to ascertain the dates with the help of printed copies, which might have succumbed to errors, modifications, and extrapolations, with the passage of time. This task of ascertaining the dates can be done only by a team of experts well versed in the various disciplines such as philology, history, linguistics, comparative literature, etc.

One thing that is striking about the Tamil Muslim literary productions before 1835 is that the Tamil Muslim authors produced their works on palm leaves like the other Tamils. Though the Arabs had no doubt frequented the southern coasts since at least the beginning of the Islamic era if not earlier, as we have seen, it is surprising that they had not introduced paper into the Tamil country although the Arabs were familiar with its use from the eighth century. Neither does it seem that the Arabs had introduced the art of calligraphy, so important in the Muslim mainlands into the Tamil country. As a result, Tamil Muslims continued to write on palm leaves, until paper was made available to them by the west Europeans.

It is possible that some other works by Tamil Muslims belonging to the period before 1835 might have existed. Though some might have been lost others might be existing in private holdings or libraries, either in manuscript or printed form. I have identified a few such manuscripts on palm leaves in the National Library of Paris. The first one is a fragment of Islamic catechism in Tamil in *ola* form, written on both sides. It is made of just six leaves. It was deposited in the library of the King of France by a certain Gautier d'Arc Edouard. The manuscript appears to belong to the period before 1830.

There is also another manuscript titled, *Visumillagit Tagum Manithagim* in Tamil which contains 54 olas. It is also a work on Muslim catechism, most probably meant for new converts. A third manuscript entitled, *Turukkamatha Puttagam*, meaning 'The Book of Turukkar religion', containing 226 olas is also found in the library's collection. Generally these religious manuscripts contain a good number of Arabic words, that makes it unintelligible to a person who does not know Arabic.

A fourth manuscript containing 44 olas is titled, '*Tulukkatamizhmojipeyarpu*'. In this we find many Hindustani words translated into 'Tulukkatamizh' or Muslim Tamil. It is actually a Hindustani-Tamil dictionary, probably the first of its kind by a Tamil Muslim. We also find in this library a paper manuscript, numbering 186 pages, without a title. This is actually a Tamil-Hindustani-Telugu pharmaceutical dictionary, produced in 1850. There are other manuscripts available at the Government Oriental Library, Madras.

It is absolutely clear now that the literary works produced by the Tamil Muslims before 1835 were not very numerous. In the face of the great mass of non-Islamic Tamil literature, especially Hindu literature that has accumulated from at least 250 B.C. up to 1835, Tamil Muslim literature as such, before 1835, is no doubt extremely limited. Perhaps on account of the liberal usage of Arabic words (and to a lesser extent Persian words), Tamil Muslim works were never in a position to attract the attention and interest of mainstream Tamil scholars. No wonder Simon Casie Chitty, in his enumeration of Tamil poets published in 1859, did not mention a single Tamil Muslim poet including Umaru Pulavar. This situation seems to have continued well into the twentieth century when Tamil scholars of repute such as M. Arunachalam could only devote about two pages to Tamil Muslim literature in his *An Introduction to the History of Tamil Literature*, published in 1974.[9]

As noted earlier, various religious currents had contributed to Tamil literature such as Hinduism, Buddhism, and Jainism. The converts to these faiths had their own sacred languages such as Sanskrit and Pali. When words of Sanskrit and Pali origin were used in Tamil literature by the Tamil poets, they were used generally in their Tamilised form, so that it almost never strikes anyone that these words were of outside origin. They were absorbed into Tamil to a great extent. This is the result of more than two thousand years of association of Tamil with Sanskrit and Pali.

But Arabic and Persian do not have such a long-standing association with Tamil, though the Arabs seem to have reached Tamil Nadu from at least the beginning of the Islamic era, if not earlier. There is no indication that the Arabs who were frequenting Tamil Nadu had shown any interest in Tamil and they hardly seem to have produced any work in it, unlike the Christian European missionaries, who arrived in Tamil Nadu in the sixteenth century. From this period itself, they started producing Christian Tamil works. In their zeal to propagate Christianity among the Tamils, they translated the Bible into Tamil during the first decades of the eighteenth century itself. Missionaries such as Beschi and Pope authored monumental works in Tamil, which have been recognised for its greatness and high quality. Contrary to this, the Arabs seem to have been more interested in trade, rather than aggressive proselytisation like the Christian missionaries.

But what is most surprising is that, unlike the Christian missionaries who strove to keep the Tamil they used in their works as pure as possible, sometimes even going to the extent of de-sanskritising Tamil, the Tamil Muslim authors did not have any inhibition whatever in using Arabic and, to a lesser extent, Persian words in their works. This they did to such an extent that their works can be characterised generally as Arabic-Tamil works, written in Tamil script, instead of purely Tamil works.

This of course has served to distinguish their literature from the rest of Tamil literature. But this rendered their literature so unintelligible to the non-Muslims (and even to the Muslims who did not know Arabic), that Tamil Muslim literature remained either more or less in obscurity till well into the twentieth century or was simply marginalised or neglected. We will see later whether the Tamil Muslims adopted this strategy of using Arabic words deliberately to distinguish themselves from the others or whether it was due to other reasons.

Nevertheless, there are two distinct factors that emerge from the following: Firstly, the extensive usage of Arabic words gave the literary works a distinct identity. Secondly, the fundamental concern of the works of these Tamil poets was Islam, its principle beliefs, traditions and values, its prophets and saints, and its stories and tales. The Tamil Hindu features found in their works were purely an adjustment they had to make in a predominantly non-Islamic Hindu milieu. This adjustment may not have been a permanent feature, for there seems to be no permanency in anything, especially in the field of culture. But through this adjustment, Tamil Muslims seem to have asserted themselves as a distinct group in the south Indian society.

These two factors of Tamil Muslim literature before 1835 constitute the fundamental conditioning factors of Tamil Muslim psyche and life in the course of their historical evolution. They affirm their attachment to both Arabic and Islam, which are like two eyes, inseparable from each other, and with which they had to live and evolve.

In the next chapter, we will examine the Tamil Muslim literature produced after 1835, when the British Acting

Governor-General, Charles Metcalfe, relaxed the press restrictions, up to 1920, when Tamil Muslims participated in large numbers for the maintenance of the Caliphate in Turkey. With this, our task of determining the Islamic identity of the Tamil Muslims in the course of their evolution will become easier and clearer. Besides, we will also be in a position to analyse the influence of modern print technology on Tamil Muslims and Tamil Muslim literature, which is the other main concern of this book, and also to find out if print had brought about any changes in the psychological set-up and identity of the Tamil Muslims and the fundamental concerns of Tamil Muslim literature as mentioned above.

Notes

1. Abdul M. Rahim, 'Islam in Negapatam', *Bulletin of the Institute of Traditional Cultures*, (Madras, July–December 1974), 92; Ali Ameer, *Vallal Seethakathiyin Vazhvum Kaalamum*, (Madras, 1983), 39; K.M. Sheriff, *Vallal Seethakathiyin Varalaru*, (Madras, 1985), 66–75.
2. G. Bouchon, *Les Musulmans du Kérala à l'époque de la Découverte Portugaise*, Mare Luso-Indicum, (Genève, 1973), II, 14–15; G. Bouchon, *Regent of the Sea—Cannanore's Response to Portuguese Expansion, 1507–1528*, trans., Louise Shackley, (Delhi, 1988), 6–7.
3. M.M. Uvais, P.M. Ajmal Khan, *Islamiyat Tamizh Ilakkiya Varalaru*, (Madurai, 1986), I, 94–98.
4. M.M. Uvais, *Islam Valartha Tamizh*, (Madras, 1984), 107–108.
5. David Schulman, 'Muslim Popular Literature in Tamil: The Tamimancari Malai', in *Islam in Asia*, Yohannan Friedman, ed., (Colo., 1984), I: 176.
6. Abdul M. Karim, *Sirapurana Thiranaivu*, (Madras, 1980), 33–34.
7. R.P.M. Kani, *Islamiyat Ilakkiya Karuvulam*, (Madras, 1963), 155; K.M. Sheriff, *Vallal Seethakathiyin*, 134–37.
8. J.M. Sali, *Islamiyat Tamizh Kaaviyangal*, (Madras, 1978), 37–38.
9. M. Arunachalam, *An Introduction to the History of Tamil Literature*, (Tiruchitrambalam, 1974).

CHAPTER THREE

Tamil Muslim Printed Literature after 1835

As we have seen, Tamil Muslim literature seems to have existed from the late sixteenth century at least. Much of this literature was printed and published during the nineteenth and twentieth centuries.

Reverend William Taylor had stated that up to 1835, the only Tamil works printed by Tamils were the *Kural* and some trifles by the Tamil poetess, Auvaiyar.[1] If Taylor's information is right, then it implies that the Tamil Muslims did not produce any printed literature before 1835, while the Hindus had already started to put some of their old literature in print form. But with the relaxation of press restrictions in 1835 and the abolition of Persian as the court language and its replacement with the vernaculars of the country two years later, the English transformed the literary scene in India and the Tamil country.

It is not surprising that from the 1830s onwards, and especially during the second half of the nineteenth century, Muslim newspapers, magazines, different translations of the Quran, and other Islamic books were published in Urdu.[2] In Madras, the seat of the Tamil country, Urdu journalism had started in 1841 itself with the publication of the first Urdu newspaper, *Jamiul Akhbar*. This was at a time when Urdu journalism had not touched many of the Urdu centres of northern India, apart from Delhi and Calcutta.[3] In 1851, a translation of the Quran into Urdu was published from Madras.[4]

In 1825, a certain P. Gnanaprakasa Mudaliar, probably from Pondicherry, translated and published the *Arabian Nights Entertainment* in twelve volumes, which had the English and Tamil versions in parallel columns. This probably was the first work in Tamil related to the Arabic and Islamic countries by a Tamil, though the author was not a Tamil Muslim.

The first most important work that the Tamil Muslims themselves got published was the *Sira Puranam* in 1842, in a Hindu press. The next year a poetical work by the name, *Nakaiyantati* was published in the antati literary style, by Abdul Qadir Nainar Lebbai of Kayalpattinam. It described the pilgrimage to the *dargah* of saint Shahul Hameed of Nagore. It was also printed at a Hindu press. It is strange that the Tamil Muslims did not approach the Urdu-speaking Muslims of Madras for use of their press, though they were their co-religionists, in order to get their works published. Instead, they approached Hindu presses for the great majority of the works published in the nineteenth century and in the later years.

The Quran or the Hadith were certainly not the first works to be printed by the Tamil Muslims. Works with an Islamic theme by Tamil Muslim authors were the ones to be first printed. Old Tamil manuscripts on palm leaves were printed and published mostly during the second half of the nineteenth century. We were told by elderly, well-informed Muslims that once the old manuscripts were printed (and sometimes even when they were not printed), it was customary to consign them to the depths of wells or to the waters of fast flowing rivers, so that they would never be trampled by human feet. Thus, it was thought that their sacredness would be preserved forever. Demeerseman informs us that a similar situation prevailed in the various Islamic countries, including north Africa, where the people so revered the manuscripts that if they found one on the road, they would immediately retrieve it and put it in some safe place where it would not be trodden upon.

Whatever may be the truth in such contentions, the difficulty of locating old Tamil Muslim manuscripts, apart from those collected by the west Europeans, renders a certain credibility to such contentions. With the unhindered beginning of the Indian printing era in 1835, not only were old manuscripts put in print, but new Muslim authors also appeared in the Tamil Muslim literary horizon during this period. It is quite obvious that this would not have been possible without the advent of print culture. The accessibility to print technology had literally induced an appreciable number of Tamil Muslims to take to writing. This resulted in the production of such a large number of works and its printing and publishing, especially during the last quarter of the nineteenth century, that it would not be an exaggeration to conclude that Muslim literary activity was far greater in proportion to the total population, especially when compared to that of the Hindus. It seems as though they were trying to make up for their low literary productivity of the earlier centuries, which was limited till then, owing to the fact that the printing technology was primarily associated with Christianity and was restricted to the circle of missionaries and colonisers.

Tamil Muslim works produced after 1835 follow more or less the same pattern as the works produced before 1835. As far as the literary styles are concerned, they followed, as before, the literary styles, borrowed from Tamil, Arabic, and Persian.

The Tamil literary styles remain the most prominent. But the borrowing seems to be more varied. They have generally adopted styles like malai, antati, Chindu, Virutham, Pillait tamizh, kirttanam, patham, vannam, kovai, kummi, kalampakam. They seem to have a special preference for the malai style (see Appendix). Regarding Arabic and Persian styles, masala and munajat are Arabic styles, and nama and kissa styles are Persian. Thus, as far as style is concerned, Tamil Muslims had literally borrowed, almost everything from Tamil, Arabic, and Persian sources, with the exception of the pataippor style, which they seem to have invented themselves.

Though the majority of the Tamil Muslim works are in Tamil literary styles, yet these works contain a lot of Arabic and, to a lesser extent, Persian words. Thus, there is a continuity between the literature produced before 1835 and after. On account of this, these works continued to remain largely unintelligible to the non-Muslim Tamil reader. The noted Tamil Muslim scholar M.M. Uvais tells us that except for the *Sira Puranam*, and the works by the Tamil Sufi poet, Mastan Sahib, no Tamil Muslim work has attracted the attention of non-Muslim Tamil scholars.[6]

No other language is more intimately connected to a religion than Arabic and as noted earlier, Arabic and Islam are almost inseparable. The rejection of one entails the rejection of the other. Therefore, wherever Islam had gained a foothold in the world, Arabic too gained a foothold. This was true in the Tamil country too. But unlike Egypt, Syria, and the Maghreb countries, which were not only Islamised but also Arabised linguistically, the Tamil Muslims were never fully Arabised, i.e. they never adopted Arabic as their mother tongue, at the cost of Tamil.

This does not mean that Arabic did not find a place in their lives. They recited their daily prayers in Arabic, they read the verses of the Quran in Arabic, they used many Arabic words in their daily language. They sent their children to Arabic schools called *maktabs* or *madrasas* to learn not only about Islam but also Arabic. So the knowledge of Arabic was always considered to be essential to the knowledge of Islam itself.

This inseparability of Arabic from Islam had naturally led many Tamil Muslim scholars to use Arabic works extensively, and Persian, to some extent, in their works even after 1835, when printing was becoming more common. The resulting inconvenience was its unintelligibility to non-Muslims. This, thus, continued to distinguish fundamentally the Tamil Muslim works right through the nineteenth and twentieth centuries.

But the Tamil Muslim scholars did not stop mixing Arabic and Persian in their works. Some of them even adopted the Arabic script, in order to write their Arabic-Tamil works. Thus, their works became completely unintelligible and even inaccessible to non-Muslim Tamils. Yet, it appears that the adoption of the Arabic script by some Tamil Muslim scholars was not totally coincidental. Of course it showed their devotion to both Arabic and Islam, but it also demonstrated their desire to distinguish themselves more and more from non-Muslims and affirm their distinct identity in the Tamil religious landscape. Thus, it emerges that apart from the admixture of Arabic and Persian words in their works, Tamil Muslims had cultivated a marked predilection for the adoption of Arabic script to write their Arabic-Tamil works.

Tamil Muslims may have borrowed the Tamil literary styles and even adopted some other Tamil Hindu features in the creation of their works, but the extensive usage of Arabic and Persian words has no doubt given them a predominating non-Tamil and Islamic flavour. It brings out the importance given by the Tamil Muslims to Arabic and Persian, because of their intimate association with Islam. Moreover, Tamil Muslim authors seem to have resorted more and more to Arabic and Persian literary styles after 1835, such as the nama and kissa styles, which once again shows their penchant for using these languages. By doing this, they had probably unwittingly introduced new varieties of literature of Persian and Arabic origin. But, it appears that the mainstream Tamil scholars have taken no note of them as yet.

Though the literary worth of most of the Tamil Muslim works still remains to be ascertained by some accomplished Tamil scholar who is also well-versed in Arabic and Persian and also Islamic knowledge, the existence of these works themselves demonstrate that many Tamil Muslim authors did possess a certain knowledge of Arabic and Persian and also of classical Tamil. But unfortunately they failed to provide an adequate basis for a systematic study of their Tamil or rather Arabic-Tamil in the form of an Arabic-Tamil dictionary or a vocabulary book or a grammar book. There was also no grammar book forthcoming on the Arabic language. This too seems to have contributed to the general isolation of the Tamil Muslim literature. Actually, the first grammar book in the Arabic language by a Tamil Muslim was not even published from Tamil Nadu. Instead, it was published from Kandy in Ceylon. It contained 112 pages and was authored by Muhammad Kassim Ibn Siddik Lebbai. He wrote two other Arabic grammar books, which were again published from Kandy. All these three copies are available in the India Office Library, London.

In 1910, a 96-page booklet on the etymology in Arabic grammar, titled, '*Tohufathul Tullab*', was published from Cuddalore. The author was a certain Moulvi Khadir Ahmad. Three years later, Abdul Nahab Sahib brought out a short Arabic-Tamil primer containing just 18 pages, from Madras. In 1919, Shahul Hameed Lebbai, brought out another short Arabic grammar book of 96 pages. Thus, as far as Arabic grammar books in Tamil are concerned, it is quite obvious from the preceding, that Tamil Muslim efforts were totally lacking and indeed insignificant in this regard. Besides, there was also no Persian grammar book in Tamil, as far as I know, during this period.

As far as Arabic-Tamil dictionaries are concerned, the first attempt seems to have been made only in 1905, by one of the most famous Unani practitioners of Madras in those days, Hakim Muhammad Abd Allah Sahib. But this dictionary contains just 144 pages and is largely incomplete. Another attempt seems to have been made only in 1918 by Muhammad Ibrahim Ibn Hassan Lebbai. It contains more than 425 pages. Unfortunately, the Tamil in the dictionary is written in the Arabic script and is therefore not useful or intelligible to a person who does not know Arabic. These two copies can also be found in the India Office Library.

It appears that another attempt was made by Moulana Syed Yassin around 1950 in Ceylon. But the Tamil in this dictionary too was written in the Arabic script. M.M. Uvais himself admits the inadequacies of these three dictionaries and brought out his own Arabic-Tamil dictionary in the Tamil script containing nearly 300 pages in 1983, published by the Madurai Kamaraj University.[7] But, no attempt seems to have been made to prepare a proper Persian-Tamil dictionary. It is crystal clear from the above that the efforts deployed by the Tamil Muslims in the production of Arabic grammar books in Tamil and Arabic-Tamil dictionaries were highly deficient and totally inadequate, particularly when we take into account the amount of literature produced by them in Tamil or Arabic-Tamil.

The question now arises about the quality and nature of the Arabic and Persian that the Tamil Muslim authors used in their literary works. One of the staunchest critics of the Arabic-Tamil was P. Dawood Sha, the editor of the Tamil Muslim periodical, *Dar-ul-Islam*. He was a product of modern English education and held a B.A. degree. He was also a recognised Tamil scholar, having won the coveted gold medal of the famous Madurai Tamil Academy (Sangam). He took to task the *alims* and *moulvis* for their inadequate knowledge of both Tamil and Arabic-Tamil, which he said was 'kitchen Tamil'. He also dismissed the works produced by them in Arabic-Tamil, which he claimed can be understood only if their authors were present. He also directed his ire against some Muslim publishing houses in Madras, which published such Arabic-Tamil books.[8]

More recently, Moulana Syed Yassin of Ceylon, who is also reputed for his knowledge of the Islamic faith, wrote that the main reason why he wrote and published his Arabic-Tamil dictionary in 1950, was his desire to help the development of Arabic and give Arabic-Tamil a new life among Tamil Muslims. Many of the works of Tamil Muslim Arabic scholars in Arabic-Tamil were full of mistakes and the true meaning of the Arabic verse, when rendered into Arabic-Tamil, was distorted or obscured. It was in order to remedy this state of affairs to some extent that he had written and published an Arabic-Tamil dictionary.[9]

The foregoing proves that P. Dawood Sha's condemnation of Arabic-Tamil was not after all an exaggeration. He was probably the first Tamil Muslim scholar who pointed out the inadequacies of the Arabic-Tamil or the Tamil admixture of Arabic and Persian of the Tamil Muslim authors. M.M. Uvais himself does not seem to contest the claims of Moulana Syed Yassin. Instead his silence seems to endorse the Moulana's view.

The implication of this is that in spite of all the inadequacies of Arabic-Tamil, the very fact that the Tamil Musim authors, right from the sixteenth century, strove to integrate both Arabic and Persian into their Tamil, however perfectly or imperfectly, clearly demonstrates their intention of drawing a line between their literature and the rest of the Tamil literature. So the question of clubbing their literature together with the non-Muslim Tamil literature never arose and probably may never arise, unless the Tamil Muslim authors choose to stray away from their original preference for Arabic and Persian words in their works. This has contributed, historically, not only to the unique identity of Tamil Muslim literature, but also to the Tamil Muslim society whose innermost longings and feelings has been greatly reflected in its literature.

As noted earlier, the second half of the nineteenth century, saw the production and publication of a rich variety of Islamic literature in Tamil Nadu, by a galaxy of Tamil Muslim authors and publishers. I have been able to enumerate about 60 books and booklets between 1835 and 1866 (see Appendix I and Appendix II). But, from 1867 to 1920, there was an extraordinary increase in the production, printing, and publishing of Tamil Muslim books, booklets, pamphlets, and tracts. During this period, I have been able to enumerate more than 1,300 Tamil Muslim works that were published. The several re-editions that were brought out now and then are not included in this list. All these works were created by several Tamil Muslim poets and writers. My enumerations as found in the Appendix, should contain the great bulk of Tamil Muslim printed works from 1835 to 1920.

If we take a closer look at those works, apart from the great number of the publications we will find many surprising and revealing features. There is no better way to do this than to group and classify them subject-wise. In doing this, as has been done in the Appendix, the literary activity of the Tamil Muslims during this period, will reveal itself clearly even to a casual reader.

One cannot fully understand the life history of a community

or society, the way it behaves and functions, its core and peripheral values, especially when it is a question of understanding its past, by studying just one or two Tamil Muslim books or by concentrating on a particular literary style or a particular author or by choosing a small Muslim village and studying the few Muslims who live there. This can only give a very limited and sometimes even a lop-sided view of Tamil Muslim society and literature. This has been unfortunately the paradise of many anthropologists and sociologists. They have always liked to study a particular aspect of a society and then make, sometimes, the broadest of generalisations. Of course this is a far easier method than the time-consuming method that I have employed in this book in order to have the broadest possible view on Tamil Muslim literature and society.

This broad, all-encompassing view can be achieved only by taking into account the entire gamut of Tamil literary production, that is to say every single Tamil Muslim work published from 1835 to 1920. This is precisely what has been done. Of the more than 1,360 works published during this period, only about a hundred books deal with subjects that are secular in nature and outlook, i.e., which do not deal with religion or with Arabic and Persian, associated with Islam.

Secular Works

Before we consider these secular publications, we have to determine what is secular or secularism, especially from the Tamil Muslim point of view. Traditionally, a Hindu king was expected to uphold the *dharma* or the law according to which the individual and society functioned. He could not promulgate any law of his own conception or that of his ministers, which attempted to alter the eternal laws (*Sanatana Dharma*). In short, he was the upholder of the dharma. His failing in this duty would have had serious consequences. We have the striking example of the Pandya king in the *Silapattikaram*, who died of remorse when he came to know that he had made a serious mistake in one of his judgements.[10]

Apart from this, in dealing with foreigners (*mlechas*), who had come peacefully to India as refugees or asylum seekers or as merchants, as the Jews and the Parsis had, the Hindu kings did not expect them to renounce their culture or religion. Instead royal grants were given to them which gave them full cultural, religious and other rights, without the slightest attempt to impose 'Hindu Dharma' on them.[11]

The Muslim laws, too, had religious sanction very much like the Hindu laws. They were based on the Quran and the Hadith, the words of God Himself and his Prophet Mohammad. As a result they were not subject to alterations even by the most powerful Muslim sultans. Actually, the sultans had a religious obligation to see that the society functioned according to these laws that were derived from the Quran and the Hadith where belief in One God was central.

Thus, when the British sought to introduce their value systems based on secularism, which did not give a central place to God, and sought to substitute Persian and Arabic with English, the Muslims had reasons to worry. It appears that secularism was born in the West as a reaction to Christianity. Historically, its main object seems to have been to counter Christian values and Christian influence over the State. A genuine secular State is actually the antithesis of a religious State, for the former does not accept God and His laws as the central guiding principle of the State. Similarly, a genuine secular education does not allow religion or God to occupy the central place in the educational curriculum or system.

Thus, while the secular State fundamentally contradicted an Islamic State centralised upon God and based on His laws, secular education neglected religion and concentrated on secular subjects such as arithmetic, science, the study of languages, history, geography, etc. Even the study of religion was reduced to a sort of secular subject. Thus the very idea of secularism directly threatened the historical conditioning of the Muslims in which Islam occupied the central place. As a result, Muslims, especially the Tamil Muslims, kept away from modern secular education and continued to instruct their children in the traditional madrasas and maktabs, where they acquired some knowledge of Islam. Many such madrasas and maktabs were opened during the nineteenth and twentieth centuries.[12]

This did not prevent the British from opening more and more secular schools. Very soon it became obvious that a secular, English education was the key to employment in the British Indian administrative structure. Hindus were definitely stealing a march over the Muslims in the employment field, because of the reservations the Muslims had over secular education.

Very quickly, i.e., from 1851 at least, Muslims realised that secular subjects such as science and mathematics, history and geography might be non-religious in character, but they were certainly not anti-Islamic. Therefore, from the Islamic point of view, there was nothing wrong in studying them as long as they did not challenge or threaten the fundamental religious grounding.[13]

Printing was also regarded as fundamentally secular in nature and was in fact the basis for the spread of secular education, through the printing of books on secular subjects at the government and missionary presses. Secular education implied the acceptance of printing and printed books on secular subjects by the Muslims. There is no evidence of Tamil Muslim opposition to printing, as far as can be ascertained, on the grounds that printing was secular and therefore anti-religious.

The first Tamil Muslim secular book that I was able to trace was published sometime before 1866 dealing with cookery. This was a work translated into Tamil from Persian and probably the same was re-edited in 1903 and 1908. The second work was probably a Tamil-Urdu vocabulary book, published in 1874. A few, similar works were published in the subsequent years. In 1876, even a Burmese-Tamil vocabulary book was brought out by a certain Muhamattu Kautu. A few other books were authored by Tamil Muslims on the handling of pearls. Some songs were also sung by them, about natural calamities and epidemics (see Appendix J).

These works in spite of their secular character seem to have been dictated by the needs of the Tamil Muslim community rather than anything else. For instance, the book on cookery translated from Persian dealt with Muslim cuisine rather than Hindu cuisine. Similarly the publication of the various vocabulary books were meant for the exclusive use of Tamil Muslims. The books published on pearls were also meant primarily for the use of Tamil Muslims, who were traditionally traders in pearls. During times of epidemics, for e.g., the plague, and at times during natural calamities such as floods, Muslims were as affected as the Hindus. Hence some Muslim authors came out with songs lamenting these natural calamities. A few reports on schools and *sabhas* were also published in the form of books and booklets, but these reports were exclusively on Muslim-run schools and sabhas.

But, there were other types of secular books such as those on arithmetic, handwork, magic, hypnotism and mesmerism, humorous stories and fiction, which were directed towards a larger public, consisting of Hindus, Muslims, and Christians. But, such works were extremely few and I have been able to enumerate only about a forty or so, up to 1920. This indubitably demonstrates that the Tamil Muslims, on the whole, were not interested in the publication of books on genuine secular subjects for the benefit of the general public consisting of Muslims and non-Muslims. Even when they did appear to publish some works with a secular character, it was primarily meant for the Muslims. Thus, it would not be out of place to conclude that though printing was undoubtedly secular in character, yet it did not contribute much to the promotion of secular knowledge among the Tamil Muslims and the publication of more secular books.

The situation does not seem to be very different in the field of medicine, which is also a secular subject. John Murdoch had mentioned a medical work of 28 pages by a Tamil Muslim, titled, *Vaittiya Satakam*, (see Appendix II), published before 1866. But, during the last quarter of the nineteenth century and the first quarter of the twentieth century, we have been able to enumerate more than 40 medical works by Tamil Muslims. The great majority of these works deal with *yunani* medicine, which is considered to be of Muslim origin. Only a few works by Tamil Muslims deal with indigenous medicines. Further, some Tamil Muslims take pride in claiming that one of their co-religionists, Yakobu Sithar, had made a major contribution to the indigenous *siddha* system of medicine (see Appendix G). Whatever it may be, the line dividing medicine practised by the Muslims from the rest of Indian medicine is quite obvious from the publications devoted to the former by the Tamil Muslims and the importance given by them to the yunani system of medicine.

Controversial Works

The preceding works on secular subjects were definitely not controversial in nature. But there were many controversial publications, authored by Tamil Muslims during the period under study. The controversial publications are of various sorts.

From the time printing was introduced into India by the west European missionaries, controversies in the religious field seem to have acquired a new dimension. The missionaries, in their zeal to propagate Christianity, attacked both Hinduism and Islam through the print media. Some of the publications against Islam were brought out by the various missionary organisations from the early decades of the eighteenth century itself. We do not have any records about the response of the Tamil Muslims during this early period until 1835, when print restrictions were relaxed and Indians took to printing in right earnest. This, nevertheless, does not mean that there was no opposition to Christian criticisms of Islam.

During the first half of the nineteenth century or a little later, a full-blooded work of 140 pages which condemned Christianity was printed and published. The author of this work was the famous Tamil Muslim Sufi philosopher, Mastan Sahib, who lived in Tiruchirappalli, probably in the first half of the nineteenth century. He is believed to have been a local Hindu convert to Islam and was held in high regard by both Hindus and Muslims. He is believed to have disputed with the Christian missionaries and catechists. In his work, which he claims to have written after careful examination of the Bible, he asserts that Christ is man and not God, that the Bible is not the word of God and that Christians were wrong in saying that Jesus Christ came to this world to suffer and die for the sins of men, etc. (see Appendix II). This work can be considered to be the most elaborate criticism of Christianity by a Tamil Muslim.

Probably, at least a few tracts or pamphlets criticising Christianity must have been published by Tamil Muslims during this period given that Christian missionaries continued to publish their works against both Islam and Hinduism. But, from the last quarter of the nineteenth century, when printing had developed much more among Indians, Muslims dared to publish more works running down Christianity and replying to the Christian tracts against Islam in the same vein. We have been able to enumerate more than ten such works (see Appendix I).

During this period, Tamil Muslims also criticised Hinduism, by pointing out its defects and drawbacks. I have been able to enumerate five such works (see Appendix I), though it shows that the intensity of criticism was much stronger against Christianity than against Hinduism.

There were many other controversial works involving the Muslims exclusively. For instance a certain Mukamattu Icumayil Sakipu wrote and published a work against Wahabism, and another tract refuted the heretical teachings of a Shaik. Still another tract criticised the *ulemas* and the alims. Wrong interpretation of a particular religious work or verse or even a controversial speech by a Muslim were occasions for the publication of tracts, pamphlets, and sometimes even books by Tamil Muslims. Later, we shall deal more extensively with these controversial aspects and the role played by printing.

The most controversial of the works, authored by a few Tamil Muslims, were the works which were overtly Hindu in character and content. They openly sang the praise of Hindu gods and goddesses such as Sakti, Subramanya, Palani Antavar, Sulakkal Mariamman, Kulamayi, Vishnu and Shiva and the Hindu gurus such as Swami Avaraiananda and sacred rivers like the Cauvery. They seem to have particularly liked Hindu pilgrim songs.

I have been able to enumerate 24 such works published up to 1920. A good number of them were pilgrim songs. This seems to suggest that at least some authors would have written and published such songs for the Hindu pilgrims, especially during festival times, in order to make some quick money. This was confirmed by some of my elderly Muslim informants. So only very few Tamil Muslim authors probably wrote out of genuine devotion for Hindu gods and goddesses. Such authors are so few and far between, and as they seem to have written only for a Hindu public, their influence on Tamil Muslim society as such has to be deemed to be very marginal and even insignificant.

Of these secular and controversial works, the former were not anti-religious, as we have seen. As for the latter, many were written in defence of Islam or against Christianity or Hinduism. Some were the products of intra-Muslim debates. Therefore, fundamentally they were religious works. On the whole, these works constitute only a minor portion of the literary production of the Tamil Muslims. Next, we shall go into the remaining major portion of Tamil Muslim literature.

The Bulk of Tamil Muslim Literature

Islam is a historical religion. Prophet Mohammad himself and his companions and descendants are all historical personalities. The various Muslim rulers and saints of the Islamic heartlands were also historical personalities. Muslims give great importance to history. This has given rise to a literature in the form of legends, tales, histories and biographies woven around these historical personalities and their heroic deeds in battles and their lives. Their opponents were generally those who opposed Islam and who were finally overcome. Thus, we have poems that describe the successful expeditions of Prophet Mohammad, poems on the Prophet's companions, relatives, and descendants like Hassan, and their battles waged in favour of Islam, and poems on the Prophet himself describing his life as in the *Sira*

Puranam. Then we have legendary poems on the lives and feats of various Islamic personalities, caliphs and saints of the Islamic countries of Egypt, Persia, etc. Most of these works revolve around the legends of a single Islamic personality. But there are also a few works such as the *Kasasulanbiya* which recount the stories of various Islamic personalities and prophets. Such stories constitute the first group in Tamil Muslim religious literature.

The second group consists of poems and works generally in praise of the Prophet, his companions and descendants and other Islamic personalities such as saints, kings, etc. They are mostly written in the Tamil literary style, but the contents are fundamentally Islamic and are invariably centred around Islamic personalities. Sometimes a poem might contain verses in praise of several Muslim saints including the Prophet too. Most of such works are not very lengthy, unlike the works of the first group. The above two groups alone account for more than 350 publications during the period under study (see Appendix A and B).

The third group consists of more than 220 works, on Islamic doctrines, prayers, law, ethics, theology, rituals, marriage and other aspects of Muslim culture. There are some works specifically meant for Muslim women and even children. Generally, Tamil Muslims seem not to have taken much interest in writing commentaries on the *fiqh* (law). Most of their works were brief and not lengthy (see Appendix C). A few works seems to have been translated from the original Hindustani, Persian, or Arabic such as the *Fikhul Akparin Tarjuma* (*Al fikh al Akbar*) or Al Ghazalli's works. There has been no attempt to comment on these translated works. Some Tamil Muslim translators such as Nellikuppam Abd al Raman had resorted to translating Islamic works such as the '*Kimiyai sa'adt*' of Al Ghazalli, from its Hindustani version into Tamil, rather than directly from the Arabic original. This, in a way, shows the inadequate knowledge of Arabic by the Tamil Muslims.

Actually this inadequacy appears to be more glaring in the translation into Tamil of the Quran and the Hadith literature, and in the commentaries written about them. We shall deal with this fourth group of Tamil literature later and separately.

The fifth group includes the mystical works and other religious works. The mystical works have great importance for the Muslims of India. It is asserted that probably on no other aspect of Muslim religious life was more literature produced in India than on mysticism.[14] This may be true of north India, but in the south, going by the number of publications on mysticism this contention does not seem to be wholly true as far as Tamil Muslims are concerned. But, these works have a very special importance in the Tamil Muslim religious life as well.

One of the foremost of the Islamic mystics of the Tamil country was of course Mastan Sahib. He is believed to belong to the Qadiriyya Sufi order. His most famous works were published under the title, *Tirattu*. Several editions of these works have been published since then. Hindus were particularly involved in the publication of his works.

Fewer Arabic words used in his poems seem to be one of the reasons why Hindus showed interest in them. Besides, Mastan Sahib has used several Hindu religious words and ideas such as Nandiswaran, Siva, Sakti, Brahman, Ganapati in his poems and also seems to have imitated the great Tamil Hindu poet, Tayumanavar, which, as John Murdoch points out, probably pushed the Hindus to consider him as one of their sages (see Appendix II). These two factors go to support the view that Mastan Sahib was a Hindu convert to Islam, who was unable to eliminate his Hindu background in his poems.

But it should not be forgotten that his poems are in full praise of Prophet Mohammad and the Muslim saints like Abdul Qadir Jilani. It should also not be forgotten that he was probably the first Tamil Muslim to bring out a book against Christianity by asserting that Christ is man, which is the traditional Muslim point of view. He thus established his Islamic identity, though controversies about his religious views still persist.

Apart from this controversial Sufi, the rest of the Tamil Muslim Sufis seem to be in the traditional Islamic mould. Of these, two are more famous than the others. They are, Tarkalai

Pir Muhammad and Gnaniyar Sahib. The former is believed to have lived in the seventeenth century and was buried at Tarkalai in Kanyakumari district. The latter seems to have lived in the eighteenth century at Kottaru in Tirunelveli. They have published several mystical works in Tamil, but Gnaniyar Sahib seems to have used more Arabic words in his works.

Then there were the other Sufis of lesser fame or rather of local fame. They seem to have used Arabic words extensively in their works. Some of them are Sheik Muhammad Madina Sahib, who died at Kottaru in 1936, Mouna Gur Sheik Mastan, whose tomb is at Tondi, Kalvathu Nayakar of Kilakarai, Macharekai Sithar of Tirunelveli and Sam Shihabuddin of Kayalpattinam.[15]

Though the literature produced by Tamil Muslim Sufis are not abundant, yet the biographies of the Sufis, written in Tamil or Arabic-Tamil, has a certain importance. In Tamil Nadu, we find Sufi dargahs not only in cities and towns but also in remote villages. Their numbers and influence are so great in the Tamil Muslim society that one can say that the dargah-oriented Muslim traditions have a life of their own, apart from the mosque-based traditions. Naturally, this has given rise to a literature in the form of biographies of the Sufis.

If one goes through these biographies carefully, one cannot fail to note the centrality given to Allah, the superiority of the Prophet, and the other Islamic principles such as brotherhood and equality. In their biographies, it has been repeatedly stated that the supernatural and the healing power of the Sufis and their punishing and rewarding capabilities are all due to the grace of Allah.[16] Moreover, the Sufis hardly contested the superiority of the Prophet. They behaved like any other Muslim, saying their prayers and even going to Mecca. Their biographies portrayed them as more powerful than Hindu deities, yogis, and even kings.[17]

In the light of this, it is simply out of place to argue, as some tend to do, that the power of the Sufis was similar to that entailed in the concept of female and male power in Hinduism and to try to prove that Sufis were Hinduised, which is no doubt the line of thinking of Louis Dumont. Of course one can pursue this argument as an academic debate and there have been many such arguments that lead nowhere. But one should be clear on the point that the Islamic identity of the Sufis, including even that of a controversial personality such as Mastan Sahib, contrary to all scholarly notions and feelings, is irrefutable.

In the sixth group, we have included stories, novels, dramas, and books on maxims. Many of these books are actually translations from Hindustani, Arabic, or Persian. The characters of these stories, dramas and novels are purely Islamic. Generally, the stories are set in the Islamic countries, except for a few as those of P. Daud Shah (P. Dawood Sha). It is surprising to note that the Tamil Muslims hardly took note of the Hindu stories in Sanskrit or any other Indian language, other than Urdu, during this period. The lone exception that I was able to figure out was a prose rendering of the Hindu story of *Vikramathithan*, by P.V. Muhammad Ibrahim. This once again shows the Tamil Muslim's attachment to Arabic, Persian, and Hindustani, which they considered as being intimately associated with Islam.

Apart from the above printed works, there exists a special category of Muslim books, which are lithographed. I have been able to enumerate about 300 such works. Lithography was invented in Germany in the eighteenth century by Alois Senefelder. Very quickly, it seemed to have spread across the Muslim world, especially because it needed the services of the copyists and calligraphists to some extent, unlike printing.[18] Demeerseman even argues that Turks, Persians, Hindus, Egytians, and north Africans got used to printing only by adopting lithography first.[19]

It appears that lithography was introduced into India during the first decades of the nineteenth century itself and the first lithographed book was brought out in India or rather northern India, probably in 1801.[20] This is not surprising because while Diehl lists fourteen printing presses in Madras during the first half of the nineteenth century, there seems to have been as many lithographic establishments in Lucknow during the same period.[21] Muslims in north India seem to have taken a liking to lithography at the expense of typography and Diehl maintains that several hundred north Indian poets, whose spiritual home was Lucknow got their works lithographed. Bombay Brahmins also seem to have used lithography until at least 1840, because of the reservations they had about the usage of printing ink.[22] But Diehl, who had in her collection nearly 300 Madras-printed books, did not seem to have possessed a single lithographed book, which might mean that lithography reached the Tamil Muslims only after 1850.[23]

Unlike the north Indian Muslims, Tamil Muslims appear to have been extremely slow in adopting lithography. This is not surprising because like the Tamil Hindus, they too were accustomed to writing on palm leaves. They probably felt neither the need for calligraphists, or copyists, or lithographists, because of such traditions. They might have gradually taken to lithography under the influence of the Urdu-speaking Muslims of Madras. I have been able to trace the first lithographed Arabic-Tamil work which was published only in 1862. There may be other books lithographed before this, but in the present state of our knowledge we are unaware of them.

Between 1862 and 1920 nearly 300 lithographic works were published (see Appendix), in Tamil or the Arabic script. The principal concern of almost all of these works was Islam and all subjects related to it. Rarely did the Tamil Muslim publish or author books, whether lithographed or printed, which did not have a relationship with Islam, or Arabic, or Persian. Such was the Tamil Muslims' attachment to Islam and all that was Muslim.

The preceding survey of Tamil Muslim literature, both before 1835 and after it, brings out clearly that the vast majority of the Tamil Muslim literary productions, except for a few controversial works and some genuine secular works, were fundamentally religious in character or were associated with Islam, or Arabic, or Persian in one way or the other. This literature was produced by members of the three Tamil Muslim sub-divisions, the Marakkayars, Ravuttars and Lebbais. The works have been created, printed and published from different parts of Tamil Nadu, such as Melvisharam in north Arcot,

Kottaru in the deep south, Salem in the west, Madras and so on. Some works have been also published from Ceylon.

But the two fundamental traits of the immense majority of these works are the extensive usage of Arabic and Persian words and the importance given to Islam and all that is related to it. We have also seen that there has been a historical continuity of these traits from the sixteenth century up to the twentieth century, in spite of the popularisation of printing from 1835. Of course, Tamil Muslims had used Tamil literary styles and features in their works. But they never overwhelmed the fundamental Islamic nature of these works. This survey definitely supports this finding.

Actually there is no better method to study the past of a particular community than to rely upon the literature produced by the members of that community. It is here that the innermost feelings and thoughts, their preoccupations and worries, their longings and desires are reflected. It should also be remembered that the poet or writer, writes above all for others to read. He plays a great role not only in shaping the minds of the people, but he also reflects the minds of the people through his writings. As a result, it is absolutely reasonable to rely on them, not only to understand their literature, but also to understand the society that is reflected in that literature. This has been pursued here with regard to Tamil Muslim literature and society.

So, in the course of their historical evolution, as reflected in their literature, Tamil Muslims have been conditioned by two core or predominant factors. Firstly, Islam itself and all that it stands for fundamentally, and secondly, Arabic and to a lesser extent Persian which are associated with Islam. It is these two factors that distinguish not only their literature but also their community from the rest of Tamil literature and society. Besides, we cannot talk of Islamic literature, Islamic society, or Islamic identity without the core factors, being fundamentally Islamic.

There already seems to be a domain in which a certain dilution is taking place. For instance, today, writing in Arabic-Tamil, using the Arabic script is no more desirable. Moreover, many modern Islamic writers such as the poet

K.M. Sheriff, owing to various circumstances, have taken to writing in a Tamil that is understandable to the larger public, i.e., the Hindus, which implies that the usage of Arabic words on a large scale is no more in vogue in their works with Tamil gaining the upper hand. They have been lately winning awards instituted by the Tamil Nadu state government for excelling in Tamil literature. But the taking to a more chaste Tamil does not mean that their prime conditioning factors, i.e., Islam itself and its fundamental values, have also been put aside. In fact, it appears that the medium of Tamil itself is being put to good use to strengthen the prime core factors. This strengthening is also reflected in the fact that today hardly any Tamil Muslim writes songs in praise of the Hindu gods and goddesses, etc., unlike during the period of our survey.

Francis Robinson is, of course, right to some extent when he claims that Islam's reformist zeal will eventually weed out all un-Islamic features. He has fixed no time limit for this to happen. But he seems not to give much importance to the fact that it can also be the other way round. These trends are unpredictable at this point in time.

Imtiaz Ahmad's knowledge is derived through 'snapshot techniques' as Robinson would call it and therefore it is extremely limited in time and space. But if he takes a longer view into the past, as we have done, he will be in a better position to have a broader understanding of Islamic communities in India, which are not at all homogeneous.

My survey also does not permit me to assert, like Louis Dumont, that beneath the ultimate Islamic values lie the non-Islamic Hindu values. On the contrary, this survey has found the unquestionable predominance of Islam and all that is related to it, and the subordination of Hindu features and aspects in spite of the fact that Tamil Muslims lived and continue to live in a predominantly Hindu society.

It is surprising that Dumont, in spite of having done field work in Tamil Nadu, did not notice the presence of Tamil Muslims there and had not taken note of the principle of egalitarianism prevalent in Tamil Muslim society, which had nothing to do with the Hindu hierarchy. This is the drawback of many anthropologists and sociologists. They either do not care to look backwards into history or they do not care to look beyond the particular village or temple of their study. Sometimes they depend too much on their informants and they even generously attribute the authorship of their books to the lone informant or a few informants. This is understandable to some extent, because many of them are not well-versed in the language of their informants and are therefore at a loss to understand the innermost thoughts and feelings of the informants or the communities whom they represent. But it appears that some scholars had sought to turn this disadvantage into an advantage by representing the informant himself as the author of the book. Thus, if there were any factual or interpretative errors in the book, the real author could blame the informant or informants and escape criticism. I think, Louis Dumont has been more or less a pioneer of this, apparently innocent, but cunning method of research.[24]

If the situation of the old breed of scholars of western origin such as Louis Dumont, who had the distinct advantage of having the colonial experience or having just emerged from the colonial experience, was such, then we need not speak of the new breed of scholars, who do not have the colonial experience and who have to start from scratch. These scholars, who, for the most part, are not well-versed with the Indian languages and acutely lack indepth experience and knowledge and the feeling about things Indian, apart from bookish knowledge, will have a tendency to rely heavily on local informants and interpreters and will generally select a very restricted area or aspect of the Indian society and make it the object of their study. They will tend to understand Indian society through their restricted or even truncated studies.

It is certain now that print technology had brought about a transformation in the production of Tamil Muslim literature, especially with regard to the number of works published. The predominant interest of most of these works was, as we have seen, Islam and all that was related to it, which testified to the fact that all Tamil Muslims were no doubt predominantly 'Islamic-minded'.

Print technology had actually come to Tamil Nadu from western Europe. It had played a great role there, first in the field of religion and later in the development of science and industry and in the evolution of society.

But in Tamil Nadu, print, a western technological product, had been put to use by the Tamil Muslims from 1835 to consolidate their Islamic identity, through the publication of hundreds of books with an Islamic theme. Probably, this would not have been the case, if they had relied only on oral or written methods of transmission and communication of knowledge.

It would not be an exaggeration to say that this consolidation of Islamic identity through the print media, had helped the Tamil Muslims to readily identify themselves with the wider Islamic world and participate in the Khilafat movement launched in order to protect the Caliphate in Turkey. Neither modern science nor industries, nor the modern values like secularism, could either submerge or weaken the Islamic identity of the Tamil Muslims during the period under study and even later, when the Tamil Muslims in their large majority, supported the creation of Pakistan.

Thus, it becomes necessary to delve into the influence that printing exercised on Tamil Muslims and their literature. We would have to assess, above all, what sort of changes and debates printing brought about in Tamil Muslim society. In the course of our survey, we have taken only passing note of the various controversies and debates in Tamil Muslim society during their historical evolution. These controversies and debates seem to have been made possible or accentuated by the advent of printing. Therefore, it is necessary to go into this in detail. We have to find out the nature of the influence of print technology on Tamil Muslims and whether the latter resisted it because it was a product of the Christian West. We have also to find out the real reasons that hindered the adoption of printing by them and what role printing played in strengthening or diluting the Islamic identity and conditioning of the Tamil Muslims. Besides, we have also to explore why they had to wait until the 1940s before a full translation and publication of the Quran into Tamil could be made.

All of this will not merely be based on oral testimony, which of course has its own value, but will be based on the usual relevant, authentic/archival and library material. Anthropologists tend to rely on oral testimonies. But, these are liable to errors by the informants owing to circumstances, passage of time, lack of memory, deliberate twisting of facts, etc. But the historian cannot be content with such a method. He always has a longer view and probably broader view as well which will be pursued in this study.

Notes

1. William Taylor, *A Catalogue Raisonné of Oriental Manuscripts*, (United Scottish Press, Madras, 1862), III, 21.
2. Barbara Metcalf, *Islamic Revival in British India Deoband, 1860–1900*, (Princeton University Press, Princeton, New Jersey, 1982), 202–204; Francis Robinson, 'Technology and Religious Change: Islam and the Impact of Print', in *Modern Asian Studies*, I (1993): 27, 233.
3. Safiullah Syed, 'Urdu Journalism in Tamilnadu from 1840 to 1850', in *Annals of Oriental Research*, XXVII, Part I and II, 7–9.
4. Christian, W. Troll, *Islam in India: Studies and Commentaries*, (New Delhi, 1982), 135–142.
5. A. Demeerseman, *Imprimerie en Orient et au Maghreb: Une Etape Décisive de la Culture et de la Psychologie*, (Tunis, 1954), 66.
6. M.M. Uvais, *Tamizh Ilakkiya Arabu Sol Akarati*, (Madurai, 1988), 7–8.
7. Ibid., 18–19.
8. *Dar-ul-Islam*, I (January, 1923).
9. M.M. Uvais, *Tamizh Ilakkiya*, 19.
10. Ramachandra, V.R. Dikshitar, *The Cilapatikaram*, (Madras, 1978).
11. See, for e.g., Geneviève Bouchon, *Regent of the Sea—Cannanore's Response to Portuguese Expansion, 1507–1528*, trans., Louise Shacley, (Delhi, 1988), 6–7.

12. J.B.P. More, *The Political Evolution of Muslims in Tamilnadu and Madras, 1930–1947,* (Hyderabad, 1997), 52–56.
13. Ibid., 57.
14. *The Encyclopaedia of Islam,* (Leiden, 1971), III, 435.
15. G.M. Abdul Karim, *Islamaum Tamizhum,* (Tirunelveli, 1985), 89–110.
16. J.B.P. More, *The Political Evolution of Muslims,* 60.
17. Ibid., 29–30.
18. A. Demeerseman, *La Lithographie Arabe et Tunisienne,* (Tunis, 1954), 16.
19. Ibid., 1.
20. Ibid., 19.
21. K.S. Diehl, 'The Printing Press—An Agent of Strength', in *Journal of Tamil Studies,* II (October 1970), 2, Part II: 11–12.
22. Ibid., 11, 13; *Encyclopaedie de l'Islam,* (1986), 795–796.
23. K.S. Diehl, *The Printing Press,* 11.
24. Louis Dumont, *A South Indian Subcaste—Social Organisation and Religion of the Pramalai Kallar,* this is the doctoral dissertation of Louis Dumont written in 1954, and translated into English in 1986. (Delhi, 1986). For a more recent work of this nature, please see the book by Viramma Josiane, Jean Luc Racine, *Une Vie Paria: Le Rire de Asservis, Inde du Sud,* (Paris, 1995).

PART II

Print Culture among the Tamil Muslims

CHAPTER FOUR

Print History

In order to study the print culture among the Tamil Muslims and ascertain the influence of print technology over them, it is necessary to know a little about the history of printing, especially printing in the Islamic countries of the Muslim heartlands. This will help us to situate the position of Tamil Muslims with regard to printing in comparison with other Islamic communities in the Indian sub-continent and abroad.

Much work has been done on the history of printing in the west European countries. But its influence on human evolution in general and human thinking in particular is still a subject of great controversy. There are those who hold that print technology was at the service of man, while some others think that print was a part of the intellectual activity of man.[1]

Gun powder and the compass were two great and ancient Chinese inventions. Its adoption by the west Europeans, who were until then in the backyard of world civilisation, facilitated their development and their expansion across the world and contributed probably also to the development of new technologies in Europe.

Globalisation is not a recent phenomenon. It has been taking place from time immemorial, in the technological, economic, social, and religious spheres. Though gun powder and the compass were Chinese inventions, yet only their adoption by the west Europeans led to their globalisation. Today many people, on account of the globalisation of these inventions, do not even know that they were originally Chinese inventions.

The transformation wrought by these inventions are enormous and incalculable. Whether it was man who brought about these transformations through his intelligence and capacity, or whether it was the dynamics of the inventions themselves, which through their interaction with man provoked these transformations will remain a debatable question.

Like gun powder and the compass, printing, too, was one of the ancient Chinese inventions. Japanese, Korean, Chinese, and Uighur Turks were already printing several hundred years before printing made its appearance in western Europe in the fifteenth century through Johann Gutenberg. By the end of the second century A.D., the Chinese had invented a method for printing texts by utilising the three elements necessary for printing that they had at their disposal, namely, paper, ink, and surfaces bearing texts carved in relief.[2]

The first surviving example of the printed word comes from Japan, in the form of Buddhist charms printed from copper blocks around A.D. 770. Some of the early printed texts were actually classics of Buddhist thought. In 1907, Sir Aurel Stein, discovered a Buddhist book in the caves of the Thousand Buddhas in China titled, *Hiraha Sutra*, which dates back to A.D. 868. This was probably the first book ever printed in the history of man. In the tenth century, when the technique of block printing was perfected in China, the entire Buddhist canon, *Tripitaka*, was published.[3]

About 1040, Pi Sheng invented moveable type printing. He used moveable type made of ceramic material. It is stated that he also made tin types. The next step was taken by Weng Chang, also a Chinese, in 1314, when he prepared wooden types. Moveable metal type was extensively used for government printing in Korea from the thirteenth century onwards.[4]

It is generally believed that print was adopted by the Islamic world only in the nineteenth century.[5] But paper-making, which was also a Chinese invention, dating back probably to the beginning of the Christian era, seems to have reached the Arabs only in the eighth century. It appears that paper was manufactured for the first time in Baghdad only in A.D. 798 and in Cairo in A.D. 900. Paper began to be made in Europe by about A.D. 1200.[6]

Printing with the use of moveable types began in Europe only in the fifteenth century. The Bible of Johann Gutenberg came out of the press in 1455. It can be said that printing reached Italy by about 1465, France in 1470, Spain in 1474, England in 1477, Denmark in 1482, Sweden in 1483, Portugal in 1495, and Russia in 1553.[7]

Though paper reached the Arab world from China at least three or four centuries before it reached Europe, yet strangely, printing of the moveable type, made its appearance in Europe well before it was adopted by the Arabs and Muslims. It is also a historical fact that the Muslims of the Arab heartlands, Persia, and Central Asia were in close contact with the Chinese several centuries before the west Europeans established contact with them over land and by sea.

In fact, Prophet Mohammad himself had called on the Muslims to go to China in search of knowledge in the seventh century itself. Arab land forces had actually reached the western frontier of China in the subsequent period. With western Turkestan in Central Asia converted to Islam and under Arab rule, and eastern Turkestan being a Chinese territory, trade and cultural intercourse between the Chinese and the Arabs was a possibility. This has given rise to Muslim populations of mixed descent in various parts of China.

Islamised Arab merchants had also reached China by sea and were trading there from at least the eighth century. The coastal cities of south China had been in contact with these Arabs and today they include large Muslim populations of mixed descent. Chinese writers such as Chou-Tu-Kua, who wrote about half a century before Marco Polo's visit to China, and Ibn Battuta, the great Arab traveller have left us detailed accounts of this Arab presence in China. Thomas Carter writes that Rashiduddin, who was the grand *vizier* of Persia during the Mongol period and who wrote a clear account of Chinese printing in his world history, seems never to have contemplated having his history printed, in spite of his knowledge of it.[8]

Thus, in spite of such contacts, Muslims never really took to printing. If Muslims had adopted Chinese printing on a large scale, it would have reached Europe well before the fifteenth century, given that Muslim rule had persisted in Spain for several centuries before it was finally evicted in 1492.

While the transmission of the knowledge of paper-making was done through the Muslim world which stood between Europe and East Asia, the fact that the Muslim world failed to adopt Chinese printing seems to have given way to the contention, in some quarters, that Gutenberg had re-invented printing of the moveable type quite independently of the Chinese inventions. But there also appear to have been other possibilities for the transmission of this knowledge of printing to Europe, e.g., during the wars of the Crusaders which took west Europeans to West Asia, and later during the Mongol invasions which reached Poland and to the doors of Germany, the land of Gutenberg.

The rise, decline, and fall of civilisations are not always easy to predict. Arabs and Muslims had reigned supreme from the seventh century to at least the fifteenth century. They were the dominant world powers during this period in the political, cultural, and intellectual spheres. Their civilisation possessed globalising characteristics, based on the universal ideals of Islam. But somehow, for various reasons, some known and others unknown, the rot set in and the decline became inevitable.

Ibn Khaldun (1332–1406) of Tunis, the veritable founder of modern scientific thinking in the social sciences observed that such changes occur so imperceptibly and take so long to make themselves felt, that they are very difficult to discern.[9] Ibn Khaldun probably would never have dreamt that Arab domination in the world would decline in the fifteenth century. Probably one of the major unnoticed reasons for Arab decline was the general Muslim reluctance to adopt printing, a technology that would have helped disseminate the Arab and the

Muslim achievements in the various fields more efficiently and would have acted as an impetus to prop up their sagging fortunes and remain in the vanguard of human civilisation.

What the Arabs and the Muslims lost by not adopting printing, the Europeans stood to gain. This was no doubt a water-shed or a turning point in the fortunes of nations and civilisations. No wonder Lord Bacon had included printing, along with gun powder and the compass as the three factors which changed the face of the world. These three factors are not merely technological inventions. They had their own dynamics and life. They actually conferred not only knowledge, but also a certain power to those who possessed them and made use of them in various ways. Thus, technology had become a real source of power in the hands of those who wielded it.

With printing being neglected by the Arabs, despite their knowledge of it, it was left to the west Europeans, (who had borrowed so much from the Muslims in the past such as Chinese paper-making and Indian numerals and zero), to inaugurate printing in Arabic. The first text printed in Arabic was a Christian prayer book, known as *Kitab Salat al-Sawai*, in 1514. This book can be found in the National Library of Paris. In 1516, a tri-lingual book of Psalms, called *Kitab al Mazamir*, was published with a preface in Arabic. In 1556, an anonymous religious treatise, titled, *I'tikad al-amana*, was published from Rome. From 1585 to 1614, on the advice of Pope Gregory XIII, a series of books in Arabic, which included the Bible, the four Gospels, and the medical canon of Avicenna, were published. Many other church establishments showed interest in publishing works in Arabic. Thus, in 1698, two big volumes of the Quran were published in Arabic with a Latin translation, on the advice of Pope Innocent XI. Two editions of the Quran in Arabic were published by Muslims for the first time in Russia, one in 1787 at Saint Petersburg and the other at Kazan in 1803.[10]

On the whole it was quite obvious that it was the Christians who were the pioneers in printing and publishing in Arabic. In the Muslim heartland itself, the Christians and the Jews were the first to be involved in setting up printing presses and in publishing books.[11]

In 1588, Sultan Murad III of Turkey issued a *firman* allowing the import of printed works into Turkey from Italy. This shows that, at least officially, Turkey or rather the Ottoman Empire was not against printing during this period.[12] In 1727, the ulemas under Sultan Ahmed III of Turkey appear to have delivered a verdict that it was against the religion and honour of Islam to allow printing of the Quran, because it rested only upon the hand-written tradition and must not be passed down in any other way. As a result, Sultan Ahmed III issued a firman which allowed the establishment of a press for the printing of books other than the fiqh, Hadith and the Quran.[13] Consequently, considerable printing activity seems to have been carried on in the eighteenth century.[14] Thus, it is clear that Islam in Turkey did not really prevent the printing of books, but it no doubt prevented the printing of the Quran.

Otherwise, it seems that print gradually became established in the Muslim world only in the nineteenth century. Until then it appears that oral and written traditions coexisted in the entire Muslim world.

A branch of the Mongols, which had conquered almost all of the then known world, was trying to enter the Indian sub-continent in the thirteenth century itself. It finally succeeded in its venture in the early sixteenth century, but only after the Mongols had been converted to Islam. The Mongols do not seem to have brought with them the art of printing.

Ancient Indian Buddhist monks had been travelling to China from at least the beginning of the Christian era. When the Indian Buddhist monk, Kumarajiva, arrived in China in the fourth century A.D., along with many other monks, Buddhism had struck strong roots there.[15] In the year A.D. 520, Boddhidharma, a native of Kanchipuram near Madras sailed to Canton in China and established the Ch'an or Zen sect of Buddhism. He was even granted an interview with the Liang Emperor, Wuti. Similarly, several Chinese travellers and pilgrims have been travelling to India. The most famous among them were of course, Fa Hien, who was in India in the fifth century and Hiuen-Tsang who visited India, when the Tang dynasty was ruling China. Fa Hien was actually sent out to India by the Chinese Emperor to procure authentic copies of the Buddhist Holy Books, which were found only in the monasteries of Pataliputra and Ceylon, in order that they would not have to rely solely on oral traditions. Max Weber asserts that in a land of literati like China, Buddhism could gain a foothold only as a book religion. He also opines that the putting down in writing of the Buddhist scriptures, probably during the reign of Emperor Asoka, meant a great deal for its preservation, and of course also its transmission.[16]

In 1015, the great Chola Emperor, Raja Raja Chola sent a royal embassy, consisting of 52 members led by his vice-minister, Chola Samanta, to China. Harprasad Ray conclusively showed the presence of Chinese settlers in the Tamil country and the frequent exchange of envoys between south India and China during this period and afterwards. There were missions to China from the Pandya country in the thirteenth century as well. In September 1280, there was a mission from the Pandya country, led by a certain, Zha-ma-li-ding, probably the Arab Muslim merchant, Jamaluddin, the brother of Takiuddin, who was an influential person at the Pandya court. Moreover, during this period, a Chinese Buddhist temple was built at Nagapattinam on the Coromandel coast, in order to serve the religious needs of the Chinese settlers there. This temple was unfortunately demolished in 1867.[17] In the fourteenth century, Ibn Battuta embarked on a Chinese ship from the Malabar coast on a voyage to China.[18] Karashima Noburu, in his paper in the *Journal of East-West Maritime Relation*, has pointed to the trade relations between south India and China in the thirteenth and fourteenth centuries.[19] During 1405–1433, Zheng He made seven voyages to south India.[20]

But, in spite of such continuous and intimate contacts with the Chinese, Chinese print technology does not seem to have reached the Indian sub-continent. In fact, Indians, especially the

Tamils, who were so well acquainted with China, never seemed to have thought of importing the technology to India.

In the early part of the fifteenth century, when the Venetian traveller, Nicolo Conti visited India, he noted that of all the inhabitants of India, only those of Cambay (in Gujarat) used paper, while all the others wrote on leaves of trees of which they made very beautiful books.[21] Thus, even though paper was used in western India in the fifteenth century, yet printing was never known.

Things, though, were not going to remain static. Some upcoming west European countries on the Atlantic sea-board, finding the land route and even the sea route to India through the Red Sea blocked by the Arabs and the Turks, were forced into the Atlantic ocean to find a sea route to India. As noted earlier, the Portuguese, belonging to a small maritime nation of western Europe, were the first who were successful in this venture. Probably guided by an experienced Arab seaman, they reached Kappakadavu near Calicut on the Malabar coast in 1498. Very soon they put an end to Muslim domination in the entire Indian Ocean region.

There were a number of zealous missionaries among the Portuguese who wanted to spread Christianity across the world. Their zeal pushed them to adopt various ways and methods to propagate Christianity. The Portuguese actually adopted printing of the moveable type in 1495. Some missionaries thought that this technology could be utilised to serve the cause of Christianity in India and elsewhere.

As early as 1540, the great missionary, Saint Francis Xavier, who was known to have converted thousands of Parava fishermen on the Coromandel coast and Travancore, expressed his desire in a letter that printing should be used to publish Christian literature in Asia. Consequently it appears that some ships carrying a printing press and some technicians left for India in 1556.[22] Later in the year, the first printing press was established at St. Paul's college in Goa by Jesuit missionaries from Portugal, to the great indifference of the Indians.[23]

However, the 'Cartilha' of 1554, printed at Lisbon indubitably established the fact that Tamil, of all the Indian languages, was the first to be printed.[24] The efforts of early missionaries such as Alexandro Valignano, Rev. Henrique Henriques, Joao Goncalves, and Rev. John Faria were responsible for the creation of the first Tamil press in south India. The credit for preparing matrices for the Tamil types goes to the Spaniard, Joao Goncalves. This was perfected by Rev. Faria. We find an impression of these earliest Tamil types made by Goncalves and Faria in the last page of a book on prayers, titled, *Tampiraan Vanakkam.* This work was put to print in the first Tamil press which came into existence at Quilon, because of the efforts of the missionaries. It is rather surprising to know that Rev. Henrique Henriques had collected 400 cruzados from the Tamil Parava fishermen for making the Tamil press. Thus Tamilians seem to have participated, at least financially, in the making of the first Tamil printing press or rather the Indian press.[25]

This *Tampiraan Vanakkam* or 'Doctrina Christa', as it was also known, consists of 16 pages and is a Tamil translation by Henrique Henriques of Saint Francis Xavier's Portuguese work of the same name, which was printed in Goa in 1557. It appears that the press in which the work was printed was soon shifted to Cochin.

In 1579, another Tamil Christian work prepared by Rev. Henrique Henriques was published from Cochin. A third Tamil Christian book, again by him, printed probably at Punnaikayal on the southern Tamil coast in 1586 can be found in the Vatican library.[27] Thus, it can be said that Rev. Henrique Henriques was the pioneer in the printing and publishing of Tamil works.

After this initial spurt in printing, there seems to have been a lull in the Tamil printing activity. One has to wait for about another century, before the Indian printer Aichamoni Ignacio, brought out Antao de Proenca's Tamil-Portuguese dictionary in 1679, and also three volumes of the Jesuit, Robert de Nobili's Catechism in Tamil.[28]

When the *Nayak* of Tanjore allowed the Danes, belonging to a small maritime nation of north-western Europe, to establish a trading settlement in Tranquebar (Tarangapadi) on the southern Coromandel coast, he would never have thought that the settlement would develop into a great centre of Protestant missionary and printing activity in India.

Apart from the Hindu population, Tranquebar had a number of Muslims. Unlike the Portuguese who waged wars against the Muslims, the Danes appear not to have faced opposition from the Muslims in south India. Nevertheless, it appears that this did not prevent the Danes in Tranquebar from despising the Hindus and above all their temples. They entered the small Hindu temples in different parts of the town and indulged in acts of profanation. Similarly, the Tamil Muslims too were at the receiving end. On account of setbacks in trade, the Danes seem to have taken to piracy between 1641 and 1673. They confiscated several Indian ships, especially Muslim-owned, and confiscated their goods.[29]

But in 1636, an incident occurred in Tranquebar, which greatly wounded the Muslim community. In that year the Danish pastor, Udbyneder chased, caught, and tied a dynamic and honourable Muslim merchant of Tranquebar known as Chinna Marakkar, to a tree and beat him mercilessly. The reasons that provoked the anger of the missionary are not known. But the event shook the Muslim community emotionally.[30] This incident shows that all was not well in the relations between the Danish Protestant Christians and the Tamil Muslims. Such a high-handed Danish attitude was going to have its effect also in the literary field as we are going to see.

In 1712, a printing press arrived at Tranquebar from the 'Society for Promoting Christian Knowledge' of England. It was meant for the Tranquebar Mission. The first work printed in Tamil by this press was a small tract, titled, *The Abomination of Paganism and the way for the Pagans to be Saved.* Subsequently, some other small works seem to have been published, such as, *A General Description of Malabar Heathendom, Four Gospels and Acts* and *Accursed Heathendom*. These were works generally criticising aspects of Hinduism. In the year 1715, the translation and printing of the New Testament was completed at Tranquebar.[31]

Unlike the Portuguese, who do not seem to have published works criticising Hinduism or Islam in Tamil, at least in the initial stages, the Danes from the very beginning of their printing activities in Tamil Nadu had started to publish works attacking Hinduism. Given their confrontation with the Muslims in the Bay of Bengal and in Tranquebar itself, it was but natural that they made use of their printing press to publish material against Islam. The first work thus published in Tamil, was titled, *Islamanavanchuvadi* (Book of Islamism) and was published in 1727. This is probably the first book in Tamil, printed and published on Islam in Tamil Nadu or anywhere in the world. But the author is without doubt a Christian missionary. The work was no doubt meant for the Muslims, but was directed against Islam. One interesting thing about this work is that its title page contained a small citation of the New Testament, engraved in wood, in Arabic. This is believed to be the first specimen of printing of Arabic characters, not just in Tamil Nadu, but in the whole of India.[32]

The French were the last of the new west European powers to appear on the Indian lands. They established a settlement at Pondicherry, on the Coromandel coast, which served as their headquarters. Following the Portuguese and the Danes, they too seem to have been imbued with a good dose of Christian inclinations. Very soon, under the instructions of the French Jesuit missionaries, they began to obstruct the Hindus and Muslims in their religious pursuits. They wanted to remove all Hindu temples and Muslim mosques in Pondicherry as they felt that they hindered the spread of Christianity. The French governor of Pondicherry, Dupleix, seems to have contributed much to the implementation of this line of thought. He gave orders to destroy the massive Shiva temple, which stood somewhat in the middle of old Pondicherry. At the same time, he also wanted to destroy the mosque, which stood behind the Capuchin church, near the seashore. While the Shiva temple was brought down by the missionaries and others in September

1748, the French were unable to destroy the mosque because the Muslim troops that were at the service of the French threatened to rise in revolt. But this mosque seems to have been destroyed later, before Dupleix left Pondicherry in 1754.[33]

Four years later, a printing press was brought over from France to Pondicherry by Count de Lally. Before this printing press could really function, the English, the traditional rivals of the French, invaded Pondicherry in 1761. They laid waste French Pondicherry and did not even spare the French churches. But they had a prize catch in the French governor's printing press. They confiscated it and took it over to Madras. They handed it over to Johann Philipp Fabricius, a Danish missionary of the Society for Promoting Christian Knowledge, who knew the technique of printing, with the understanding that it would be used for the East India Company's publications as well as missionary publications. Thus was born the first printing press in Madras in 1761.

Though it was officially a government press, much missionary material was printed here. It even appears that the intention of Fabricius was to make the press an exclusively Tamil missionary press. Fabricius informs us that the problem of shortage of paper, which was usually imported from Europe, was solved in Madras with indigenous effort. It appears that some Indians of Madras, took to manufacturing paper in the 1760s itself with some help from the English.[34] Whether these early Indian manufacturers of paper were Hindus or Muslims, or Tamils or Telugus cannot be confirmed.

During the first half of the nineteenth century, the missionaries began to deploy their efforts more vigorously by establishing various missionary societies and printing presses. Some of them are the Madras Tract Society, the Nagercoil Tract Society, the Neyoor Tract Society, Tamil Christian Book Society, the Palamcottah Mission Press, the Nagercoil Mission Press, the American Mission Press, the Christian Vernacular Education Society, the Pondicherry Roman Catholic Press, the Jaffna Tract Society, etc.[35] These societies and presses, owned by the west European Christians, published not only a great number of Christian literature meant for the Christians, but also a good deal of literature criticising Islam and Hinduism, which was supposed to help the missionaries in their proselytising activities. Thus, we have the *Indian Pilgrim* a 36-page book by Mrs Sherwood, criticising Islam, published in 1826, the *Letter to the Mahomedans,* consisting of just 8 pages, published by the Nagercoil Tract Society, *The Conversation* (12 pages) meant for Muslims by Rev. E. Daniel, *Abdul Messee* (20 pages) by Punari Moodeliar, *The Inquiry* (24 pages), meant for Muslims by Rev. Spaulding and published by the Jaffna Tract Society, etc.

All such activities would have no doubt contributed to the association of printing technology with the Christian missionaries and colonisers. These societies and presses, by their very structure, were directed towards the promotion and propagation of Christianity. As a result, Hindus and Muslims could not depend on them to get their religious works printed and published. Neither could they rely on the government presses which had started functioning in Madras and Pondicherry in the 1830s.[36] Actually the government press took up printing for the public only at the end of the East India Company rule in 1857.

Though the Indians at Madras had started fabricating paper in the 1760s itself, printing presses owned by Hindus or Muslims were still not a reality, in spite of the fact that the personnel of the government and missionary presses were largely Indians.[37] Thus, we know that in the eighteenth century itself Hindus and probably also some Muslims possessed the expertise and experience to operate a printing press.

In 1806, at the instance of the East India Company and probably also under the influence of Rev. Christian Frederick Swartz, the royal press, known as Nava Vidya Kala Nidhi, was established by Serfoji Bhonsle, the Maharaja of Tanjore. A few Sanskrit and Marathi books were published between 1806 and 1817, after which the press ceased to exist.[38]

It appears that the first fully Indian or Tamil-owned press was functioning at Kanchipuram during the second decade of the nineteenth century. It was owned by K. Thiruvenkata Mutaliyar and the name of the press was Iyartamizh Vilakka Press.

Probably the first Tamil book to be ever printed and published was from this fully Indian-owned press. The book was compiled by Periyasami Pillai from Pondicherry and a certain Sabapathi Pillai, and was titled, *Purvacakravarti Vacakappa.* It was published in 1819.[39] Kesavan seems to maintain that the *Kalvi Vilakka Achukootam,* run by the famous Tamil scholar, Thirutannigai Kandapaiyar was also one of the early Tamil presses, probably older than Iyartamizh Vilakka Press.[40] By 1850, at least 14 Hindu-owned presses had been established in Madras, but not a single Tamil Muslim-owned press came into being during this period.[41]

But, the establishment of Hindu printing presses during this period seem to have made the Muslims less reluctant to take to printing, which was until then exclusively associated with the Christian missionaries and colonisers. As a result, we find that from the 1840s onwards, Tamil Muslims were getting their works published from the Hindu presses and actually the great majority of their works during the period under study, were printed in presses owned by the Hindus, who had no inhibitions in printing Muslim works, unlike the Christian missionaries.

The Hindus of the Tamil country did not have any reservations about the use of printing ink, unlike the orthodox Bombay Brahmins who rejected ink because they thought it contained animal fat.[42] Neither did the Tamil Muslims seem to have had any such reservations. It has also been suggested that the Muslims generally suspected that there were hog bristles in the brush used for cleaning the block, which prevented them from taking to printing. But Demeerseman has shown that the brush in question was not an integral part of the printing machine itself and it could have been easily substituted with some other material.[43] Thus, this cannot be the real reason for the Muslims not taking to printing quickly. There is no indication whatever that Tamil Muslims had raised such problems at any point of time.

Ironically, the real opposition to printing, especially Indian printing, seems to have come from the British government. On one side there were the British critics of the government policies in India. Unable to contain them the government under Lord Wellesley the Governor-General in 1797, introduced press censorship and formulated stringent rules for the editors and printers to follow. On the other, there were the missionaries who in their zeal to propagate Christianity were offending the religious sensibilities of the Indians—both Hindus and Muslims, especially through printed material, and was actually threatening the stability of British rule.

In 1806, there was a revolt of the Sepoys in Vellore, in Tamil Nadu, which resulted in the massacre of Colonel Faucourt and nearly a hundred other officers. A section of the British administration in India attributed the revolt to the resent caused by the activities of the missionaries. In 1807, the attention of the government was drawn to some pamphlets decrying the Hindu and Muslim religions. As a result, the missionaries were obliged to submit all their publications for approval to the British government. The British government apparently wanted to give the impression that they were not siding with the missionaries though they were connected to them, in order to allay popular suspicions against them.

In the year 1818, press censorship was abolished during the governor-generalship of Lord Hastings. Finally, under pressure from the Court of Directors in London, the government at Calcutta, promulgated a Press Act, which was extended soon to all territories under British rule, which laid down stringent rules and regulations for printing.[44]

The British also seems to have had serious misgivings about allowing Indians to take to printing, which could ultimately threaten their supremacy in India.[45] They seem not to have taken any visible steps to curb the spread of printing among the Indians except for the imposition of press restrictions and censorship. How far this prevented the Muslims from taking to printing cannot be known, though we think that it might have had some effect on both Hindus and Muslims. Besides, in the present state of research, we do not know if the missionaries played a role in preventing the Indians from gaining access to printing technology, though we know that Hindus and Muslims as a rule did not get their works printed from their presses in the Tamil country, at least in the earlier stages.

Now, all of a sudden a liberal breeze began to blow through British India. In 1835, Sir Charles Metcalfe succeeded Lord William Bentinck as the governor-general. He abolished many of the restrictions on press freedom, without worrying about its consequences for British domination. He actually declared, 'If India could be preserved as a part of the British Empire only by keeping its inhabitants in a state of ignorance, our domination would be a curse to the country and ought to cease.'[46]

This was a turning point in the history of printing in India and the Tamil country. Hindus and Muslims got their works in Tamil printed and published mostly in the Hindu-owned printing presses. In 1863, apart from the many wooden presses, there were at least three or four iron presses owned by the Hindus, which hot-presed sheets.[47]

Another factor that needs to be taken into account at this juncture is the fact that the British had retained Persian as the court language until 1837. So it appears that the British in Calcutta took an interest in printing and publishing in Persian, Arabic, and even Urdu from the 1780s itself. In Madras, translations of the Company rules into Persian were regularly published from 1802 onwards. The Fort St. George press at Madras too started publishing works in Persian, Arabic, and Urdu from 1826 onwards.[48]

However, following Lord Macaulay's education policy, the British abolished Persian as the court language in 1837 and replaced it with the vernaculars and English. This in turn seems to have had a salutary effect on the development of printing in the vernacular languages that even Tamil Muslims, a few years later, got their poetical work, *Sira Puranam*, printed and published in 1842. It is notable that the Tamil Muslims straightaway took to printing, instead of lithography, which they utilised to some extent only later.

Notes

1. See Elisabeth Eisenstein, *La Révolution de l'Imprimé dans l'Europe des Premiers Temps Modernes*, Edition La Decouverte, (Paris, 1991).
2. T.F. Carter, 'Islam as a Barrier to Printing', in *The Moslem World*, XXXIII: 213; *The New Encyclopaedia Britannica*, (Chicago, 1990), 26, 69.
3. A.K. Priolkar, *The Printing Press in India*, (Bombay, 1958), 1, vii; *The Cambridge Encyclopaedia of China*, 2nd edition (Cambridge, 1991), 340.
4. See T.F. Carter, *The Invention of Printing and its Spread Westwards*, (New York, 1931); Priolkar, *The Printing Press in India*, 1–2; *The Cambridge Encyclopaedia of China*, 341.
5. Francis Robinson, 'Technology and Religious Change: Islam and the Impact of Print,' *Modern Asian Studies*, (1993), I: 27, 232.
6. Priolkar, *The Printing Press in India*; *The Cambridge Encyclopaedia of China*, vii, new edition, (Cambridge, 1991), 340.
7. Priolkar, *The Printing Press*, vii–ix.
8. T.F. Carter, 'Islam as a Barrier to Printing' in *The Moslem World*, XXXIII: 214–216; Thomas F. Carter, *The Invention of Printing in China and its Spread Westwards*, (New York, Columbia University Press, 1925), 113.
9. Charles Issawi, trans., *An Arab Philosophy of History: Selections from the Prolegomena of Ibn Khaldun of Tunis*, 2nd edition, (London, 1955), 30.
10. *Encyclopaedie de l'Islam*, (Leiden, 1986), VI, 784–786; J. Balagna, *L'Imprimerie Arabe en Occident*, (*XVIe, XVIIe et XVIIIe siècles*), (Paris, 1984).
11. Kingsley, Birge, 'The Printing of Books in Turkey in the eighteenth Century', *The Moslem World*, XXXIII: 292–294; see also Carter, *The Moslem World*, 112–113; see also Toderini, *De la Littérature des Turcs*, Poincot, (Paris, 1789); *Encyclopaedie de l'Isam*, Tome VI, (Leiden, 1986), VI, 786, 789.
12. *Encyclopaedie de l'Islam*, 789.
13. Ibid., 790; Kingsley Birge, *The Moslem World*, 292–294; see also Carter, op cit., 112–113.
14. Kingsley Birge, *The Moslem World*, 293–294; *Encyclopaedie de l'Islam*, 790–791.
15. Joseph Needham, *Science et Civilisation en Chine, Une Introduction*, (Paris, 1995), 93.

16. *The New Encyclopaedia Britannica*, (London, 1998), II, 315; James Legge, trans., *A Record of Buddhistic Kingdoms. Being an account of the Chinese Monk Fa Hien of His Travels in India and Ceylon* (*A.D. 399–414*) *in Search of the Buddhistic Books of Discipline*, (New York, 1965); Catherine Meuwese, ed., *L'Inde du Bouddha: Vue par les pélérins Chinois sous la Dynastie Tang* (*VIIe siècle*), (Paris, 1968); Max Weber, *The Religion of India: The Sociology of Hinduism and Buddhism*, (Glencoe, Illinois, 1958), 241.
17. See for e.g. Harprasad Ray, 'Indian Settlement in China', in *Indian Ocean and Cultural Interaction*, ed. K.S. Mathew (Pondicherry University, Pondicherry, 1996), 52–81; Husain Mahdi, ed. *The Rehla of Ibn Battuta*, (Baroda, 1976), lvi–lvii; Walter Elliot, 'The Edifice Formerly known as the Chinese or Jaina Pagoda at Nagapatnam', in *Indian Antiquary*, VII: 2247.
18. Ibid., lvi–lvii; W.W. Rockhill, 'Notes on the Relations and Trade of China with the Eastern Archipelaego and the Coast of the Indian Ocean during the 14th century', *Toung Pao*, XV, 419–47.
19. Karashima Noburu, 'Trade Relations between South India and China During the 13th and 14th Centuries', in *Journal of East-West Maritime Relations*, (1989 (2)), vol. I, 9–81.
20. Harprasad Ray, *Indian Ocean*, 66–67 (fn. 12).
21. R.H. Major, *India in the fifteenth Century: The Travels of Nicolo Conti in the East in the Early Part of the fifteenth Century*, (New York, n.d.), 31.
22. Priolkar, *The Printing Press*, 2, 4.
23. *Encyclopaedie de l'Islam*, 794.
24. B.S. Kesavan, *History of Printing and Publishing in India, South Indian Origins of Printing and its Efflorescense in Bengal*, (New Delhi, 1985), 16.
25. Priolkar, *The Printing Press*, 9; S. Rajamanickam, ed., *Vanakkam*, (Tuticorin, 1963), Preface; 'Padre Henrique Henriques, The Father of the Tamil Press', paper presented at the 2nd Tamil International Seminar, (1968).
26. Priolkar, *The Printing Press*, 9–10.
27. Ibid., 11.
28. Kesavan, *History of Printing and Publishing*, 35; S. Rajamanickam, *Vanakkam*.
29. J.B.P. More, 'Some Maritime Aspects of the Indian Ocean Region, 1660–1760' and Martin Kriegers, 'Danish Country Trade on the Indian Ocean in the seventeenth and eighteenth Centuries' in

Indian Ocean and Cultural Interaction (A.D. 1400–1800), ed. K.S. Mathew, (Pondicherry, 1996), 125, 141.

30. Jacques Macau, *L'Inde Danoise—La Première Compagnie, 1616–1670,* (aix-en-Provence, n.d.), 75.
31. Kesavan, *The History of Printing and Publishing,* 57; Priolkar, *The Printing Press,* 43–44; John Murdoch, *Classified Catalogue of Tamil Printed Books,* (The Christian Vernacular Education Society, Vepery, Madras, 1865), lvii; K.S. Diehl, *Early Indian Imprints,* (New York, 1964), 63.
32. *Encyclopaedie de l'Islam,* 794; John Murdoch, *Classified Catalogue,* 22.
33. J.B.P. More, 'A Tamil Muslim Sufi', in *Islam and Christian-Muslim Relations,* vol. 10, no. 1, 1999, 21(fn. 9).
34. Gerard Duverdier, 'L'Apparition de l'Imprimerie à Madras et sa Disparition à Pondichèry', in *Sonder Druck Aus Dem Gutenberg,* (Jahrbuch, 1976), 351–52, 356, 359, 362–63.
35. John Murdoch, *Classified Catalogue,* xli, xlii, 13.
36. B.S. Kesavan, *The History of Printing and Publishing,* 67.
37. K.S. Diehl, 'The Printing Press—An Agent of Strength', in *Journal of Tamil Studies,* vol. II, no. 2, part II, (October 1970): 9.
38. Ibid., 10; Priolkar, *The Printing Press,* 46.
39. B.S. Kesavan, *The History of Printing and Publishing,* 67.
40. Ibid., 69.
41. K.S. Diehl, *Journal of Tamil Studies,* 10.
42. Ibid., 11; Priolkar, *The Printing Press,* 128.
43. T.F. Carter, 'Islam as a Barrier to Printing', 213; Demeerseman, *L'Imprimerieen Orient et au Maghreb,* (Tunis, 1954), 12–14.
44. Priolkar, *The Printing Press,* 107–108, 111, 114.
45. Ibid., 126.
46. Kesavan, *The History of Printing and Publishing,* 67.
47. John Murdoch, *Classified Catalogue,* lx.
48. *Encyclopaedie l'Islam,* 794–795.

CHAPTER FIVE

Obstacles to the Adoption of Printing

Oral and Written Transmission

Now we are in a position to determine the various other obstacles that hindered the adoption of printing by the Muslims. We will first determine the role of oral and written transmission of knowledge in the Islamic world and find out if they were, especially the former, obstacles to the adoption of printing in the Muslim world, including the Tamil Muslim world.

Until the beginning of the nineteenth century, Christian literature in Arabic, Persian, and Urdu was imported straight from Europe. In 1580, the Mughal emperor, Akbar, received a copy of the Bible printed in Belgium as a gift from the Jesuits as part of their efforts to convert the Emperor to Christianity. But neither Akbar nor the Mughal court adopted the technology of printing.[1] There is no evidence to prove that Akbar and his court did not adopt printing because they favoured the oral transmission of knowledge. In fact, during Akbar's reign and even before and after his reign, Muslim historians were writing voluminous works. If they had relied only on oral transmission of knowledge, we would have never probably known about a

Barni, or a Ferishta, or an Amir Khusru. But there is evidence to prove that throughout the Muslim period, there were a number of calligraphists, copyists, and artists, who made a living out of the works of these Muslim historians and writers.[2] Such was the hold of written tradition during the Muslim period in India.

At about the same time, i.e., in 1588, Sultan Murad III had permitted the import of printed books into Turkey. Almost about one and a half centuries later in 1727, as noted earlier, the ulemas in Turkey decided to disallow the printing of the Quran because it rested upon written tradition and could not be handed down in any other way. It is surprising to note that the learned ulemas of Turkey did not mention anything about the theory of oral transmission of knowledge in Islam when they disallowed the printing of the Quran. Moreover, the Sultan of Turkey, paying heed to the verdict of the ulemas had allowed the printing of all other books except the Quran in the Ottoman Empire, which covered a good part of the Muslim world. Thus, here too there is no factual evidence in favour of the oral transmission of knowledge that prevented the adoption of printing by the Muslims.

However, there seem to have existed in Turkey powerful corporations of calligraphists, copyists, miniaturists, book-binders, and other professionals.[3] The adoption of printing would have naturally undermined the livelihood of these professionals. Therefore, they had every reason to resist the introduction of printing. Old professions, like old habits, die hard. This naturally resulted in the late adoption of printing and its development in Turkey and the Ottoman Empire.

In Persia, too, the situation was very much the same as in Turkey and the Ottoman Empire. A form of Chinese printing had actually been introduced in Persia in A.D. 1294 itself. Rashiduddin, who wrote his world history, when Persia was under Mongol rule, never seems to have been attracted by this novel technology, in spite of his knowledge of it. Instead, he willed and left funds for the purpose that each year two full copies of all his works, should be made by hand, one in Arabic and the other in Persian, until gradually there would be a complete copy of it in the mosque of every large city of the Muslim world.[4] That Rashiduddin, the author himself, had to leave money for the purpose of copying his own works shows that even copying was a fairly costly affair. Rashiduddin as the grand vizier of Persia, was financially sound enough to be able to leave money for copying his works. But there may have been many other writers in Persia, who would have been less fortunate than Rashiduddin and were unable to afford the copying of their works.

However, it is interesting to note that Rashiduddin, though he did not adopt printing and never gave his reasons for it, was a prolific writer and greatly encouraged the copyists through his will and thus helped them to earn a living. It would appear, then, that as there were many persons who depended on copying to earn a living, it would not have been in their interests, if writers like Rashiduddin had resorted to printing.[5] Rashiduddin, the grand vizier, more than any other Persian writer, was probably conscious of this simple economic and material factor involved in the adoption of printing and chose to distance himself from it, though he knew about it.

Ibn Khaldun of Tunis, was never against the writing of books, though he considered the existence of a large number of books on a particular subject to be an obstacle to the mastering of that subject.[6] He had never explicitly mentioned in his works that Islam favoured the oral transmission of knowledge. To my knowledge, no Muslim writer or thinker had ever left us an irrefutable indication that Islam favoured such transmission.

The Arab and Muslim historians, travellers, geographers, philosophers, mathematicians, physicians, and writers, right from the eighth century up to at least the fifteenth century have left us voluminous records of their knowledge. If they had depended only on oral transmission of knowledge, much of it would have been lost. So they were judicious enough to cultivate the art of writing in the various fields of knowledge. Of course, there were the copyists who have done a wonderful job in the preservation and transmission of knowledge.

Though the Quran itself means 'recitation' and Prophet Mohammad is known to have recited the Quran and not put it down in writing himself, yet the initial morality of the revelation appears to have given way to written forms in the course of time. But the text of the Quran was not written fully during the Prophet's lifetime. It was Caliph Abu Bakr, who made an attempt to collect what was written till then and what was retained in memory by the companions of the Prophet. There were four other versions of the Quran produced by the companions of the Prophet. As these versions were not identical, they created dissensions and discord among Muslims. In order to solve this problem, Caliph Uthman appointed a commission under the direction of Zaid and established the official text of the Quran, which is accepted as the authentic text by all Muslims. Thus, Uthman's written text of the Quran put an end to all the controversies arising out of other versions of the Quran, oral and written.[7]

Probably, it was when the Quran was put down in writing that the Muslims began to style themselves proudly as *Ahl-el-Kitab*, meaning 'People of the Book'.[8] A Tamil Muslim scholar, Alla Pichai, had written some time back, about the importance of 'Book' in Islam. The Quran itself was also known as the 'Mother of Books'.[9] Further, neither in the Quran nor in the Hadith, do we find a clear statement, in favour of the oral transmission of knowledge in Islam.

Thomas Carter had pointed out that the Uighur Turks, who were Muslims, seem not to have suffered from such economic inhibitions and material or spiritual constraints, as could be found in the Ottoman empire, Persia, and the Indian sub-continent.[10]

The preceding clearly militates in favour of the fact, that the late adoption of printing by the Muslim world was more due to economic and material factors, rather than spiritual. Such economic and material reasons for the late adoption of certain modern technologies still hold in various parts of the world. For example, in India, the introduction of modern technologies and equipment in the agricultural and construction sectors would have resulted in large-scale unemployment and impoverishment. One cannot argue that Indians have a special predilection for the old methods of construction and farming, which thus would be responsible for retarding the adoption of modern technologies. The same was true of the Muslim world with regard to printing.

But, this does not mean that recitation and memorising of the Quran and other sacred and non-sacred literature was not part of Islamic learning. At the time of its inception, Islam seems to have laid stress on these twin factors, probably because writing on paper was not yet introduced into the Arab world and popularised. Obviously, the only safe way for the transmission of knowledge among the vast majority of the early Muslim world would have been orally. Hence the importance given to recitation and memorising in Islam, given that there is no learning itself without memorising, and which implies recitation in one form or the other, either aloud or without raising the voice. Moreover, it should not be forgotten that Prophet Mohammad had recited the Quran to his companions. This apparently seems to have created a situation which gives credence to the theory that oral transmission of knowledge is preferred in Islam, though this is not backed by any Quranic or Hadith injunctions or the *fatwas* of the ulemas.

This theory seems to have received some scholarly recognition because Muslims adopted printing quite late. But we have seen earlier some of the more down-to-earth reasons, arising from economic and material conditions. In the light of this, the theory that the preference for oral transmission of knowledge has retarded the adoption of printing by the Muslims, has to be set aside.

Further, while the Islamic literature and the secular literature produced by the Muslims have been generally put in writing, there is a special category of Islamic knowledge centred around the personalities of the Sufis, who seem to have had a predilection for the oral transmission of knowledge or rather esoteric knowledge on the basis of a teacher-disciple relationship. This knowledge is open to speculation and is often secretive, passed on from the teacher to the disciple.

Even here, as we have seen, we have the *tazhkiras* or the biographies of the Sufis which have been put in writing. It has got also its own philosopher-writers such as Ibn al Arabi and

Al Ghazzali, and it has also given birth to a rich lore of mystical poems and literature. But, the tendency for the oral transmission of knowledge in the Sufi orders might have misled some scholars to believe that the whole of Islam preferred oral transmission of knowledge.

Now, where do the Tamil Muslims stand in all this? Though they were part of the Indian Muslim world, yet we have seen their peculiar evolution in Tamil Nadu. They were actually an independent Muslim group who evolved outside the sphere of the great northern Muslim empires. They actually owed their origin to the Arab merchants and sailors. Besides, they had never ruled any part of Tamil Nadu in the course of their historical evolution.

At the present state of research, we do not know for sure if these Arabs brought along with them copies of the Quran and other Islamic literature when they were on their trade missions to south India. Probably, it was the Sufis, who seem to have reached Tamil Nadu, at least from the eleventh century from north India and beyond, and who brought with them Quranic literature, etc. There is also a possibility that the Quran and other literature might have penetrated Tamil Nadu during the Turkish invasions and their rule in the fourteenth century. Nothing seems to be certain anyhow for want of hard evidence.

But what is most probable is that Tamil Muslims had taken to writing from at least the late sixteenth century. The poetical works that they composed from this period onwards were most of the time sponsored by rich Tamil Muslim philanthropists. This confirms that the Tamil Muslims were not against writing. In other words, they did not show any particular preference for the oral transmission of Islamic knowledge.

Moreover, the Tamil Muslim works produced from the sixteenth century up to 1835, when the British had relaxed press restrictions, were not numerous, as we have seen. They never seem to have needed copyists, or calligraphists, or binders, as in other parts of the Muslim world. They generally seem to have adopted the traditional Tamil method of writing on palm leaves, as the Arabs, who frequented the southern coasts, never seem to have introduced paper into the Tamil country. As the Tamil Muslims had never wielded political power, there was thus no need for official calligraphists, or copyists, or binders, as in the Ottoman or Mughal empires. Thus, the economic and material reasons responsible for the late adoption of printing in other parts of the Muslim world did not apply to the Tamil Muslim society.

As we have already shown that the theories advocating a preference for the oral transmission of knowledge can only be hypothetical, mainly owing to the absence of Quranic or Hadith injunctions in favour of it, we therefore have to search for reasons elsewhere. That is what we propose to do next.

Association of Printing with Christianity

We are aware of the contact that India had with China; but, for reasons that we do not know, despite these contacts Indians did not adopt Chinese printing. According to one theory it is because of the association of printing with Christianity, that Indians failed to adopt even the western printing. This assertion needs some verification as far as the Muslim world and the Tamil Muslims are concerned. For this we need to go a little bit more into the history of the Muslim world, of which the Tamil Muslims are a part.

We know about the confrontation of Islam with Christianity and Judaism, during the Prophet's lifetime itself. The Quran is living proof of this.[11] Later, in the course of Islam's spectacular expansion, Arabs reached India and China in the east, while they conquered the whole of north Africa and penetrated into western Europe up to France. All these conquests took place in the eighth century A.D. Spain and Portugal were under Arab rule for several centuries. It was an accident of history that the rest of Christian Europe did not succumb to the Arab Muslim power, probably because the Arabs had moved too far from their homelands and mingled with the local populations wherever they went, resulting in the depletion of their expansive spirit. This proved to be their undoing, for from the fifteenth century, Muslims began to lose out to the Christian Spaniards. By the end of the fifteenth century, the Christians overcame the Muslims in Spain and pushed them back into Africa.[12]

On the other hand, in the earlier phase of their expansion, the Muslims had conquered Syria and Jerusalem bringing the Holy City of the Christians under their influence. The Christians of Europe started what was known as the Crusades in order to retrieve the Holy Land from the Muslims.

But in the east, they were kept at bay by the Seljuk Turks, especially under the famous, Saladin, who conquered Jerusalem in A.D. 1187. But this conquest was made only after the Christians had indulged in one of the most terrible massacres in world history when Muslims and Jews were slaughtered in the name of religion and Jesus Christ.[13] This incident and the entire Crusades, seem to have left an indelible mark on the Muslim psyche, which further alienated them from the Christians. While the Muslims were confronting the Christians in their very heartlands, they were also suffering under the brutality of the Inquisition on the Spanish frontier.

It was during the last phase of the expulsion of the Muslims from Spain that print technology spread in western Europe. We have seen that the first most important book printed by Johann Gutenberg was the Bible. It appears that it was the Church, rather Christianity in all its various forms, which first capitalised on this new printing technology. It was the Church which translated Christian books into Arabic and published them before any one else, in order to help the propagation of the Christian faith among the Muslims. Surprisingly, it was the Christians, particularly the missionaries, and the Jews who established the first printing presses in the Muslim lands.

This association of Christianity with the technology of printing is a fact of history. There is every possibility that the Muslims, who were resisting and fighting Christian Europeans and Christianity, thought that printing was a sort of weapon or tool in the hands of the Christians to undermine the Muslim interests. This might have made them hesistant to adopt printing from the western Christians, who were bent upon undoing them by all means, including propaganda through printing.

A similar sort of situation seems to have prevailed in the Indian sub-continent too. The Portuguese arrival on the southern Indian coast was not altogether a peaceful one. They had destroyed the Arab and the Indian Muslim domination of the maritime trade of the Indian Ocean region. They attacked Muslim interests on the Malabar and Coromandel coasts. They pulled down mosques and even forcibly converted Muslims to Christianity in some places like Quilon.[14] In a way, it was a terrible situation for the Muslims of the Malabar and Maabar during the sixteenth century, which can be seen especially from the accounts of Sheik Zainuddin al-Mabri.[15]

Incidentally, it was during this period that the Portuguese set up their printing presses in Goa and on the Malabar coast and published material in order to propagate Christianity among Indians. I think that the Muslims of south India had no reason to adopt printing technology from the Portuguese because it was they who had brought about the downfall of the Muslims. Printing was associated with the Portuguese missionaries and was being used against the Muslims and others. Probably, the Muslims might have thought that there was no reason to adopt a technology which was being used against them. But, even if they had wanted to use printing, they had no means to gain access to the technology as it was a Portuguese preserve.

Once again in the seventeenth century, when the Danes had settled at Tranquebar, the Muslims came under attack on sea and land from the Danes, as we have seen earlier. When the Tranquebar Mission Press was started in 1712 by Danish missionaries, from its very inception the publications were directed against Hinduism and Islam. The literature published by this press was meant as Christian propaganda to convert the Hindus and Muslims. Probably, because of this, the Muslims like the Hindus never seem to have shown any interest in printing which was associated with Christianity and the missionaries, who were bent upon destroying their identity.

When the Vepery press was established near Madras in 1761,

again, it was largely a missionary press, though it was nominally controlled by the Company government. They seem to have been more interested in printing Christian literature, especially in Tamil, rather than anything else. The Muslims had no access to it in order to publish their works. There is no indication anywhere that the Muslims approached any of these presses to get their works published. Thus, these early printing presses and the missionary presses and societies established during the first half of the nineteenth century were all presses that were associated with Christianity and therefore by implication they were all directed against Islam and Hinduism. In other words, a situation seems to have prevailed where printing itself was considered to be against Islam, especially by the Tamil Muslims. This would have no doubt rendered them hesitant and skeptical about printing.

Why the Muslims did not Adopt Chinese Printing

At this juncture, the question arises why the Muslims who did not adopt European printing because of its association with Christianity, did not borrow the same from the Chinese a few centuries earlier. We have to do a bit of historical re-tracing once again to answer this question.

The Chinese were manufacturing paper, at least from the time Jesus Christ was born. The technology involved in paper-making had largely remained a Chinese or East Asian preserve until at least the seventh century A.D., though Central Asia seems to have had access to it even before, through the Uighur Turks.

In the eighth century, the Arabs after conquering Central Asia, were knocking at the western frontiers of the Chinese empire. In the battle that took place between the Arab forces headed by Ziad ben Salah and the Chinese in A.D. 751 at Atlakh, the Arabs took many Chinese as prisoners. It appears that among them were a few who knew the art of paper-making. Thus paper was made by them at Samarkand during this period. That the Chinese prisoners were utilised for the purpose shows that the technology of paper-making was not to be had for the asking and had remained more or less a preserve of East Asia until that time. It had actually taken more than nine centuries before the Arabs could force this technology out of the Chinese.

The Indians who had been travelling to China by land and by sea even before the seventh century, seem to have shown no interest to import the art of paper-making into India. Neither did the Chinese travellers who came to India during this period such as Fa Hien and Hiuen Tsang, ever talk about it.

From Samarkand, the art of paper-making spread to Baghdad towards the end of the eighth century. But it reached Egypt only a hundred years later and Morocco in A.D. 1100. It was only in the twelfth century that Sicily and north Italy came to know about paper-making. France came to know about it only in the course of the fourteenth century. Thus, we can see that the transmission of the knowledge of paper-making was an extremely slow process, even within western Europe. Similarly, block printing (xylography) reached the Muslims from China only towards the end of the ninth century or rather the tenth century. It took another four centuries to reach France.[16] This too was an extremely slow process.

The technology of printing of the moveable type was invented by Pi Sheng only in the eleventh century. It was a major invention. It would be naive to expect that the Chinese, who took seven centuries to divulge the art of paper-making to the Arabs, would disclose the art of printing immediately to the first foreigner they come across. Besides, the invention itself would have taken sometime to mature and gain recognition within China itself. So, it would also be naive to expect that Pi Sheng's invention would dash across the Muslim world and reach western Europe within the space of few years, when paper-making and block-printing had taken several centuries to reach the Arabs and Muslims, and some centuries more before it reached the west Europeans.

In the thirteenth century, when the Arabs and Chinese were the two major powers of the world, the Mongols gate-crashed into the world scene. They dealt a devastating blow on the Arabs, razed Baghdad, the greatest seat of learning in those days, to the ground, conquered China, Persia, and Russia, entered Poland and it was by sheer chance that they chose not to enter western Europe, which was on the threshold of being a world civilisation.

The Arabs could never fully recover from that blow, even though in the course of time many Mongols converted to Islam. But the Mongol invasions had unsettled almost the whole of the then known world, especially the Muslim world. Consequently, the conditions were not appropriate during this period for the transmission of knowledge. Pi Sheng's invention thus remained exclusively with the Chinese for some more time. Further, about the same time, the decline of Muslim rule in the Iberian peninsula had begun with their expulsion from Cordoba, by Ferdinand of Castille. This expulsion was executed in the most violent manner in 1492, when the Muslims were either killed or thrown out of Spain.

The Arabs, though, continued to have trade contacts by sea with the Chinese during the fourteenth and fifteenth centuries. The Chinese, too, visited Indian shores during this period, where they met a number of Arabs. In fact, Ibn Battuta had boarded a Chinese ship from the Malabar coast on his way to China. One may ask why the Arabs did not learn Chinese printing during this period. The answer is not difficult to find.

Apart from the Arabs, there were Indians, especially the Tamils, and other peoples of South-East Asia who had regular trade and cultural intercourse with the Chinese during this period. But, they also never adopted Chinese printing technology. It appears that the Chinese either did not divulge their printing technology to the Indians or the Arabs, or that the Indians and Arabs were intent only upon trading, at least during this period.

Further, it should be noted that the Tamils, who were in close contact with China, especially during the Chola and Pandya periods, neither adopted print technology nor the art of paper-making. Preference for the oral transmission of knowledge, which was prevalent not only among the Arabs but also among the Hindus, was argued by some to be responsible for the late adoption of printing. But, this argument is not applicable to paper-making, for the Arabs had adopted paper without any problem. Therefore, as far as the Hindus or the Tamils are concerned, the real reasons for their not adopting either paper or printing have to be found elsewhere.

Yet, one relevant observation should be noted, which could give the real reason why the Indians did not adopt Chinese paper-making or printing. It was an observation made by one of the greatest Indo-Persian poets of India, Amir Khusru, in the thirteenth century. He credits India for the numerical system, the symbol zero, the game of chess, etc., but, above all he had noted that from time to time scholars from all parts of the world had come to study in India, but no Indian scholar had found it necessary to go abroad in the quest of knowledge.[17] Such was the confidence that the Indians had in those days about their science and knowledge in the various fields that it probably prevented them from borrowing technologies such as paper-making and printing from China. Amir Khusru may be after all right in his observation regarding the Hindus. We will not go further into this for it will be beyond the scope of this book. Nevertheless, we would like to point out that such a superiority complex would have probably existed among the Arabs too, who until the fourteenth century had hardly borrowed anything spectacular from the Europeans and had been on the contrary the transmitters of knowledge to them. This attitude would have also contributed to their adopting printing from the Europeans rather late, who in their eyes would have been not only infidels, but also inferior to them in every way.

Thus, it becomes clear from the above, why the Indians and the Muslims did not adopt Chinese printing technology and also why they took some time to adopt European printing. On the other hand, as we have shown earlier, it is important to keep in mind that the Muslims did not adopt printing technology from the west Europeans because of its association with Christianity. This was true of the Muslim world and also of south India. With Tamil Muslims, even the economic reasons such as the threat that the introduction of printing would be for the calligraphists or copyists does not hold water.

The south Indian Muslims, in general, had to bear the brunt of the Portuguese incursion in the Indian Ocean region which caused their trade to suffer. They were persecuted and harassed by the Portuguese and later by the Danes. Further, printing was used against them by the missionaries. Therefore, there was no reason for them to adopt such a technology, which was associated with the *firangis*, who were out to destroy their culture and religion. This also seems to have been the case in the Muslim heartlands.

Besides, Tamil Muslims never had access to the European-owned presses, especially the missionary presses. The various press restrictions clamped by the British authorities might have also discouraged them from taking to printing earlier. It appears that it was only when the press restrictions were abolished in 1835, and when English and vernaculars such as Tamil replaced Persian, which was until 1837 the court language, that Tamil Muslims seriously began to take to printing.

Quranic and Hadith Literature

We have seen above some of the real reasons that have contributed to the late adoption of printing by the Tamil Muslims. But, now we will explore what factors really prevented the Tamil Muslims from translating the Quran and the Hadith into Tamil and getting them printed and published. This will shed further light on the various theories being advanced for the late adoption of printing by the Muslim world, which includes the Tamil Muslims.

The Indian Muslims like the Muslims the world over were never a homogeneous group. They belonged to various ethnic and linguistic groups ranging from the Pushtoo-speaking Pathans of the north-west to the Tamil-speaking Muslims of south-east India. During the Mughal period and also until 1837, Persian was the court language of India. One of the most renowned and respected Muslim scholar-saints of India, Shah

Waliullah had translated the Quran into Persian in 1737, when the Mughal empire was on the decline and the upcoming west European maritime powers were making their presence felt all over the Indian sub-continent. Shah Waliullah undoubtedly exercised a great influence on Muslim religious thought in north India and even in the Muslim heartlands, but his influence on the Tamil Muslims still remains to be ascertained.[18]

In the early nineteenth century, the Quran was translated into Urdu and commented upon by the two sons of Shah Waliullah, Shah Rafiuddin Saheb and Shah Abdul Qadir.[19] In 1851, an Urdu translation of the Quran was published at Madras in the Tamil country.[20] But the translation of the Quran into the languages of south India was still not forthcoming. One had to wait until 1949–50 for a complete translation and publication of the Quran into Tamil.[21]

This appears to be an anomaly particularly when translations of the Quran into Urdu were being published from the early part of the nineteenth century in north India and when Tamil Muslim literature was being regularly published from the 1840s itself. As it would be unreasonable to say that the Tamil Muslims were ignorant of the Urdu translations and publications, an attempt to uncover the real reasons will be made below.

Quranic and Hadith literature occupy the prime place in Islamic literature. The Quran was known as the 'Mother of Books'. Therefore, it is only reasonable to start by first making an assessment of the publications on the Quran and the Hadith, in both the Arabic and Tamil script. It appears that the earliest Tamil Muslim attempt to translate the Quran into Arabic-Tamil written in the Arabic script was by a certain Mustapha Alim Hajyar of Kayalpattinam. It was titled, *Fath al-Rahman fi Tarjumat-i-Tafsir al-Quran.* It contains a commentary of the last portions of the Quran. It was printed from Bombay in 1873 and contains 653 pages.[22]

The next attempt seems to have been made by a certain Habib Muhammad al Bakhri al Kahiri during 1879–84. This book in Arabic and Tamil is also written in the Arabic script. In 1882, a commentary of the Quran again in Arabic-Tamil, containing 626 pages was published from Bombay. In 1881, Nuh Alim Sahib wrote the commentary of the entire Quran under the title, *Fath al Karim*, again in Arabic-Tamil in the Arabic script which was published from Bombay in the year 1890.[23] But a full Tamil translation of the Quran was not yet published.

On the basis of the information in hand, it appears that the first attempt in this direction was made by Christians of the Madras Religious Tract society and it was printed at the Society for the Propagation of Christian Knowledge Press, in 1897. It contained just 20 pages and was titled, *The Quran* (see Appendix). But we do not know what its exact contents were, though it is quite possible that it contained missionary views about the Quran.

In the same year, a translation into Tamil of Surahs 78 to 114 was published from Colombo. It was authored by Sulaiman Ibn Muhammad al Sailani. This work which contained 112 pages was a Ceylonese Tamil Muslim work.

In 1908, a short commentary on *Surat Ya Sin*, was authored by Muhammad Fazlullah and the very next year an interpretation of *Surah al Fatiha* was published. In 1910, Sheik Abdul Qadir, brought out his interpretation of *Surah al Fatiha*, which is a preface to the Quran, and in the same year another commentary of *Surah e Yasin* by Naina Mohammad Sahib was published. In 1911, Haji Jilani Fakir bin Monna Muhammad, translated the last five sections of the Quran into Tamil.

Another Tamil Muslim attempt in Tamil Nadu to translate parts of the Quran, with commentaries in Tamil, seems to have been made by Ramnad Qadir Muhyi al Din Muhammad Ibrahim and was published in 1913 at Madras under the title, *Quran Sharippu Tamizh Tafsir*. In the same year, Shahul Hamid Lebbai, edited and published, Surah XXXVI of the Quran with the Arabic text in Tamil characters and the Tamil translation of one prayer. This contained only 30 pages. Two years later, a certain Muhammad Tahir, translated into Tamil the first chapter of the Quran. Hazrat Moulvi Haji Sheiku Miran Mohideen Sahib's exposition of the *Surat Ya sin*, in Tamil script, with a

Tamil translation was published in 1917. In 1918, a commentary on a portion of the Quran, was published in the Arabic script. But all such publications do not constitute a veritable and full translation of the Quran into Tamil. At most, they were feeble and scattered attempts to translate and publish the Quran.

In 1926, A.K. Abdul Hamid Baqavi translated (and published) the first portion of the Quran into Tamil, but without the Arabic text. A second edition of the same was published from Tiruchirappalli in 1929, with the Arabic text.

In 1934, Moulvi S.S. Muhammad Abdul Qadir Sahib Baqavi of Uthamapalayam, son of Ramnad Muhammad Ibrahim, published more or less the first eight Surahs of the Quran, under the title *Bayan al Quran*. In 1940, the same author, translated Surahs 5 to 9 of the Quran and published them with a detailed commentary in Tamil.

But a full translation of the Quran in Tamil was still not forthcoming. This finally saw the light of day in two volumes, published in 1948 and 1950 respectively, titled, *Tarjumatul Quran*. Copies of these two volumes can be found at the Ecole Française d'Extrême Orient at Pondicherry. Thus, in spite of the number of translations and commentaries upon the Quran published in north India, the Tamil Muslims were extremely slow in emulating and printing the Quran into Tamil.

A similar situation also prevailed in the studies, translation, and publication of Hadith literature into Tamil. Tamil Muslims appear to have been slow to bring out a full translation of the Hadith into Tamil and to write commentaries upon them. The first renderings of some Hadith into Tamil was done by Pettai Amur Abd al Qadir and published in 1875. In 1908, Shahul Hamid Lebbai wrote and published a treatise on the Hadith from Madras. In 1904, a Tamil translation from the original Arabic work by Ahmad bin Abdallah, which contained a collection of 400 sayings of the Prophet, was published.

In 1910, a translation of 40 Hadiths with explanations was published by Shahul Hamid Lebbai. Two years later, an account of some traditions of the Prophet was published under the title,

Jawahir ul-Hadis by Muhiuddin Abdul Qadir. Another work by Muhammad Ibrahim Sahib, explaining some sayings of the Prophet, was published in 1913. A similar work was published in 1915–16. Such was more or less the situation regarding the studies, translations, and publications of Hadith literature until the 1920s and even later.

These minor achievements pale in comparison to the monumental studies on the Hadith done in northern India by Shaik Abd al Huq of Delhi and later by Shah Waliullah. Actually it was in the sphere of Hadith literature that Indian Islam, rather north Indian Islam, had made a remarkable contribution to the Islamic world. The great Muslim scholar, Rashid Rida, had maintained that when the science of Hadith literature was dying out in the Arab world, it was in India that it was revived in the sixteenth century.[24] But it goes without saying that Tamil Muslims had no role to play in this revival.

It is quite obvious from the above that the Tamil Muslims were lagging behind the north Indian Muslims not only in the translation and publication of the Quran and the Hadith into Tamil, but also in studying and in commenting upon the Quranic and Hadith literature. It is necessary to examine the reasons for this situation by looking at some hard evidence, which has to be once again in the form of literature and not at theories and speculations such as those pertaining to the untranslatability of the Quran and Hadith because of its complicated language or sacredness.

In order to throw some light on this aspect, there is no better way than to turn our attention towards Muslim scholars and intellectuals themselves. These scholars generally were products of modern education or were influenced to some extent by the modern scientific ideas and values. They were not of the same breed as the ulemas, who were products of the madrasa education.

The ulemas were the traditional dispensers of knowledge of Islam. Naturally, the responsibility of translating the Quran or the Hadith into Tamil, writing commentaries upon them, and publishing them, lay primarily with them though for one reason or other in Tamil Nadu they lagged behind.

Thus, it was not surprising that the Muslims, who had received modern education and who had acquired a certain new awareness about themselves as Muslims, started questioning the authority of the ulemas with regard to Islam itself. They laid all responsibility for the absence of a Tamil Quran on the ulemas. They accused them blatantly of not taking any steps to translate the Quran and the Hadith fully into Tamil when in north India such books had already been translated and published several decades earlier. They held that though there were many ulemas who took pride in their Islamic learning and knowledge, it was really distressing for the Muslims that a Hindu company of Madras, by the name of Sri Valli Nayakan, had come forward to translate and publish the Quran and the Hadith into Tamil.[25]

They gave two reasons for the ulemas' disinterest in the translation and publication of the Quran and the Hadith. They opined that the ulemas did not want such translations because they were afraid either that their influence among the ignorant Muslim mass would be undermined or because the ulemas did not have the knowledge to do the translations.[26] These two accusations seem to have great relevance because they came out of the pens of responsible modern Muslims, who used the print media to air their views.

It should be noted that such modern Muslims had wanted any Muslims who were lagging behind the Hindus and other Muslims in modern education to become proficient in both English and Tamil, and considered the education dispensed in the Arabic madrasas by the ulemas as inappropriate for the new situation.[27] They wanted the madrasas to have several classes like those in the modern schools. They also wanted to hold exams on a regular basis, so that only those who pass the higher exam could become a ulema. They heavily criticised the then state of education in the madrasas, where there were no exams and where every student became a moulvi or ulema in just a few days, without any method or way to verify his knowledge.[28]

These were questions that attacked the heart of the madrasa type of education, where any Ahmad or Dawood could become a moulvi or a ulema, without any adequate training or knowledge. If the state of the students was thus, then the responsibility for such a situation must lie with the ulemas who imparted such an education and their religious knowledge, including their knowledge of Arabic which is almost inseparable from Islam.

Singling out the ulemas for such a state of affairs, they accused them further of living a comfortable life by collecting money in the name of the madrasas and mosques or by saying that they belonged to the Pir's house, etc., or sometimes even by lending money on interest.[29]

P. Dawood Sha, the editor of the Muslim periodical, *Dar-ul-Islam*, was in the forefront of the attack against the ulemas. He was the *bête noire* of the ulemas. He was an accomplished Tamil scholar, having even won a gold medal for his proficiency in Tamil, from the famous Madurai Tamil Academy (Sangam). He voiced, through the print media, one of the most strident criticisms of the ulemas' inadequate knowledge of Tamil. In *Dar-ul-Islam*, he wrote:

> We believe that the Tamil spoken by the Marakkayars and the Rawthers will render shy any student of Tamil. Their religious teachers called moulvis and their knowledge of Tamil is very shameful. These Alims do not know the fundamentals of Tamil. They do not try to learn this language of the kafirs. Such people knowing to speak some Tamil, and wanting to put their dirty kitchen Tamil in writing, have named it 'Arabic-Tamil'. Such books written in Arabic-Tamil can be understood only if their authors were present.
>
> How can such moulvis, not knowing Tamil, teach about Islam to others?
>
> At the *Majlis-ul-ulema* conference in Tamil Nadu, organised with the help of Tamil Muslim money, they speak in English

> and Hindustani. In such meetings, some Alims dare to speak in the Tamil of their houses.
>
> Only a few Alims really know to read and write in Tamil. Even newspaper reporters can't understand their [pure] Tamil.
>
> ...Tamil Muslims do not know anything more than some of the useless Arabic-Tamil books of such Alims and their story-telling....But now in Madras, some are publishing books. If they do not publish such books written in bad Tamil, they will be doing a great service to Islam and Tamil...[30]

Dawood Sha was a recognised Tamil scholar. He had written several books in Tamil (see Appendix). He was editing Tamil Muslim journals from the time of the Khilafat movement and even after the independence of India. He had actually translated the Quran into Tamil in his later years and commented upon it. He was probably dissatisfied with the complete translation into Tamil of the Quran by A.K. Abdul Hamid Baqavi, which pushed him to re-translate the entire Quran and interpret it along rational lines. Six volumes of his translation and commentary of the Quran were published between 1962 and 1971, but the seventh and final volume still awaits publication.[31] Given such a background, it certainly will not be out of place to rely upon his assessment of the ulemas' knowledge of Tamil and their Arabic-Tamil.

However, Dawood Sha admits that only a few alims really knew to read and write in Tamil. One can probably include among them, Mustafa Alim Hajiyar and Nuh Alim Sahib, whose Arabic-Tamil works on the Quran was published in 1881 and 1890 respectively. The quality of such and other works in Arabic-Tamil remains yet to be ascertained fully.

However, during the 1920s, Dawood Sha himself translated the Quran into Tamil, from Mohammad Ali's English version.[32] This attempt to translate the Quran into Tamil from the English version rather than directly from the Arabic original seems to demonstrate that even the modern Muslim scholars were not well equipped in the knowledge of Arabic (not to speak of the ulemas' inadequacies in it) in order to translate directly from Arabic into Tamil and get it printed.

In the light of the above, it appears more plausible that one of the real reasons why the Quran and the Hadith were not translated fully into Tamil using the Tamil script and then published, seems to be the lack of adequate knowledge of Tamil, especially classical Tamil, as claimed by Dawood Sha and his school and probably also a lack of adequate knowledge of Arabic among the ulemas in the Tamil country despite the fact that Tamil Muslim works were regularly published from the 1840s. What is remarkable is that, this explanation is based not on speculation or theoretical assumption, but on actual irrefutable literary evidence.

Reasons as the untranslatability of the Quran because of the difficulty in rendering the highly sophisticated Arabic language into another language, or because of the sacredness of the Quran, which when translated cannot be published in print form, as written forms were the only acceptable form for the Muslims, do not seem to hold water because of an acute lack of factual evidence, especially from the party which is directly concerned, i.e., the Tamil Muslims. Further, such reasons are not valid because in northern India, the Quran had been translated into Urdu in the early eighteenth century itself and at least a dozen different translations of the Quran were published in the second half of the nineteenth century.[33] An Urdu translation of the Quran was even published from Madras in 1851.

We cannot reasonably hold that the Tamil Muslim ulemas were unaware of these translations into Urdu, especially the one at Madras, at a time when several other works in Persian or rather Urdu, (see the Appendix) had been translated into Tamil and also printed. There is no ground to claim also that the Tamil Muslims were more orthodox than the north Indian Muslims or the Urdu-speaking Muslims of Madras, and that it was this which prevented them from translating and publishing the Quran.

However, we are aware of the Tamil Muslim opposition to the secular values of the British, especially in the field of education.[34] But, there is no factual evidence, either in the form of a fatwa or any other literary evidence which establishes their opposition to the printing of the Quran or the Hadith. Even if they were opposed to printing, it ought not to have prevented them from translating the full Quran into Tamil and writing in the Tamil script on palm leaves or on paper, something which they never did until the 1940s. This once again lends credence to Dawood Sha's contentions.

The preceding discussion brings out the fact that the late translation of the Quran into Tamil without which no printing was possible, was also due to reasons which are peculiar to the Tamil world. Such a peculiarity does not allow for generalisations applicable to the entire Muslim world. This, however, does not undermine other reasons for the late adoption of printing, as the association of printing with Christianity. But what has to be emphasised is that the peculiarities of every Muslim society round the world have to be also taken into account when determining why Muslims were slow in taking to print as we have done in the case of the Tamil Muslims. Thus, an area-wise study of the various parts of the Muslim world is imperative to understand the slow penetration of print culture and its impact to prevent the risk of committing errors due to undue haste and over-simplification of the issues involved.

Notes

1. *Encyclopaedie de l'Islam,* (Leiden, 1986), VI, 794.
2. Ibid.; Amir Khusru, *Khaza'inul Futuh*, (Madras, 1931), vi.
3. *Encyclopaedie de l'Islam*, 790.
4. T.F. Carter, 'Islam as a Barrier to Printing', *The Moslem World*, vol. XXXIII: 216.
5. *Encyclopaedie de l'Islam*, 793.
6. Ibn Khaldun, *An Arab Philosophy of History*, John Murray, (London, 1955), 159; *The Muqaddimah*, vol. III, (Princeton University Press, Princeton, New Jersey, 1958), 288–89.

7. Dominique Sourdel, *L'Islam*, (Paris, 1981), 42–43.
8. Johannes Pedersen, *The Arabic Book*, (Printeton University Press, Princeton, New Jersey, 1984), 14.
9. Alla Pichai, *Just a Peep into the Muslim Mind*, (Madras, 1972), 2nd edition, 35–59; R.P.M. Kani, *Islamiya Ilakiyak Karuvulum*, (Madras, 1963), 10.
10. T.F. Carter, *The Moslem World*, 213.
11. A.K. Abdul Hamid Bakavi, *Tarjumatul Koran*, 6th edition, published by A.K.A. Abdus Samad, (Madras, 1986).
12. E. Lévi-Provençal, *La Civilisation Arabe dans l'Espagne Musulmane*, (Paris, 1948).
13. Dominique Sourdel, *Islam*, 28.
14. S. Delacroix, Mgr., *Histoire Universelle des Missions Catholiques—Les Missions Modernes*, (Paris, 1957), II, 44; K.S. Latourette, *A History of the Expansion of Christianity, 1500–1800*, (New York, 1971), 3, 251.
15. M.J. Rowlandson, *Tohfut-ul-Mujahideen*, (London, 1833).
16. A. Demeerseman, *L'Imprimerie en Orient et au Maghreb: Une Etape Décisive de la Culture et de la Psychologie*, (Tunis, 1954), 18–19, 21.
17. M.W. Mirza, ed., *The Nur Sipihr of Amir Khusraw*, (London, 1950), xxix–xxx.
18. *The Encyclopaedia of Islam*, (Leiden, 1971), vol. III, 435.
19. W. Christian Troll, *Islam in India: Studies and Commentaries*, (Vikas Publishing House, New Delhi, 1982), 135–142.
20. Ibid.
21. A.K. Abdul Hamid Bakavi, *Tarjumatul Koran*, 6th edition, published by A.K.A. Abdus Samad, (Madras, 1986), 13–15.
22. R.P.M. Kani, *Islamiya Ilakiyak Karuvulum*, (Madras, 1963), 10; W. Christian Troll, *Islam in India: Studies and Commentaries*, (New Delhi, 1982), 136.
23. Ibid.
24. *The Encyclopaedia of Islam*, 435.
25. *Muslim Sangha Marukamalam*, 1st April 1920.
26. Ibid.
27. J.B.P. More, *The Political Evolution of Muslims in Tamil Nadu and Madras, 1930–1947*, (Hyderabad, 1997), 50–87.
28. *Muslim Sangha Marukamalam*, 1 April 1920.
29. Ibid., August 1920.
30. *Dar-ul-Islam*, 1 January 1923, 30–32.

31. W.C. Troll, *Islam in India*, 137.
32. *Taj-al-Islam*, (Tamil Muslim Journal), May 1924.
33. Barbara Metcalf, *Islamic Revival in British India: Deoband, 1860–1900*, (Princeton, New Jersey, 1982), 202–203.
34. J.B.P. More, *The Political Evolution of Muslims*, 50–87.

CHAPTER SIX

Debates and Controversies

Some of the controversies, briefly dealt with in the third chapter, regarding the introduction of printing and its adoption by the Tamil Muslims will be discussed in detail in this chapter. The impact of print on Tamil Muslim literature, type of influence exerted by it, and the transformations that it brought in the Tamil Muslim society and in the identity of the Tamil Muslims will be studied.

Debates, dissensions, and differences had existed almost throughout Islamic history. The differences between the Sunnis and Shias, which appeared very early in Islamic history are well known. As far as India is concerned, the Mahdhawi sect in the fifteenth century posed a challenge to orthodox Islam. A certain Sayyid Muhammad Jaunpuri had declared himself as *mahdi* (messiah) and was executed for apostasy by the Turkish sultan of Delhi, Firuz Tughluq.[1]

But in the subsequent century, during Emperor Akbar's reign, another major religious controversy erupted that pitted orthodoxy against innovators like Emperor Akbar and his grandson, Dara Shikoh. Actually, during his reign, Akbar used to organise religious debates between scholars of Islam and various other religions, in his *Ibadat Khana* (House of Worship). This had even led to the formation of a new religion known as

Din i Ilahi, which provoked the opposition of the ulemas, the custodians of orthodox Islam. After the death of Akbar in 1605, orthodoxy gradually got the upper hand and maintained its position, in spite of Dara Shikoh's liberal and mystical predilections.[2]

All such transformations had taken place without the least influence or aid of print. So it will not be altogether right to assert that print alone had the capacity to bring about change and transform society.

Similarly, during the colonial period, various movements of a controversial nature, had risen with or without the aid of print technology in India, including in the Tamil country. These can generally be classified under three heads, viz., (i) pan-Indian controversies and debates, (ii) pan-Islamic or international controversies, and (iii) controversies and debates at the local level. We will go into each of them.

Pan-Indian Debates

Of the pan-Indian movements, i.e., movements which had some influence in various parts of India, the two most popular and most controversial ones are the Ahmeddiya movement and the Nechari (Naturist) movement. The former was founded by Mirza Ghulam Ahmad of Qadian in Punjab, during the last decades of the nineteenth century, while the latter was led by Sir Sayyid Ahmad Khan, during the second half of the same century.

Mirza Ghulam Ahmad, originally a landowner, declared himself as the new Prophet and Messiah, to the great horror of the orthodox ulema. By this declaration, he defied the fundamental doctrinal belief of the Sunni Muslims that Mohammad was the Last Prophet. There is no basis to claim that this self-styled prophet of northern India and the founder of the Ahmeddiya movement, which still has millions of followers in the Indian sub-continent and beyond, was a product of print culture, given the fact that prophets had existed for thousands of years before the invention of print technology by Pi Sheng in China.

But, Mirza Ghulam Ahmad's movement and his disciples and followers had no doubt made use of printing as a propaganda aid. It should be emphasised that even without print technology, personalities such as Sayyid Ahmad and Mirza Ghulam Ahmad would still have made an impact.

However, we cannot deny the fact that the advent of Mirza Ghulam Ahmad during the colonial period, represented a controversy within Islam in India, which provoked much debate and conflict. This controversy seems to have spread even to Tamil Nadu in the deep south all the way from the Punjab, where the orthodox ulemas rose against the Ahmeddiya movement and its principles. This controversy was aided and abetted by print and the print media to a great extent in the Tamil country.

It had become common with such prophets and founders of sects in the modern age, to have a printing press at their disposal, which could be used to publish their radical thoughts and writings. Thus, while the Ahmeddiya movement produced a wide range of missionary literature in various languages, there were other similar movements of a sectarian nature, such as the Arya Samaj founded by Dayananda Saraswati, or the Sri Aurobindo sect in Pondicherry, which usually laid claim to a certain universality, and which made good use of the press to propagate their views.

Regarding the Ahmeddiya movement in the Tamil country, it appears that at one stage, the Tamil scholar, Naraiyur P. Dawood Sha, was singled out and accused of being an Ahmeddiya by the orthodox ulemas and Muslims. *Dar-ul-Islam*, of which P. Dawood Sha was the editor in 1923, maintained that every religion was God's religion and even cited the Quran to affirm that there was no people who had no prophets.[3]

Dawood Sha began to interpret the Quran and explain Islam according to his own understanding. He had actually founded a Muslim *sangam* (association) at Natchiarkovil in the Tanjore region, during the second decade of the twentieth century and had even started a Tamil Muslim paper, known as *Tattuva Islam* (Philosophical Islam), with a certain Khaja Kamaluddin as the co-editor.[4]

The policies propagated by *Tattuva Islam* and that of the Natchiarkovil Muslim Sangam came to be known in Tamil as *Sutta Sathya Sanmarkam* (Pure and True Religion).[5] From the very beginning, Dawood Sha used the press to attack the traditional ulema, whom he accused of blatantly exploiting the poor and ignorant Muslims and of having very little knowledge of Islam.[6]

Probably, because of such criticism and because Dawood Sha was not a moulvi of the Arabic madrasa, but was a product of modern English education, the ulemas were obliged to defend themselves. So in their turn, they started newspapers and periodicals to counter the criticisms of Dawood Sha. One such monthly magazine was the *Hifazatul Islam*. Its editor was Moulvi S.S. Muhammad Abdul Khader Sahib Baqavi, who as we have seen earlier, had translated the Quran into Tamil from the Arabic script. He himself admitted, in his journal, that *Hifazatul Islam* was started to defend Islam against the false views and interpretations of Dawood Sha.[7] Another Tamil Muslim monthly favourably disposed to the ulema was the *Al Kalam*. It too came down heavily on Dawood Sha in defence of the ulema. *Saiphul Islam*, which was started in 1921 by Moulvi Sayyid Ahmad was also not sympathetic to the Ahmeddiya movement. In fact, a *Saiphul Islam* publication of 1935 pointed out the erroneous principles of the Ahmeddiyas.[8]

Generally, such journals depicted Dawood Sha as an Ahmeddiya, working against Islam.[9] Vigorous propaganda was carried on against the Ahmeddiya movement in general and Dawood Sha in particular. On the basis of the material in hand, it is not possible to determine, whether there was any truth in the contention of the ulema that Dawood Sha was an avowed Ahmeddiya.

Nevertheless, it appears from his early publications that he was not a full-fledged Ahmeddiya. Dawood Sha had asserted on 1 May 1920 that the Quran wants to rid man of superstitions.[10]

He criticised the *mahans* (great men in Islam who are venerated as Sufis) and stated that there were no contemporary records to prove the miracles of the mahans nor any genuine biographies of their lives, which were generally shrouded by myths.[11] Given this strong criticism of the mahans and their miracles, it is doubtful that Dawood Sha would have endorsed the miracles believed to have been performed by Mirza Ghulam Ahmad. Thus, there is a strong possibility that the accusation of the ulemas that Dawood Sha was an Ahmeddiya, was nothing but a ploy to discredit the personality who had challenged their traditional authority, invested in them by the Tamil Muslims.

The fact remains that Dawood Sha in the 1920s had translated the Quran into Tamil, from the English version by Lahore Moulvi Mohammad Ali, under the title, *Jawahirul Burhan pi Tarjamattil Quran*. Similarly, he had also translated Lahore Moulvi's English version of the Hadith into Tamil, under the title, *Sahiba Bukhari*. A shorter version of the same called, *Nayaka Vakkiyam*, was also published by him.

But this Lahore Mohammad Ali, along with Kwaja Kamaluddin, had broken away from the main Ahmeddiya sect in 1914, and had created their own group. Ahmad Aziz maintains that this Lahori group regarded Mirza Ghulam Ahmad as a mere reformer (*mujaddid*) and not a prophet and, in general, was very close to Sunni Islam.[12] Thus, we can reasonably conclude that Dawood Sha was never an Ahmeddiya and that he had resorted to translate Mohammad Ali's English version of the Quran and the Hadith into Tamil as a matter of convenience, primarily because he himself obviously did not possess adequate knowledge of Arabic for a direct translation from Arabic-Tamil. However, it is quite possible that he might have had some sympathy for the breakaway Lahori group, which actually, as noted by Ahmad Aziz, was very close to Sunni Islam.

On the other hand, Sir Sayyid Ahmad Khan's Nechari philosophy, was also roundly condemned by the ulemas in northern India. Actually, he was called a kafir by the moulvis for having adopted the English style of dressing and eating.

Sir Sayyid Ahmad Khan thought of rationalising Islam by asserting that Islam was in accordance with the laws of nature. There was considerable opposition to Sayyid Ahmad Khan's views, especially among the ulemas of Deoband, a traditional madrasa established in 1867, and also from other traditional Islamic schools.[13]

But the influence of the Nechari philosophy over the Tamil Muslims seems to be extremely limited. I have not come across any publication in Tamil until 1920, which shows the impact that Sir Sayyid Ahmad Khan's views on Islam might have had. It is quite possible that there might have existed some literature before this date. But it was only after this date that some literature seems to have been produced in Tamil, that reveals the influence of Sir Sayyid Ahmad Khan's Nechari philosophy. Thus, Moulana A.K. Abdul Hameed Baqavi wrote the *Iyarkkai Matham* (Natural Religion). It was published by the Islamic Prachar (Propaganda) Sabha of Tiruchy in 1930. Again, from Tiruchy, a book titled, *Iyarkkai Vazhi Islam* (Natural-Path Islam), was published. Its author was Moulvi Hafiz Syed Masood Kasimi. It appears, also, that in Tamil Nadu during the 1920s and 1930s many Muslims, especially their leaders, took pride in calling Islam a 'Natural Religion'.[14] Such a situation, though limited, would not have arisen without the influence of Sir Sayyid's teachings.

P. Dawood Sha, who was also a product of modern education like Sir Sayyid Ahmad Khan, hardly refers to the Nechari philosophy, as far as I know. This does not mean that he, who was no doubt one of the leading, modern Muslim intellectuals of south India and Tamil Nadu, was never influenced by Sir Sayyid's views, though he generally seems to have adopted a certain rational approach to Islam.

The Dutch scholar, J.M.S. Baljon has characterised Lahore Mohammad Ali's English translation of the Quran as one of the best known works of a modern Indian apology for Islam. He has shown that the religious thought of Mohammad Ali had much in common with that of Sir Sayyid Ahmad Khan's. Actually, he asserts that Mohammad Ali's views were a curious mixture of Mirza Ghulam Ahmad's spiritualism and Sir Sayyid's rationalism. This mixture had desupernaturalised his English-Quran commentary (Baljon 151–52). Dawood Sha, who was imbued with a certain rationality already, found in Mohammad Ali's English Quran, a version corresponding to his own penchant for a rationalist approach to religion. This prompted him to translate Mohammad Ali's English Quran into Tamil. But, in the process he was indirectly influenced by Sir Sayyid's Nechari philosophy, for, Mohammad Ali's source material in writing his English Quran was based substantially on Sir Sayyid's views. This prompts me to conclude that Dawood Sha's religious ideas had been influenced not only by Lahore Mohammad Ali, but also by Sir Sayyid Ahmad Khan.

In order to propagate his ideas, he had of course made good use of printing, though we cannot say how far print shaped his ideas. It rather appears that print, though it was the basis for stocking and diffusing information more efficiently, was only a part or rather an instrument of modern scientific knowledge and values, which had a decisive utility for Dawood Sha.

Pan-Islamic Debates

Now, let us move on to pan-Islamic and international controversies and debates in which the Tamil Muslims were involved. Tamil Muslims, as we have seen, were always an independent Muslim group, who had originated and evolved outside the spheres of the great northern Muslim empires. We have also seen through the analysis of their literature, their attachment to Islam and whatever was related to this, including Arabic and Persian.

Therefore, it is not surprising to find that the Tamil Muslims or at least some of them were attracted by movements and currents that had their origin in the Muslim heartlands. One such movement was the Wahabi movement, born in Nejd, in Arabia. The British believed that the Wahabi movement which spread to India was directed against them. But it appears that the religious ideas of the Wahabis were not appreciated by a majority of the orthodox Muslims in India. Orthodox theologians like Karamat Ali Jaunpuri, openly attacked the ideas of the Wahabis. Several works were written and published against them in the late nineteenth century.[15]

Though the Wahabis did not have much of a following in the Tamil country, yet we may find a few works against Wahabism in Tamil, such as the one by a certain Muhammad Ismail, condemning Wahabism, though it was actually compiled from Urdu sources (see Appendix). There seems to have been some vigorous Wahabi activity in the French territory of Pondicherry which was part of the Tamil country. There, the Wahabis seem to have broken ranks with the Sunnis and built their own mosque, known as Mohammadiya Palli, during the second half of the nineteenth century.[16] We were not able to trace any literature which was either produced by the Wahabis or was against the Wahabis in Pondicherry during this period. We, however, think that the diffusion of printed material would have played a role in bringing about such divisions in the Tamil country.

But the Tamil Muslim involvement of a more serious nature in pan-Islamic affairs occurred during the early decades of the twentieth century. During this period, they were greatly concerned with the fortunes of Turkey, which was not only the seat of the Caliphate but also of the Ottoman Empire. Tamil Muslim feelings and thoughts with regard to Turkey can be easily gauged by the publications, both in prose and in poetry, about affairs concerning Turkey.

They sang ballads when the Turks won the war in the Balkans, they wrote books about the Turkish-Balkan war to instruct Tamil Muslims about the problems faced by Turkey, they wrote about the Turkish involvement in the First World War on the side of Germany, and later they lamented the pitiable condition of the Turks in Asia Minor. (see Appendix). Such was their attachment to Turkey, the seat of the Caliphate, and also to the fortunes of Islam. Thus when moves were afoot to abolish the Caliphate once and for all, they participated extensively in the agitations that were launched, by the Congress and Gandhi in the 1920s, for the maintenance of the Caliphate at all costs. Tamil Muslim publications gave much importance to the Caliphate, which was a world Muslim affair.[17] Print of course seems to have played its role in strengthening and consolidating the Islamic identity of the Tamil Muslims during this period, when they began to feel that their future as Muslims was related to what was happening in Turkey and the Muslim heartlands, rather than what was happening in their immediate surroundings. It would have been almost impossible to ascertain this feeling of the Tamil Muslims during this particular period without the existence of literature produced by the Tamil Muslims themselves, during the same period.

Local Debates

Apart from the preceding pan-Indian and pan-Islamic controversies and debates in which the Tamil Muslims were involved in varying degrees, there existed a third dimension which was strictly local and intra-Muslim in which Tamil Muslims seem to have taken particular interest. Thus, the interpretation of a particular passage or even a verse in the Quran or some other Islamic sacred text by a Tamil Muslim had the potential to become a cause for debate. Such controversial debates were generally carried on through the publication of pamphlets and tracts. Traditional ulemas and even ordinary Muslim individuals seem to have been involved in such controversies.

Such controversies did not stop with the interpretation of verses and passages of the Quran. Sometimes it concerned the teachings of a Muslim holy man or a *sheik*. Thus a certain Ahmad Ibrahim published a tract from Tuthukudi (Tuticorin), refuting the heretical teaching of a sheik, called Mottu Sheik, during the first decade of the twentieth century. During the same period, we find a certain Muhammad Mohideen of Muthupettai, a Muslim holy place, coming out with his own religious teachings in the form of a pamphlet called, *Jivaratna Jagajothi Malai*. This was immediately followed by another pamphlet by a certain Muhyuddin Fakir, condemning the teaching of Muhammad Mohideen, as contrary to Islam.[18] Many other similar controversial pamphlets and tracts, of a strictly local value, seem to have been published now and then by Tamil Muslims during this period of which only a few seem to have come down to us.

Printing and publication were of course a vital means for these controversies and debates, even if they were of a very local nature, to stay in the limelight. Though one cannot say that print was at the origin of these controversies, because controversies and differences can arise even without the involvement of print as we have shown earlier, yet it appears that printing because of its inherent capacity to stock and diffuse information had given an extra vigour and life to at least some of these local and even trivial controversies and in the process consolidated them in one form or the other for posterity. Otherwise they would have withered away and died a natural death in the course of time, as all morality is liable to.

Reformist Tendencies

Another crucial dimension of controversies and debates seems to have been in the domain of reforms and Islamic identity in Tamil Muslim society. For most Muslims, reforms in Tamil Muslim society meant getting rid off all un-Islamic and Hindu habits, customs, and traditions that were lingering on in the lives of the Muslims, as survivals of ancestral traditions.

It should be noted that under the influence of the British and also the European Christians and their values and rational traditions, the necessity of reforms was felt in Indian society. Thus we have social reformers like Raja Ram Mohun Roy in the eighteenth century, among the Hindus. In the nineteenth century, we have Sir Sayyid Ahmad Khan among the Muslims, who strove to rationalise Islam and took a position against issues such as slavery and usury.[19]

The pioneer among social reformers in Tamil Muslim society appears to have been a certain Shamu Shihabuddin Waliullah of

Kayalpattinam, who probably lived during the eighteenth century. He had written several poems in Arabic-Tamil, of which a few such as the *Rasul Malai, Adabu Malai, Nenjarivu Malai, Meeran Malai, Kalyana Pith Attu Malai, Kanturi Pith Attu Vilakku Malai,* have survived to this day.

Through the poems, he severely criticised the un-Islamic habits prevailing among Tamil Muslims. He was particularly critical of the *Kanturi* festivals, celebrated in honour of the Muslim saints, which was replete with un-Islamic customs and traditions. Similarly, he wrote against the un-Islamic practices often found during Muslim marriage ceremonies. He rose especially against the Hindu dowry system among the Muslims, according to which the bride's parents were expected to gift money, houses, jewels, etc., to the bridegroom's family. This was obviously contrary to Islamic principles and Shamu Shihabuddin vehemently condemned those who accepted dowry as Satan's disciples.[20] He did not stop with this. He took to task the Lebbais (Tamil Muslim theologians) and the ulemas who were tolerating such un-Islamic habits and even supporting them.[21]

He was even critical of various other corrupt actions in the daily lives of some Muslims. He took a position against usury, against making money through foul means such as selling adulterated milk and rice, and even against smoking tobacco.[22]

It is notable that Shamu Shihabuddin, if we are to believe the Tamil Muslim scholars, was not a product of modern education like Raja Ram Mohun Roy or Sir Sayyid Ahmad Khan. He never travelled abroad like the latter two. He was born in Kayalpattinam and died at Kayalpattinam. We cannot also say, on the basis of the material available, whether he was exposed to British values and whether it may have influenced his writings. He was probably exposed to Christian missionary efforts and values. But it appears certain that Shamu Shihabuddin was probably among the first and foremost of the Muslims, who felt the need for reforms in Tamil Muslim society. What his reforms entailed was to get rid off the un-Islamic and Hindu habits and customs that were infecting Tamil Islam and thus be in conformity with the true Islamic principles. He never advocated innovations, outside the sphere of the Islamic scriptures.

It should also be noted that Shamu Shihabuddin wrote at a time when the Tamil Muslims had no access to print technology, which was the preserve of the missionaries and colonisers. It was only after 1835, that some of his manuscripts that had survived were put to print.

Moreover, the Arabic-Tamil utilised by Shamu Shihabuddin in his works had made them unintelligible not only to Hindus, but also to the great majority of the Tamil Muslims who did not know Arabic. It might be because of this that his works never became popular, not to speak of the fact that he did not write in English like Sir Sayyid Ahmad Khan.

In the light of the above, it will be incorrect to claim that print had any influence over his zeal for reforms. In fact, his reformist tendencies seem to be independent of not only print, but also modern values and traditions. Therefore, it will be incorrect to claim that reforms in Muslim society were made possible only with the advent of print technology.

Besides, as we have seen, the authority of the ulema had been repeatedly challenged and criticised even before printing became popular in India. In Tamil Muslim society, Shamu Shihabuddin, who even today is revered as a Sufi saint in Kayalpattinam, had unleashed a volley of criticism against the ulemas, and thus challenged their authority, though he never openly rose against them. This he did in spite of not being a product of modern education or a part of print culture. Therefore the theory that the authority of the ulemas was challenged only because of those who had received modern education or were part of the print culture has to be set aside. Instead, it will be more reasonable to admit that modern education and values and print culture, helped to consolidate and diffuse more widely the spirit of reforms in Tamil Muslim society, which in turn, naturally collided with the interests of the traditional ulemas. Print rather than hand-written palm leaf or even paper manuscripts was, of course, a more effective tool, mainly because of its capacity for large-scale diffusion, to challenge the authority of the ulemas, and to promote reforms. This shall be dealt with now. I have been able to trace a rare pamphlet containing just eight pages in verse form, titled, *Alim Al Fasikin Jahul al Maskarkhin*, by a certain Muhyi al Din Ibn Hamid Muhyi al Din of Nagore in the Tanjore region, published in 1906. It was from Madras and Colombo, and it contains the most undiluted criticism of the ulemas of Tamil Nadu. (see Appendix I) We do not know much about the background of the author, but the fact that he was from Nagore, one of the greatest Islamic spiritual centres of south India, proves that there were forces in Tamil Nadu, pitted against the authority of the ulemas during this period, and that demanded for reforms in the Tamil Muslim society.

There might have been many such pamphlets directed against the ulemas and their hold on Tamil Muslim society, published even before 1906. These are not available now, for even printed material, if it is not properly preserved, is liable to perish and disappear. But what is certain is that the print media had been put to good use by the early Muslim pamphleteers of Tamil Nadu to counter the ulemas' position as the traditional leaders of Tamil Islam.

During the second decade of the twentieth century, Naraiyur P. Dawood Sha, who had already established himself as a Tamil scholar and writer, founded the Muslim Sangam of Natchiarkovil, also located in the Tanjore region. In 1919 and 1921, this association published two volumes, which was a collection of several leaflets dealing with Muslim educational and religious matters, the Khilafat and world affairs.[23]

Dawood Sha as we know, was a product of modern education. He even seems to have served as a sub-magistrate before he began to take interest in the Tamil Muslim society.[24] He was particularly sensitive to the state of Islam in Tamil Nadu. His concern led to the establishment of the Muslim Sangam of Natchiarkovil, which was run primarily by scholars and intellectuals such as Khaja Kamaludeen, the first editor of *Tattuwa Islam*, the prime publication of the association.[25] Dawood Sha who was influenced by western values, ideas, and methods, showed a keen interest in cleansing Islam of impurities or un-Islamic habits and traditions.

It is here that the issue is of interest. The association, mainly through its press organ, rather than public meetings, launched a multi-pronged attack on the various aspects that were infecting Islam in the Tamil country. It held that the Quran wanted to get man out of all superstitions.[26] This assertion, though simplistic, has a certain importance because, according to it, the necessity for reforms in Tamil Muslim society arose from the Quran itself and not from modern ideas and values. But it appears probable that the latter might have pushed modern Muslim intellectuals and scholars to turn to the Quran itself, to find answers to the un-Islamic ills and superstitions affecting Islam and, thus, try to rationalise Islam itself rather than admit openly that the source of reforms in Tamil Muslim society, resided outside Islam.

Whatever the cause may have been, the association did not fail to direct its criticism against the dargah or tomb-oriented tradition in Islam, as practised in Tamil Nadu. It even went to the extent of discrediting the miracles performed by the saints of these dargahs and questioned not only their authenticity, but also the rationality behind them.[27] It criticised those who organised the Kanturi (*Urs*) festivals for their own self-pride and also adopted an uncompromising posture against the unnecessary expenditure involved in the celebration of ceremonies like *Kaathu Kuthal* (piercing of the ears) and *Peyar Vaithal* (christening).[28] Some other Muslims, also, wrote against worshipping at the dargahs.[29]

Later in November 1931, *Dar-ul-Islam* came down heavily on the *Dargah Sharif* festival at Nagore as anti-Islamic. The Erode Muslim Youth conference also criticised the Nagore festival.[30] The Dravidian publications such as *Kudiarasu*, gave ample coverage in its papers to this position of *Dar-ul-Islam* and others against the Nagore festival.[31] *Dar-ul-Islam*, whose editor was P. Dawood Sha, lamented the pathetic condition of Muslim women, who were used just as objects of reproduction and to do household work. It also lamented the atrocious Islamic knowledge of these women and criticised the attitude of some fathers who took pride in saying that their daughters had finished saying prayers in Arabic and Arabic-Tamil.[32]

It held as inhuman the way of dress of the Muslim women and their habit of piercing a large number of big holes in the ears, called *allikothu*, which resembled more the Hindu habits rather than Islamic. It called upon the Muslims to abandon this practice and claimed that Islam was not like traditional Hinduism. But when it came to the abolishing of child marriage, which was common among some Muslims also, *Dar-ul-Islam* cautioned the government to examine whether this abolition would affect the Islamic Shariat laws.[33]

Another Islamic association, known as Samuga Seer Thirutha Sabha (Association for Social Reforms), located at Koothanallur, also in the Tanjore area, took to task the ulema and the Muslim elderly, for not questioning this practice of piercing the ears of young Muslim girls of five to six years, in the name of beauty and custom. Ten to eighteen holes were pierced, in order that they might wear some years later, the gold jewellery, called *allikothu arasilai*. The children were slapped to prevent them from crying while the holes were pierced in their tender ears. This gold jewellery that they had to wear deterred them from playing, with the result that they became physically weak. Besides, they were a great hindrance while sleeping and also the noise they made caused the little girls to cover their ears with their hands and other people had to talk loudly to them to be heard.

Some women endured great suffering when the holes became septic, while some others who had delicate ears ended up with two or three holes stretching into one big hole. The Samuga Seer Thirutha Sabha wanted sincerely to abolish these customs and called upon the old Muslim grandmothers not to subject their children to such pain and suffering.[34] Journals such as *Dar-ul-Islam*, gave adequate publicity to the activities of such Muslim social reform associations like the one at Koothanallur and brought to the fore the need for reforms in Tamil Muslim society.[35]

Thus, there were clear signs of modern Muslim reformist

tendencies in the Tanjore region. These tendencies, which had their influence on other parts of Tamil Nadu also, especially through the publication of journals like the *Tattuwa Islam* and *Dar-ul-Islam,* can be rightly termed as the Tanjore School of Islamic Thought. Though, we cannot affirm outright that these tendencies would have come into existence without print technology, it will not be incorrect to note that print had contributed largely to their staying power and to their popularisation, unlike to the reformist works of Shamu Shihabuddin.

But what is more interesting is that the Tanjore School of Islamic Thought, generally held the ulemas responsible for the preceding state of affairs. By doing so, it challenged the Islamic knowledge of the ulemas. It came down heavily on the moulvis, who claimed that there was no knowledge other than what they wrote in some of their *kitabs* (Arabic-Tamil books) which was not regarded by the school to be Islamic. It considered the education dispensed in the madrasas by such moulvis as completely inadequate to the present situation and wanted to reform the madrasa educational system, where every student could become a moulvi in a few days, on modern lines, by conducting examinations, etc., and stressed the importance of learning both English and Tamil, which had been neglected by the ulemas.[37]

It also claimed that in the Quran it was not written that the alims should live all the lives on other people's money. It attacked them for taking money from poor Muslims in the name of the madrasas or masjids or by saying that they belonged to the Pir's house, etc. The Tanjore School of Islamic Thought put the blame on the ignorant Muslims for such a state of affairs.[38]

Dar-ul-Islam accused the moulvis for their inadequate knowledge of Tamil, which was a great obstacle to their teaching Islam to the great majority of the Muslims who were not well-versed in Arabic or Arabic-Tamil. If the alims' knowledge of Tamil was such, *Dar-ul-Islam* wondered about the state of religious knowledge of the Tamil Muslims. Actually *Dar-ul-Islam* declared:

> ...Among the Muslims of the world, the Tamil Muslims know less about religion. The Tamil Muslims do not know anything more than some of the Arabic-Tamil books of such alims and their story-telling... Even the *pesh Imam* does not know what he is reading, leaving aside the listeners in the mosque, who just go to sleep.... Is it enough to perform some rituals just for the sake of tradition? Why don't the alims talk about national problems in the mosques, as it was in the days of the first four Caliphs? The moulvis are responsible for keeping the Tamil Muslims in ignorance.... Except for some (Tamil Muslims) who go to foreign countries, and those who do business, the rest are betel-nut growers and live very frugally....[39]

Even the Samuga Seer Thirutha Sabha of Koothanallur took to task the ulemas, whom it accused of not caring for the state of Tamil Islam. Others, like Kambam Khan Sahib N.K.P.P. Rowther held, like Dawood Sha, that the Muslims did not know their religion and instead of unnecessary expenditures, they should concentrate on education.[40] Thus, on the whole, the Tanjore School of Islamic Thought accused the ulemas of having no enthusiasm to introduce and encourage reforms in Tamil Muslim society along strict Islamic lines.

It should be noted, anyhow, that the Tanjore School of Islamic Thought, in spite of all its enthusiasm for reforms in Tamil Muslim society, did not really want any reform measures in Tamil Islam outside of what it considered to be true Islam and what it considered to be of alien origin. It merely wanted to do away with all the un-Islamic habits and traditions in Tamil Muslim life, so that it was more in conformity with the genuine principles of Islam based on the Quran and the Hadith. Even in the abolition of child marriage, for instance, what they wanted was that it should be in conformity with the Shariat laws. In all their activities, they used the print media to buttress their views.

Thus, print was being used not against Islam, but for purifying the Islam practised by the Tamil Muslims. In this, they might have challenged the authority of the ulemas, whose knowledge was considered inadequate in the changing situation. But there was no question, at any time, of doing away with the institution of the ulema itself, which was the traditional custodian of Islam. All that they seem to have wanted to stress was that the ulemas needed to reform themselves and equip themselves with the necessary knowledge, not only about Islam, but also about Tamil, Arabic, English, etc., in order to be in a position to respond more adequately and rationally to the changing situation. In short, for them, reforming Islam never meant weakening Islam, but strengthening and consolidating it. Print had certainly played a great role in all this.

The Tanjore School of Islamic Thought, spearheaded by P. Dawood Sha, did not just print and publish to reform Islam, but it also wrote in defence of Islam against attacks from Christian critics. It took interest even in analysing Christian theological points such as the belief that Jesus Christ was the son of God. *Dar-ul-Islam* also rose against the vilification of Islam and the Prophet by the Christian missionaries.[41] It also published articles on the fallacies of the Hindu *karma* philosophy and asserted that our sorrows and happiness were not because of our last birth's karma (action).[42]

Also, it wanted to put across the point that religious tolerance and freedom of conscience was more present in Islam than in other religions. It even opined that there was no need for military might in Islam and it did not spread through coercion like some other religions.[43]

What is interesting is that this school wanted the expansion of Islam across the world. It actually wrote:

> It is not enough to propagate Islam in England alone, but it has to be done in France, Russia, America, Australia, Japan… Muslims have to help those who work for the expansion of Islam.[44]

During this period, Muslims seem to have been worried by the activities of the Arya Samajists, a Hindu proselytising organisation, which was quite active in south India.[45] Dawood Sha, who was very keen on the expansion of Islam across the world, was particularly worried about this. This prompted him to write and publish books like the one titled, *Ariyarkku Oru Vedikundu* against the Arya Samaj.[46] He also feared the *Ram Rajya* of Mahatma Gandhi and asked the Muslims to strive and strengthen the reign of Islam the world over, rather than witness the establishment of Ram Rajya desired by the Hindus, who were bent on rooting out Islam from India.[47]

It is amply clear that the Tanjore School of Islamic Thought not only wanted reforms and strengthening of Islam, but also its expansion across the world. Print, as we have seen, was a major weapon in their armoury to achieve these aims. Of course, Tamil Muslims had modernised themselves by adopting printing, but its use by them seems to point in the direction of the strengthening and consolidation of their historical Islamic identity and conditioning rather than anything else.

In this connection, it would not be impertinent to note that the adoption of printing by the west Europeans in the fifteenth century, did not lead to their de-christianisation, though print played a role later in the development of science and industry, which in their turn, challenged Christianity and its values. It should be noted that print was also used by the Christians in Europe, as we have seen, from its very inception and therefore it will be absurd to claim that it was print that was responsible for its weakening.

Orthodox Reaction

However, the traditional ulemas were not going to take the criticisms of Dawood Sha and others lying down. In their turn, the ulemas had their own publications such as the *Saiphul Islam* (editor, Moulvi Ahmed Sayyid), *Hifazat-ul-Islam* (editor, Moulvi Abdul Kader Sahib Baqavi and later Moulvi A.R. Abdur Rahim Baqavi) and the *Al Kalam* (editor, K.A. Abdul Majid) in order to defend themselves and attack their detractors such as the Tanjore School of Islamic Thought spearheaded by P. Dawood Sha. The latter's attack on the ulema organisations such as the *Majlis-ul-Ulema* of south India, whose first conference was held in 1917 at Tiruchy, and the Jamiat-ul-Ulema of all India was seen by them as being detrimental to Islamic interests.[48] Dawood Sha's refusal to accept the fatwas or judgements of the Jamiat-ul-Ulema, if they did not seem correct, and his overt disrespect towards the prestigious ulemas of the preceding two organisations was condemned.[49]

Another Tamil Muslim journal, *Al Kalam* stood for the defence of Islam against the Ahmeddiyas and Christians. It was against the *Panja Kondattam* (Panja festival) and other un-Islamic practices among the Tamil Muslims. Further, it favoured Hindu-Muslim unity, supported the views of Moulana Abul Kalam Azad of northern India, and was against P. Dawood Sha for his allegedly Ahmeddiya leanings.[50] It appears that under pressure from the reformist zeal of modern Muslims, the traditional ulemas were obliged to take some steps to rid Tamil Islam of its impurities and thus bring about some reforms. They claimed too that they were against the un-Islamic habits of the Muslims such as the *Santhanakoodu* procession and other un-Islamic habits associated with it.[51] Also, they defended themselves against the criticisms of the modern Muslims, who accused them of extracting money from poor Muslims and leading a comfortable life without earning a living of their own.[52]

Hifazatul Islam, too, directed its attack against the Ahmeddiyas and their seer, Mirza Ghulam Ahmad, who was supposed to have done great damage to Islam.[53] Its editor claimed that the *Hifazatul Islam* was started primarily to counter the Ahmeddiya views expressed in a Tamil Muslim journal called *Tattuva Islam*, of which Khaja Kamaludeen was the first editor, and P. Dawood Sha was the second, and thus protect Islam among the Tamil Muslims. It also reiterated the necessity for conversions to Islam in Tamil Nadu and Travancore, where many people were willing to convert. It asked the rich Muslims to help with money to welcome these conversions.[54] *Saiphul Islam* too expressed great interest in the matter of the conversion of Harijans.[55]

But *Taj al Islam*, a monthly Tamil Muslim journal from Erode took a position against the modern or modernised Muslims and wanted Muslims to conform to the genuine Islamic principles and customs.[56] There were also some orthodox Muslim sangams in Tamil Nadu, such as the one at Tirunelveli, and the *Rabikul Islam Society* of Adiyamangalam, which were in favour of *purdah*.[57] Later, some writers seem to have even brought out books and booklets in favour of the purdah system and argued that it was the best solution to prevent prostitution.[58] Such journals, writers, and associations were certainly intolerant to the views expressed by modern Muslims in some modern Islamic Tamil journals such as *Al Islam*, whose editor, M.A. Abul Hudha, was particularly interested in the promotion of modern education among Muslims, especially female education. This journal was so modernist that it wanted the establishment of clubs for all women as in foreign countries, including purdah-clad women, for them to discuss their problems.[59]

Taj al Islam regretted the lack of a Tamil Muslim daily. It complained that the *Saiphul Islam*, started in 1921, could not sustain itself as a daily because of Muslim apathy. This situation, it said, was pleasing to the Arya Samajists. During the fourth conference of the Majlis-ul-Ulema, held in Tirunelveli, P. Khalifullah, a leading Muslim lawyer and personality from Tiruchirappalli, voiced the necessity of starting a Tamil Muslim daily. Some other Tamil Muslim journals such as the *Livavul Islam* and the *Muslim Thoothan*, started a few years earlier, had to stop publication owing to lack of support from the Muslims.[60] Moulvi Ahmed Sayyid's *Saiphul Islam* was satisfied that vernacular Muslim newspapers such as *Azad Hind* and *Saiphul Islam* were doing good work among Muslims, but regretted the absence of English language newspapers in Tamil Nadu run by Muslims for Muslims. It thought that it was not advisable to rely upon non-Muslim English papers to ventilate Muslim grievances and promises.[61] All this shows that orthodox Muslims including the mullahs had fully realised the importance of the print media, not only to defend themselves and their causes, but also to protect and advance the interests of the Muslims in general.

Many mullahs and moulvis were no doubt in favour of the print media in order to serve their interests and that of the Muslims. But they were also against certain journals, representing the rationalist Dravidian movement, which they considered to be directed against them and Islam. So, it appears that they had dissuaded Muslims from buying and reading such papers.[62] Thus the print media seems to have become an arena where various interest groups clashed in order to advance or defend their interests.

The preceding as well as some of the controversial works listed in the Appendix, show that print was not only utilised by the modern intellectuals or the modernists, but also by the traditional ulemas to advance and popularise their views and causes. What differentiates print from the oral and written methods of transmission of knowledge was its capacity for mass diffusion of information and ideas, whether it was religious or modern. Though debates and controversies had always existed in Islamic history, yet I think that the preceding developments could not have taken place in Tamil Nadu without the aid of print and the influence of modern values.

It also appears that print and its capacity of mass diffusion had irreversibly undermined the authority of the ulemas, who until then were almost the sole custodians of Islamic knowledge and its transmission. Those Muslims exposed to modern values and technology like print challenged more and more the authority of the ulemas and their interpretations of Islam. They came out with their own explanations and interpretations of Islam, based generally on a certain rational approach to religion. In fact, as Francis Robinson has so aptly put it, any Ahmad, Mahmud or Muhammad could claim to speak increasingly for Islam from now.[63] Such a situation had risen no doubt owing to the influence of print and other modern or rational values. But it can also be attributed to the absence of an internal mechanism within Islam as found in Roman Catholicism, which formally prohibited or prevented any Ahmad, Mahmud or Muhammad from interpreting the Quran and the Hadiths, according to his own understanding. This had naturally resulted in the proliferation of various groups, sects, and schools such as the Deobandis, Wahabis, Nadwatis, Ahmeddiyyas, Ahl-e-Hadiths, Necharis, Jamiatiyyas, Natchiyarkovilis and the Tanjoris (Tanjore School of Islamic Thought), modernists and traditionalists.

If religion had taken a back seat in many parts of Europe, it was certainly not just because of print, because even religion had used print to advance its interests. If tomorrow, religion once again becomes a force to reckon with in Europe, which seems to be one of the possibilities, one cannot say it will be because of print technology alone. Thus, though print is considered to be a product of modernity or of a certain intellectual renaissance, yet it can be at the service of everything that is not modern or not part of the intellectual renaissance at all, as we have seen in the Tamil country.[64]

Our survey and analysis of the origin and evolution of Tamil Muslims and their literature, of their identity, and the role played by print will not be complete without taking into account the extraordinary relationship that developed between the Tamil Muslims and the non-Brahmin Dravidian movement. The movement was under the leadershp of E.V. Ramasamy or *Periyar* (Great Sage), as he was popularly known, from the 1920s onwards and later under C.N. Annadurai, popularly known as *Anna* (elder brother). We have already established, what constituted the Muslim identity in Tamil Nadu. The next two chapters will help to establish more emphatically the identity of the Tamil Muslims, especially after independence up to the 1960s. Print, as we are going to see, had a great role to play in the assertion of this identity.

Notes

1. Ahmad Aziz, *An Intellectual History of Islam in India*, (Edinburgh, 1969), 27.
2. M. Mujeeb, *The Indian Muslims*, (London, 1967), 247.
3. *Dar-ul-Islam*, (1 January 1923), 23.
4. *Hifazatul Islam*, (February 1930), vol. I.
5. *Muslim Sangha Marukamalam*, (1 June 1920).
6. *Dar-ul-Islam*, (1 April 1920, 1 August 1920).
7. *Hifazatul Islam*, (February 1930).
8. *Al Kalam*, (April, May 1925); *Qadianikalin Tavarana Kolkaikal*, (Madras, 1935).
9. *Al Kalam*, (April, May 1925).
10. *Muslim Sangha Marukamalam*, (1 May 1920).
11. Ibid., (1 May, 1 October 1920).
12. Peter Hardy, *The Muslims of British India*, (Cambridge, 1972), 172; Ahmad Aziz, *An Intellectual History of Islam in India*, 33; R.P.M. Kani, *Islamiya Ilakiyak Karuvulum*, (Madras, 1963), 220.
13. Ahmad Aziz, *An Intellectual History of Islam in India*, 14; M. Mujeeb, *The Indian Muslims*, 412, 449; see also J.M.S. Baljon, *The Reform and Religious Ideas of Sir Sayyid Ahmad Khan*, (Lahore, 1970) (reprint).
14. *Kudiarasu*, 24 February 1935.
15. Ahmad Aziz, *An Intellectual History of Islam*, 10; Peter Hardy, *The Muslims of British India*, 83.
16. Jacques Weber, *Les Etablissements Français en Inde au XIXe Siècle* (*1816–1914*), (Paris, 1988), IV, 2058, 2953.
17. J.B.P. More, *The Political Evolution of Muslims*, 46; see *Marukamalam*, 1921.
18. See Appendix.
19. M. Mujeeb, *The Indian Muslims*, 451.
20. *Islamiyat Tamizh Ilakkiya Katturai Kovai*, (Tiruchi, 1978), 23–25.
21. Ibid., 24–25.
22. Ibid., 26–27.
23. See *Muslim Sangha Marukamalam*, (Natchiarkovil, 1919), 205; *Muslim Sangha Marukamalam*, (Natchiarkovil, 1921).
24. *Dar-ul-Islam*, (September 1923).
25. *Hifazatul Islam*, (February 1930).
26. *Muslim Sangha Marukamalam*, (1 May 1920), 73.
27. Ibid., (1 May 1920), 62; (1 October 1920), 142.

28. Ibid., (1 August 1920), 116.
29. *Kudiarasu* (Dravidian newspaper), (25 February 1934, 1 November 1931).
30. *Dar-ul-Islam*, (30 October 1931); *Viduthalai*, (7 August 1937).
31. *Kudiarasu*, (1 November 1931).
32. *Dar-ul-Islam*, (1 January 1923).
33. Ibid.; *Dar-ul-Islam*, [16 November 1929 (NNPR, 1929)].
34. *Dar-ul-Islam*, (July–August 1923).
35. Ibid.
36. *Muslim Sangha Marukamalam*, (1 April 1920), 59.
37. Ibid., 57–59.
38. Ibid., (1 August 1920), 106–112.
39. *Dar-ul-Islam*, (1 January 1923).
40. Ibid., (July–August, 1923); *Viduthalai*, (15 February 1938).
41. Ibid., (September 1923); *Dar-ul-Islam*, [19 January 1935 (NNPR, 1935)].
42. *Muslim Sangha Marukamalam*, (1 December 1920).
43. Ibid., (January–April 1920), 31, 52.
44. Ibid., (1 March 1920), 41–42.
45. *Al Islam*, (September 1927); see F.R., 1st half of April 1934.
46. P. Dawood Sha, *Aariyarukku Oru Vedikundu*, (Madras, 1927).
47. *Dar-ul-Islam*, [17 April 1931 (NNPR, 1931)].
48. *Al Kalam* (Tamil Muslim Journal), (April 1925); *Al Kalam* (Tamil Muslim Journal), (September 1927).
49. *Al Kalam*, (April 1925).
50. *Al Kalam*, (April–May 1925).
51. See for e.g., *Hifazatul Islam*, (February 1930).
52. *Hifazatul Islam*, (November 1930).
53. Ibid., (December 1934).
54. Ibid., (February 1930; March–July, December 1934).
55. G.O. No. 1098, (21 June 1937); Tone of Tamil Newspapers in 1936, TNA.
56. *Taj al Islam*, (October 1923, May 1924).
57. *Swadesamitran* (30 September 1933); *Viduthalai*, (3 September 1937).
58. Rasool, *Pardha Enge?*, (Dindigul, n.d.).
59. *Al Islam*, (November 1926; July, September, December 1927; January 1928);
60. *Taj al Islam*, (November 1924).; *Al Islam*, (September 1927).
61. *Kudiarasu*, (28 August 1927).

62. Ibid., (3 March 1929).
63. Francis Robinson, 'Technology and Religious Change: Islam and the Impact of Print', *Modern Asian Studies*, (1993), 27, 1, 245.
64. See Elisabeth Eisenstein, *La Révolution de l'Imprimé dans l'Europe des Premiers Temps Modernes*, (Paris, 1991).

PART III

Muslims and Dravidians up to the 1960s

CHAPTER SEVEN

Hindu Role in Social Reforms among Muslims

It was not just the Tanjore School of Islamic Thought spearheaded by Dawood Sha, which through print media was clamouring for reforms in the Tamil Muslim society and lashing out at the ulemas for their indifference to the state of Islam in Tamil Nadu. During this period, there began another major movement that contributed in no small measure to the need for reforms in the Tamil Muslim society. This movement was known as the Self-Respect Movement. It was founded in 1925, by E.V. Ramasamy Naicker, a high caste non-Brahmin Hindu, hailing from a wealthy merchant family of Erode in Tamil Nadu.

E.V. Ramasamy had actually parted company with the Indian National Congress of which he was one of the leaders in south India, primarily because he was unwilling to tolerate its Brahmin leadership. Instead, he founded the non-Brahmin Self-Respect Movement with the avowed objective of doing away with Brahminism, the Hindu caste system, and its Gods. He characterised the Brahmins as Aryans, and the non-Brahmins including the Tamil Muslims as Dravidians. He also held that Dravidians and Muslims were of the same mother.[1] In order to achieve his objectives, he did not just rely on propaganda through public meetings. Instead, he like Mirza Ghulam Ahmad of Punjab and Dawood Sha of Tamil Nadu, put to good use the print media. Through this he carried on his propaganda war against all aspects of Hinduism throughout Tamil Nadu and elsewhere. The principal press organs of his were the *Kudiarasu* and the *Viduthalai*. Tamil Muslims were allowed to express their thoughts, feelings, and views in these journals. A perusal of these journals will demonstrate indubitably the extent of importance given to the Muslims and their affairs.

E.V. Ramasamy's contemporaries such as Swami Vivekananda, Rabindranath Tagore, Mahatma Gandhi, and Sri Aurobindo, all of whom hailed from northern India, were more interested in fostering the *aastika* traditions. Though, some of them were critical of the extreme forms of the caste system, none dared to wage a total war against it. While Vivekananda turned to the virtues of the Vedanta, Gandhi preferred to engage himself in the anti-untouchability campaign, leaving unperturbed the rest of the caste system. Tagore was known for his universal ideals and Aurobindo suddenly became a superman and formulated a religious synthesis influenced decisively by the works of the French philosopher, Paul Richard, with whom he was in close contact. Ramasamy appears to be the only Indian or rather Hindu social reformer, hailing from south India, who was pitted not only against the entire aastika traditions of Hinduism and Christianity, including the caste system, but also against the irrationalities and un-Islamic habits infecting Islam. This naturally seems to have drawn the Muslims of Tamil Nadu towards him.

E.V. Ramasamy and his movement, not only championed the causes and grievances of the non-Brahmin Hindus, especially through the use of the press, but also that of the Muslims. He participated in various non-Brahmin and Muslim meetings, especially the Prophet's birthday meetings, where he aired his rationalistic views about religion, society, and politics. He considered the Muslims to be more progressive than the Hindus, who he said were steeped in superstitions. He and his movement extolled the lofty principles of Islam such as equality and brotherhood and asked the Muslims to admit into their fold the depressed sections of the Hindu society, in order that they might enjoy the equality and brotherhood of Islam.[2]

Usually E.V. Ramasamy's speeches in such meetings were systematically printed and published through his movement's publications and circulated throughout Tamil Nadu. Ramasamy's sympathetic attitude towards the Muslims, in spite of being an avowed atheist, led the Muslims to consider him as a well-wisher of their community. Editors of Tamil Muslim newspapers such as Moulana Moulvi Ahmed Sayyid Sahib of *Saiphul Islam*, came out openly in support of the Self-Respecters, especially E.V. Ramasamy, and supported his participation in Muslim meetings. Moulana Moulvi Ahmed Sayyid Sahib held that when the Hindus who worshipped thousands of gods and Christians who believed in the Trinity, were allowed to speak at Muslim meetings, there was nothing wrong in allowing the atheist Self-Respecters to speak at Muslim meetings as long as they did not contradict Islamic principles.[3] Thus, print media, both Muslim and Dravidian, played a crucial role in bringing the Tamil Muslims closer to E.V. Ramasamy and his movement. This would probably not have been possible if E.V. Ramasamy had relied only on public speeches to propagate his views.

As noted earlier, Muslims were allowed to express their views in the publications of the Self-Respect Movement. Some local Muslim personalities identified the Tamil Muslims as Dravidians. A certain E.V.T. Sheik Abdul Khader of Salem wrote in the *Kudiarasu*:

> One who has Tamil as mother tongue from the very beginning, one who has migrated and settled in Tamil Nadu, was a Tamil. Among them there may be Saivites, Vaishnavites, Buddhists, Christians and Muslims, atheists and believers; they were all Tamils.

Another Muslim, B.A. Ismail of Athur, claimed that racially too the Muslims were Dravidians.[4]

Even P. Dawood Sha, the most vociferous of the Muslim social reformers, seems not to have been totally impervious to this Dravidian dimension in south India. He openly claimed that Tamilians, Christians, and Muslims were all Dravidians, though they had different customs and habits.[5] One could say that Dawood Sha had more or less subscribed to E.V. Ramasamy's view as far as the latter's Dravidian theory was concerned.

Tamil Muslims did not stop with expressing their Dravidianness through the print media. Actually some of the local Muslim personalities and stalwarts such as Tiruchi Haji Subagu Mohideen Sahib and Erode Abdullah gave vent to their desires for initiating radical reforms in Tamil Muslim society, through articles published in the *Kudiarasu*. They wanted the abolition of the purdah system and called for women's education and their upliftment for the good of the Muslim community.

Haji Subagu Mohideen Sahib even went to the extent of writing in favour of family planning and contraception. He quoted verses from the Quran and stated that the Quran was not against them.[6] He condemned the position taken against family planning by western-educated Muslim stalwarts of Madras such as Basheer Ahmad Sayeed, and spoke of the necessity of recognising reason in everything including religion. He wrote:

> ...Where has rationalism gone among those who have taken B.A. and M.A. degrees. ...When we take into consideration the economic situation of India, family planning becomes a necessity. ...The Islam I know wants to resolve the problem of the poor in the most rational manner. ...Quran says not to kill your children for fear of poverty (6:152 and 17:32, Quran)...The Quran does not oppose contraception considering the economic situation.

Like Dawood Sha, he too drew attention to the pathetic and subordinated condition of the Muslim women and widows and lamented that while the Hindus were openly admitting their faults and reforming themselves, Muslims were covering up their drawbacks by asserting that all the rights were already given to women.[7]

Some Muslims, under the influence of the Self-Respect Movement, such as Colombo's A.L. Mohammad Tameem, even went to the extent of questioning the rationality of Islam, in publications like *Viduthalai*.[8] T.M. Ibrahim, another Muslim stalwart from Colombo, wrote in the *Viduthalai* that Prophet Mohammad himself was a communist.[9] He condemned the false equality prevailing among the Muslims. He held that equality where there was no economic equality was false equality and that giving two and a half per cent of one's income as alms was not suited to modern times. Dindigul K. Abdul Hameed wrote that, 'If there was no equal dharma, there was no equality'.[10] Such writings appeared in the *Kudiarasu*, when E.V. Ramasamy himself was flirting for some time with communism, after his return from a visit to Russia in 1932.[11]

It would not be an exaggeration to say that such Muslims, apart from those of the Tanjore School of Islamic Thought, were the pioneers in highlighting the need for reforms in Muslim society, the upliftment of Muslim women, and the promotion of their rights. The Self-Respect Movement's press organs had no doubt played a crucial role in bringing the thoughts and feelings of such Muslims to the attention of the general public. We would have never known about the existence of such radical Muslim stalwarts, who desired to reform their society, had the Self-Respect Movement not used the print media.

The Self-Respect Movement trained its guns not only on Hindu religious beliefs and practices, but also directed its criticisms against certain customs of the Muslims, which were not in conformity with Islam. They did not even spare the religious teachers of the Muslims, that is the mullahs, and wrote about the necessity for them to be reformed.[12] It condemned habits as worshipping at saints' tombs (dargahs) and extravagant participation in the *Allasamy Pandigai* (Mohurram).[13] It wanted the abolition of purdah, because it prevented Muslims particularly women such as Begum Amiruddin of Madras, who was a member of the Madras Legislative Assembly, or Aruna Asaf

Ali, Congress Socialist leader of the United Provinces, from participating freely in public life. Moreover, purdah was also considered to be unhygienic for Muslim women, as it prevented access to sunlight and fresh air, which led to the spread of contagious diseases like tuberculosis. It also held that it was inhuman and that human values could not be sacrificed merely to satisfy some conservatives. It called upon the men to think about the gross injustice being meted out to the women of the society.[14]

The editorial of the *Viduthalai* of 29 November 1947 called upon the print media to help reform Muslim society by writing against *Allasamy Pandigai*, Panja dances, and the custom of fakir's blessing with peacock feathers. It also wanted the Dravidian Muslims to follow Mustapha Kemal Pasha of Turkey and Amanullah of Afghanistan who rose against purdah and other irrational customs.[15] *Kudiarasu* even reproduced in Tamil, articles written against purdah by Muslim women like Laila Bano Begum.[16]

Further the Self-Respect Movement compared the dominance of the mullahs over the common Muslim to that of the Hindu *purohits* (priests) or the Brahmins. It described the mullahs as the Muslim purohits or the Muslim Brahmins. It pointed out that whereas their dominance still continued, that of their Hindu counterparts was being destroyed. It held that the Hindu non-Brahmins had awakened, while Muslim non-Brahmins continued to live in ignorance and brought about such a state where the common Muslims were bound to the Islamic Brahmin because of a lack of education.[17]

E.V. Ramasamy compared the situation of Muslims in Turkey with that of India and Tamil Nadu; while the latter believed in religion, and upheld the ideals of Khilafat, Turkey had put an end to religion and mythology and had adopted modernism or westernism. He exhorted Indian Muslims to follow the example of Turkey and Afghanistan and accept reforms. This, he maintained, would pave the way for Islam to become accepted as a world policy.[18]

Generally, during this period the Self-Respect Movement and its leaders and its publications such as *Kudiarasu* and *Viduthalai* took a radical position not only against Hindu Gods, the Brahmins, and the caste system, but also expressed, frequently, their views about the grandeur of Islam and the necessity for the untouchables to convert to Islam to obtain equality and liberty. The editorial of *Kudiarasu* of 24 February 1935 held that Islam was suitable for the Tamils.[19]

The *Kudiarasu*, in its extreme zeal to destroy the Hindu caste aberrations more than its love for Islam, encouraged the untouchable Hindus to take refuge in Islam, if they really wanted freedom and equality, which according to it was not possible either in Christianity because of its caste structure or in Hinduism where there was no freedom at all.[20] *Viduthalai* thundered that the real way to freedom and equality lay in the conversion of the untouchables to Islam so that the Muslim population would rise to 16 crores.[21]

This was happening at a time when Mahatma Gandhi was warning the Hindus that if untouchability was not abolished, Hinduism would disappear.[22] The recognised untouchable leader, B.R. Ambedkar was advising the Harijans to break away from the Hindu fold.[23] Besides, Abdulla Gandhi, one of the sons of Mahatma Gandhi who had converted to Islam, was touring south India, presiding over conversion of low castes to Islam. He actually declared.... 'I am convinced that whoever becomes a *Mussalman* does a distinct service to himself and to humanity'.[24]

In a speech delivered on the occasion of the Prophet's birthday at Satyamangalam in 1929 and published in the *Kudiarasu*, E.V. Ramasamy declared,

> My Dear Hindu and Muslim brothers,
>
> Today is celebrated the birthday of a great Mahan (the Prophet). But many among us may think that this Mahan belongs to Muslims alone and so they alone have got the right to celebrate his birthday. They may also think how a Hindu like me may preside over such a meeting. When I clarify this,

though my Hindu brothers may suspect me for talking in favour of the Muslims and Muslim religion, yet I thank first of all heartily my Muslim brothers for giving me the opportunity to participate in this meeting and also giving me the honour of presiding over this meeting.

Brothers! I consider that religions were created by the sages of the past for the good and pleasure of the people in this world and not as a *Sadhana* of the soul or as something endowed with divine nature or something beyond this world...I never accept that any religious policy created by a God is suitable for all times and that it cannot be altered to suit the changing times. In the same way, I consider all religious leaders as social workers...I least accept the religious leader as God-like or messengers of God or God's incarnation...

So the celebration of Thiru Mohammad Nabi's birthday today, as I told before, is the celebration of a great man's birthday. To say more explicitly, of all the great men that we call our religious leaders, Thiru Mohammad Nabi is superior and I can even say boldly that he is worth to be followed by all people. Thiru Mohammad Nabi's religion is the latest of all religions. Therefore I would say that it had removed all the drawbacks and faults in other religions and can be accepted by more or less all as a reformed religion.

...I have not read those books (sacred books of other religions). Nevertheless, whatever great things may be found in these books, it is not going to be useful to us. Will sugar be sweet, if we write 'sugar' on a paper and lick it?

Muslim religion is a national religion. Besides it is an egalitarian religion i.e. in Muslim religion there is no division by birth as high and low. Setting aside the differences between rich and poor, learned and illiterate, weak and strong, it gives equal rights to all....

It can redeem the Chandalas. The people rejected by us as Chandalas have found refuge in the Muslim Religion and are given all the rights...

Today in our country, if six and a half crore untouchables convert to Islam, I can say forcefully that the next day itself the government needed for the good of India will come into being...Muslims cannot think in terms of getting out of India or get rid of the Hindus from India. Both have to exist in this country. ...For the good of the nation the Muslims must also have to cooperate with the Hindus: I think that the several drawbacks among the Hindus will cease to exist shortly. Then, there will not be much difference between the Hindus and Muslims...[25]

During this time at Seeliyampatti in southern Tamil Nadu, the untouchables unable to tolerate high-caste Hindu oppression, converted to Islam. E.V. Ramasamy and the Self-Respect Movement welcomed these conversions. E.V. Ramasamy actually declared:

I am not happy because 69 Adi Dravidas (untouchables) by their conversion to Islam would have all their sins forgiven or be nearer to heaven or have mingled with God. I do not believe in such things and I do not ask others to believe in it...For these 69 people untouchability has ceased to exist. Nobody can insult them anymore by calling them Paraya, Sakkili or Chandala. They need not...stand at a distance from others. They need not prostrate before the others. They need not live outside the *Ur* (village). They suffer without water to bathe and drink. They need not go about with dirty clothes and uncut hair, without dhobis or barbers, repugnant to others. They can walk in all the streets. They can take up any job. They can compete with anyone. They can participate in politics. ...They can go henceforth into their temples and can read the sacred books. Above all they need not worship stones, vessels, baskets and broomsticks as Gods. ...When I think of all these things I cannot but be happy...

Therefore as long as there is no equality and unity in the Hindu society, untouchables have no other alternative except to convert to Islam. We are not in a position to oppose this...'[26]

The *Kudiarasu* also held that E.V. Ramasamy was asking the untouchable Hindus to convert to Islam not just because they can worship *Allasamy* (Allah) or go to heaven, but to abolish untouchability and achieve equality.[27] E.V. Ramasamy considered Islam as the best antidote to counter the caste feeling and even wondered if there was any better antidote than this.[28]

In its editorial of 6 February 1938, *Kudiarasu* held the following:

> For the past 20 years, we have been asking the Adi Dravidas (untouchables) to become Muslims. We are not interested in their (Muslims') notions of heaven or reward... But for the Adi Dravidas to become human, to get self-respect, to be free from the oppression of the Hindus and the cowardice of the Christians, there is only one way for the Adi Dravidas, i.e. to free themselves from Hinduism and Christianity and become Muslims.[29]

On 20 June 1943, declared as the Untouchability Destruction Day in Madras, E.V. Ramasamy spoke of the necessity for the low caste and untouchable Hindus like the Tiyyas, Pulayas and Nayadis to convert to Islam, in order to get rid off their inferior status. At the same time he stressed that by Islam, he did not mean Islam's God or Prophet or Quran, but its capacity to confer dignity on the untouchables and low-caste people.[30]

Later, at the Tiruchi meeting held on 18 March 1947, he declared:

> I am not speaking in support of Islam or doing propaganda in its favour. This is true! I do not have more love and affection for the Muslims than for you (Hindus), more confidence in Muslims than in you (Hindus), more cooperation with the Muslims, than to you (Hindus). But in order to kill the cruel and horrible snake which is Brahmanism or remove the poison from it this (Islam) is the best medicine...Islam does not mean Mohammad Nabi's religion or the *lungi*-clad or the 'measured bearded' people...'[31]

From the preceding, it becomes quite clear that E.V. Ramasamy and his movement were actually utilising Islam as the most effective weapon in their armoury to destroy or at least weaken the hereditary Hindu caste system and the hold of Brahminism to reform the Hindu society. The call for the conversions of low caste and untouchable Hindus to Islam was considered by E.V. Ramasamy and his movement as the most effective method to shake Hinduism's aastika traditions and uproot it, if possible. E.V. Ramasamy, though, had grave doubts about the possibility of reforming Hinduism at all, unlike Islam. he wanted to destroy Hinduism completely and held that it was foolish to think that it was being reformed. He declared:

> There is no place for reforms in Hindu religion; nobody has the right to reform it.
>
> The structure of Hinduism lies in what is known as the Vedas, Shastras and Puranas and is dependent on them, and not on the self-styled Swamijis and Mahatmajis, craving for publicity.[32]

While E.V. Ramasamy tried to undo Hinduism, he and his movement, directly or indirectly, also lent a helping hand to the Muslim reformists, rationalists, and modernists, such as Dawood Sha, to reform Muslim society along Islamic lines. But it would be incorrect to maintain that Dawood Sha's reformist zeal was inspired by E.V. Ramasamy. His reformist tendencies appear to have started during the second decade of the twentieth century, i.e., before E.V. Ramasamy left the Congress and founded the Self-Respect Movement in 1925.

It should be noted that until 1938, Dawood Sha was a staunch Congressman and leader and was even the president of the Madras District Congress Committee. He regularly spoke in meetings in favour of Congress policies. He even declared that the national song *Vande Mataram* was not against Islam, at a time when many Muslims in the Madras Assembly and outside were opposed to it.[33] This was at a time when many Muslim papers such as *Saiphul Islam*, favourable to the Muslim League, wrote against reciting *Vande Mataram* on the grounds that it was *shirk*, i.e., against Islam.[34]

Dawood Sha was such a staunch supporter of the Congress until 1938 that Muslims in some places in Tamil Nadu even decided to boycott his paper, *Dar-ul-Islam*, and support papers such as *Saiphul Islam, Viduthalai* and *Uthaya Sooriyan* which were considered to be favourable to Muslims and the Muslim League.[35] Even an Urdu-speaking Muslim leader, Abdul Hameed Khan publicly asked Muslims to support *Saiphul Islam* and also *Viduthalai*.[36] The Self-Respecters referred to Dawood Sha as 'Ramayana Sahib', for being in the Congress and giving lectures on the *Ramayana* and *Mahabharata* like the Brahmins.[37]

But on 1 January 1939, Dawood Sha did a volte-face. He joined the Muslim League and accused the Congress of ill-treating and cheating the Muslims. In the same year, he came out in favour of the development of Urdu or Hindustani as the language of the Muslims.[38] Dawood Sha was known to one and all as a Tamil scholar. He had always campaigned for the development of Tamil among the Muslims, including the moulvis of Tamil Nadu. But suddenly in 1939, he switched over to the Muslim League from the Congress and even extended his support to the separatist Pakistan demand of Mohammad Ali Jinnah and the All India Muslim League. Now, as a Muslim Leaguer, Dawood Sha, like P. Khalifullah of Tiruchirapalli and other prominent south Indian members of the Muslim league, did not oppose Urdu or Hindustani, though, like them, he agitated against the introduction of Sanskritised Hindi into the south by joining hands with E.V. Ramasamy—for Ramasamy, though, Urdu, Hindi, or Hindustani, were of the same north Indian Aryan extraction, and were seen as the enemies of Tamil.[39] Naturally, people such as Dawood Sha and Khalifullah seem to have been obliged to pay at least lip service to Urdu in order to be in line with the policies of the All India Muslim League, which was dominated by Urdu-speakers, and to be in the good books of north Indian (Urdu-speaking) Muslim leaders.[40] So it would not be incorrect to conclude that the support extended by some Tamil Muslim leaders to Urdu during this period, was not out of any genuine love for it.

Further, Dawood Sha held that the interests of the minorities could not be safeguarded, without supporting the Pakistan scheme.[41] Following, Jinnah and the All India Muslim League, he, like most of the Leaguers, distanced himself from the separate *Dravidanadu* or *Dravidasthan* demand of E.V. Ramasamy, in spite of the latter's consistent support to the creation of Pakistan and to the conversion of untouchables to Islam.[42] This was to have serious consequences between the Self-Respecters and the Muslims of Tamil Nadu, especially after independence.

It should also be noted that though E.V. Ramasamy attacked Hinduism in the most uncompromising terms, certainly much more than any other social reformer of India hitherto, and praised Islam and even asked the untouchables to convert to Islam for their deliverance, yet he himself never became a Muslim or disowned his Hinduness completely. When he was asked, why he did not join Islam, his answer was: '...I consider myself as belonging to Islam as far as its philosophy of Oneness is concerned...'[43] Later he said, 'I will destroy the Hindu religion by remaining in it. If I change my religion, I will lose the right to reform it and save the people who are caught in it...'[44]

It is interesting to note at this juncture, that when a few Muslim youth, who were highly influenced by the Self-Respect movement, apprised E.V. Ramasamy of their intention to leave Islam, the latter had advised them against it. Instead, he had asked them to indulge in social reform activities like Mustapha Kemal Pasha and get rid of all superstitions in Islam. He even suggested that they work for the removal of the Muslim priestly class by establishing an anti-purohit sangam. It was also his opinion that Mutapha Kemal Pasha would never have been able to reform Turkish Muslims if he had chosen to abandon Islam.[45] It would then seem that E.V. Ramasamy was simply following the line of Mustapha Kemal Pasha, by choosing to remain in Hinduism in order to reform it and asking the Muslims also to do the same. But, many Muslims appear to have been expecting E.V. Ramasamy to convert to Islam during this period. Sultan

Bagdhadi Sahib, a local Muslim leader from Ramnad, where conversions to Islam were taking place, refuted the allegation that E.V. Ramasamy was an atheist or was insincere when he advised the untouchables to convert to Islam. He said that E.V. Ramasamy was at heart a Muslim and he had not adopted the Muslim faith because he wished to inspire conviction among the untouchables by remaining within the Hindu fold.[46] Such a posture seems to have been adopted by certain Muslim leaders, who were sympathetic to the Self-Respect Movement, in order to ward off the criticisms of certain Congress Muslim leaders, such as the staunch nationalist Haji Mohammad Moulana Sahib of Madura and K.M. Sheriff, Tamil Muslim member of the All India Congress Committee. The former held:

> Reactionaries and anti-Congress groups like the Self-Respect Movement were misleading the Muslims by saying that the Congress was irreligious, while on the other hand, the Self-Respecters, who professed friendship towards the Muslims, were the people who disowned all divinity and mocked at all religions.[47]

It is highly improbable that the propaganda of E.V. Ramasamy and his movement, in favour of reforming Hindu and Muslim societies, would have achieved the popularity and the success that it really achieved in south India without the print media. It would not be an exaggeration to say that print technology and culture had directly contributed not only to the acceleration of the pace of reforms in Hindu and Muslim societies, but also to the coming together of the Self-Respecters (who never disowned their Hinduness) and a sizeable section of the Tamil Muslims.

Notes

1. *Kudiarasu,* (15 July 1947).
2. Ibid., (24 August 1930).
3. Ibid., (6 February 1938).
4. Ibid., (30 April 1939; 21 June 1947).
5. *Mail,* (18 April 1940).

6. *Kudiarasu*, (26 November 1933; 25 March 1934).
7. Ibid., (28 January 1934; 26 November 1933).
8. Ibid., (29 April 1934).
9. Ibid., (17 September 1933).
10. Ibid., (31 December 1933).
11. Under-Secretary's Secret File, Government of Madras, Secret, No. 896, (22 June 1934), TNA; *Kudiarasu*, [20 November 1932, (NNPR, 1932)].
12. *Kudiarasu*, (27 October 1929).
13. Ibid., (3 March 1929; 14 June 1931).
14. Ibid., (14 October 1928); *Viduthalai*, (29 November 1947).
15. *Viduthalai*; Ibid.
16. *Kudiarasu*, (14 October 1928).
17. Ibid., (3 March 1929).
18. *Dravidan*, (5 August 1929); *Kudiarasu*, (23 August 1931).
19. *Kudiarasu*, (24 February 1935).
20. Ibid., (19 April; 31 May; 25 October 1931).
21. Ibid., (12 January 1936).
22. *Swadesamitran*, (11 June 1936).
23. *Madras Mail*, (25 October 1935).
24. Ibid., (2 September 1936).
25. *Kudiarasu*, (25 August 1929).
26. Ibid., (20 October 1929).
27. Ibid., (2 February 1936).
28. Ibid., (12 March 1947).
29. Ibid., (6 February 1938).
30. *Viduthalai*, (26 June 1943).
31. E.V.R. Periyar, *Ina Izhivu Ozhiya Islamay Nanmarunthu*, (Erode, 1947), 17; *Kudiarasu*, (12 March 1947).
32. *Viduthalai*, (26 September 1943).
33. Ibid., (24 November 1937).
34. *Viduthalai*, (7 August 1937), quoted from *Saiphul Islam* of 4 August 1937.
35. Ibid., (15 November 1937).
36. *Kudiarasu*, (26 June 1938).
37. *Viduthalai*, (4 April 1947).
38. *Kudiarasu*, (25 December 1938; 1–2 January 1939); *Sunday Observer*, (1 June 1939); *Viduthalai*, (2 January 1939); *Madras Mail*, (24 January 1939).
39. See J.B.P. More, 'Tamil Muslims and Non-Brahmin Atheists', in

Muslim Communities of South Asia: Culture, Society and Power, ed., T.N. Madan (Delhi, 1976), 349–358; *Swadesamitran*, (17 April 1937).

40. *Kudiarasu*, (16 June 1940).
41. *Mail*, (16 April 1941).
42. J.B.P. More, *The Political Evolution of Muslims in Tamil Nadu and Madras, 1930–1947*, (Hyderabad, 1997), 173–181.
43. *Kudiarasu*, (10 July 1947).
44. Mangaiyarkarasi, *Varalaru Kanda Vaikom Veerar* (Tamil), (Madras, 1980), 134.
45. *Kudiarasu*, (15 February 1931).
46. *Madras Mail*, (10 January 1939).
47. Ibid., (14 April 1938).

CHAPTER EIGHT

Muslims and Dravidians: Strains and Frictions

We have already seen how the Tamil Muslims and the Hindus of the Self-Respect Movement drew closer to each other, in spite of acute ideological differences. Print media had undoubtedly played a crucial role in cementing this alliance. Yet, differences remained and cracks developed.

Moulvi Ahmed Sayyid of *Saiphul Islam* had asserted that there was nothing wrong in joining hands with the Self-Respecters, as long as the latter did not contradict the Islamic principles and as long as they were helpful in the attainment of the aims and objectives of the All India Muslim League.[1] Even the prominent theologian, Moulana Moulvi Abdul Hameed Baqavi, who translated fully the Quran into Tamil for the first time, did not hesitate to participate in meetings in which E.V. Ramasamy and other Self-Respecters spoke.[2] The Self-Respect Movement enjoyed the support of other prominent Muslim moulvis during this period, such as Moulana Moulvi Sherfuddin Sahib of Vellore, who joined hands with Ramasamy in 1938 in his agitation against the imposition of Hindi or Hindustani, in spite of the latter's tirades against the mullahs.[3] P. Khalifullah, the prominent lawyer and Muslim League leader from Tiruchirappalli, had cautioned the Self-Respecters to eschew atheist propaganda, if they wanted an understanding with the Tamil Muslims.[4]

Another prominent Muslim local leader, Sultan Baghdadi Sahib went to the extent of refuting the allegation that Ramasamy was an atheist or was insincere when he advised untouchables to join the Muslim faith and asserted that Ramasamy was at heart a Muslim.[5]

E.V. Ramasamy himself had opined in 1931, that he had met several moulvis and a few moulanas and many Muslim youths and discussed with them the policies of Islam and the Self-Respect Movement. He held that most of them never openly expressed their opinions about God, probably out of fear, and that they had even requested him to stop propaganda that was against God.[6]

Thus, the Muslims defined the contours of their ties with the Self-Respect Hindus and imposed limitations on their relationship with them. It appears that from the foundation of the Self-Respect Movement, E.V. Ramasamy was guarded about openly attacking the fundamental beliefs of Islam. He was always evasive in his replies about his position vis-à-vis these fundamental beliefs. Instead, he seems to have always held the view that what was necessary then was to do away with the superstitions and the various gods and goddesses of the Hindus, who married, had children and even had love affairs.[7]

Sometimes, it appears that E.V. Ramasamy never really took a categoric position against Islam and its beliefs like the belief in One God, probably because he was enamoured of its social principles of equality and brotherhood, which he thought was the best antidote to counter untouchability among the Hindus. It is also possible that during the 1920s and 1930s, E.V. Ramasamy deliberately did not want to adopt a categorical position against Islam and its beliefs, though he did not fail to decry its superstitious beliefs which he believed to be survivals of Hindu traditions. This was because public meetings organised by Muslims offered a convenient and comfortable platform for Ramasamy and the Self-Respecters to air their religious views, especially on Hinduism, without restriction.

Though E.V. Ramasamy did not adopt a hardline position against Islam, he nevertheless seemed to have maintained an ambiguous position in his relationship with it. As a result, Ramasamy would on the one hand praise the lofty principles of Islam, declare that Islam was very suitable for the Tamils, and exhort low castes to join Islam,[8] and on the other he maintained that 'no religion was suitable for life',[9] which naturally included Islam, or that '...the unity of people was more important than religion and heaven', or that 'the feeling of defending religion was a wrong feeling',[10] or things such as '...Believing that the Prophet cannot have spoken against reason...and being stubborn is worse than being superstitious'.[11]

On his part, Ramasamy declared that his call for low-caste Hindus to convert to Islam was motivated by Islam's capacity to confer equality and dignity to the low castes and not because one can go to heaven, or because of the Quran, the Prophet, etc.[12] Thus he maintained his distance from those Islamic religious beliefs which he thought did not appeal to reason. Muslim expectations in some quarters that Ramasamy will convert eventually to Islam, never materialised.

Instead, Ramasamy and the movement always maintained that Dravidian culture and religion were similar to Islamic culture and religion. He asserted that Islam was based on the principle of One God, one caste, and one community and that these principles belonged to the Dravidians too and were needed by them.[13] Knowing fully well that some Tamil Muslims, influenced somehow by Sir Sayyid Ahmad Khan, were trying to portray Islam as a natural religion, he asserted that his *naastikam* (atheism) was about research into nature and therefore Muslims also were atheists.[14]

He further opined, '...Muslims should be ready to call all rationalists their brothers.... The Muslims should try to make the whole world into one religion i.e., the rational religion. ...Only when religion is destroyed, world peace and unity can be achieved in the opinion of many scholars...'[15] The English publications of this Dravidian movement, edited by

E.V. Ramasamy and S. Ramanathan, wrote that 'Islam like other world religions is feeling the thirst of rationalism'.[16]

It is quite obvious from the above that during this period, Ramasamy maintained an ambiguous attitude about Islam, so as not to antagonise the Muslims and deprive himself of their support. Many Tamil Muslims, though they did not relish his atheistic propaganda, seem to have preferred to maintain a close relationship with him mainly for political reasons. Opposed to the Congress, E.V. Ramasamy was their most important ally in Tamil Nadu. He contributed to the assertion of their Tamil identity, in the face of domination of Urdu-speaking Muslims in Madras public life until 1930. Further, they probably also stood to benefit from the conversions to Islam, which Ramasamy and his movement encouraged incessantly.[17]

This scenario was in for a change when in March 1940, the All India Muslim League and its president, Mohammad Ali Jinnah, raised the demand for Pakistan, a separate State for Muslims in the north-west and north-east of India. E.V. Ramasamy was quick to endorse this demand, expecting that Jinnah and the Muslims would support his demand for a separate Dravidasthan, which would consist of Tamil, Malayalam, Telugu, and Kannada areas. This was raised two years earlier in December 1938, when E.V. Ramasamy assumed the presidency of the Justice Party founded earlier in 1916, to protect the interests of the non-Brahmins. In general, the Muslim press of Tamil Nadu including *Dar-ul-Islam, Saiphul Islam*, and *Al Kalam* came out in support of the Pakistan scheme.[18]

On 27 August 1944, the name of the Justice Party was officially changed to Dravida Kazhagam or Dravidian Federation.[19] The immediate objective was the attainment of a Dravidasthan under the direct control of the Secretary of State in London, which would finally evolve into a separate State.[20] Tamil Muslims do not seem to have played any role either in the changing of the name or in the fixing of objectives.

In spite of Ramasamy's unreserved support for the demand of Pakistan and the conversion of untouchables to Islam, Jinnah, preoccupied with the Muslims, decided to distance himself from the Dravidasthan demand. This dissuaded the Muslims, mostly the Tamil Muslims sympathetic to the Muslim League, from participating in the agitation for Dravidasthan. This was a severe blow not only to the objectives of Ramasamy and the movement, but also to the relationship between Tamil Muslims and the Dravidian movement, which until then was more or less smooth.

Very soon, following E.V. Ramasamy, his former Brahmin colleague in the Congress, C. Rajagopalachari, considered to be the southern lieutenant of Mahatma Gandhi, adopted a position in favour of the demand for Pakistan. In the course of time, Rajagopalachari produced a formula, known as the Rajaji Formula, which not only envisaged the partition of Bengal and Punjab on religious lines, but also in the process reduced the role of Bengal and Punjab in national politics, cut down the size of northern India, and increased the political, economic, and other prospects of south Indians at the national level. In 1947, Lord Mountbatten, who was sent to India to wind up the British Empire in India, more or less adopted Rajaji's formula in order to break the constitutional deadlock and partition India. Sarat Chandra Bose, Congress leader and the brother of Subhas Chandra Bose, accused Rajagopalachari of letting down both Punjab and Bengal and held that the Indian partition was C. Rajagopalachari's plan.[21]

E.V. Ramasamy, though he was Rajagopalachari's arch political rival in south India, had earlier maintained that Rajagopalachari's moves regarding Pakistan could not be dismissed outright without examination.[22] Besides, he had never severed his personal ties and friendship with Rajagopalachari since the days when they were the chairmen of the Erode and Salem municipalities respectively.[23]

Later in a meeting at Salem held on 23 June 1947, E.V. Ramasamy made the following startling statement:

> ...I am not dependent on our Dravidian comrades alone, for the separation of Tamil Nadu. Many may not like that what I am going to say. But I will say what is in my heart. We are going to soon get the cooperation of my friend and comrade,

Acharya (Rajagopalachari), for the separation of Dravidanadu. Not only him, but all Brahmins...are going to support our demand for separation. Some of our comrades may wonder, if one can believe in Rajagopalachari's words; some may say that his affairs are always doubtful. But till today he has kept all the words that he had given to me...When comrade Acharya and myself met, he told me forcefully... 'Whether we get *swarajya* or not, the troubles given by the north Indians must be got rid off.'[24]

What is puzzling is that this crucial statement of E.V. Ramasamy and his meeting with Rajagopalachari was neither denied or contradicted by the latter. This goes to prove that there was some sort of an understanding or an identity of views, regarding the future of India, between Rajagopalachari and Ramasamy.

Now, where do the Tamil Muslims and their identity stand in all this? They were happy that they had the support of both Ramasamy and Rajagopalachari in their struggle for Pakistan. They voted overwhelmingly in favour of Pakistan and the Muslim League in the 1946 assembly elections. The very fact that those who were against partition, such as the Muslim Congressmen, were unable to mobilise the Muslim masses either through the press or by staging public meetings is proof enough that even the rank and file were in favour of Pakistan. Anyhow, neither the Government fortnightly reports nor the newspapers, both in English and Tamil during this period, give any indication that the masses were against Pakistan. This overwhelming support for Pakistan among the Muslims of Tamil Nadu and south India would not have come about without the historical conditionings of the Tamil Muslims, as we had seen through the survey of their literature where the fundamental principles of Islam always held the central or most important place. This actually constituted the basis of their identity.

However, the fact that Tamil Muslim leaders, stalwarts, and even the masses never came out fully in support of the

Dravidasthan demand, in spite of E.V. Ramasamy's consistent support for Pakistan and for the conversion of untouchables to Islam, gradually appears to have exasperated not only E.V. Ramasamy but the entire Dravida Kazhagam (DK) establishment. This will become obvious, if we go through the newspapers and magazines, published during the 1940s and after. Now, why did the Tamil Muslims who so vociferously supported the anti-Hindi agitations launched by Ramasamy when Rajagopalachari was the prime minister of the Madras Presidency, not come out in favour of the Dravidasthan demand, which was but a logical outcome of the anti-Hindi agitations?

The reasons for this might be attributed largely to the political situation. The All India Muslim League under Jinnah had steered clear of the Dravidasthan demand. The Madras Presidency Muslim League, under the influence of Mohammad Ismail, a Tamil Muslim, had no other alternative but to toe the line of the League high command in this matter. Besides, the non-Brahmin DK under Ramasamy had put itself out of the reckoning as a political force, by deciding not to contest the 1946 provincial elections, probably owing to lack of mass support. Being no longer a political force, the party had naturally become less attractive to the Tamil Muslims. This was not the situation in the 1920s and to a great extent in the 1930s, when Tamil Muslims allied themselves in great numbers with the non-Brahmin movement. Further Mohammad Ismail had consistently supported Pakistan and had become the president of the Indian section of the Muslim League known as the Indian Union Muslim League after independence. Staunch nationalists as Abul Kalam Azad, advised the winding up of the League as it had supported partition.[25] By supporting the Dravidasthan demand, Ismail did not want to see himself and his party as anti-nationalists or separatist any more. Mohammad Ismail refrained from joining hands with the DK, when Ramasamy declared 15 August 1947, the day of Indian independence, as 'Day of Sorrow' for Dravidians and expected his followers to raise black flags everywhere on that day.[26] Immediately after independence, *Viduthalai*, the publication of the DK heavily criticised

Mohammad Ismail for his ambiguous attitude, regarding the Muslim League, its objectives, and future.[27]

All these factors naturally had a destabilising effect on the DK's policies towards Muslims. This began to reflect more and more in the public postures of E.V. Ramasamy and his followers and also in the Dravidian publications. Probably, from the time the name of the Justice Party was changed to Dravida Kazhagam, there was a perceptible change in the policies of Ramasamy and the movement that he was heading. The earlier stress of the 1920s and 1930s on atheism seems to have been diluted to some extent by Ramasamy and his followers because of the changed political circumstances and equations. Instead of the previous unequivocal stand against religion and God, Ramasamy and his movement began to lay greater stress on a new-found Dravidian religion, which was claimed to have existed even before Buddha, Mohammad, Jesus Christ, and the Aryan Krishna and Rama. *Kudiarasu* actually claimed that the Dravidian religion, like Islam, had concepts such as One God, a God without image, a God of peace, unity, humility, *bhakti* (devotion) and brotherhood.[28] Probably Ramasamy and the movement thought that in this way they could retain the support of the Muslims for their party, even though they did not support the Dravidasthan demand in great numbers.

The editorial of *Viduthalai* of 15 July 1947 reproduced Ramasamy's speech at Tiruchi as follows:

> Muslims are following the ancient philosophies of the Dravidians. The Arabic word for Dravidian religion is Islam. When Brahmanism was imposed in this country, it was Mohammad Nabi who opposed it, by instilling the Dravidian religion's policies as Islam in the minds of the people.[29]

The editorial also asserted that on the basis of old Dravidian literature, it was possible to conclude that the Dravidian religious and social policy was based on the principle of *Onre Kulam Oruvane Devan* (One Community, One God). This principle had been obscured by an alien Aryan culture and only with the attainment of a separate Dravidasthan would this ancient policy of the Dravidians come into effect; then Islam would be able to join hands with them and become one with them.[30] A few Muslim stalwarts such as B.A. Ismail, were more or less in agreement with this new ideological trend of Ramasamy and the DK. Ismail affirmed that the fundamental principle of the Dravidians and that of Islam was the same, for both worship One God.[31]

This momentary ideological shift on the part of Ramasamy and the DK. during this crucial period leading to the partition of India, had serious implications. During the 1920s and 1930s when the main thrust of Ramasamy and his Self-Respect Movement was atheism and rationalism and the bulk of their criticisms was directed against Hinduism in all its aspects, and when the fundamental Islamic beliefs were left unperturbed because of the deliberate adoption of an ambiguous attitude vis-à-vis these beliefs, there was not much room for any collision between the historical conditionings of the Tamil Muslims and the ideological stand of the Self-Respecters. Besides, during this period, the Self-Respecters were of great political utility to the Tamil Muslims, as we have seen.

But, during the 1940s, Ramasamy and the Self-Respecters began to equate more and more the fundamental principles of Islam, such as the concept of One God, with their Dravidian religion, which was supposed to have antedated Islam. Naturally, this was cause for great anxiety among Tamil Muslims, for the God of Islam cannot be equated or associated with any other concept of One God, especially when it fell outside the Judeo-Christian-Islamic belief system. As long as Ramasamy restricted his criticism to the un-Islamic habits of the Muslims, praised certain lofty features of Islam, asked untouchables to convert to Islam, and did not challenge directly the fundamental principles of Islam or attempted to amalgamate Islam within an atheistic mould, there was not much of a problem in the Muslim relationship with the Self-Respecters, for the historical identity and conditionings of the Muslims were not under threat. Even some prominent Muslims like Moulvi Ahmed Sayyid of

Saiphul Islam and Moulana Moulvi Sherfuddin Sahib of Vellore supported Ramasamy's movement, probably because its views regarding Tamil Muslim society were sometimes not totally wrong. But this was not the situation in the 1940s when Islam was being associated and amalgamated within a supposedly more ancient Dravidian religion. This posed a threat to their very identity as Muslims. Naturally, the Muslims reacted in order to reaffirm their identity.

Besides, the Self-Respect Movement, which had consistently since the 1920s championed the causes and grievances of the Muslims and supported separate treatment and separate electorates for Muslims, including Dravidian Muslims, suddenly seems to have changed its policy vis-à-vis Dravidian Muslims during the days leading to the partition of India. At a meeting addressed by Ramasamy, held in the French colony of Karikal in the Tanjore region, on April 1947, he opined that in the 'Dravidanadu' of his conception, there was no question of religious divisions rearing its head.[32]

The editorial of *Viduthalai*, dated 17 April 1947 asserted that,

> in the event of a separate Dravidian government, there was no question of giving special treatment and privileges to any religion or man. The Muslims and the Christians for e.g., will be considered as Dravidian friends. As far as religion was concerned, everybody can behave as he likes, without giving trouble to anyone. ...As Muslims are Dravidians they had the right to remain in Tamil Nadu. Except for the small affair of 'religion', in all other matters of human existence and efforts, they have to join hands with the Dravidians... In the event of a separate Dravidian Government, Hindu religion will not dominate in any way. Individually in their houses, Hindus, Saivites and Vaishnavites can swim in the gutter of religion, but we will not allow them to pollute the public pond and relish evolving in it. ...In such a State, Muslims will not have any grievances in any department.... In short, Muslims and Dravidians will mix with one another...so that Muslims and non-Muslim Dravidians will become inseparable and our

society will be reformed, not on the basis of religion, but on the basis of a certain humanity. Therefore it is necessary that Muslim friends support the Dravidanadu demand.'[33]

Another *Viduthalai* editorial dated 24 October 1947, wrote:

> ...why do the Muslims of south India turn towards the Muslims of north India now? The problems of the Hindustan (north Indian) Muslims are different from the problems of the Muslims in Dravidanadu. ...Mohammad Ismail (leader of MPML) says that this (the question of Leaguers joining the various political parties) has to be decided by the AIML council meeting.
>
> What do the north Indian Muslim leaders know about south Indian political parties and their programmes? They will only advise according to their own advantages and disadvantages. ...How can they know that all the Muslims here support Dravidanadu, except for some leaders who are like the cat on the wall? Therefore the Muslims should organise a Tamil Nadu Muslim League meeting to decide whether the Muslims should join the Congress or the DK...
>
> But as far as we are concerned, ...we have not started the agitation for separation believing that the Muslims will support us.... We welcome those Muslims who still want to cooperate with us. We are not against the Muslims who want to join the Congress. But considering their welfare, we want them to come to a decision quickly.'[34]

Not only the *Viduthalai*, but also the other Dravidian publications published articles and editorials about the necessity for Dravidian Muslims to join the agitation for the creation of Dravidanadu and not offer support to the Congress which was a Brahmin-dominated, Aryan establishment. They reminded the Muslims of the close association between them and the Dravidian movement from the 1920s and wanted it to continue in the future.[35]

But towards independence and after, the political scenario changed rapidly. The political utility of the DK, especially after partition, had ceased to exist mainly because the latter had failed to emerge as a viable political force after independence. Naturally the DK and its secular approach to the problems of society, where Muslims were no longer entitled to separate treatment, appeared to be less attractive to the Muslims, especially after independence. This coincided with the fact that the DK was trying during this period to absorb Islam into a sort of Dravidian religion and the Muslims themselves into a larger Dravidianism, threatening their very separate identity which was conditioned by centuries of history. All these factors led to the estrangement of Tamil Muslims from Ramasamy and the DK.

Besides, 1949 was marked by an acute inner party struggle in the DK.[36] Some young lieutenants of Ramasamy such as C.N. Annadorai, Neduncheziyan, Anbazhagan, N.V. Natarasan, and Muthuvel Karunanidhi (the former chief minister of Tamil Nadu), raised the banner of revolt against Ramasamy. They formed their own party called the Dravida Munnetra Kazhagam (DMK) under C.N. Annadorai. Some of the prominent leaders of this party were interested in participating in the political process by contesting elections, contrary to the DK which preferred to remain a social reform movement.

This split naturally weakened the DK and its leader, Ramasamy. This probably encouraged the Muslims to adopt a more strident position against the DK. But, the DMK too did not give up the demand for a separate Dravidanadu. Instead, it continued, like the DK, to woo and seek the support of the Tamil Muslims.[37] Following the DK, the DMK too subscribed to a certain rationalism. It also adopted the slogan, *Onre Kulam Oruvane Devan*, but the DK's enthusiasm was on the wane.[38] For many Muslims, this, however, meant once again an association of the fundamental belief in the One God of Islam with an alien belief system, drawn from ancient Dravidian lore.

At least since the 1940s, C.N. Annadorai, like Ramasamy, had been speaking more frequently in Muslim meetings. On 13 April 1945, he participated in the Seethakathi anniversary ceremony.[39] Seethakathi was the most renowned philanthropist in Tamil Muslim history. At the Tanjore district Muslim League conference held on 3 August 1943, Annadorai held that Muslims were not strangers to his country and that racially they were also Dravidians, though they had a different religion.[40] This acquaintance of Annadorai with the Muslims while he was in the DK, appears to have stood him in good stead, so that when the split in the DK came about, Annadorai was able to attract many Muslim sympathisers, especially the Muslim youth, to his fold from the DK. Thus, while Ramasamy claimed that he had the support of the Tamil Muslims to continue his fight for Dravidanadu,[41] Annadorai and the DMK too seem to have enjoyed the support of many Tamil Muslims.[42]

As noted earlier, the 'One Caste, One God' slogan of the DK and later the DMK threatened the Islamic identity and historical conditioning of the Muslims of Tamil Nadu, because it sought to subordinate or amalgamate Tamil Islam within the larger Dravidian belief system. But, there were many more causes of friction. The DMK not only stood for Dravidanadu, but was also passionately attached to the Tamil language and its development. C.N. Annadorai, Nedunchezhiyan and M. Karunanidhi were not only great orators in Tamil, but were so well-versed in Tamil that their talents were there for everyone to see, in the form of numerous publications authored by them, and the various Tamil dramas and films for which they wrote the scripts. Generally, they took great pride in ancient Tamil literature and extolled its virtues profusely.

Though the Tamil Muslims, as we have seen, had their own literature, the DMK stalwarts hardly showed any interest in it. This was once again a difficult situation for the Tamil Muslims who were expected to extoll ancient Tamil literature, which was not only non-Islamic, but was in many ways also very Hindu in character. Moreover, the literature produced by the DMK stalwarts themselves had nothing very Islamic about it. Instead it was more of a secular character, with great emphasis on reason. We have seen earlier that the Tamil Muslims were extremely interested in Islamic literature of various kinds and took very little interest in non-Islamic literature. Thus, it was natural that the stand of the DMK stalwarts vis-à-vis literature, became a cause of friction between the DMK and the Tamil Muslims.

Nedunchezhiyan, one of the foremost leaders of the DMK and Annadorai's right-hand man, was known for his mastery of the *Tirukkural*, an ancient Tamil literary work, that dated back to the beginning of the Christian era. The *Tirukkural*, written in the form of couplets, dealt with human life and existence, and is considered to be a masterpiece of Tamil literature and world literature, and also as a great work of wisdom and genuis. The author of *Tirukkural* was a low-caste Hindu, known as Tiruvalluvar. Nevertheless, he and his work have been held in high esteem by all, including the Brahmins.

Nedunchezhiyan, being an expert on the *Tirukkural*, was invited to speak at the seventh annual celebration of the Mylapore Tiruvalluvar Kazhagam. It appears that during his speech, Nedunchezhiyan was supposed to have held that the Quran was not suitable for the times prevailing in 1952, whereas the *Tirukkural* was.[43] Tamil Muslims did not wait long to rise against this statement of Nedunchezhiyan's, which if true, belittled the Quran. The editor of *Dar-ul-Islam*, P. Dawood Sha, who had taken an uncompromising position against both the DK and the DMK, especially after independence, was in the forefront in opposing Nedunchezhiyan's statement. Dawood Sha who was never really sympathetic either to Ramasamy or Annadorai, dismissed Nedunchezhiyan's statement as the irresponsible statement of an ignorant person who knew nothing about Islam.[44] Besides, he was never confident about Annadorai's goodwill towards the Muslims.[45]

The prolonged silence of Annadorai regarding Nedunchezhiyan's statement raised further doubts about the intentions of both of them, with regard to the Muslims. It appears that this silence lent some credence to the theory that Annadorai like Nedunchezhiyan was against the Muslims, though we do not know the truth about this.[46] The Muslim weekly, *Shah Jehan*, accused Nedunchezhiyan of even inciting the Muslim youth sympathetic to the DMK to talk against the Quran.[47] The general Muslim opposition to Nedunchezhiyan's statement was such that Nedunchezhiyan in a solemn declaration stated that he had not intended to hurt the Muslims nor had he meant that the Quran was unsuitable for those times. In the DMK's Third Year Souvenir of 1952, Neduchezhiyan replied to the criticisms levelled against him by the Tamil Muslims. He wrote:

> ...the misunderstanding about my reference to the Quran, had been clarified and published in the *Muslim* of 4 September 1952.
>
> I really did not want to hurt Muslims or criticise the Quran. I referred to the Quran while explaining my opinion about the *Tirukkural.* This was not done with a spirit of criticism and the meeting was not held for that purpose.
>
> Among the Muslims there are two sections. One section wants to destroy the Dravidian and Rationalist movement. The other section has a close relationship with the Dravidian movement and participates in its work. I am giving this explanation to the latter and not to the former.
>
> In the *Tirukkural* meeting, if my speech had been aimed at finding out which religion is rationalistic and protects and develops rationalism, then I would have said 'Islam'. We have said the same thing till now and there is to be no change in it.
>
> But I did not then speak of religious research. In the field of public morality, *Tirukkural* scores over other religious books, percentage-wise. I just wanted to show the uniqueness of *Tirukkural.*
>
> If Bharathi (the national poet of Tamil Nadu) tells that in the languages that he knew, there was nothing sweeter than Tamil, it does not mean that he looks down upon other languages. Similarly, I wanted to show the *Tirukkural* from a certain plane. It was done not to criticise Quran....
>
> To divert the Muslim youth from supporting the Dravidian movement my speech at Mayilai (Mylapore) is being used. Especially the Muslim Leaguers want the support of this youth.
>
> The unity between the rationalism of the Dravidian movement and the Muslim life principles were the reasons

why the Dravidian movement and the Muslim League lived in cooperation.

We had consistently supported Pakistan, in spite of Congress criticism and we had appeared in Muslim League platforms to propagate this principle.

Till now, we rationalists of the DMK have been invited to Nabi's birthday celebrations and Umaru Pulavar celebrations by the Muslims. The rationalists who went there did not accept the prayers said there, and did not accept the mysteries expounded there. We have always spoken of the Prophet as a rationalist and the difficulties he underwent to spread his policies, viz., his prohibition principles, interest-free policy, principles against unnecessary decorations, widow re-marriage property for women... These rationalists even today are the same...

When the situation is such, the Muslim League's call asking Muslim youth to leave the Dravidian movement is due to the Muslim-Congress relationship. As some important Muslim people need the Congress, which is in power, for ensuring their future and because the alliance with Congress could help some of them to become members of municipalities and Assemblies, same Muslim bigwigs are trying to woo the Muslim youth from the Dravidian movement...

Otherwise to suppose that I said that the Quran is not fit for 1952, and the *Kural* is fit and...all this is just false propaganda.

Therefore my Mayilai (Mylapore) speech was not at all with the intention of hurting the Muslims.[48]

I have reproduced the above statement more or less verbatim, because it clearly brings out the position of not only Nedunchezhiyan, but also of the DMK in their relationship with the Muslims, during this period. It also throws light on the new, evolving political equation in the Tamil country, where the Muslim League sought to ally itself with the Congress, and the Congress leader. K. Kamaraj himself sought the Muslim League support in 1954, when he wanted to get himself elected from the Kudiyatham constituency to the Madras State Assembly.[49] Kamaraj had held as early as 1949, that Muslims would not have anything to do with anti-God organisations like the DK.[50] This could very well have meant that Kamaraj was courting Muslim support for himself and the Congress from this period itself.

However, the entire controversy over the *Kural* and the Quran proves yet again how touchy the Tamil Muslims were, with regard to issues of Islam or anything associated with it, which constituted their historical identity. They could never accept or digest any reference where the Quran and Islam were belittled or subordinated to some other non-Islamic factor. Even the slightest reference or action that could be construed as disrespectful to the Quran or Islam was enough for the Muslims to react. There was no question of accepting secondary status for the Quran in the Tamil country and no question of altering the boundaries that separated the Muslims from the rest.

In 1937, the Tamil Muslims had already risen against one of their own co-religionists, the Urdu-speaking Moulana Yakub Hasan Sait, who was a Minister in Rajagopalachari's Congress ministry, for the alleged disrespect exhibited by him towards the Quran during the course of a Muslim meeting at Coimbatore. It appeared that when the Quran was being recited during the meeting, Yakub Hasan Sait failed to stand up and pay respect to it as was the custom. Some Muslims had even decided to boycott the minister on account of this. They claimed that religion and culture were more important to them and they asked Yakub Hasan Sait to tender a public apology for his disrespectful act.[51]

Similarly, when the controversy over the *Kural* and the Quran arose, Muslim leaders were bent upon proving that the Quran was superior to the *Kural*. P. Dawood Sha, the erstwhile editor of *Dar-ul-Islam* categorised Tiruvalluvar as somebody who does not know God and the *Tirukkural* as a literature which was not a product of 'revelation'. He did not think even that the author of *Tirukkural* was Tiruvalluvar. He attributed it to a naked Jaina saint. He blamed the *Kural* for not showing any interest in spiritual development or in life after death.[52]

Another prominent Muslim writer, who seemed to have spared no effort to prove that the Quran was superior to the *Kural* was Madani of Tiruchirappalli. He assisted Janab Rasool in editing the Muslim journal *Shah Jehan,* which was in circulation from 1951 to 1954. Though he was just a matriculate, he brought out a whole book in 1968, attesting the superiority of the Quran.[53]

In this book by Madani, we also find a reference to some remarks of the DMK stalwart, M. Karunanidhi, who seems to have stated in 1969, in the DMK publication, *Murasoli,* that the 1,300 couplets of the *Kural* were not acceptable or applicable to one and all in its entirety.[54] In this connection, it is interesting to note that in 1954, Karunanidhi's mentor, Ramasamy, had held a similar view about the Quran, when he said that the Prophet was the last believer who introduced reforms in the society and in the same breath maintained that everything one said was not acceptable at all times.[55] Naturally some Muslims were not happy with Karunanidhi's statement and accused him of indulging in 'percentage belief', i.e., believing in only some parts of the *Kural.*

The extent of identification of Muslims with Islam during this period was very great. All this would not have been possible and cannot be explained satisfactorily without taking into consideration their historical origin, evolution, and conditioning, both before the printing era and after the Muslims accepted print.

Newspaper Wars

We have seen how the Tamil Muslims and their print media were pitted against the DK and DMK and its leaders and policies. We have also seen how the print media had aided and sustained these controversies, which had serious implications for the Muslim identity in Tamil Nadu. On the whole, it appears that after independence a considerable section of the Tamil Muslim print media had become more defiant and hostile towards the DK and the DMK. The editor of *Dar-ul-Islam,* P. Dawood Sha seems to have been the most hostile against the designs of both the DK and the DMK towards the Muslims. He used the press to launch a systematic attack against both of them. On the other hand the Dravidian publications also went on the offensive to checkmate Dawood Sha and ward off Tamil Muslim criticism and hostility in general.

As noted earlier, the DK under Ramasamy had modified its policy towards the Tamil Muslims, towards 1946–47. Contrary to their earlier stand they did not want to extend special privileges to Muslims any more. Instead, they expected them to cooperate in their agitations for Dravidanadu. The minds of the Tamil Muslims seem to have been very exercised by this volte-face of Ramasamy.

From this period onwards, articles began to appear in some Tamil Muslim newspapers against the new policy of the DK vis-à-vis the Muslims. They began to set conditions for participating in the agitations for Dravidanadu. These conditions were more or less the same as before independence. They wanted separate electorates, the right to profess their language, culture, and religion without interference, and the assurance that the majority community will not be an obstacle to the development of the Muslims.

Dar-ul-Islam asked Ramasamy to accept these conditions, if he wanted Muslim support for Dravidanadu.[56] It held that the Tamil Muslims were still backward in education and in other aspects and therefore they needed special consideration and separate electorates. It was not considered right to deny these privileges to the Muslims, while they were being given to the Harijans.[57]

But Ramasamy and the DK never really accepted these conditions. The opposition of the Muslims to this stand was at first mild, but later it became more pronounced. They began to consider Ramasamy himself as the greatest obstacle that prevented the Muslims from supporting the Dravidanadu cause. Contrary to their earlier stand, they even began to deride the racial foundations of the Dravidian movement and held that the Muslims could not support such a racially motivated cause.[58]

Besides, *Dar-ul-Islam* took a position against the few Muslim newspapers such as *Muslim* (weekly) and *Ishate Islam* (monthly), which somewhat favoured the DK and the DMK. It accused the Muslim editors of these papers of stooping so low as to attack those who opposed the DK. It also accused them of trying to defend Ramasamy as when they claimed that 'Periyar never said that God does not exist', though the whole world knew about his stand. It refuted the claims of these papers which held that it was because of Ramasamy that the Muslims were safe in Tamil Nadu. Instead, it pointed out that at Erode, the seat of Ramasamy's Dravidanadu, some Muslims were forcibly converted to Hinduism and it was at Ramasamy's strongholds such as Tiruvannamalai and Salem that Muslim properties and mosques were damaged or destroyed.[59]

Ramasamy was further accused of openly indulging in propaganda against Islam, in spite of his earlier stand in favour of it. He was also accused for his ambiguous attitude towards Islam in which he had warned that if the Muslims were not vigilant, *Tirukkural* would become their religion and Tiruvalluvar their Prophet. *Dar-ul-Islam* wondered why some Muslim editors were supporting Ramasamy when they knew that Ramasamy had decided, as early as 1932, to destroy Islam and had even passed a resolution to that effect at the Second Conference of Self-Respecters held at Mannargudi in the Tanjore District on 17 June 1932.[60]

It is to be noted anyhow that neither Ramasamy nor the movement had annulled this resolution passed in 1932, despite the fact that pro-DK Muslims such as the publishers of *Ishate Islam*, from Athur near Salem, had actually asked for its annulment in 1946.[61] The arguments put forward by these pro-DK Muslim editors that Ramasamy had been responsible for the conversions of thousands of Hindus to Islam were also squarely refuted by journals like *Dar-ul-Islam*.[62]

In the *Viduthalai* of 5 April 1949, it appears that once again Ramasamy had reverted to his earlier atheist stand. He held that in the event of a separate Dravidian state, there would be no place for 'God' and 'religion', as in the old Tamil literature such as *Tirukkural* and *Tolkappiyam*, where there was no place for such words.[63]

Taking his cue from this statement of Ramasamy's *Dar-ul-Islam* wrote that in case Dravidanadu came about, then its constitution would be based on the *Kural* and *Tolkappiyam* and there would be no place for God or the Quran there. It was useless to think that Ramasamy would give special protection to Islam, Muslims, and God, when he had decided to abolish all gods. *Dar-ul-Islam* warned that it was high time that the Black Shirt (DK) Muslims realised this situation and parted company with Ramasamy, the enemy of Islam, the Quran, and God. Ramasamy was even considered as the foremost enemy of the Muslims.[64]

Similar attacks were directed by Tamil Muslims against C.N. Annadorai, the founder of the DMK. Dawood Sha accused Annadorai of misguiding the Muslims on Dravidasthan and God and of wanting to burn the Quran and adopt the *Kural*, of wanting to destroy mosques and build schools instead, to abolish prayers and worship, so that the Muslims would go to factories. Sha maintained that for the past 1,383 years, Islam had defeated so many rivals and would vanquish Anna (Annadorai) and E.V. Ramasamy too.[65]

Even Mohammad Ismail, the president of IUML, seems to have wondered why Muslims invited people like Annadorai for the Prophet's birthday meetings, and even paying them for that, when he denied the very existence of God.[66] This stand of Mohammad Ismail was not surprising because reliable sources reveal that he was deeply steeped in the Islamic religion and never failed to refer to or talk endlessly about the Quran and Islam even in Muslim political meetings.[67] Besides, during this period Mohammad Ismail was moving closer to the Congress, at the cost of distancing Muslims from the rationalist DK and the DMK. It was also held that Annadorai and his DMK were no different from Ramasamy and his DK.[68]

It appears that some other Muslim journals such as *Shah Jehan,*

Samarasam, and *Marumalarchi*, published from Tiruchirappalli during this period, also took a strident position against the policies of the DK and the DMK. The *Marumalarchi* was singled out for praise by another Muslim journal, *Muslim Murasu*, for its stand against atheism and atheists.[69] *Shah Jehan*, whose editor was Janab Rasool, actually criticised both the DK and the DMK for their anti-Islamic postures and opined that it was not wrong to punish these Muslims who acted against Islamic principles and swore by the DK.[70]

Generally speaking, Tamil Muslim journals and periodicals were late in appearing in Tamil Nadu. They seem to have appeared earlier in Ceylon and in South-East Asia, where a number of Tamil-speaking Muslims were settled. In 1892, Seethi Lebbai Marakkayar of Ceylon started the *Muslim Nesan* in Colombo. Later, he published another journal, known as *Gnana Deepam*. *Muslim Nesan* seems to have been the successor of another Muslim journal, known as *Ceylon Muhammadan*, started in the 1880s. It seems to have been published twice a week.[71]

It was only in 1906–07 that a Haji Jilani Pakir Alim started the *Livavul Islam* from Madras. It appeared first as a daily then as a weekly. In 1908–09, journals such as *Muslim Thoothan* and *Islam Nesan* (edited by Sultan Sayyid Ahmed Rauttar from Madura) were started. In 1916, Moulvi Ahmed Sayyid started the *Saiphul Islam*. In 1918, the *Thondan* was published, followed by the monthly, *Ajayibul Alam*, edited by A. Muhammad Tahir Sahib from Tanjore and *Al Kalam* from Bangalore. In 1921, P. Dawood Sha started the monthly, *Tattuva Islam*, which became *Dar-ul-Islam* the very next year. This was followed by *Vajirul Islam, Al Islam*, etc.

During the 1930s were published the *Taj al Islam*, *Hifazatul Islam, Hakhul Islam, Shamsul Huda, Muslim Nesan, Desa Nesan, Desasevagam, Jawaharul Islam, Gnana Sooriyan, Muslim Pathukavalan, Sathya Islam Kalvi, Musalman, Al Hidaya, Al Haq, Nural Islam, Tablikul Islam*, etc.[72] During the 1940s and 1950s, there were several other Muslim weeklies, fortnightlies, monthlies, and even a daily in circulation in Tamil Nadu. They were the *Balyan, Ezhuthani, Samathanam,*

Ishate Islam, Islam, Thozhan, Penamunai, Ilainjan, Tharagai, Nanban, Marka Vina Vidai, Sanmarka Sanku, Marumalarchi, Kalanjiyam, Durbar, Sempirai, Bakavi, Islamiya Sooriyan, Velli Malar, Manisudar, Shakir, Unmai Uthayam, Sandeep, Sutantira Kadir, Nervazhi Ilampirai, Munnetram, Manivilakku, Pakistan, Milap, Arul Jothi, Nurul Huq, Uthama Puthiran, Sutantira Nadu, Uthayam, Muslim, Kathir, Muslim League, Siraj, Puthulagam, Sutantira Intiya, Bukhari, Muslim Murasu, Dinat Tabal, Valipa Muslim, Islamiya Mithiran, Deenul Islam, Rahmat, Urimai kural, Pirai, Santhi Vikatan, etc.[73]

Almost all of these journals published from various places in Tamil Nadu were shortlived. Even *Muslim* which came out as a daily from 1946, with K.T.M. Ahmed Ibrahim B.A.B.L., the brother of Mohammad Ismail, president of IUML, as editor, lasted only for nine years. But of the whole lot none was favourable to the DK or DMK, except the *Muslim*, the *Ishate Islam* and also the *Muslim Murasu*, which were somewhat neutral or even sometimes sympathetic to the Dravidian movement.[74]

Many other journals such as *Nurul Haq* of Madurai, edited by Kadir Mohideen Marakkayar, were deeply interested in Muslim religious matters, while some others such as the *Ilainjan* and the *Valipa Muslim* were directed towards the Muslim youth. The bi-monthly, *Huqqul Islam* and the weekly, *Sathya Islam* (editor, Aali Janab M.M. Pavaḷar Sahib) stood for the upliftment of Muslims and the propagation of Islam.[75] Several other journals during this period, such as the radical weekly, *Pakistan*, from Erode, edited by M.A. Rahiman and the *Muslim*, edited by K.T.M. Ahmed Ibrahim, were so deeply immersed in politics and electoral affairs that they hardly had any time to cater to the other needs of the Muslims, especially the spiritual.[76] The *Muslim* in 1948 itself seems to have called for a separate political organisation for the Muslims left in India.[77]

Some other journals such as *Marumalarchi* and *Pirai* were more or less in favour of the Muslim League. *Marumalarchi*, founded at Tiruchirappalli in 1952 by A.K. Jamali with A.M. Yousuf as editor, appears to have contributed a lot to propagate the message of the Muslim League among the Tamil Muslims.

Mohammad Raza Khan, in his book, *What Price Freedom*, maintained that every village subscribed for at least one copy of *Marumalarchi.*[78] *Pirai* also contributed to the strengthening of the Muslim League.[79]

On the other hand the *Muslim Murasu* justified Muslim support for the DK, by arguing that all the Hindus who supported the DK were not atheists and that this was true of the Muslims too. It maintained that several lakhs of Hindus, including some prominent God-believing ones supported the DK on account of its political postures and economic policies and not because Ramasamy was an atheist. Similarly, thousands of Muslims supported the DK, which did not mean that all of them were atheists. It further asserted that if there was communal peace in Tamil Nadu, unlike in north India, even after partition, it was because of Periyar (Ramasamy). Therefore, it concluded that it was not correct to prevent the Muslims from supporting the DK and Ramasamy, by accusing them of being atheists.[80]

Contrary to the position of the Muslim League leader, Mohammad Ismail, *Muslim Murasu* opined that south Indians had contributed a lot to the League Fund. Therefore the funds could not be left for the use of some self-interested Muslim League leaders of Pakistan; the IUML too had the right to claim a part of it. The *Muslim Murasu* wanted to utilise this fund for the development of Muslim education, especially women's education.[81] At the same time, it gave full coverage in its paper to the position of the Muslim League leader, Mohammad Ismail.[82]

The *Muslim Murasu* seems to have shown more interest in the DMK and its policies. It advised the DMK (whose leader, Annadorai, had lately criticised the framing of the new constitution as undemocratic) to concentrate its attention more on politics, than on criticising the Aryans or the *Ramayana*, which did not interest the people.[83] It also expressed its approval of the DMK's policy of 'One Caste, One God'.[84] It dismissed the DK as being more interested in unimportant social details.[85] It came down heavily on the *Viduthalai*, which published an article claiming that caste existed in the Tamil Muslim society and held that there was no such thing as caste among Tamil Muslims.[86]

Another important Muslim journal of the 1950s, which espoused the cause of the Muslim League, was the *Manivilakku*. It was edited by A.K.A. Abdus Samad, M.A., son of A.K. Abdul Hameed Baqavi, the translator of the Quran into Tamil. It gave adequate coverage not only to the activities of the League, but also to its leader, Kayithe Millath Mohammad Ismail. At the Tamil Nadu Muslim League Conference held at Tiruchirappalli on 11 January 1958, Mohammad Ismail spoke of the necessity of maintaining the Muslim League to protect Muslim interests, to prevent the government from interfering in the Muslim Shariat laws which were God-given, for the necessity of maintaining English as the official language of India, etc.[87] He also criticised the idea of promoting a single culture, which stifled the other cultures existing in a society.[88]

Pirai did not stop at supporting the Muslim League. It also took a firm stand against the DMK and its leader, Annadorai. It accused them of belittling Islamic principles and the Quran. It even accused the local DMK leaders of behaving disrespectfully towards Islam and the Muslims. It pointed out that in the *Dravida Nadu* issue of 15 February 1959, C.N. Annadorai had subtly criticised the Muslim purdah system.[89]

The *Santhi Vikatan* of Karikal A.M. Ali could not tolerate even cartoons in DMK journals, like those found in the *Thaniarasu* of DMK stalwart, Asaithambi, which cast the Muslims in a poor light.[90] *Santhi Vikatan* also took Ramasamy to task for his wavering policies and principles.[91] It also came down heavily on C.N. Annadorai for his criticisms of others and for what he said at the Kanchipuram conference of 29 March 1960, with regard to his relationship with women.[92]

All this incessant propaganda through the print media seems to have led to the strengthening of the Muslim League, which, among other things, wanted to protect the religious identity of the Muslims. It led to continuous depletion of Muslim support for DK and Ramasamy and the weaning away of Muslim youth from the DMK to a considerable extent. But, the abandonment of the demand for a separate Dravidanadu in 1962 by the DMK, seems to have removed one of the major obstacles for the Muslims and also the Muslim League to subsequently collaborate with the DMK. During this period, with bright prospects of political power in sight, the DMK also seems to have considerably toned down its rationalist and social reform propaganda, as it became more and more drawn into electoral politics.

The propaganda carried on by the Muslim journals, especially after independence, against the DK and the DMK mainly to wean away Muslim support from them, seems to have yielded fruit in the 1950s itself. The Dravidian publications such as the *Viduthalai* seem to have tried their level best to ward off such propaganda and maintain support for the DK among the Muslim youth during this period.[93]

It seems, that on account of the sustained propaganda against the DK, the Muslims who supported it and subscribed to its atheist views had become unwanted in various Muslim community circles. They were socially boycotted by many aastika (God-believing) Muslims. It also appears that they were not addressed by their Islamic names any more. The were not allowed to enter the houses of believers, their wives demanded and obtained divorce from them and in some places those Muslims who had subscribed to the values of the DK were deemed as dead by their parents and relatives who performed death rites in their names. In some places such as Ayyampettai in Tanjore district, they had even been subject to violence. *Viduthalai* had even complained that two of its supporters, Madar Sha and Haja Mohideen had been threatened. Madar Sha seems to have been even fined Rs 10 and was beaten 10 times with chappals, in conformity to the decision of some local Muslim groups.[94]

Clearly, exasperated by such a situation, *Viduthalai* was obliged to publish a warning to the non-DK Muslims in its issue dated 31 July 1953. It held that since some Muslims were working against the Dravidian people, an agitation would be launched against them. The first step of which would be that processions with drums would go past the Muslim mosques. It further held that if a mullah who did not enjoy the support of the people spoke against the DK, it did not imply that all Muslims were against the DK. It also maintained that such Muslims were not interested in the national good.[95] Whether E.V. Ramasamy was directly involved in the publication of this warning seems to be doubtful, though there is room to believe that such a notice could not have been published without the prior knowledge of Ramasamy. The editor of *Muslim Murasu* thought that the editor of *Viduthalai* alone was responsible for this provocation and hatred against the Muslims.[96]

From its very inception, the DK and DMK had not only put the print media to good use, but they had also effectively used theatre and film media to propagate their values and policies among the common people throughout Tamil Nadu.

During the British period (and even after independence in the 1950s and 1960s), Tamil masses were largely illiterate. Female illiteracy was particularly rampant.[97] So the social reform movements and the political parties in Tamil Nadu could not depend only on the print media and public speeches in order to convey their messages to the illiterate masses of Tamil Nadu. But, theatre and the introduction and development of film technology and media during the first half of the twentieth century, were an effective means to reach the masses for the social reforms movements and the political parties.

In order to propagate its radical ideas, one of the early steps the DK took seems to have been to stage dramas. One of its leading personalities, M.R. Radha, was a great actor. DK's values and policies were spread by him through radical dramas such as *Por Val, Ratha Kanneer, Thooku medai* and *Ramayanam*.[98] But the DMK was probably the first political organisation in India, to fully utilise the film media to its advantage. Its leading personalities such as Annadorai and Karunanidhi were great story and script writers for films. They communicated their social-reform zeal through the silver screen and captivated large sections of the Tamil masses, including Muslims, with their revolutionary ideas and values. Some of the DMK stalwarts took to acting in the films and also wrote revolutionary and other songs for the films. One of the rising stars of the DMK in the film world during the 1950s was M.G. Ramachandran (M.G.R.). Similarly, another DMK stalwart, Kannadasan, emerged as a great poet, scoring a number of songs for films.

It will not be an exaggeration to say that films, in general, had a great impact on the Tamil society, including the Muslims. Apart from being a media for transmitting revolutionary ideas, values and intentions, cinema had become a media of mass entertainment. It had also become an arena in Tamil Nadu where one's social and political opponents were criticised, chided, and derided. The Muslims, having very little hold on the film media during this period, were sometimes at the receiving end. Realising fully well the effects or possible effects of the film media on the Muslims, some Muslims sought to counter it through the print media, by publishing books about the bad effects of films on people.[99]

Towards the end of the 1950s, an occasion arose when the Muslims felt threatened and hurt by a film titled, *Raja Tej Sinku*, with M.G.R. in the lead role. Muslims were terribly agitated by the way they had been portrayed in this film, which was produced by Hindus such as the DMK stalwart, Kannadasan. Raja Tej Sinku was actually a historical personality of the early eighteenth century, Tamil Nadu. He was in charge of the Gingy fort, not far from Pondicherry. He was known for his bravery and courage in the Tamil legends and folk tales.[100]

But the Muslims asserted that the film was not based on the traditional stories about Raja Tej Sinku, prevalent in the Tamil country, but was an invention of atheist Hindus like Kannadasan. They held that the storyline of the film was not historically correct and that the entire film was an exercise in distorting and denigrating the Islamic culture and principles.[101]

It appears that with the release of *Raja Tej Sinku*, the Tamil Muslim print media had swung into action and registered its opposition to the screening of the film in Tamil Nadu. Journals such as *Marumalarchi* and *Santhi Vikatan* seem to have stood in the forefront in their condemnation of the film, which they considered to be an insult to Islamic culture and religion.[102] Even the IUML under Mohammad Ismail, passed resolutions, condemning the film.[103] In spite of Muslim opposition, the film was screened throughout Tamil Nadu.

Muslim journals singled out Kannadasan and M.G.R. as responsible for the film and subjected them to heavy criticism. Kannadasan retorted in his Tamil magazine, *Thendral*, that the Muslim League could henceforth function as an organisation that conducted research on Tamil films such as *Raja Tej Sinku*, *Anarkali or Akbar*. This naturally infuriated the Muslim print media, especially those favourable to the League, which threatened Kannadasan with dire consequences.[104] It even accused M.G.R. of having acted in films like *Baghdad Thirudan* (the Thief of Baghdad), which was supposed to have derided Muslim culture and feared that future films as *Chitoor Rani Padmini*, might contain derogatory remarks about Islam and Muslim society.[105]

The foregoing once again shows how sensitive the Muslims and their print media were to anything that belittled or hurt Islam and the Muslim society. As seen above, the Muslim print media was once again in the forefront to defend Islamic interests, culture, and society, and by implication to maintain and re-affirm the boundary separating the Muslims from the other groups. As we have seen, even the Muslim League was involved in this course of action.

Another area in which the Muslim print media was overtly active during this period, though to a lesser extent, was in the field of cleansing Islam of its impurities and making Muslims conform to the true Islamic principles. Every journal, from the old *Dar-ul-Islam* and *Saiphul Islam* down to *Santhi Vikatan*, focussed on this in one way or the other.

In the 1920s, P. Dawood Sha, the editor of *Dar-ul-Islam*, accused the editors of orthodox journals such as the *Al Kalam* and *Saiphul Islam* of indulging in propaganda against him. But during the second half of the 1930s, his opposition to such journals, especially *Hifazatul Islam* and to the moulvis and alims seems to have mellowed down considerably.[106] These orthodox journals on their part appeared to have stopped deriding Dawood Sha as an Ahmeddiya, though the latter had never stopped translating the works of Lahore Moulana Mohammad Ali such as the *Religion of Islam* and *The New World Order* into Tamil.[107]

During the 1940s, especially after independence and during the 1950s, some Muslim journals (both orthodox and modern) voiced their protest against the un-Islamic practices and customs of the Muslims though with a lesser intensity. Many others such as *Muslim Murasu*, *Pirai*, and *Manivilakku* concentrated on political and electoral matters. Further, there were other Muslim journals which wrote against *samadhi* (tomb) worship and the un-Islamic practices prevalent in the dargahs and the celebration of *Urs* festivals.[108]

During the 1950s, Dawood Sha wrote against the Tamil pirs and *auliyas*, who claimed to possess special miraculous powers by the grace of Allah, through which they could satisfy the desires and solve the various problems of the Muslims, especially women who could not conceive. Muslims who believed in their powers offered money and gold to these pirs in order to become their *murids* (disciples). The pirs, taking advantage of the credulousness of the Muslims, exploited them. Dawood Sha held that they even abused the Muslim women, by promising pregancy through their miraculous interventions. So, he asked the Muslims not to believe in such false pirs and to turn instead directly towards Allah, for anything they desired.[109]

We do not know, the exact position of *Dar-ul-Islam* and Dawood Sha with regard to family planning and contraception. But it is interesting to note that *Dar-ul-Islam* carried advertisements regarding books explaining the necessity of contraception.[110] Dawood Sha would not have allowed such advertisements to appear in his paper, had he been against family planning and contraception. It is quite possible that his position would have been similar to that of Haji Subagu Mohideen Sahib of Tiruchirappalli. It is useful to note in this context that Dawood Sha always wrote in favour of Muslim women's education.[111]

Shah Jehan was another Muslim journal, which seems to have shown great interest in the abolition of the un-Islamic practices of the Muslims, especially the ceremonies related to the tombs and the festivals and processions conducted in honour of the Sufis. *Shah Jehan* even started an association known as Anachara Ozhippu Iyakkam (Association for the Abolition of Un-Islamic practices) at Tiruchirappalli, in order to carry on the battle against these practices. It appears that a certain A.K. Pasha of *Shah Jehan* took an active part in this venture. In 1948, he organised a meeting in the very compound of the famous dargah of Nathar Vali of Tiruchirappalli, condemning the un-Islamic festivals and ceremonies, conducted to honour the saint. Though nothing concrete seems to have emerged from this spectacular agitation, yet *Shah Jehan* maintained that it had sent shock waves among the *pujaris* (priests), who organised such ceremonies in the various parts of Tamil Nadu.[112]

Marumalarchi, one of the most widely circulated Tamil Muslim journals, seems to have also stood steadfastly against all un-Islamic habits of the Muslims.[113] *Santhi Vikatan*, on its part criticised the custom of allowing women to kiss the tombs of Muslim saints or sojourning to the dargahs in fulfilment of some prayers, which were thought to be Hindu in character and against Islam.[114] It condemned the un-Islamic act of charging interest for loans.[115] In its zeal to develop both modern and religious education among Muslims, it advised the Muslims to imitate the Hindus and transform the big dargahs into centres of education or universities, teaching religion, science, and the crafts.[116] It also condemned the behaviour of some Muslims, who gave a wrong impression to the Hindus, not only about Islamic worship, but also about the Islamic belief in One God. It wanted that the considerable income derived from the dargahs be spent not on unproductive matters as festivals, ceremonies, and song recitals, but on useful things such as education, in order to enlighten the great number of ignorant Muslims.[117] Thus, the *Santhi Vikatan* and its editor, Karai A.M. Ali strove to purify Islam among the Tamil Muslims and to educate them, lest the

Muslims should fall even lower than the untouchables (dalits) in the course of time.[118]

There were some other journals such as *Muslim Murasu*, which even justified polygamy in Islam, by asserting that in a country where the female population is greater than the male population, the principle of monogamy would lead to social disaster. It also asserted that monogamy was not compulsory in Islam. It opined that even Sir C.P. Ramaswamy Iyer, the erstwhile Diwan of Travancore State, had advised Hindus to follow Islam in this respect. It also drew attention to the statement of Kanchi Sankaracharya (Periaval) made in February 1953, in which he had declared that if Hindus adopt monogamy as law, it would contribute to a decrease in the Hindu population and an increase in the Muslim population, which practiced polygamy. It asserted that this would finally transform India into another Pakistan.[119] It is clear that even in such matters as marriage and polygamy, Muslim journals stuck to the Islamic principles.

The preceding two chapters are revealing in various ways. They clearly bring out the conditions and limits under which cooperation between the Tamil Muslims and the non-Brahmin Hindus was possible. As a rule, the Muslims never wanted to compromise the fundamental Islamic beliefs, principles, and customs in their relationship with the non-Brahmin Hindus. They accepted the latter's criticism of the un-Islamic practices of the Muslims, but rarely did they contemplate a move which could jeopardise their religious principles and their Islamic identity.

They of course wanted to reform Islam on the basis of the Quran and other Islamic scriptures. But, generally, they did not think that it was necessary to reform Islam on the basis of un-Islamic norms however rational or modern, for they considered that Islam in its essence was a rational religion and had an answer to all the problems of existence. Even a great Islamic social reformer as P. Dawood Sha did not deem it necessary to tamper with the Shariat laws. Besides, when some Muslims took a position in favour of contraception or family planning, they sought justification in the Quran itself and quoted verses from it in support of their stand. But they never abandoned or altered their religious principles, in order to make room for some alien ideas, however progressive and modern they might have been in their lives as Muslims.

As a result, their intimate relationship with the non-Brahmin Hindus seems to have been one of convenience, principally for political reasons and also because the latter spoke most of the time in glowing terms about Islam.

On the other hand, the non-Brahmin Hindus, led by Periyar E.V. Ramasamy, were not particularly enamoured by Islam, or its Prophet, or the Quran. Instead, on the whole, their objective had been to utilise what they considered as the good features in Islam to cure the ills of Hinduism and Hindu society such as the caste system and the many superstitious practices. In the later stages, especially towards independence and after, they even went to the extent of glorifying the Dravidian religion, which was supposed to have existed before even Islam or, Christianity, or Hinduism.

The above stand naturally perturbed the Muslims. It made them distance themselves from the objectives of the non-Brahmin Dravidian movement, not only of E.V. Ramasamy's, but also of C.N. Annadorai, who broke away from the former and founded his own Dravidian movement in 1949. In their relationship with the latter movement, as we have seen, the Muslims could never accept secondary status for the Quran or the assertion that the Quran was only partly right. They did not accept that the Quran could be altered and equated with the *Kural* or any other ancient Tamil text, even for the sake of argument. This yet again highlights the fundamental Islamic identity of the Tamil Muslims during the 1950s and 1960s. Up to this period of our study, one can say that the separate identity of the Tamil Muslims, shaped by centuries of history, had not weakened or slackened, at least in Tamil Nadu if not in the whole of south India. One striking aspect of the relationship between the Tamil Muslims and the non-Brahmin Hindus is the extraordinary role played by the print media. But, the very existence of all those newspapers and periodicals published from various parts of Tamil Nadu from the 1920s onwards (apart from the several books and booklets published after 1920 for Muslims, as could be seen from the Catalogue of Albertine Gaur and other Tamil Muslim catalogues), exclusively catering to the needs of the Tamil Muslims, confirms once again the distinct foundation of the Tamil Muslim society.

This foundation was laid centuries earlier and has evolved gradually adding to its strength day by day, as is evident, from our survey of the Tamil Muslim literature. Tamil Muslims gradually took to writing late in the sixteenth century after an initial oral phase. This written phase continued more or less until the 1840s, when the Tamil Muslims took to printing in right earnest.

Newspapers and periodicals belonged to the phase of printing. They generally had a circulation which was wider than that of books or booklets and reflected the day-to-day preoccupations and problems of the Muslims. All the Tamil Muslim newspapers invariably catered to the protection and promotion of Muslim interests in various fields. There might have been differences of opinion about how to promote and protect these interests, but there was no controversy over the necessity of promoting or protecting them. The establishment of a Tamil Muslim newspaper was also an assertion of the Islamic identity in an overwhelmingly Hindu society. It would not be an exaggeration to conclude that print, though of Chinese or western origin, played a crucial role in the spread of Islam and in the establishment of the identity of the Tamil Muslims.

Further, we do not find any convincing evidence, as far as the Tamil Muslims were concerned, which suggests that print challenged Islam and its genuine traditions. Instead, as we have seen, print has contributed to reforming and strengthening Islam in Tamil Nadu. The retention of the All India Muslim League in the form of the Indian Union Muslim League, in Tamil Nadu (and Kerala) when it was defunct in the rest of India, and the support enjoyed by it among the Muslims (as proven by the successive elections held in Tamil Nadu and Kerala after independence), is no doubt an emphatic public expression of the separate historical, social, cultural, and religious identity of the Tamil Muslims.

Notes

1. *Kudiarasu,* (6 February 1938).
2. *Kudiarasu,* (24 August 1930).
3. *Sunday Observer,* (28 August 1938).
4. *Swadesamitran,* (29 November 1937); *Madras Mail,* (30 November 1937).
5. *Madras Mail,* (10 January 1939).
6. *Kudiarasu,* (15 February 1931).
7. *Viduthalai,* (16 July 1946).
8. K. Veeramani, *Periyar Kalanjiyam,* (Madras), II, 68, 140.
9. *Kudiarasu,* (11 August 1935).
10. Ibid., (24 August 1930).
11. *Kudiarasu,* (9 August 1931).
12. Ibid., (2 February 1936); *Viduthalai,* (26 June 1943).
13. *Kudiarasu,* (5 April 1947).
14. *Viduthalai,* (16 July 1946).
15. *Kudiarasu,* (23 August 1931).
16. *Revolt,* (12 May 1929).
17. J.B.P. More, 'Tamil Muslims and Non-Brahmin Atheists', in *The Muslim Communities of South Asia: Culture, Society and Power,* (New Delhi, 1995), 333–360; see for e.g., *Kudiarasu,* (16 February 1938).
18. Report on the tone of newspapers and periodicals published in 1940 and 1941; Extracts from G.O. related to anti-war and Quit India Movements, *History of Freedom Movement* (TNA); F.R., 1st half of September 1940.
19. *Kudiarasu,* (29 September 1945).
20. Ibid., (2 September 1944).
21. *Viduthalai,* (7 August 1947); J.B.P More, review of C.R. Narasimhan's 'Rajagopalachari, A Biography', *Journal of South Asian Studies,* (Australia, 2 December 1996), XIX.
22. *Madras Governor's Reports*: (1942, L/P&J/5/205, IOL); F.R., (1st half of June 1942).
23. *Kudiarasu,* (14 June 1936); see Review, J.B.P. More, *The Muslim Communities.*

24. *Viduthalai*, (24 June 1947).
25. *Mail*, (15 November 1947).
26. Ibid., (9 August 1947).
27. *Viduthalai*, (29 October 1947; 8 October 1947).
28. *Kudiarasu*, (27 March 1947; 12 March 1947).
29. *Viduthalai*, (15 July 1947).
30. Ibid.
31. *Viduthalai*, (24 June 1947).
32. Ibid., (17 April 1947).
33. Ibid.
34. Ibid., (24 October 1947).
35. See, for e.g., *Kudiarasu*, (25 September 1948).
36. See *Fortnightly Reports*, 1949.
37. F.R., (1st half of March, 1950).
38. F.R., (1st half of January 1950).
39. *Dravida Nadu*, (8 April 1945); *Viduthalai*, (24 November 1940).
40. *Viduthalai*, (17 August 1943).
41. Ibid., (24 June 1947).
42. See for e.g., *Dravida Nadu*, (25 May 1952; 1 June 1952).
43. *Dravida Nadu*, 1953.
44. *Dar-ul-Islam*, (September 1952).
45. Ibid.
46. *Shah Jehan*, (15 October 1952).
47. Ibid.
48. A.S. Venu papers, *Dravida Nadu*, DMK Third Year Souvenir, 1952, 9–11, N.M.M.L.
49. *The Hindu*, (14 July 1954); Wright.
50. *Deccan Times*, (27 February 1949).
51. *Viduthalai*, (22 October 1937).
52. *Dar-ul-Islam*, (October 1952); Arignar Madani, *Pothu Marai Ethu? Kurala? Kurana?*, 1st edition, 1968, (Dindigul, 1974), 151–154.
53. Ibid.
54. Ibid., 158–159.
55. *Muslim Murasu*, (January 1954), 10.
56. *Dar-ul-Islam*, (October 1947), 26.
57. Ibid., (December 1947), 37–40.
58. Ibid., (October 1948), 9–11.
59. Ibid., (January 1949), 46–48.
60. See *Kudiarasu*, (26 June 1932); *Dar-ul-Islam*, (March 1949).
61. Ibid.

62. Ibid., (February 1949), 39–42.
63. *Viduthalai*, (5 April 1949).
64. *Dar-ul-Islam*, (May 1949), 4–7; August 1949, 17–24; June 1952, 4.
65. Ibid., (January 1951), 46–48.
66. Ibid., (January 1951), 48.
67. Based on Interviews with some elderly informed Muslims.
68. *Dar-ul-Islam*, (March 1952), 13–15.
69. *Muslim Murasu*, (October 1953), 58.
70. *Shah Jehan*, (15 October 1952), 5–7.
71. R.P.M. Kani, *Islamiy Ilakiyak Karuvulum* (Madras, 1963), 244; Julien Vinson, 'Un Journal Musulman en Langue Tamoule', *Revue du Monde Musulman*, 1, 4, 622.
72. Ibid., 244–245.
73. See Ibid., 245–246; see also A.M. Sami, *Tamizhil Islamiya Ithazhkal* (Tamil) (Madras, 1994).
74. See *Dar-ul-Islam*, (January 1949), 41–48; see *Muslim Murasu*, 1958 issues.
75. See G.O. 1098, (21 June 1937); Statement of newspapers.
76. See *Dar-ul-Islam*, (March 1952), 13–15; *Deccan Times*, (24 February 1946), 8; (14 July 1946), 10.
77. F.R., 1st half of January 1948.
78. Mohamed Raza Khan, *What Price Freedom*, (Madras, 1969), 475(fn).
79. *Pirai*, (June 1959).
80. *Muslim Murasu*, (September 1948), 14–16.
81. See Mohamed Raza Khan, *What Price Freedom*, 364–365; Peter Hardy, *The Muslims of British India*, (Cambridge, 1972), 165; *Muslim Murasu*, (June 1949), 7.
82. See for e.g., *Muslim Marasu*, (April 1949).
83. *Muslim Marasu*, (February 1950), 8–9.
84. Ibid., (April 1957), 7.
85. Ibid.
86. *Muslim Murasu*, (April 1957), 9–11.
87. *Manivilakku*, (February 1958).
88. *Santhi Vikatan*, (October 1960), 3.
89. *Pirai*, (April 1959), 5–7.
90. *Santhi Vikatan*, (May 1960).
91. Ibid., (December 1960), 13.
92. Ibid., (May 1960), 37; (June 1960), 37–38.

93. *Muslim Marasu,* (July 1953), 13.
94. *Viduthalai,* (3 October 1952); *Shah Jehan,* (15 October 1952).
95. *Muslim Marasu,* (July 1953), 11–13.
96. Ibid., (July 1953), 12.
97. J.B.P. More, *The Political Evolution of Muslims in Tamilnadu and Madras, 1930–1947,* (Hyderabad, 1997), 173–181.
98. Mangaiyarkarasai, *Varalaru Kanda Vaikom Veerar* (Tamil), (Madras, 1980), 171; F.R., 2nd half of 1949.
99. Rasool, *Seerazhiya Cinemavai Paarunkal,* (Dindigul, n.d.).
100. *Santhi Vikatan,* (October 1960), 10.
101. Ibid., 9–19.
102. *Santhi Vikatan,* (November 1960), 18; *Marumalarchi,* (4 November 1960).
103. Ibid., 34.
104. See for e.g., *Santhi Vikatan,* (November 1960), 34.
105. *Santhi Vikatan,* (October 1960), 19.
106. *Al Kalam,* (April 1925), 2, 4, 121; *Hifazatul Islam,* (September 1934), 331.
107. *Dar-ul-Islam,* (January 1953), 18.
108. Ibid., (January 1956; May 1950), 45–46; (April 1952), 24.
109. *Dar-ul-Islam,* (July 1956), 4–6.
110. See, for e.g., *Dar-ul-Islam,* (October 1947), 26.
111. See *Dar-ul-Islam,* (April 1954).
112. *Shah Jehan,* (15 November 1952), 9–10.
113. Interview with A.M. Yousuf.
114. *Santhi Vikatan,* (May 1960), 23.
115. Ibid., 37.
116. Ibid., (March 1960), 33.
117. Ibid., 39–40.
118. Ibid.
119. *Muslim Murasu,* (March 1953), 2–5.

Conclusions and Observations

The Tamil Muslims, as is evident, have undergone the twin processes of evolution and conditioning, like any other community or society round the world. We have traced the story of this evolution and conditioning with the help of the literature produced by the Tamil Muslims themselves, apart from travellers' accounts and other primary and secondary sources. As said earlier there is no better way of studying the past of a community than to take into consideration the literature produced by the members of that community.

The past conditionings largely regulate the present. Therefore, the study of the past of a society is necessary to study even the present of a community. The historian is better equipped in this respect than the anthropologist or the sociologist.

Our survey and analysis of the origin of the Tamil Muslim society and their literature clearly points to the separate foundations on which they have been evolving from the time they originated and the conditionings to which they have been subjected in the course of their long history. These conditionings, as we have shown were fundamentally Islamic. This distinguishes them invariably from the rest of the Tamil Hindu society contrary to the views of many anthropologists and sociologists such as Louis Dumont, Imtiaz Ahmad, T.N. Madan, and Susan Bayly.

On our part, we consider that it is irrational, inhuman, and against nature to deny the identity of a people, for whatever reason, whether it is in the name of a nation or some fantastic universal idea. By this we do not mean that people from different communities cannot live together. They have to because they are products of the same twin processes of evolution and conditioning that are common to all mankind and existences. It will be irresponsible to refute this truth. Anthropological theories like the 'Great Divide' theory which distinguishes the so-called 'civilised' western societies from the primitive or traditional or non-western societies, in which scholars from the west such as Louis Dumont and his followers are so deeply embedded, consciously or unconsciously, though they may pretend to be impartial or scientific, has to be discarded once and for all to the dust-bin of history as unscientific and untrue in the light of what we have seen above.

Anthropology is above all the science of knowing oneself and not just the knowing of others. Both are in fact inter-related and inseparable. This will become more obvious if we accept the fact that the whole of humanity is in the same boat of evolution and conditioning, whether we like it or not. The realisation of these fundamental facts by every individual and community will be in itself a revolution. Besides, it is necessary to view the whole first and then the details and not the other way round which is the traditional way. The fact of evolution and conditioning is the whole. All the rest are details and scholars of various 'hues and cries' have made it a habit of dwelling on details and making a living out of it. But, we do not prevent scholars from dwelling on details, provided they do not lose sight of the whole.

We have seen how the identity of the Tamil Muslims had gathered strength in the course of its evolution. The popularity of the Khilafat Movement and the All India Muslim League before independence, and the Indian Union Muslim League after independence in Tamil Nadu is a powerful expression of the separate social, cultural, religious, and historical identity of the Tamil Muslims.

Social reform efforts in the Tamil Muslim society contributed in their own way to the strengthening of this identity, for generally these reforms were directed against the un-Islamic practices and customs of the Muslims, which were mostly survivals of their ancestral traditions. The reforms were never against the Islamic principles and norms based on the Quran and the Hadith. In fact, the objective of the reforms in the Muslim society was to render the lives of the Tamil Muslims more in conformity with the true Islamic principles rather than introduce some alien principle, however modern or progressive, to regulate their lives.

In their attempts to reform the Tamil Muslim society, Tamil Muslims were helped by the non-Brahmin Hindus or the Dravidians, led principally by E.V. Ramasamy, from the 1920s. We have seen that no synthesis took place between the non-Brahmin Hindus and the Tamil Muslims, in spite of the intimate relationship that existed between them. The frontier separating them was never blurred and was in fact clearly demarcated. When these frontiers, which safeguarded the identity of the Tamil Muslims, were undermined by certain postures of the non-Brahmin Hindus, especially towards and after the independence, the Tamil Muslims naturally reacted to assert their separate identity and to remind the non-Muslims of the frontiers that existed between them and the others.

We do not however suggest that the strength of this identity or conditioning is permanent. This identity may weaken or on the contrary may gain further in strength, depending on the circumstances. It is worthwhile at this juncture to keep in mind that Clifford Geertz had pointed out that the Islamisation of Morocco and Indonesia was in danger not only of becoming stagnant but also of receding,[1] whereas in Pakistan and Bangladesh, Francis Robinson had noted the strengthening of the Islamic identities of the Muslims.[2]

The introduction of print technology into the Tamil country had brought about significant changes in the Tamil Muslim society and its literature. Print, as we know, originated in China and reached south India in the sixteenth century through the west European missionaries and colonisers. The late adoption of printing by the Muslim world in general, led to the formulation of various theories and much speculation on the causes responsible for this delay.

Our study has conclusively demonstrated that the late adoption of printing by the Tamil Muslims was more due to the association of printing with Christianity, governmental restrictions, and the inaccessibility of the printing presses, which were in the hands of the missionaries and colonisers, until at least 1835, when Charles Metcalf abolished the restrictions on printing, especially native printing. We have shown that the other reasons such as the Muslim preference for oral transmission of knowledge (which Francis Robinson seems to hold as true for the entire Muslim world) is not valid for the Tamil Muslim world. Neither can we say conclusively that the Tamil Muslims had a marked preference for the written transmission of knowledge, which prevented them from taking to printing earlier.

Further, reasons such as the untranslatability of the Quran because of its sophisticated language or its sacredness is not tenable when we have clear evidences as those advanced by P. Dawood Sha, the foremost Muslim social reformer of south India, about the real reasons that prevented the translation of the Quran and the Hadith and its publication.

But when we compare the quantity of literature produced before 1835 and the quantity of literature produced and published after 1835, when the Tamil Muslims adopted printing, it is quite obvious that the technology of printing had brought forth hundreds of Tamil Muslim authors and literary productions into the Tamil literary scene. This phenomenal increase in the number of authors and literary productions and publications can be largely attributed to the facilities provided by print technology like the wider diffusion of printed material, the easier stocking of knowledge, and also the possibilities of commercial benefits.

But, the adoption of printing, which was of an alien or rather an un-Islamic origin, and the enormous increase in Tamil Muslim literary productions and publications from the last quarter of the nineteenth century, and the appreciable number of periodical publications such as newspapers and magazines from the 1920s, were never at the cost of jeopardising the fundamental Islamic identity and the historical conditionings of the Tamil Muslims.

Of course printing, along with modern education and values, made it possible for any Ahmad, Mahmud, or Mohammad, as Francis Robinson had written, to interpret Islam according to his own understanding, and challenge the authority of the traditional ulemas. But in the Tamil country, as we have seen, this was not done at the expense of Islam itself. Actually these modern Muslim interpreters of Islam wanted to reform the Tamil Muslims by removing all the practices which were not Islamic and make the Tamil Muslims live a life which was more in conformity with the genuine Islamic principles, and in the process strengthen Islam.

The very production of an enormous quantity of literature by the Tamil Muslims, grounded in Islam and also Arabic and Persian, lends credence to the fact that printing itself and the ensuing literary productions were utilised to distinguish Tamil Muslims from the rest of the society. Thus printing and printed literature had contributed greatly to the strengthening of the frontiers separating the Tamil Muslims from others. So, though printing has been hailed as a progressive technology or as part of the intellectual activity of man, as held by Elizabeth Eisenstein, yet it seems to possess its own dynamics and has the potential to contribute to the strengthening of the frontiers between communities and possibly also exacerbate the divisions in society, as we have seen in the case of the Tamil Muslims.

It is true that print had made the wider diffusion and stocking of ideas and knowledge possible. But, ideas, knowledge, and information have been travelling across the world even before the printing era. Old religions as Buddhism and Hinduism had spread across the Indian sub-continent, South-East Asia and many parts of East Asia, without the aid of print. Christianity too spread in Europe without the aid of print. Islam in its turn had spread from Asia to Africa and Europe without the aid of print.

But, when the European Christians adopted printing in the fifteenth century and took it across the world in the subsequent centuries, and used it to propagate Christianity, it seems quite certain that Christianity did not make much headway either in India, or in South-East Asia, or in East Asia. The reasons for this may be many. But, what is quite obvious is that the possession of print technology by the European missionaries did not give them a distinct advantage, in spite of its great propaganda value, to convert the local Hindu, Buddhist, or Muslim populations to Christianity.

It was claimed in the Tamil country, that earlier missionaries such as Saint Francis Xavier had effected more conversions to Christianity,[3] when printing was still unknown in Tamil Nadu or was at its nascent stage, than the later missionaries of the late eighteenth and nineteenth centuries, when European colonisers had established themselves more solidly in south India and when printing was becoming popular and was adopted by both Hindus and Muslims in greater numbers. This demonstrates yet again that printing, in spite of all the virtues heaped upon it, still has its own strange limitations and ways of functioning, which arc not easily detectable.

Yet, we can be sure of one thing, i.e., modern print technology and the possibilities offered by it did play a considerable role in the strengthening of the Islamic identity of the Tamil Muslims. In its turn, the strengthening of the Islamic identity had its own consequences which also contributed to the participation of the Tamil Muslims in great numbers in the agitation for the maintenance of the Caliphate during the 1920s and, later in the 1940s, to the overwhelming support extended by the Tamil Muslims to the creation of Pakistan. Thus, it would not be totally correct to say that the division of India was solely the work of some individuals or groups. Instead, it will be more judicious to admit that print and the possibilities provided by it played an important role, especially in the division of India.

Before the adoption of printing in Tamil Nadu, we have seen that the written word i.e., literature had served to distinguish and divide Tamil Muslims from the rest of the society. But after the adoption of printing, we have also seen how printing contributed to the strengthening of this distinction and division. Neither Pi Sheng nor Gutenberg would have ever imagined that printing, which is nothing but memory in the form of words stored up outside the brain, was going to emphasise and demarcate more than ever the identity of the Tamil Muslims, and also at the same time divide them from the rest of the society.

Besides, though printing may be a product of modernity and a part of the intellectual activity of man, as Eisenstein has held, yet it is above all the product of human thought. Before the printing era, thought had invented the alphabet and the written word. Later it invented printing. But like the word and the written word, the printed word too had acquired the function of dividing and distinguishing one community from another and one group from another. Whether it is the written word or printed word both are products of thought. Therefore, it would not be an exaggeration to hold that one of the fundamental functions of thought itself is to divide. Thus, tools such as printing, which has the capacity to divide or accentuate divisions, as we have seen in the case of Tamil Muslims, cannot be deemed as altogether progressive from the human point of view, though it is undoubtedly a progress from the technological point of view.

Notes

1. Clifford Geertz, *Islam Observed: Religious Development in Morocco and Indonesia*, (1968).
2. Francis Robinson, 'Islam and Muslim Society in South Asia', in *Contributions to Indian Sociology*, 1983, 17, 2, 201.
3. S. Delacroix, ed., *Histoire Universelle des Missions Catholiques-Les Missions Modernes*, (Paris, 1957), II, 43–48; P. Thomas, *Christians and Christianity in India and Pakistan*, (London, 1954), 44–75.

APPENDIX I

A Compiled List of Tamil Muslim Printed Works

A: Islamic Legends, Tales, History and Biography

Umaru Pulavar, *Sira Puranam*, Madras, 1842 (copy in the private collection of Janab 'Hasan', Madras). A poem on the life of Prophet Mohammad, edited by Sheik Abdul Qadir Nayinar Lebbai, known as Sekana Pulavar.

Umaru Pulavar, *Ciravenkinra Puranam,* Madras, 1849, 515, IOL. A Poem on the life and legends connected with the Prophet Mohammad, edited by Abd al Qadir Nayinar Lebbai.

Ceykaptul Katirnayinar, Kayarpattinam, *Putukuccamculama Puranam* (*s.l.*), Madras, 1857, 7 (1), 706, RMRL. A Muslim legend.

Caiyitapupakharp Pulavar, Kottaru, *Cirakirttanam*, Madras, 1863, 516, RMRL. An Islamic legendary poem.

Kunnamucu Pulavar, M., *Caiyithathu Pataippor*, Madras, 1863, 62, IOL; another edition, Madras, 1864, 62, IOL; Pungathur, 1872, 62, INALCO; Madras, 1878, a.e., 56, IOL. A Poem on an Islamic legend.

Kunnamucu Lebbai Kazi Alim Pulavar, *Iravuculkul Pataippor*, Madras, 1869, 264, IOL, INALCO; Madras, 1877, a.e., 262, IOL. A Poem on female heroism in Islam.

Veerasamy Naidu (publ.), *Kan Sahib Sandai,* Madras, 1870, 106, MP; Madras, 1878, a.e., 96, MP; Madras, 1880, a.e., 92, MP. The Story of Khan Sahib, a soldier under the Nabob of Madura.

Aliyar Pulavar, son of T. Kantapillai, *Intirayan Pataippor*, Madras, 1871, Pt. II, 56, IOL; Madras, 1873, Pt. 2, a.e., 46, IOL; a.e., MSB, 1878; a.e., MSB.

Aliyar Pulavar, *Uchi Pataippor*, Madras, 1871, MSB; Madras, 1878, a.e., 358, MSB. An Islamic legend.

Aliyar Pulavar, son of Kanta Pillai Aliyar, *Ipunniyantan Pataippor*, Madras, 1871, 66, MP; Madras, 1873, a.e., 49, IOL; Madras, 1874, a.e., 50, IOL; Madras, 1876, a.e., 66, IOL. A poem on a fight between Ahman Nabi of Medina and another Muslim prince.

Muhyidhin Pulavar, Varicai, *Sackoon Pataippor*, Madras, 1871, 61, IOL, MP; Madras, 1874, a.e., 48, IOL, MP; Madras, 1878, a.e., 48, IOL, MP; Madras, 1900, a.e., 48 (copy in my possession). A ballad poem, edited by Muhammad Ibrahim.

M. Ibrahim Pulavar (ed.), *Iratna Muhammadu Karana Carittiram*, Madras, 1873, 56, IOL; see also MP, 1873. A prose account of Prophet Mohammad.

Abu Bakr Pulavar, S., *Ipulicu Nama*, Madras, 1874, 46, IOL; see also MP, 1874. The story of a Muslim called Ipulisu.

Ceytakkati Pulavar, *Apu Sakamaa Malai*, Madras, 1874, 48, IOL; a.e., Madras, 1877, 48, IOL; Madras, 1878, a.e., 48, MP. A poem on the Islamic legend of Apushakama.

Kontalakan Pulavar, Vedalaiyur, *Paluluna Sukapi Malai*, Madras, 1874, 43, MP, MSB. Story of Palulun.

Mahomed Pulavar, *Kasim Padaippor*, Madras, 1874, 24, MP. A work on King Kasim and his holy expedition.

Mira Pulavar Saiyyid, son of Urai Nayinar, *Papparattiyar Ammanai*, Madras, 1874, 48, IOL; Madras, 1875, a.e., 48, IOL; Madras, 1877, a.e., 44, MP; Madras, 1878, a.e., 48, IOL; Madras, 1882, a.e., 48, MP. The story of the marriage of Aliyar with Pappataiyar.

Karunananda Sawmigal, *Khan Saib Sandai*, Madras, 1875, 2nd edition, 96, MP; see also EFEO. An account of a battle.

Neyina Muhammad Pulavar, *Meeran Sahib Antavar Charitra Surukam*, Madras, 1875, 4, MSB; Madras, 1877, a.e., MSB. A brief story of Meeran Sahib.

Qasim Pataippor and Kasim Malai, Madras, 1876, 20, IOL; a.e., Madras, 1878, 20, IOL. Two poems on Islamic legend.

Abdul Qadir, *Sadu Gnanikal Charitram*, Madurai, 1877, 67, MSB. A history of four persecuted sages.

Muhammad Mastan Pulavar, *Yunussu Napiutaiya Kissa*, Madras, 1877, 24, MSB. Story of Prophet Yunus.

Abdul Khadar Sahib, *Sakarat Nama*, Madras, 1878, 40, MP. A poem on the sad adventures of Sakara.

Aliyar Pulavar, *Aintu Pataippor*, Madras, 1878, MSB; Madras, 1883, a.e., MSB; Madras, 1887, a.e., MSB. An Islamic war legend.

Aliyar Pulavar, Taki Pataippor, Madras, 1878, 180, MSB; Madras, 1883, MSB; Madras, 1887, a.e., MSB. An Islamic legend.

Aliyar Pulavar, *Vadochi Pataippor*, Madras, 1878, 315, MSB; Madras, 1883, a.e., MSB.. An Islamic legend.

Agammadu Mira Sahib E., *Ravusulkul Padaippor*, Madras, 1878, 352, MP. An account of the battle fought by Mohammad Nabi after his departure from Mecca to Medina.

Kannagu Mahomed Pulavar, *Puttu Kussam*, Madras, 1878, 2nd edition, 596, MP. History of the Prophet and His triumphs.

Madar Sahib, *Mikurasu Nama*, Madras, 1878, 32, MP; Madras, 1887, 4th edition, 32, MP. A poetical legend.

Mahomed Ibrahim Sahib, *Kasim Malai*, Madras, 1878, 20, MP. A poem on the victories of Kasim over his enemies.

Makhdum Muhammad ibn Makhdum Pilla, *Iravuculkal Pataippor Vacana Kaviyam*, Madras, 1878, 352, IOL. A prose version of an Islamic legend.

Makhdum Mohammad ibn Makhdum Pilla, *Puttukussam Vacana Kaviyam*, Madras, 1878, 580, IOL, A collection of Islamic legends and history compiled from Arabic sources.

Muhammad Ibrahim, *Papparattiyar Ammanai*, Madras, 1878, 48, MP. The legend of a prince transformed into a woman and who ultimately married Ali, the champion of Islam.

Muhammad Ibrahim, *Aindu Padaippore*, Madras, 1878, 156, MP. A poem describing the successful expeditions of Nabi, the King of Medina, against five other kings.

Seikaptul Kadir Nayinar, *Puthukussam Vacana Kaviyam*, Madras, 1878, 580, MSB. An Islamic legend.

Seku Tambi Pulavar, *Sira Natakamenru Vazhanga Ninra Karanamalai*, Madras, 1878, 268, MSB. A history of the Prophet.

Neyina Muhammad Pulavar, *Meeran Sahib Antavar Charitram*, Madras, 1879, MSB. A history of Meeran Sahib.

Sheik Easap Labbai, *Riyalul Kikkam*, Madras, 1879, 3rd edition, 102, MSB. A history of the king of Khorasan.

Aidurusu Nayina Pulavar, *Navamani Malai Enru Vazhankum Mukiyitin Puranam*, Madras, 1880, 302, MP; see also MSB. A work on saint Mukiyitin Abdul Qadir.

Seikaptul Kadir, Tenkasi, *Munajattu*, Madras, 1880, MSB. A war legend.

Seyeedu Mukamattu, *Katiya Malai*, Madras, 1880, MSB. The story of the fight between Ipulicu and Iman.

Umaru Pulavar, *Siravenkinra Puranam*, Madras, 1880, MSB; Madras, 1886, a.e., MSB. An Islamic legend.

Sheik Abdul Khadar Saib, *Mukarapattulakin Charitram*, Madras, 1881, 56, MP. A poem on a sacred expedition of Sultan Imam and on his triumphs.

Abdul Qadir, *Saithun Kissa*, Madras, 1882, 172, MSB. A story translated from Hindi into Tamil.

Abdul Saib, *Maluku Mulikkin Padaippor*, Madras, 1882, 80, MP. An account of the religious war between Caliph Ali and a chief named Malukul Malik.

Kunju Musa Pulavar, *Kunju Musa Pulavar Padal*, Madras, 1882, 56, MP. A work on the battle between Hassan, the grandson of the Prophet, and a hostile tribe.

Mahomed Ibrahim Sahib, *Tajjal Nama*, Madras, 1882, 16, MP. A work on the last man who is to appear at the end of the world and the premonitory indication of his advent.

Mahomed Ibrahim Sahib, *Ayanayinan Kathai*, Madras, 1882, 48, MP. The story of a Muslim saint.

Kannagu Mathu Muhammad Pulavar, *Ravusulkul Padaippor*, Madras, 1883, 2nd edition, 352, MP. A description of the different battles fought during the lifetime of the Prophet, with some accounts of the individuals who were converted to Islam.

Umar, *Ciravenkinra Puranam*, Madras, 1885, viii, 536, IOL. A poem on legends relating to Prophet Mohammad, edited by Allah Pitchai Pulavar.

Kannakumathu Makathu Mukamattu Pulavar, *Kasasulanbiya*, Madras, 1886, 1st part, 780, MP, MSB. History of the prophets.

Mahammadu Pulavar, *Kasim Padaivettu*, Madras, 1887, 5th edition, 20, MP. A poem on a religious war.

Makuthu Mukamattup Pulavar, *Sira Vacana Kaviyam*, Madras, 1887, 1290, MP; see also MSB, 1887. A work based on *Sira Puranam*.

Kalvi Kalanjiya, Madras, 1888, 52, MP; see also RMRL. Pulavar, Melur, N.K.V., *Siravannemum, Sittirakavikalum*. A work on the history of the Prophet.

Kalvi Kalanjiya Pulavar, *Tavupa Malai and Makkal Vasagam*, Madras, 1888, 80, MP. A poem on the Prophet.

Mukamattu Ismail, M., *Sham Hun Raliyallahu Ankutaiya Kissa*, Madras, 1889, 40, MP; see also MSB. A legend.

Citti Levvai Maraikkayar and Mukamattu Kasim Maraikkayar, *Asan Pé Utaiya Charitiram*, Madras, 1890, MSB. History of Asan Pé.

Umaru Pulavar, *Siranapi Avatara Patalam*, Madras, 1890, 125, MSB. An Islamic legend.

Mukamattu Aptulla, *Akitayé Islam Ennum Shamsul Islam*, Madras, 1892, 135, MSB. A history of Islam.

Kannakumatu Kakutu Mukapattup Pulavar, *Periya Kasasulanbiya*, Madras, 1892, 964, MSB. A work on the prophets.

Sheik Muhammad Lebbai Alim Sahib, *Nangimankal Charittira Vasana Rupagam*, Madras, 1892, 384, MP. A saintly work.

Ghulam Kadiru Navalar, *Nagore Puranam*, Tirichinapuram, 1893, xii, 202, EFEO. A work on the saint of Nagore.

Muhammad ibn Muhammad, al-Mu'izz, *Futuh al Misr wa'l Bahnasa or Kissat al Bahnasa*, Madras, 1894, vi, ii, 432, IOL. A legendary history of the town of Bahnasa in Upper Egypt, translated from the Arabic by Muhammad Labbai Alim Sahib.

Periya Nuh Lebbai, Kayalpattinam, *Vedapuranam*, Madras, 1894, v, 138, i, IOL. Muslim legends and teachings, edited by Kann Ahmad Makhdum Muhammad.

Sheik Muhammad Lebbai Alim Sahib, *Sira Vilakku*, Madras, 1894, 48, MSB. A religious work on the Prophet.

Shaik Mugamadu ibn Muhamadul Muasurakumadulla, *Pathukul Misir*, Madras, 1895, MSB. The history of the capture of Misr, during the reign of the second Caliph, Umar.

Sulaiman Levvai M., Jaffna, *Carupantha Mekapatharthovam Tarukka Nirakaranam*, Jaffna, 1895, 8, IOL. An Islamic legend.

Muhammad Sultan ibn Ahmad Umar Maraikayar, *Sira Satakam* followed by *Tottira Padigam* (devotional verses), Penang, 1900, 16, 4, IOL. Hundred verses founded upon the Sira of Umar.

Abdur Rahman Sahib (trans.), *Tuhfatul Hindu, Part I and II*, Madras, 1902, 240, MP. A work translated from Hindi.

Badr al Din Pavalar, *Muhyi al Din Puranam*, Madras, 1901–1903, 2 parts, IOL; see also Madras, 1901, 338, MP. A poem on the life of saint Muhyi al Din, edited by Shaikh Tambi Pavalar, Kottaru, Fakir Miran.

Umar Pulavar, *Cira Puranam*, Madras, 1902, vol. I, 88, 753; vol. II, 1026, IOL; Madras, 1904, a.e., RMRL. Legend, edited with commentary by Sheikh Tambi Pavalar.

Hasan Ali Pulavar, Kalai, *Husain Pataippor Vacana Kaviyam*, Madras,

1903, 208, illus., IOL; see also MP. A prose version of a poem on Islamic history.

Pillai, Kandasamy, *Jagandarsha Charittiram*, Madras, 1903, 78, EFEO. History of Jagandar Sha.

Shaik Tambi Pavalar, *Sirapuranam, Part I*, Madras, 1904, 944, MP. A religious legend, with paraphrase.

Selvakesavaraya Mudaliar, T., *Akpar Nur*, Madras, 1907, 140, IOL; Madras, 1914, a.e., IOL; a.e., 1917, IOL; a.e., 1918, IOL. A biography of Mughal Emperor Akbar.

Kottaru Meeran Sahib (ed.), *Sirapuranam*, Madras, 1908, 2 vols., 88, 855 and 1026, RMRL. An Islamic story.

Shaik Tambi Pavalar, *Sirapuranam, Part II*, Madras, 1908, 2, 1026, MP. A poetical work with a commentary giving an account of the life of the Prophet and the early history of Islam.

Abd al Qadir Nayinar Lebbai, Kayalpattinam and Ahmad Maraikkayar, *Cirap Puranam*, Madras, 1910, Pt II, 316, IOL. A poem on the life of Prophet Mohammad.

Bava Muhiyuddin B., *Sira Venba*, Madura, 1910, 26, MP. A poem giving an account of the birth of the Prophet.

Muhammatu Aptul Alim Sarar, Tilli Mavulana Mavulavi, *Paittul Mukattisin Yutta Carittiram*. Madras, 1910, RMRL. A war history.

Shaik Abdul Khadar Nayinar Labbai and Bani Ahmad Marakkayar, *Sirapuranam*, Madras, 1910, vol. 2, 1, 3, 316, MP. A poem embodying the later life of the Prophet being a continuation of a previous volume.

Tassaduq Husain, *Dastan, Amir Hamza Jank*, Madras, 1910, vol. I, 385; vol. II, 610; vol. III, 416; vol. IV, 403; vol. V, 205, IOL. An Islamic legend, translated by Sheikh Daud Hakim A.S. and Muhammad Shems al Din Hakim from the Urdu version.

Muhammad Ibrahim Sahib, *Rouzatul Asfiya fi Kassanul Anbiya*, Madras, 1912, Part II, 444, MP. Brief accounts of the lives of all the Prophets from Joseph to Moses.

Muhammad Kasim of Amritsar, *Bisharat Fatimah Ennum Miss Keat Charitram*, Maraikayar, Penang, 1912, ii, 14, IOL. The story of two English converts to Islam, Mr Joseph and Miss Keat and their marriage; translated from the original Urdu of Muhammad Kasim by Talavay M. Sinnavappu.

Muhammad Mappilai Lebbai, Sayyid, *Nal Imankal Pirapantam*, Madras, 1912, 364, IOL. An account of the originators of the four Sunni rites; Put into Tamil characters by M.K. Hasan Ali Pulavar.

Adam Bava, M. of Kanakkur, *Matchimai Tangya Sultanavargal*

Adrianopilil Seitha Turukki Sandai, Madras, 1914, 24, IOL. A lyrical ballad praising the victory of the Turks in the Balkan war concluding with the capture of Adrianopil.

Aliyar Lebbai, T., *Jermaniyutan Vuttam*, Madras, 1914, Pt. I, 117, ilus., IOL; see also MP, 1915. An account of the causes of the First World War.

Neyina Muhammad Pavalar, M.A. of Chevval, Tinnevely (ed.), *Ceyyidattu Pataippor Vacana Kaviyam*, Madras, 1914, 105, IOL, MP. A narrative of the exploits of Abd ul Rahman bin Abu Bakr, son of the first Caliph, who successfully fought with an infidel and married his daughter.

Shah Muhammad Ziya al Din Kadiri, *Turki Palkan Yutta Carittiram*, Madras, 1914, 265, IOL, MP. A history of the Balkan war.

Shah Muhammad Ziya ul Din ibn Muhammad Madar, Kadiri, *Turkey Balkan Yuddha Charitram*, Madras, 1914, iv, 258, 7 plates, IOL. A history of the war in the Balkans involving Turkey.

Shah Muhammad Diya al Din, T., *Muhammatu Hanifa Yutta Carittiram*, Madras, 1915, 303, IOL. A rendering from the Urdu, *Jang Namah*.

Shah Muhammad Siya-ud-din, *Hasarat Muhammad Haniba Yuddacarittiram*, Madras, 1915, 303, MP. Gives a description of the adventures of Muhammad Hanif, one of the disciples of the Prophet Mohammad; rendered from Hindustani sources.

Abdul Rahim, *Kanam Mistar Aptur Rahimin Maruppurai*, Madras, 1917, iv, 320, IOL. A Tamil rendition of Mr Justice Abdul Rahim's minute of dissent from the findings of the Royal Commission on Public Services in India written in English.

Kirusnacami Pavalar, T., *Aitar Ali*, Madras, 1919, 171, IOL. Life of Hyder Ali.

Palavarnac Cintu, Palghat, 1919, 16, IOL. A popular ballad on an Islamic legend.

Ahmad Tambi Marakkayar, *Catta Capayil Ettu Varusha Velai*, Madras, 1920, 341, IOL. An account of eight years of work in the Madras Legislative Council.

Muslim League, Kuttanallur (publ.), *Asia Minoril Turukiyarin Parithapa Malai*, Negapatam, 1920, 8, MP. An account of the pitiable condition of the Turks in Asia Minor; also contains a Tamil rendering of the Report on the same together with an appeal for funds by the Muslim League.

Srinivasa Aiyankar C.R., *Mahamat Napi*, Madras, 1920, 56, IOL. A life of the Prophet Mohammad.

B: Works on Prophet Mohammad, the Saints and Other Muslim Personalities and Events

Abd al Qadir Nayinar Lebbai, Sheik, Kayalpattinam, *Nakaiyantati*, Madras, 1843, 8, 122, IOL; Madras, 1872, a.e., 83, IOL; Madras, 1887, a.e., 144, MP; Madras, 1912, a.e., 145, RMRL. A poem on the pilgrimage to Nagore, with the author's own commentary.

Mahomed Labbai Alim, Kayarpattinam, *Arumai Karana Malai*, Madras, 1865, 45, RMRL; Madras, 1874, 38, MP; see also IOL.

Nagore Mahomed Pulavar, *Kesadipaatha Malai*, Madras, 1868, 161, MP, MSB. A work in praise of a Muslim saint.

Abdul Khader Sahib, Pettai Amur, *Sacharattu Nama*, Madras, 1869, 38, MP; see also MSB 1868–69. A work in praise of the Prophet and God.

Qasim Pulavar, *Tiruppukazh*, Madras, 1870, 73, IOL; see also MP, 1871; Madras, 1880, a.e., 76, MP; Madras, 1911, a.e., 80, RMRL. A poem in praise of Prophet Mohammad.

Abeem Saib, *Nabi Malai*, Madras, 1871, 11, MP. A poem in praise of the Nabi.

Nayinamuhammatup Pulavar, Pacipattinam, *Kuttupul Akparakiya Apul Acan Alicatili Rakumattulaki Alaiki Avarkal Peril Patiya Manimalai*, Madras, 1871, 8, RMRL. A song in praise of Abul Hasan Ali Shadili.

Pir Muhammad Tarkalai, *Picumilkkuram*, Madras, 1871, 44, IOL; a.e. edition, Madras, 1874, 44, IOL; Madras, 18, 76, a.e., MSB; a.e., Madras, 1877, 44, IOL; a.e., Madras, 1878, 44, IOL, RMRL; see also MP, 1871, 1874, 1878, 1887. Poem in praise of the Prophet and Islam.

Samu Naina, Kayalpattinam, *Naalima Malai*, Madras, 1871, 55, MSB. A poem in praise of four Imams.

Mahomed Mahomed Pulavar, *Puhalpa Malai*, Madras, 1872, 18, MP. A work in praise of a certain Syed Mahomed Marakkayar.

Shahabuddin, *Orupa Orupadu*, Madras, 1872, 4, MP. A work in praise of Nagore Antavar.

Alli Marakkayar, *Seytha Kadi Nonti Natakam*. Madras, 1873, 149, MSB. A dramatic sequence in praise of Seethakathi.

Abd al Qadir Nayinar Lebbai, Sheik, Kayalpattinam, *Tirumani Malai*, Madras, 1873, 219, IOL; see also INALCO. Songs in praise of Muslim personalities like Abraham, Ismail, and Isaac.

Katirmukaiyatin Pulavar, *Sahulhamitantakai Peril Munajattu*, Madras, 1873, 29, RMRL. A work in praise of Shahul Hameed.

Selvakannu Kavirayar, Thennur, *Rasullulah Peril Pukazh Pamalai*, Madras, 1873, 31, MP; see also MSB, 1873. A work in praise of Rasalullah.

Abd al Qadir, Amur Valaibava, *Karanap Pukazh*, Madras, 1874, 14, IOL; see also MP, 1874 and 1882. A religious poem in praise of the Prophet.

Abu Bakr Pulavar, S., *Seyeedu Anbiya Sakipu Pulavar Napisalvallahu Alaikivasalvam Avarkal Peril Pillai Tamizh*, Madras, 1874, MSB. A work on the Prophet in pillai style.

Abdul Khadar Sahib, *Musal Iman Konda Karanam*, Madras, 1874, 3rd edition, 12, MP. A story of Nagore Mira Sahib.

Abdul Khader Sahib, *Hakayat Nama*, Madras, 1874, 33, MP; see also MSB, 1874. A work in praise of the Prophet and his followers.

Abdul Qadir, Pettai, *Mukamattu Napi Sallalaku Alaihuvasalavam Avarkalutaiya Karanap Pukazh*. Madras, 1874, 62, MSB. A work on the Prophet.

Annaiyya Pulavar, Sayyid, *Napiyin Peril Pillaitamizh*, Madras, 1874, 28, IOL. A lullaby related to the Prophet.

Kadiru Mukiyittin, O., Puducheri, *Napiyulla Perir Karanakkummi*, Madras, 1874, 26, MSB. A work in praise of the Prophet.

Ḳontalakan Pulavar, Vedalaiyur, *Paluluna Sukhapi Malai*, Madras, 1874, 47, IOL; see also MP, 1874; Madras, 1878, a.e., 43, IOL. A poem on the successors of Prophet Mohammad.

Madar Pulavar, Aiyanpettai, *Yucapu Napi Malai*, Madras, 1874, 28, IOL. A poem on an Islamic Prophet.

Mohideen Sayubu, *Yusuppu Nabi Malai*, Madras, 1874, 28, MP, MSB. A work on Prophet Yusuf.

Mugiyadin S., *Tavugidu Malai*, Madras, 1874, 20, MP. A tract in praise of the Prophet and other champions of Islam.

Muhammad Mastan Pulavar, *Innicai*, Madras, 1874, 16, IOL, MP. Devotional poems on certain Muslim saints.

Muhammad Mastan Pulavar (ed.), *Pulukkiyavutaiya Kissavum Yunucu Napiyutaiya Kissavum*. Madras, 1874, 32, 24, IOL; a.e., Madras, 1877, 32, 24, IOL. The story of Pulukkiya and Yunucu Napi.

Makumattu Mastan Pulavar, *Seiku Dawoodoli Sakipu Avarkal Peril Innicai*, Madras, 1874, 50, MSB. A work on saint Seiku Dawood.

Makumattu Mastan Pulavar, *Seiku Dawoodoli Sakipu Avarkal Peril Padiya Nerissai Venba*, Madras, 1874, 25, MSB. A work on saint Seiku Dawood.

Makumattu Mastan Pulavar, *Fathima Amma Avarkal Peril Padiya Venba*, Madras, 1874, 31, MSB. A work on Mother Fathima.

Mukamattu Usmayil Alim Sayib, *Musal Iman Konda Karanumum Meeran*

Sahibu Charittramum, Madras, 1874, 16, MP, MSB. A story of Nagore Mira Sahib, mixed with a lot of Hindustani words.

Naina Mukamattu Pulavar, *Teenilai Thangam Pattu*, Madras, 1874, 3rd edition, 24, MP. A work on Muslim personalities.

Nayana Muhammad Pulavar, *Munajattu*, Madras, 1874, 78, MP. Verses in the yannam metre in praise of the Prophet.

Neyina Muhammad Pulavar, *Yunusu Napiyutaiya Kissa*, Madras, 1874, 26, MSB; Madras, 1876, a.e., 22, MSB; Madras, 1877, a.e., 24, MSB. A story of the Prophet Yunus.

Saiddakadi Pulavar, *Abushakamé Malai*, Madras, 1874, 48, MP; see also 1882. A poem in praise of a saint.

Saikolu Saibu, *Munajattu*, Madras, 1874, 14, MSB. Hymns in praise of the Prophet.

Shaik Ibrahim Sahib, *Arunmani Malai*, Madras, 1874, 16, MP. A tract in praise of the Prophet's celebrated followers, full of Persian and Arabic expressions.

Samu Nayinar Lebbai, Kayalpattinam, *Piruca Ammal Katitu, Tokaimalai*, Madras, 1874, 183, IOL. A story of Piruca Ammal; it also contains *Aisal* by Ahamadu Lebbai Alim Sahib, *Seyku Aptulla Oli Kathai* and *Kuru An Sutratai Kontuntakiya Munajattu*; all in poetic style.

Samu Nayinar Lebbai, Kayalpattinam, *Seiku Aptula Olirakimatulla Avarkal Kathai*, Madras, 1874, 104, MSB. A story of saint Seiku Aptulla.

Samu Nayinar Lebbai, *Miran Malai*, Madras, 1874, 12, IOL, MP. Religious verses.

San Nayinar Lebbai and Sam Shihab ul Din ibn Sulaiman, *Piruca Ammal Katitu*, Madras, 1874, 56, IOL. Religious poems and story of Pirucca Ammal.

Sataku Mukamatabtul Kadirup Pulavar, *Maimaik Kappiyam*, Madras, 1874, 22, IOL; see also MP, 1874. A work on a Muslim saint.

Savatu Pulavar, *Pillai Tamizh*, Madras, 1874, 36, MP. A work on the Prophet's childhood.

Seyed Anapiya Sahib Pulavar, Tenkasi, *Napisallahu Aliki Salem Avarkal Peril Pillai Tamizh*, Madras, 1874, 28, MP. A work on the Prophet's childhood.

Shaik Mahomed Pulavar, *Kiyamattu Nalutaiya Visalam*, Madras, 1874, 70, MP. A work on the latter days of the Prophet.

Sheik Ibrahim Sahib Pulavar, *Dastagir Avargal Peril Munajat*, Madras, 1874, 8, MSB. A work on saint Dastagir.

Sheik Ibrahim Sahib Pulavar, *Napi Nayakathin Peril Munajattu*, Madras, 1874, 1, MSB. A work in praise of the Prophet.

Syed Abdul Khader, *Adaikkala Malai*, Madras, 1874, 24, 2nd edition, MP. Hymns in praise of the Prophet and Allah.

Abd al Kadir, Amur, Valai Bava, *Iratna Muhammadu Karana Charitram*, Madras, 1875, 55, IOL; a.e., 1877, IOL. Life history of the Prophet Mohammad.

Allapichai Pulavar, *Musal Yiman Karanam*, Madras, 1875, 16, MP. A biographical sketch of Nagore Meera Sahib.

Madar Pulavar, Aiyanpettai, *Mikurasu Nama*, Madras, 1875, 32, IOL, MP; Madras, 1878, 32, a.e., IOL; Madras, 1882, a.e., MSB.

Muhiyittin Antavarkal Sakul Hamitu Antavarkal Peril Taukitu, Madras, 1875, 96, IOL; another edition, Madras, 1877, 96, IOL. Devotional songs on a Muslim saint.

Pakir Mohideen, *Pulukkiya Kissa*, Madras, 1874, 60, MP; Madras, 1875, 4th edition, 59, MP; Madras, 1877, a.e., 56, MP.

Nayina Muhammatup Pulavar, *Meeran Sahib Antavar Charithira Surukkam*, Madras, 1875, 4, MSB. A brief biography of Meeran Sahib.

Sheikh Lebbai, *Tamimancari Malai*, Madras, 1875, 64, IOL; see also MP, 1875, 1887. A poem on a legendary Muslim saint.

Abdul Khadar Marcaya Pulavar S.K., *Sorga Nidhi*, Madras, 1876, 20, MP; see also MP, 1878. A compilation of three tracts containing prayers and praise of the Prophet.

Author unknown, *Kasim Malai*, Madras, 1876, 20, MP; Madras, 1888, a.e., MSB. Two poems praising Kasim, who vanquished the infidels who attacked the followers of the Prophet.

Kannakumathu Makuthu Mukamattup Pulavar, *Kasim Malai* (*Imam Kasim Pataippor*), Madras, 1876, 41, MSB; Madras, 1878, a.e., MSB. In praise of Imam Kasim.

Kasim Pulavar, *Innicai*, Madras, 1876, 29, MSB. In praise of the Prophet.

Muhammad Imam Ghazalli ibn Muhammad Ali Maraikkayar of Nagur, *Hazrat Miran Sahib Andavar Avargal Karana Charitram*, Karikal, 1876, 3, 165, IOL. A biography of Miran Sultan Shah al Hamid, a Muslim saint of the 16th century, compiled from Persian, Hindustani and other sources.

Muhammad Saib Kadir Modin Uduma Nina, *Doukidu Malai*, Madras, 1876, 20, MP. A kind of Tamil song in praise of the Prophet and a saint.

Neyina Mihammad Pulavar, *Pulukkiyavutaiya Kissa* (*Yunusu Napiyutaiya Kissa*), Madras, 1876, 32, MSB; Madras, 1877, a.e., MSB. A work in praise of Prophet Mohammad, translated from Arabic.

Seikabdul Qadir Nayinar, Kayalpattinam, *Innicai*, Madras, 1876, 16, MSB; Madras, 1889, a.e., MSB. In praise of the Prophet.

Ligibir Muhammad, *Titaaru Malai*, Madras, 1877, 44, MSB. A poem on Teethar, a Muslim personality.

Nooru Mukamattu, *Kayarpatnam Pallivasal Sapaiyar Peril Kavithaikal*, Islamiya Vilakka Press, 1877, 36, 4, MSB. Poems on some Muslim personalities.

Pakir Mukiyittin, *Nanmani Malai*, Madras, 1877, 16, MP. A work on Nagore Antavar.

Alla Pichai, *Alla Pichai Pulavarkal Padal*, Madras, 1878, 20, MP; Madras, 1882, a.e., 32, MP. Verses in praise of the Prophet and His successors.

Alli Maraikayar, *Imam Asankusainantaver Peril Dasarathinam*, Madras, 1878, 11, MSB. A work on Hasan and Hussain.

Alli Maraikayar, *Ammanai*, Madras, 1878, 5, MSB. Girls sing the praise of God.

Alli Maraikayar, *Hakku Peril Padarattinam*, Madras, 1878, 175, MSB. In praise of Hakku.

Alli Marakkayar, *Prabandha Kottu*, Madras, 1878, 32, MP. Hymns in praise of the leaders of Islam.

Author unknown, *Nabi Avadhara Ammanai*, Madras, 1878, 24, MP. A poem on the birth of the Prophet.

Halarat Sayeed Kutbu Shahul Hameed Meeran Ghouthu Sultan Kadiru Ganj Savaiy Sahibu Antavarkal Peril Patalkal, Madras, 1878, 12, MSB. A work in praise of Shahul Hameed.

Mahomed Ibrahim Sahib, *Karanak Kummi*, Madras, 1878, 20, MP. A poem in praise of a certain Nyna Mahomed.

Muhammad Pulavar, Nagore, *Katija Nayaki Tirumanna Vazhthu*, Madras, 1878, 46, IOL. Poems on the marriage of Katija and other aspects of the life of the Prophet.

Pir Muhammad Sahib, Tarkalai, *Bisumul Kuram*, Madras, 1878, 14, 2nd edition, MSB. Verses in praise of the Prophet.

Shaik Abdul Kadir Lebbai, Sari Attumalai, Madras, 1878, 23, MP. Hymns in praise of the Prophet.

Aidurusu Pulavar, *Aidurusu Padal Tirattu*, Madras, 1879, 76, MP, MSB. Selections from various poems in praise of the leaders of Islam.

Alla Pichai Pulavar, *Anatakalippu*, Madras, 1881, 8, MP. A work in praise of the Prophet.

Madar Saib Pulavar, *Parulu Malai*, Madras, 1881, 20, MP. A work in praise of the Prophet.

Mahomed Abdul Khader, *Munajattu*, Madras, 1881, 24, MP. Hymns and verses in praise of some of the votaries of the Prophet.

Peer Muhammad Saib, *Magaripattu Malai*, Madras, 1881, 80, MP; see also 1882, MSB. Verses in praise of the Prophet.

Mahomed Abdul Khader, *Munajattu*, Madras, 1881, 24, MP. Hymns and verses in praise of some of the votaries of the Prophet.

Abd al Kadir, Amur Valai Bava, *Iratna Muhammadu Karana Charitram*, Madras, a.e., 1882, 64, IOL. Life history of Mohammad, compiled from Persian sources by Abd al Kadir and edited by his son, Abd al Wahab.

Abdul Wahabu, *Ayubu Nabiyinutaiya Kissa*, Madras, 1882, 24, MP, MSB. A story of the Prophet Ayub.

Kalvikalanjya Pulavar, *Nabi Avatara Ammanai*, Madras, 1882, 20, MP; see also MSB, 1882. A poem on the advent of the Prophet.

Katiru Mugaaideen, O., Puducheri, *Kummi Paatu*, Madras, 1882, 26, MSB; see also 1883, 1888, MSB. In praise of the Prophet.

Mahomed Muppan, M.T., *Mahadin Malai Pattu*, Madras, 1882, 8, MP, MSB. Verses in praise of a saint.

Meeran Kaniannavi, Paraiyar, *Kuramathu* (*Sorka or Madhu Kuram*), Madras, 1882, 603, MSB. A work in praise of the Prophet.

Muhammad Hussain Pulavar, *Taukitu Malai*, Madras, 1882, 20, MP, MSB. A work in praise of the Prophet.

Naina Muhammad Pulavar, *Salavattu Malai*, Madras, 1882, 20, MP; see also 1883, MP. A work in praise of the Prophet.

Sakkili Pulavar, *Paralu Malai*, Madras, 1882, 16, MSB. A work in praise of a Muslim saint.

Alla Pichai Pulavar, *Halarat Sheik Oliyulla*, Madras, 1883, 16, MP. Songs in praise of a saint.

Alla Pichai Pulavar, *Nagor Antavar*, Madras, 1883, 12, MP. Songs in praise of a saint.

Aravamurthi U.V., *Sheiku Dawoodoliyulla Peril Patalkal*, Madras, 1883, 16, MSB. A work in praise of Sheik Dawood.

Kannagu Mathu Muhammad Pulavar, *Palapadal Tirattu*, Madras, 1883, 228, MP. A collection of poems in praise of the Prophet and Allah.

Mathar Sahib Pulavar, *Mikurasu Nama*, Madras, 1883, 2nd edition, 32, MP. A poem on the ascension of the Prophet to heaven.

Alli Marakkayar, *Bangla Sirappu Padigam*, Madras, 1884, 14, MP, MSB. A work in praise of a Nagore philanthropist, Jainulabidin Mia and his bungalow.

Seiku Mukammattu, *Rattinavilasam Nasihathullasam*, Madras, 1884, 152, MSB. On the Prophet's words.

Haja Mokhaytin Sahib, *Rasululla Munajat and Rasululla Kummi*, Madras, 1887, 8, MP. A tract on *Rasululla* (the Prophet).

Kannakumathu Makuthu Mukamattupulavar, *Rasalullah Peril Suseeda*, Madras, 1887,52, MSB. A work on Rasalullah.

Kannakumathu Makuthu Mukamattupulavar, *Subuhan Maulidu, Rasalullah Maulidu, Ya Seyeed Maulidu Yakutba Maulidu*, Madras, 1887, 92, MP; see also MSB, 1887. A work on saints.

Kannakumathu Makuthu Mukamattupulavar, *Tirumudi Irakkina Hadidu*, Madras, 1887, 40, MP, MSB. A work on the Prophet's hair.

Kannakumathu Makuthu Mukamattupulavar, *Yakutuba*, Madras, 1887, 20, MSB. A work on Mohideen Andavar.

Rasalullah Peril Kaseedah, Madras, 1887, 52, MSB. Verses in Arabic style on Rasalullah.

Kadiru Sahbu V.S., *Jemesa Oliyulla Avarkal Mel Paadiya Pavani Sirappu*, Madras, 1888, 8, MP. A work on saint Jemesa.

Nagore Muhammad Pulavar, *Unjarr Paatu*, Madras, 1888, 17, MSB. A song concerning the Prophet.

Said Mohiadin Pulavar and Sheikul Ahmadi Pulavar, *Navanita Punjam*, Madras, 1888, 176, MP; see also MSB, 1887. Munajat on Rahman and Rasalullah, Pillai Tamizh on Mohideen Antavar and Manikkamalai on the Prophet.

Said Sultan Lebbai, *Olinayakaravatara Cintu*, Madras, 1888, 102, MP; see also MSB. A work on saint Mohideen.

Sheik Muhammad Usuf Labbai Ali, *Shamsul Iman*, Madras, 1888, 296, MP. An account of the Prophet and His creed.

Abdul Wahabu, *Paralu Nama*, Madras, 1889, 14, MSB. A work in praise of Prophet Mohammad.

Kadar Naina Labbay N.V., *Abhushaka Mamalai*, Madras, 1889, 56, MP. A work on one of the Caliphs.

Mahomad Abdul Kadar Pulavar (ed.), *Muhiatin Puranam*, Madras, 1889, 52, MP. A poem on saint Mohideen.

Pacha Pulavar, *Aasiriya Virutham*, Madras, 1890, 8, MSB. In praise of Abdul Razak, a Muslim divine.

Kosu Pulavar, *Tirunakara Kanturi Vala Chindu*, Tinnevely, 1891, 12, MSB. A Kantiru song.

Muhyi al Din Karpudaiyar ibn Sinna Ibrahim, *Nabi-allah Perir Padikam*, Jaffna, 1891, 20, IOL. A lyric in praise of Prophet Mohammad; followed by *Yanai Kadal*, verses in honour of a Muslim devotee.

Marakkayar, M. *Halarat Meeran Sahibu Antavaravargal Karana Charittiram*, Madras, 1892, 144, EFEO. A saintly biography.

Sayed Mahomed Ravutar, *Nervali Vilakkam, Tinmani Muzhakkam*, Madras, 1892, 8, MP. A tract in praise of the Prophet.

Sekati Nayina Pulavar, *Tirumana Katchi.* Madras, 1892, 192, MP, MSB. A work on the Prophet and his marriage with Asia and Maryam.

Aravamurthi U.V., *Halarat Sayeed Kutbu Shahul Hamid Meeran Ghauthu Sultan Kadiru Ganj Savas Sahib Antavar Avarkal Peril Patalkal*, Madras, 1893, 12, MSB. A work on Saint Shahul Hamid.

Pakir Mohideen, *Mukamattin Vazhkai Surukkam*, Madras, 1893, 70, MSB. A brief history of the Prophet.

Abdullah Saib C.K., *Seyedu Pirkai Auliya Peril Paadiya Valinadai Patham*, Kumbakonam, 1894, 15, MSB.

Ahmad ibn Kadir, Muhyi al Din, *Tirunadai Vazhialankaram*, Colombo, 1895, ii, 8, IOL. Poem in praise of Saiyid Ibrahim Auliya.

Muhammad Ghouse Labbai Khalifa Saib Kadir, *Pathkul Misir Pakanasa Kaaviyam*, Madras, 1895, 440, MSB. In praise of Islam.

Muhammad Shamsuddin Sahib, *Tarichir Kappal Cintu*, Tirunelveli, 1895, 11, MSB. Work in praise of the Prophet and others in Kappal Cintu style.

Pavani Pulavar, Palghat (Saiyid Bukhari), *Abd al Rahman Arabi Satakam*, Madras, 1985, 58, IOL. 160 stanzas in praise of Abd al Rahman, a saint buried at Vedarandur, Madura district.

Seikaptul Kadir, S., Tirunelveli Pettai, *Abidinarpudam Aripinarpudam Ennum Tarikathul Auliya*, Madras, 1895, 2nd part, 460, MSB. A saintly work.

Seikaptul Kadir Nayinar, *Chitirakavi Mudaliya Palapatarrirattu*, Madras, 1895, 376, MSB. A work in praise of the Prophet.

Abd al Kadir Nayinar, Sheikh of Kayalpattinam, *Chitra Kavi Mudaliya Pala Padat Tirattu*, Madras, 1896, I, xxxiv, 376, 1 plate, IOL. Poems on Islamic worthies and also Islam.

Meideeno Iyer, R.R., *Mukamattu*, Madras, 1897, 22, MSB. A work on the Prophet.

Ghulam Kadiru Navalar, *Aarippu Nayakam*, Tiruchirapuram, 1896, xxxvii, 336, EFEO. A saintly work.

Muhammad Abd al Kadir, Pulavar, *Kirtanna Tirattu*, Singapore, 1896, 58, IOL. Lyrics addressed to the Prophet and various other Muslim saints.

Muhammad Ghaus, al Shafi'i, al Madrasi, *Nasr al Jawahir*, Madras, 1896, xvi, 319, IOL. The life of Abd al Kadir Jilani, originally composed in Arabic under the title of *Anbar al Mafakhir* and translated into

Hindustani by the author's son, Sibghat Allah and thence into Tamil by Muhammad Madinah Kottari.

Muhammad Meeran Mastan, *Gnana Ratinakaram*, Madras, 1896, 157, MSB. A work in praise of Allah, Prophet Mohammad, etc.

Aruvamurthi U.V., *Tottirapa*, Madras, 1898, 14 MSB. A work in praise of Gnaniyar Sahib Oliyulla.

Meeranayinar Pulavar, K., *Dhyana Manjeri*, Madras, 1898, 22, MSB. A work in praise of Gnaniyar Sahib.

Muhammad Musa Sahipu, *Hidayatul Anam*, Madras, 1898, 693, MSB. A work in praise of the Prophet and Islam.

Mukiyittin Pulavar, *Napinayakam Peril Meygnanar Cintu*, Madras, 1898, 37, MSB. A work on the Prophet.

Seikavtu Qadir, M., *Sheiku Tampi Gnaniyar Sahibu Peril Tottirap Padigam*, Madras, 1898, 10, MSB. A work in praise of Gnaniyar Sahib.

Sheiku Muhiyidin Maluku Mudaliar, *GnaniyarSakiboliyulla Meygnana Tirupadarirrattu* (*Tirukotatru Kalambakam, Tottirappa*), Madras, 1898, MSB. A work on Saint Gnaniyar.

Sultan Mukaiyitin Ravuttar, *Nakur Vazhinataic Vilakka Todar*, Madras, 1898, 18, MSB. A work on a saint of Nagore.

Mukamattu Hamsa Lebbai, *Meygnana Ratnavalankara Kirttanam*, Madras, 1899, 68, MP, MSB. A work in praise of the Prophet and also addressing other religious issues.

Sheik Mohideen Kadiru Meeran, *Meygnana Sakaram*, Madras, 1899, 96, MSB. A work on several saints such as Pettai Oliyulla, Mira Alam.

Kalai Hasanali Pulavarn, *Anukulapunjam*, Madras, 1900, 128, MP; see also MSB. A work in praise of the Prophet and the saints who followed him.

Muthu Mukamattup Pulavar, *Kattu Bawa Sakipu Ayarkal Ammanai*, Devekottai, 1900, 72, MP. A work on Kattu Bawa or saint Syed Muhammad Bava Bahuruddin.

Subbaiah Desigar, B., *Syed Tamim Gnaniyar Itam Venduthal*, Madras, 1900, 40, MSB. Prayers addressed to an Islamic saint.

Syed Abdul Nabi Sahib. *Maksamal Iman Vazhi Iculam*, Udumalpet, 1900, 80, MSB. A work on Muslim Labbais.

Tirumakkap Pallu, Tuticorin, 1900, 54, MSB. A work on the Prophet.

Muhammatu Nakur Muttupulavar, *Mukiyittinacatakam*, Madras, 1901, 32, RMRL. A work on Mukiyittin.

Ghulam Kadar Navalar V., *Kanjul Karamattu*, Madras, 1902, 576, MP. Life of Nagore Miran Sahib Hamid, based on *Kulasatul Karamattu* and *Karana Puranam*.

Sultan Abd ul Qadir Marakayar, *Napikal Pranirusiradiyin Aimbattitrurai*, Madras, 1902, 16, MP. A saintly work in praise of the Prophet.

Sultan Abdul Qadir Marakayar, *Shah Hamid Padigam*, Chidambaram, 1902, 12, MP. A work on Shah Hamid.

Ghulam Kadir Navalar, *Aripunayaga Vacanam*, Madras, 1904, 15, 294, 10, IOL, MP. Life of an Islamic saint.

Khaja Muhaiyadin Ravuttar A.N., *Rahman Malai, Tirunapi Malai, Pettai Nagar Sirappu*, Tirunelveli, 1904, 34, MP. A work in praise of the Prophet and also the Pettai town.

Koca Maraikkayar, Nakur K.M., Karikal, *Pinanku Urcava Tiruvalankarac Cintu*, Penang, 1904, 8, 28, RMRL. A song on a Muslim procession in Penang.

Abdul Khadir Pulavar, *Kattubava Sahib Antavar Karanak Kummi*, Madras, 1905, 24, MP. A work on saint Kattu Bava.

Alim Abdul Khadar Sahib A., *Sir al Salekeen*, *with Noobuzathul Favayid*, Madras, 1906, 240, MP; see also IOL, 1906. Lives of the disciples of the Prophet.

Haji Shaik Muhiyidin Alim Sahib, *Thuhfatul Ahbab Us Hadyatu Oolil Albab*, Nagerkoil, 1906, 232, MP; see also IOL, 1906. A work in praise of the Prophet.

Khali Shah Muhammad Inayatullah Lebbai, *Riyalul Matayih Bi Manakkibissa Lih Ennum Gurustottirabavi*, Madras, 1906, 12, 99, IOL; see also MP. Panegyrics in praise of the Muslim gurus.

Muhammad Jainul Ghouse Pavalar, *Prabandha Malai*, Cuddalore, 1907, MP. Stanzas in praise of the Prophet and Islam.

Pir Muhiyidin Rowtar, *Halaratu Haja Mukiyidin Andavar Peril Padigam*, Madras, 1907, 5, 10, MP. Verses in praise of saint Mukiyidin.

Shah al Hamid ibn Miran Sahib, Melapalayam, Attiyaditteru, *Muhyi al Din Antavargal Kanduri Alankara Rayil Vazhi Nadai Chindu*, Tinneveli, 1907, 12, IOL; see also MP, 1907. Verses on a rail journey to Kanduri; and verses about a local Muslim saint.

Abdul Khadir Ravuttar M.K.M., *Nakur Nayakar Pancharatham*, Madura, 1908, 2, 21, MP. Five stanzas in praise of the Nagore saint.

Abdul Rahim Sahib S., *Vilaclothun Nabi*, Madras, 1908, 16, MP. A work on the Prophet and his value to the world.

Muhammad Nuruddin, *Nurul Kalamennum Musanabi Puranam*, Cuddalore, 1908, 70, MP. The story of Moses in verse according to Islamic traditions.

Shaik Abdul Khadar Ravuttar, *Manjkulam Auliya Peril Padiya Padigam*, Palghat, 1908, 8, MP. Ten stanzas in honour of a Muslim saint.

Sikkandar Maraikkayar M., *Samsuddin Oli Avarkal Peril Padiya Padam*, Tirumandira Nagar, 1908, 6, MP. Stanzas in praise of a certain Samsuddin Oli.

Abdul Azis Marakkayar, *Kurangu Mastan Tirupadigam*, Porayar, 1909, 16, MP. Stanzas in praise of a Muslim teacher.

Khadir Muhaiyuddin Ravuttar N., *Rakshi Mastan Sahib Karanak Kummi*, Dharapuram, 1909, 8, MP, Dance songs and lament songs about the death, burial and ascent to heaven of saint Mastan Sahib.

Mira Levvai A.M.V., *Karuthapakir Avuliyakummi, Part I*, Karungalakudi, 1909, 16, MP. Dance song lamenting the death of saint Karuthapakir.

Muhammad Abdullah Lebbai ibn Muhammad Sulaiman, P., *Kirttana Ranjitam*, Madras, 1909, vi, i, 76, i, IOL. Lyrics in praise of important Muslim personalities and Islam.

Nakurukkani Ravuttar, *Meygnana Manjeri*, Madura, 1909, 6, 37, MP. Stanzas in praise of the Prophet and certain saints and teachers.

Ostamuka Abdul Hamid, *Singara Kirttanai*, Madras, 1909, 8, MP. Devotional songs in praise of the Prophet.

Ahmad Ibrahim Sahib, *Navalankara Manjeri*, Negapatam, 1910, 7, MP. Nine songs in praise of the Prophet.

Abdul Karim Sahib, *Miyanga Tarauga Vazhinadai Karana Alankaracindu, Part I*, Miyangapalli, Tirunelveli, 1910, 8, MP. Ballads and pilgrim songs to be sung on the way to the tomb of a Muslim saint.

Kabilu Muhammad Ravuttar, U.A., *Tiruparangunram Sikkandar Sayubu Oliavarkal Meitu Palasantavazhinadai Alankara Chindu*, Trichinopoly, 1910, 6, 22, MP. Songs in different metres supposed to have been recited by a pilgrim describing to his lady companion, the scenery on the way to the mosque of Sikkandar on the Tiruparangunram hill, near Madura.

Muhammad Ismakil Ravuttar, *Munajattup Padham*, Kiranur, 1910, 22, MP. Stanzas and songs in praise of the Prophet and His teachings.

Naina Muhammad Labbai, Katib, *Amirtha Meygnana Alankara Kirttanam*, Madras, 1910, 38, MP. Songs in praise of the Prophet and some other teachers of Islam.

Naina Muhammad Labbai, Katib, *Rahman Peril Munajattu*, Madras, 1910, 20, MSB. Verses in praise of Rahman.

Saiyad Bawa Rauttar, Khadar Ibrahim Rautar and Nakaya Naikar S.K., *Nalisallallakura Alaikivassalam Avarkal Peril Padankalum, Kalimavin Muzhakam, Part I*, Tr chinopoly, 1910, 2nd edition, Part I, 7: Part II, 1st edition, 7, MP. Songs in praise of a Muslim saint.

Shaik Muhammad Pavalar U.A., *Singai Juhar Prayana Kummi*,

Adiyarkaimangalam, 1910, 26, MP. A dance song describing a voyage to Singapore, with a prayer to the Prophet.

Shaik Nur Pulavar, *Nagore Khadar Auliya peril Padamum Santhana Kootin Sirappum*, Trichinopoly, 1910, 2nd edition, 7, MP. Stanzas in praise of saint Khadar of Nagore.

Sultan Abdul Khadir, *Kunankuti Mastan Sahibavarkalin Meitu Arunokkamalai*, Porayar, 1910, 19, MP. Thirty stanzas and five songs in praise of the saint of Kunankuti.

Varisai Ibrahim, *Kappal Pattu Kodichindu, Alankaram Malaikommi*, Trichinopoly, 1910, 31, MP. Dance songs in different metres in praise of one Magdum Sayyid Ahmed Auliya of Abubeker family in Andakkulam, Trichinopoly.

Fakir Muhammad Shah A.K., *Tiru Muhammadu Nabi Satakam*, Tiruppapuliyur, 1911, 52, MP. A simple didactic poem of a hundred stanzas apostrophising Prophet Mohammad.

Hasan Ali Pulavar, Kalai, (trans.), *Muhyittin Antavarkal Karana Carittiram*, Madras, 1911, 14, 320, IOL. Biography of a saint, translated from Arabic.

Kadar Muhiyuddin Ravuttar, *Cakratpadam*, Tanjore, 1911, 5, MP. Stanzas and songs of prayer to the Prophet.

Muhammad Ibrahim Sahib A.N., *Palamuthumalai Nalampatti Malai*, Palapatti, 1911, 24, MP. Stanzas and songs being prayers addressed to Prophet Mohammad and some saints.

Muhammad Jainul Ghouse Pavalar S., *Muhammadu Salikin Caranakavi*, Cuddalore, 1911, 1, 6, MP. Memorial stanzas relating to one Muhammad Salikin of Cuddalore.

Nur Ismail Sahib S., *Rayil Mastan Sahibu Karana Singara Chindu*, Trichinopoly, 1911, 7, MP. Songs in Kummi style in praise of a Muslim saint known as Mastan, said to have been living near Madras.

Saiyid Imam Sahib, *Nagore Shahul Hamid Andavargal Peril Rayilway Vazhinadai Padam*, Trichinopoly, 1911, 8, MP. Pilgrim songs in Kummi style, descriptive of a journey from Trichinopoly to the mosque built in memory of Shahul Hamid at Nagore.

Saiyid Imam Sahib, *Perinba Navarasa Kirtannamirtam*, Uraiyur (Trichy district), 1911, 1, 15, MP. Songs in popular style in praise of one Mastan, a religious devotee, who lived at Royapuram, Madras, during his last days.

Saiyid Muhammad Alim Sahib, *Munajattu Maligai*, Madras, 1911, 20, MP. Devotional songs in praise of Prophet Mohammad and various saints.

Sheik Abdul Karim Sahib, *Nagore Khadar Auliya Peril Padiya Pukazhchi Kummi*, Vaniyambadi, 1911, 12, MP. Songs in the Kummi style in praise of Khadar Auliya of Nagore.

Sultan Abdul Kadir S.K.M., *Kattu Bava Sahib Avargal Kummipattu*, Kumbakonam, 1911, 14, MP. Kummi songs descriptive of the grand mosque dedicated to Kattu Bava Sahib.

Ibrahim ibn Adham, Sultan of Balkh, *Sultan Ibrahim ibn Adham Udaiya Kissa*, Madras, 1912, 140, IOL; see also MP, 1912. A life of Ibrahim ibn Adham, a famous Muslim saint, edited in Tamil script by M.K. Hasan Ali Pulavar from a work in Arabic characters styled, *Bustan ul Ahkam.*

Muhammad Jainul Ghouse S., *Tirumana Vazhthu Malai*, Cuddalore, 1912, 13, MP. Benecdictory stanzas recited on the occasion of the marriage of one Muhammad Abu Bakr of Cuddalore.

Muhammad Mappilai Lebbai, Sayyid, Keezhakarai, *Nal Imamgal Prabhandam*, Madras, 1912, 8, 364, IOL. An account of the lives and teachings of the four Islamic jurists; edited in Tamil characters by Melapalaiyam M.K. Hasan Ali Pulavar from the original edition in Arabic script, which bore the title, *Marakib ul Mawahib.*

Piccai Pulavar, *Singara Kummi*, Mudukalathur, 1912, 8, MP. Dance songs in praise of a Muslim saint at Nagore.

Saiyid Mashud Ravuttar N., *Mummaniyarapadigam*, Sammandapuram, Rajapalayam, 1912, 4, 20, MP. Stanzas in praise of Allah, Prophet Mohammad, and Abdul Kadir Darbagir, a descendant of the Prophet.

Saiyid Muhammad Alim Sahib S.M., *Kirttanna Maalikai*, Perambur, 1912, 24, MP. Songs in praise of Prophet Mohammad.

Sikandar Rauttar ibn Mira Rauttar, Nagore, *Nagur Shah ul Hamid Andagaiyin Karana Alankara Chindu*, Kolinjambarai, Madras, Pt. I, 112, ii, ii, IOL. Lyrics on the Muslim saint of Nagore, edited by N. Shaikh Abd al Kadir Rauttar.

Abdul Qadir M. (trans.), *Rattina Nayakiyin Tirukalyanam*, Vaniyambadi, 1913, 12, MP. Gives certain facts of the marriage of the daughter of Prophet Mohammad and the lessons to be derived from them.

Abdulla Sahib P., *Vazhinadai Cindu*, Nellikuppam, 1913, 10, MP. Pilgrim songs in ballad style, descriptive of a festival held in honour of a Muslim saint at Panruti.

Alli Maraikkayar, *Munajattu Malai*, Nagore, 1913, 9, IOL, MP. Verses in praise of an Islamic saint.

Muhammad Husain Labbai, K., *Munajat*, Cuddalore, 1913, 14, MP. Stanzas invoking the grace of a famous Muslim saint.

Parimala Tasar, *Cantalabasitiara Cintu*, Madurai, 1913, 36, IOL. Songs in praise of a Muslim saint.

Shah Muhammad Ziya ul Din ibn Muhammad Madar, Kadiri, *Majmu Mu'jizat ul Rasul*, Madras, 1913, 31, 366, IOL, MP. 396 anecdotes and notices on the life and character of Prophet Mohammad.

Shaikh Labbai Sahib, *Muhamaddiya Javali*, Negapatam, 1913, 16, MP. Songs in praise of Prophet Mohammad.

Abd al Kadir, son of Sulapuram Baghdad Sahib, *Fatimah Nayakattin Malai*, Sulapuram, 1914, 27, IOL, MP. A collection of songs on Fatima, the Prophet's daughter; it also contains *Taymakal Pukazhchi* and *Nasayuhullinnissa*.

Abd al Kadir Nayinar, Sheikh of Kayalpattinam, *Nakai Antadi*, 1914, 2, 25, IOL. 101 verses in praise of the Nagore saint, preceded by 11 verses in praise of Muhyi al Din Ardacai.

Adam Khan K., *Singara Kummi*, Nangavalli, 1914, 5, MP. Ballad songs on a saint who lived in Salem village.

Jamalu Muhammad Alim Sahib T.M., *Kalvathu Nayagar Karana Charitram*, Kilakarai, 1914, 78, MP. Gives an account of the life and career of a Muslim saint.

Muhammad Jainul Ghouse Pavalar S., *Thirumana Vazhthu Malai*, Cuddalore, 1914, 12, MP. A garland of benedictory songs relating to the marriage of one Bava Sahib Marakkayar of Cuddalore.

Muhammad Ibrahim Sahib Khadiri A.M., *Marana Vilakkam*, Vellore, 1914, 48, MP. Islamic songs including penitence and devotion to Prophet Mohammad.

Muhammad Muhyi ul Din ibn Ahmad Lebbai, Kayalpattinam, *Shaduli Nayagam*, Jaffna, 1914, xvi, 168, i, IOL. A poem on the life and career of Abu'l Hasan Ali bin Abd Ullah al Shadali, a famous Muslim saint; followed by *Nava Ratna Punjam*, religious poems, edited by Muhammad Sulaiman Lebbai.

Muhammad Qadir Mirin Lebbai, *Kuruvarul Anantak Katei*, Madurai, 1914, 226, IOL. Devotional verses in praise of a Muslim saint.

Neyina Muhammad Labbai E., *Muhammadiya Javalikirtannam*, Tuticorin, 1914, MP. Songs in praise of Prophet Mohammad.

Qasim Pulavar, *Tiruppukazh and Nakaiyantati*, Madras, 1914, 6, 132, 25, IOL, MP. Devotional stanzas in praise of Prophet Mohammad and another in Antati style in praise of the Islamic saint of Nagore.

Shah Muhammad Ziya ul Din Qadiri J., *Sirat ul Faruk*, Madras, 1914, 5, 6, 370, IOL. A biography of the Caliph Umar ibn Khattab, containing translations of *Al Faruk* and parts of *Sirat ul Faruk*.

Shaik Sahib K., *Vicitra Padam*, Madras, 1914, 7, MP. Songs in popular ballad style in praise of Prophet Mohammad.

Sheikh Muhammad Khadar Miran Labbai, *Guruvarurainanda Katchi*, Gudalur, 1914, 226, MP. Stanzas and songs in praise of a Muslim saint.

Sultan Abdul Khadar Maraikkayar C., *Munajatu Sadhakam*, Porto Novo, 1914, 28, MP. One hundred stanzas in praise of Muhuiddin, the eleventh descendant of Prophet Mohammad.

Abdul Kadar Ravutar M.K.M., *Prabandhattirattu*, Madras, 1915, 36, MP. A collection of stanzas in praise of one Seyakuna Muhammad Mira Sahib of Ilayangudi.

Bava Muhaiyudin Pulavar, *Tottirappa Padikam*, Melchevval, Ambasamudiram Taluk, 1915, 8, MP. Stanzas in praise of a Muslim saint named Saiyid Abdul Khadir.

Madar Sahib, Aiyan Pettai, *Mikurasu Nama*, Madras, 1915, 32, IOL; see also MP, 1916. A poem of 234 verses on Prophet Mohammad's ascent to heaven, edited by K. Kann Ahmad Makhdum Muhammad.

Muhammad Abdur Khadar S.M., *Darga Iru Nooravadu Varushatuk Kondattamum Pukari Kanduri Vilakkamum*, Pasippatnam, 1915, 18, MP. Gives the account of the receipts and expenses relating to a feast held in honour of a Muslim saint entombed at Pasippatnam.

Muhammad Bawa Labbai M.P., *Tirukarana Singara Chindu*, Trichinopoly, 1915, 8, MP. Ballad songs descriptive of the life and career of a Muslim saint entombed at Cintamanipatti.

Muhammad Bawa Labbai M.P., *Pattapeyar Ammanai*, Trichinopoly, 1915, 8, MP. Ballad songs embodying the names and titles of the ancestors of a Ravuttar family.

Muhammad Labbai K. (trans.), *Subuhana Maulidu Tarjuma*, Madras, 1915, 64, MP. A Tamil rendering of an Arabic-Tamil work in praise of Prophet Mohammad.

Muhiyddin Ghaus, *Vazhinadai Cindu*, Chidambaram, 1915, 16, MP. Ballad songs descriptive of a pilgrimage to Nagore for the worship of a well-known Muslim saint.

Neyina Muhammad A.P. (of Colombo), *Ilankaiyil nadanda Kalakam Allathu Kolai Alankaram*, Tirumangalam, 1915, 8, IOL. Ballad songs descriptive of the riots in Ceylon.

Saiyid Imam Sahib, *Padanandak Korvai*, Trichinopoly, 1915, 65, MP. A collection of stanzas in praise of Prophet Mohammad.

Shaik Abdul Alim, Moulana Moulvi, *Minajumalai Vacana Kaviyam*,

Madras, 1915, Part I, 79, MP. A prose rendering of a metrical work in Tamil, describing the ascension to heaven of Prophet Mohammad.

Sultan Abd al Khadir M.C., *Karaiyantati*, Porayar, 1915, 19, IOL; see also MP, 1915. A centum of stanzas in the Antati style of metrical composition, in praise of a Muslim saint of Karikal.

Abdul Khader A.M., *Pukalananda Kirtannam*, Nagore, 1916, 6, MP. Songs set to various tunes in praise of the Muslim saint, Shahul Hamid of Nagore.

Ahmad P. Muhammad Sahib P.M., *Arivu Malai*, Valangaiman, 1916, 16, MP. Ballad songs descriptive of the various saints and Islam.

Cinnappa Ravuttar, *Nondi Chindu*, Pallapatti, 1916, 8, MP. Ballad songs in praise of one Abdul Karim Sahib at Aravakurichi.

Farid al-din Attar, *Takriyathal Asaiya pi Ashiratul Auliya*, Madras, 1916, 268, IOL; see also MP, 1916. A rendering of the Tazkirah al-auliya by S. Muhammad Ibrahim Alim Sahib; Biographical sketches of certain saints.

Kannagamudu Mahudu Muhammad, *Kasim Malaiyum Imam Kasim Pataipporum*, Madras, 1916, 22, MP. A poem in praise of Prophet Mohammad and another poem describing the holy expeditions of a Muslim king named Kasim.

Malik, M.A., *Mahan Muhammat Napi Avarkalin Upatesa Ratnam*, Madras, 1916, vi, 128, IOL. Teachings of Prophet Mohammad.

Malik M.M., *Upadesaratnam*, Madras, Burma, 1916, 141, MP. Gives the teachings of Prophet Mohammad, with an account of his life.

Mastan Sahib, Muhammad Shah S., *Meygnana Vikasitak Kirtannai*, Madras, 1916, 7, 95, IOL. Songs in praise of Muslim saints.

Mohiuddin Sahib, *Meygnana Arpuda Munajattu Kirtannaiyum Kunangudi Padigamum*, Tinnevely, 1916, 32, MP. A collection of devotional songs to certain Muslim saints.

Muhammad Mira Ravuttar A.M.S., *Alankara Pathankal*, Madura, 1916, 16, MP. Songs in the popular style in praise of a Muslim saint entombed at Sintahattope.

Muhammad Ravuttar M.H., *Madinapuri Malai*, Bodinayakannur, 1916, 11, MP. A garland of stanzas in praise of Prophet Mohammad.

Muhammad Shah Mastan Sahib S., *Meygnana Vikacita Kiratnai*, Madras, 1916, 92, MP. A garland of songs in praise of various Muslim saints.

Muhammadmiyya Pulavar, *Gnanapalapadal*, Sirttandumanagaram, 1916, 7, MP. Devotional stanzas addressed to Prophet Mohammad and certain other Muslim saints.

Shaik Abdul Khader M.K., *Asmavur Rahmaniyya*, Madras, 1916, 18, MP. A garland of a hundred stanzas in praise of Allah.

Sikkandar Ravuttar ibn Mira Ravuttar, Nagore, *Karanavalankara Cindu*, Kolinjamparai, 1916, Part I, 118, MP; see also IOL. Ballad songs descriptive of a well-known Muslim saint of Nagore.

Sulaiman Kadiri Sahib (S. Bawa), *Karana Munajattu Malai*, Madura, 1916, 8, MP. Devotional stanzas and songs addressed to a Muslim saint entombed on a hill near Madura.

Sultan Marakayar, *Navinalankara Javali*, Nagore, 1916, 7, MP. Songs in popular style in praise of the Nagore saint.

Abd al Qadir, Amur Valaibava (trans.), *Tamimul Ancari Avarkalin Kissa*, Madras, 1917, 40, MP; see also IOL. An account of a legendary Muslim saint, compiled from Arabic and Persian sources.

Abdul Hamid Ravuttar A.C., *Idé Miladi Nabaviyya*, Kuttanallur, 1917, 8, MP. A work on the celebration of the birthday of the Prophet.

Alim Sahir Sahib E.A., *Yanabiyumalaiyum Yarappumelai Munajattum*, Trichinopoly, 1917, 31, MP. Two collections of verses—one addressed to the Prophet and another to Allah.

Bava Kasim Vaidyar, *Napiulla Manodu Peciya Karankathai*, Madras, 1917, 32, MP. A work describing the incident in the life of the Prophet relating to the deer.

Miran Sahib P.S., *Sangita Kirttana Manjeri*, Madras, 1917, 20, MP. Songs in praise of Allah, the Prophet and some saints.

Muhammad Hanifa P.S.M., *Arulutaiyavanandam*, Melapalayam, 1917, 42, MP. A collection of devotional verses in praise of different saints.

Saiyid Iman Pulavar, *Pukazh Alankara Chindu*, Trichinopoly, 1917, 9, MP. Ballad songs and verses in praise of the proprietor of a small grinding mill at Gandarvakottai.

Saiyid Muhammad Alim Pulavar S.M., *Kirttana Malikai*, Madras, 1917, 3rd edition, 24, MP. Devotional songs in praise of the Prophet and some saints.

Saiyid Muhammad Alim Pulavar, *Madanandamalikai*, Madras, 1917, 2nd edition, 24, MP. Devotional songs in praise of the Prophet and some saints.

Shahul Hamid, *Tottira Munajattu*, Madras, 1917, 16, MP. Verses in praise of a Muslim saint.

Shaik Lebbai, Kayalpattinam, *Tamim Ansari Malai*, Madras, 1917, 80, IOL. A poem of 880 verses on the life of Tamim Ansari, a Muslim saint.

Shaik Miran Mohiuddin (publ.), *Khadija Nayaki Tirumana Vazhthu*,

Madras, 1917, 48, IOL; see also MP, 1917. Verses dealing with the wife of the Prophet.

Shaik Sayyid Muhammad Alim Sahib A.S.M., *Tottiramunajattu*, Kovilur, 1917, 8, MP. Prayers in honour of a Muslim lady saint of Tirunelveli.

Miran Sahib ibn Shah ul Hamid, Melapalayam, *Rasul Nayagam Pillaitamizh Ennum Pugazh Udaya Punjam*, Madras, 1918, iv, 66, IOL; see also MP, 1918. A poem in pillai tamizh style on Prophet Mohammad, followed by verses on other Muslim saints, edited by Mel Chevval Bava Muhyi al Din.

Mohiuddin Abdu Khadar Pulavar, *Yusuppiyya Malai*, Negapatam, 1918, 26, MP. A garland of verses on saint Yusuf of Nagore.

Muhammad Ismahil K.P.M., *Pathima Nayakiyin Pukazh*, Tuticorin, 1918, 8, MP. Songs in praise of Fathima, the daughter of the Prophet.

Muhiuddin Pakhir Pulavar, *Karanakkummi*, Tiruvalur, 1918, 24, MP. Kummi songs in praise of saint Sheik Dawood Ali worshipped at Jambuvanavar.

Muhiuddin Sahib (Alimsa Haja), *Tiruppugal Munajattupa*, Tuticorin, 1918, 12, MP. Prayer verses in the pilgrim song style on a Khaja Alauddin as worshipped at Papavurand Adiramapatnam.

Pakkir Mastan E.S., *Keertha Manjeri*, Negapatam, 1918, 26, MP. A work in praise of the Prophet.

Siniyava Ravuttar S.A., *Valinadai Chindu*, Madura, 1918, 9, MP. Songs in praise of the Muslim saint of Erupadi.

Sultan Maraikayar M.A., *Tirupukazhpamalikai*, Negapatam, 1918, 26, MP. A work in praise of several Muslim saints.

Abdul A. Maraikkayar M.V., *Tottiramanjeri*, Chidambaram, 1919, 18, MP. A work in praise of certain Muslim saints.

Abdul Aziz Maraikkayar M.V., *Tiruneri Vanakkam*, Chidambaram, 1919, 2, MP. A collection of verses in praise of the Prophet.

Hasan Ali Pulavar, Kalai, *Puvadic Cintu*, Madras, 1919, 44, IOL. Popular devotional songs in praise of Prophet Mohammad and Islamic saints.

Ismayil Ravuttar V.K.P.M., *Kirttanai Kothu*, Tiruvalur, 1919, 15, MP. Songs in praise of the Prophet and also of the Muslim saints of Nagapattinam.

Khadar Mohiuddin Ravuttar, *Navurar Padigam*, Chidambaram, 1919, 8, MP. Ballad on a Muslim saint.

Khadar Mohiuddin Ravuttar, *Nankumantri Kummi Pattu*, Chidambaram, 1919, 2nd revised edition, 8, MP. A work describing how four travellers were employed as ministers by a king.

Khaja Mohiuddin Alim Sahib, *Majmo-i-Bahar i-Gulchan Ksardi*, Madras, 1919, 64, MP. Verses in different metres in praise of the Prophet.

Muhammad Hanif K.S.K., *Alankara Chindu*, Pallapatti, 1919, 12, MP. A ballad on one Abdul Khadar of Aravakurichi.

Muhammad Jeynul Ghouse Pavalar S., *Tirukalyanavaltu*, Tiruppapuliyur, 1919, 8, MP; see also MP, 1920. Wedding benedictions relating to a Muslim marriage.

Muhayuddin Piccai K., *Majlisul Hulamé Mahatva Muttaram*, Kumbakonam, 1919, 8, MP. A work on the greatness of saint Majlisul.

Muhiuddin Abdul Khadiri Pulavar M.A., *Sangita Kirttana Malikai*, Negapatam, 1919, 8, MP. Devotional songs in praise of various Muslim saints.

Sayyid Muhammad Magdum Alim Sahib K., *Salavattu Paittu*, Tiruppur, 1919, 20, MP. A work in praise of the Prophet.

Abbas Das S.A., *Kirttana Malikai*, Negapatam, 1920, 8, MP. Songs in praise of the Prophet and saint Shahul Hamid of Nagore.

Abd al Kadir, D.K., *Cinkara Vazhinataic Cintu*, Rangoon, 1920, 111, 17, IOL. Verses in praise of a local Muslim personality.

Abdulla Sahib F.M., *Baktiralat Kirttanam*, Salem, 1920, 20, MP. Devotional songs in praise of the Prophet.

Hussain Sahib M.S. and Ahmadibrahim Muhammad P., *Alkanjil Akbar Bimanagibi Babayé Nathar*, Trichinopoly, 1920, 96, MP. An account of the life of saint Nathar of Trichinopoly.

Hussain Sharif, M.S. Ahmad Ibn Muhammad, *Alkanjil Akpar Pi Manakapi Pepeye Nathar*, Trichinopoly, 1920, 95, IOL. An account of a Muslim worthy.

Kaja Muhammad Alim Sahib P., *Pailussalam Pisiratti Alaihissalam*, Madras, 1920, 48, MP. An account of Saiyidina Abdul Abbas.

Katirvel Pillai, K.V., *Nakur Sakul Hamid Oli Antavar Tirupukazh Cintu*, Madras, 1920, 19, IOL. Popular verses in praise of an Islamic saint.

Khadar Mohiuddin Ravuttar, *Mauna Sikamani Padigam*, Ambasamudram, 1920, 16, MP. Devotional verses in praise of the Silent Saint.

Miran Sahib Pulavar, *Pathima Nayakam Pillait Tamizh*, Tirunelveli, 1920, 60, MP. Verses in pillai tamizh in praise of Fathima.

Muhammad al Kancavi, Kwajah, P., *Mu'inuttin Antavargal Karana Carittiram*, Tiruvellore, 1920, 95, IOL. A life of the Sufi, Muin al Din Chisthi, compiled from Urdu and Persian sources.

Muhammad Alim Sahib, P. Kwajah of Kanjipuram, *Faiz ul Salam Pi Sirati Kiluru*, Madras, 1920, 48, IOL. A life of he legendary saint Tchizr (Abu'l Abbas ibn Malkan).

Muhammad Kasim, *Vazhinadaialankara Chindu*, Dindigul, 1920, 10, MP. Pilgrim songs descriptive of a journey to Begampur (Dindigul), sacred to Muhaiyuddin, a Muslim saint.

Muhammad Muhaiyadin Sahib S., *Hindul Voli Atayur Rasul Kaja Muyinuddin Jisti Andavargal Karana Charittiram*, Trivellore, 1920, 95, MP. A work on the Muslim saint, Rasul Khaja.

Srinivasa Ayyankar, C.R., *Mahamat Napi*, Madras, 1920, 56, RMRL. A work on he Prophet.

C: Islamic Doctrines, Rituals, Law, and Culture

Qadir muhy al Din K.M., *Muhammadi Samaya Vilakkam*, Madras, 1851, 60, IOL; Re-edition, Madras, 1876, 45, IOL. An exposition of the Islamic doctrine.

V. Rajagopala Achariar (trans.), *Mahamaddiya la Surukkam*, Madras, 1857, 42, IOL; Re-edition, Madras, 1862, 51, IOL; Re-edition, Madras, 1869, 51, IOL. A rendering from the English of a manual on Muslim law by K. Satakopa Acharyar.

Valai Bava Sahib, Amur, *Tozhugai Hakikat Vilakkam*, Madras, 1862, 44, IOL. An adaptation of the *Hakihat al Sa'lat* of Moulavi Abd Allah; an exposition of how to conduct worship, what prayers to recite, etc.

Samu Nayina, Kayalpattinam, *Thakka Karuthendru Vazhangukinra Salathul Arukaan Malai*, Madras, 1867, 97, MSB. A work on Islamic principles.

Peer Muhammad, Tarkalai, *Mukamatiya Matatai Patriya Uraiyadal*, Madras, 1869, MSB; 2nd edition, Madras, 1871, MSB; 3rd edition, Madras, 1872, MSB. A work on Islam.

Vanna Kalanjiya Pulavar, *Teen Vilakamenkinra Puranam*, Madras, 1869, 1714, MSB. A work on Islamic principles and customs.

Muhammad ibn Ibrahim Lebbai, *Tarikattul Iculam*, Madras, 1870, 71, IOL; a.e., Madras, 1874, 70, IOL. An exposition of Islamic religion.

Munshi Ghulam Ali, Arkadu, *Viveka Vilakkam*, Madras, 1870, 44, MSB, IOL. Translated from Hindi into Tamil; contains teachings on Islam.

Muhammad Husain Pulavar, *Pen Putti Malai*, Madras, 1871, 20, IOL; Madras, 1875, a.e., MSB; Madras, 1881, a.e., MSB; Madras, 1883, a.e., MSB; Madras, 1888, a.e., MSB. Ethical verses for women.

Samu Nayina Labbai, *Arukkaan Malai*, Madras, 1871, 127, MP; Madras, 1873, a.e., MSB.

Sayed Mahomed Labbai, *Tarikathul Islam*, Madras, 1871, 73, MP; see also MP, 1874. Muslim work on religious duties and ceremonies.

Sheik Esap Labbai, *Iculam Mata Vilakkam*, Madras, 1871, 90, MSB. A work on Islam.

Kanakkumadu Mahumadu Pulavar, *Tirumani Malai*, Madras, 1873, 224, MP. A work on Islam.

Abd al Qadir Nayinar Lebbai, Kayalpattinam, *Cariattu Malai*, Madras, 1874, 21, IOL; Re-edition, Madras, 1878, 23, IOl. Verses on religious duties.

Abdul Khader Sahib, *Kipayat Isulam*, Madras, 1874, 24, MP; Madras, 1887, a.e., 20, MP. A tract on Islam and the duties of a Muslim.

Abdul Khader Sahib, *Sakkaratu Nama*, Madras, 1874, 38, MSB. Burial prayers.

Condalagan Pulavar, *Paluluna Sukhapi Pulavar*, Madras, 1874, 2nd edition, 43, MP. A poem on the successors of the Prophet.

Kattanai Seikoliyulla, *Gnana Venba*, Madras, 1874, 103, MSB. A work on Islamic principles.

Kader Mohideen Pulavar, *Kiyamattu Nal Utaiya Vicalam*, Madras, 1874, 70, IOL. A Moslem religious treatise.

Khadir Maideen Sahib, *Mukamattu Samaya Vilakkam*, Madras, 1874, 46, MP, MSB. A work on Islamic doctrines.

Malik Kisap Pulavar, *Paralu Vilakkam*, Madras, 1874, 20, MP; see also MSB. A work on Islamic principles.

Muhammad Husain Pavalar, *Pen Putti Malai*, Re-edition, 1874, 16, IOL; see also MP, 1875. Ethical verses of advice to women.

Muhammad Pulavar, *Pannirendu Malai*, Madras, 1874, 40, MP. Verses on Islamic doctrines.

Mukamattusain Pulavar C., *Taukitu Malai* (*Napiyulla Peril Karanak Kummi, Padham, Salavattu Paatu, Padham*), Madras, 1874, 48, MP; see also IOL, 1874, Madras, 1876, a.e., 20, IOL; Madras, 1879, a.e., MSB. A work on the tenets of Islam and the Prophet.

Naina Muhammad Pulavar, *Mungrin Malai*, Madras, 1874, 12, MP; see also MSB, 1874. A work on Islam.

Samu Nainar Labbai, *Nenjarivu Malai*, Madras, 1874, 8, IOL, MP. Verses on the tenets of Islam.

Seikabdul Qadir, Tenkasi, *Parulu Vilakkam*, Madras, 1874, 20, MSB. A work on Islamic ethics.

Seiku Aptul Kadir, *Tavatutu Katitu Visalam*, Madras, 1874, MSB· Madras, 1884, a.e., MSB. A religious dialogue.

Seyed Muhammad Lebbai, *Sarurul Musalimin*, Madras, 1874, 24, MP. A work on Islamic ethics and principles.

Sultan Sahib of Nagore, *Tarajattu Malai*, Madras, 1874, 21, IOL, MP; Madras, 1882, a.e., MSB. A work on Islamic principles.

Syed Abu Bakr Pulavar, *Apayé Situl Pustami*, Madras, 1874, 20, IOL, MP. An exposition of parts of the Quran and other sacred works.

Syed Abdul Khader, *Sariathu Malai*, Madras, 1874, 22, 3rd edition, MSB. On Islamic ethics and principles.

Allapichai Pulavar, *Kifayattul Islam*, Madras, 1875, 20, MP. A catechism of Islam.

Allapichai Pulavar, *Salavattu Pattu*, Madras, 1875, 20, MP. A variety of Tamil songs and verses usually recited on marriage ceremonies by Muslim women.

Alla Pichai Pulavar, *Suka Pullimanenru Vazhanga Ninra Imanutaiya Payankal*, Madras, 1875, 1211, MSB. A work explaining kalima, etc.

Madar Sahib Pulavar, Ayyampettai, *Parulu Malai*, Madras, 1875, a.e., 16, MP; Madras, 1879, MSB; Madras, 1881, a.e., MSB. A work on Islamic prayers and ethics.

Pir Muhammad Sahib, Tarkalai, *Gnanamani Malai*, Madras, 1875, 84, MP. A poem on the truth of Islam.

Pir Muhammad Tarkalai, *Maaripattu Malai*, Madras, 1875, 80, IOL; see also MP, 4th edition, 1875. A metrical treatise on Islamic culture.

Samu Naina, *Adabu Malai (or Jathi Ozhungana Adabu Malai)*, Madras, 1875, MSB; see also Madras, 1875, 80, MP. Verses on the religious practices of the Muslims.

Satakatulla, R., Kayarpattinam, *Tozhugai Adaivu*, Madras, 1875, 40, MP; Madras, 1878, 40, MP; Madras, 1884, a.e., MSB. A work on Muslim prayer and ceremonies.

Malik Kisap Pulavar, *Tozhugai Nama*, Madras, 1876, 20, MP; Madras, 1878, 16, MP; Madras, 1888, a.e., MSB. A work on praying, etc.

Marakkaya Pulavar, *Ennei Chindu*, Markapuram, 1876, 129, MSB. On an Islamic social event.

Meideeno Iyer R.R., *Mukamathiya Mathathai Patriya Uraiyadal*, Madras, 1876, 4th edition, 14, MSB. A work on Islam.

Muhammad Ibrahim, *Kipayattul Islam*, Madras, 1876, 20, MP. A collection of directions extracted from older works on the duties of a Muslim.

Muhammad Mir Hussain Rowther alias Biramahamed Saib, *Bismal Kuram*, Madras, 1876, 44, MP; Madras, 1878, a.e., 44, MP. A tract on Islam and the Prophet.

Seikaptul Kadir Nayinar, *Innicai* (*Tozhugai Nama or Sorkka Niti*), Markapuram, 1876, 34, MSB. A work on praying, for Islamic children.

Sultan, Nakar, A., *Tarajattu Malai*, Madras, 1876, 47, IOL. A religious poem.

Malikisa Pulavar, *Tozhugai Nama*, Madras, 1877, 86, MSB. A work on worship.

Seiku Avdu Qadir, S., Pettai, *Ahkamul Islam*, Tirunelveli, 1877, 81, MSB. A work on praying.

Abdul Khadar Sahib, *Sorka Niti*, Madras, 1878, 20, MP, MSB. Compilation of three religious tracts, stressing on belief in God.

Abdul Kadar Sahib, *Nasihattu Nama*, Madras, 1878, 30, MP. A Tamil tract containing the rules of conduct to be learnt and followed by Muslims.

Alli Maraikayar, *Nenjarivuruthal*, Madras, 1878, 5, MSB. Advice to Muslims.

Ligibir Muhammad, *Teettaru Malai*, Madras, 1878, 2nd edition, 32, MP; see also MSB, 1877. A work on Islamic principles and the Prophet.

Mastan Sahib, *Parulu Malai*, Madras, 1878, 16, MP. Verses containing directions for reading and writing the Muslim scriptural texts.

Pir Muhammad Sahib, *Gnanamani Malai*, Madras, 1878, 36, MP. A work intended to teach the Muslim doctrine.

Abdul Kadir, *Nasihatu Nama*, Madras, 1879, 30, MSB; Madras, 1886, a.e., 31, MSB. A work on Islamic ethics.

Samu Naina, *Salatul Arukaan Malai*, Madras, 1879, 138, MP, MSB. A garland of verses about the proper behaviour of true Muslims.

Seiku Yucupu, *Riyalunisvan*, Madras, 1879, 2nd edition, 192, MP, MSB. A work on Islamic principles and worship, translated from Hindi.

Sheik Abdul Khadar, *Tavatudu Kadidu Vislam*, Madras, 1879, 174, MP. A catechism of Islam.

Author unknown, *Kifayat ul Islam*, Madras, 1880, 46, MP. An instructive tract on the duties of life, illustrated by stories.

Kadiru Mukiyittin Pulavar, *Pancharattina Volivattam*, Madras, 1880, 76, MP, MSB; Madras, 1882, a.e., 76, MP, MSB. A work on the five precepts of Islam such as prayer and fasting.

Muhammad Usaini Pulavar, *Pen Butti Malai*, Madras, 1880, 16, MP; see also MP, 1881, 1883. A work of advice to Muslim women.

Kannaku Madu Muhammad Pulavar, *Kuramadu*, Madras, 1882, 72, MP. A work on the precepts of religion.

Minna Nurudin Pulavar, *Osith Ponnarya Malai*, Madras, 1882, 96, MP. The dying injunctions and the prophesies of the Prophet.

Muhammad Muttu Ravuttar, *Istakhubar*, Madras, 1882, 8, MP. A prayer asking pardon for sin.

Saiyed Mahomed Labbay, *Tarikkatul Islam*, Madras, 1883, 72, MP. A religious work.

Shaik Muhammad Labbai Alim, *Ratna Vilasam Nasihattulasam*, Madras, 1883, 152, MP; Madras, 1885, a.e., 156, MP. A work on meritorious devotion and the benefits to be derived from fastings, prayers, pilgrimages, almsgiving, etc.

Kannakumathu Makuthu Mukamattupulavar, *Nasihatul Islam Hanafiyya*, Madras, 1884, 80, MSB. A work on praying.

Muhammad Abdul Khader Husain Alim Sahib, *Mukamatu Mathathai Patriya Sambashanai*, Madras, 1884, 5th edition, 14, MSB. A work on Islam.

Moulana Sheik Mohadin, *Daravul Arsh*, Madras, 1885, 16, MP. Prayers with translations and commentaries in a mixed dialect of Arabic and Tamil.

Shaik Muhammad Usuf Sahib, *Arkanal Islam*, Madras, 1885, 64, MP. A work on Islam, with a commentary in a mixed dialect of Arabic and Tamil.

Shaik Muhammad Yusuf Sahib, *Bakiat-ul Fula Adabun Nika*, Madras, 1885, 532, MP. A tract containing marriage rules with Arabic interpolations.

Sheik Miran Sahib, *Farayazul Mominin*, Madras, 1885, 80, MP; Madras, 1889, 64, a.e., lith., MP. A work containing religious directions in a mixed dialect of Arabic and Tamil.

Abdul Khadar Sahib (trans.), *Nasihat Nama*, Madras, 1886, 32, MP. Rules of conduct for daily life.

Samu Nayina Seikabtul Kadir, Kilakarai, *Tozhugai Malai* (*Hidayat Innicai, Tozhugai Nama*), Madras, 1886, MSB. A work on prayer.

Sheiku Habipu Mukamattu, *Misbahul Irbanennum Gnanodaya Deepavalankaram*, Coimbatore, 1886, 56, MSB. A work asking Muslims to follow the Prophet's behaviour.

Haja Mugaideen Sahib C., *Resululla Munajatum, Resululla Kummiyum*, Madras, 1887, 8, MSB. A work on Islam.

Mahomed Mohadin Labbai Alim, *Nifaisul Kalayad*, Madras, 1887, 116, MP. A tract in prose on the religious beliefs of Muslims.

Mahomed Pulavar C.M., *Subuhana Moiludu or Rasululla Moiludu*. Madras, 1887, 80, MP. A religious work.

Muhammad Labbai Alim Haji Sahib, *Musal Iman Konda Karanam*, Madras, a.e., 1887, 12, MP. A work for Muslims.

Seiku Aptul Katiru, S., *Nervazhi Vilakkam Teenmani Muzhakam*, Madras, 1887, 400, MP, MSB. A work on Islam.

Abdul Vahab Sahib V., *Mufitatul Islam*, Madras, 1888, 3rd edition, 38, MP. A work containing the articles of belief.

Akamadu Masudi, *Tavuba Malai*, Madras, 1888, 396, MSB. A work on Islamic ethics.

Akamadu Makudi, *Makkal Vasakam*, Madras, 1888, 24, MSB. A work on Islam.

Muhammad Yusuf ibn Kadir Ahmad, Ammapattanam, *Shams al Iman*, Madras, 1888, xii, 296, iv, IOL. An elementary work on the Muslim faith.

Samu Nayina, *Toshugai Malai* (*Hidayatinnicai, Tozhugai nama*), Madras, 1888, 96, MSB. A work on praying.

Seiku Mukamattu, *Hidayataul Muslimin*, Madras, 1888, 90, MSB. A work in praise of praying.

Seiku Mukamattu, *Kipayattul Anam*, Madras, 1888, 64, MSB. A work on Islamic principles.

Shahu Mukamattu Abdul Kadiru Jainuddin, *Murid Vilakkamenum Iratinasurukkam*, Madras, 1888, 32, MP, MSB. A work on Islamic ethics.

Alla Pichai, *Unmaiyana Islam*, Madras, 1889, 24, MSB. A work on true Islam.

Kader Naina Labbai, *Ennei Chindu*, Madras, 1889, 12, MSB. A work for the youth.

Habilu Mukamattibrahim Labbai S., *Pattukul Mannan*, Madras, 1889, 88, MP, MSB. A work on prayer and Allah.

Kadar Naina Labbay N.V., *Sorka Niti*, Madras, 1889, 12, MP. Some instructive verses.

Sheik Mahomed Labbai Alim Sahib, *Tuttattul Anam*, Madras, 1889, 16, MP, MSB. A work on Islam.

Usuf Labbay Ali, *Shamsul Iman*, Madras, 1889, 448, MP. A mixture of Arabic and Tamil prose on religious beliefs and practice.

Katirasana Maraikkayar, *Sira Napiavatara Patalam*, Madras, 1890, 2, 306, EFEO. A sort of commentary on the Quran.

Muhammad Abdul Khader Husain Alim Sahib, *Tarulul Islam Marka Ratna Thulakkam*, Madras, 1890, 64, MP; see also MSB, 1890. A lullaby tract showing the way to Paradise.

Sheik Mahomed Labbai Alim Sahib, *Jawahirul Islam*, Madras, 1890, 16, MP. A work on Islam.

Kadiru Mukiyittin Pulavar, *Neethi Neriananta Kalipum Sila—Patankalum*, Madras, 1891, MSB. Teachings for Muslims.

Kannakumadu Makudu Muhammad Pulavar, *Peria Kasusulanbia*, Madras, 1891, 956, MP. A prose account of the Prophet and his saints.

Hakim Muhammad Abdulla Sahib B., *Shamsul Islam*, Madras, 1892, 134, MP. A work on Islam.

Makhdum Muhammad ibn Makhdum Pillai, Kann Ahmad, son of Kanakumatu Makutum Pillai of Kayalpattinam, *Din Neri Vilakkam Vacana Kaviyam*, Madras, 1892, vii, 412, IOL, MP. An exposition of the Islamic religion.

Mahomed Abdul Khadar Ravuttar E., *Kalyana Valtu etc.*, Coimbatore, 1892, 8, MP. Muslim songs, intended for recitation on marriage occasions.

Muhammad Kannu, Perumal Durai Vaidyam, A., *Khamsina Faridah Malai*, Colombo, 1892, 14, IOL. A metrical tract upon 50 essential observances of Islam.

Mukamattu Abdullah Mo.Thu., *Akithaye Iculam Ennum Shamsul Iculam*, Madras, 1892, 42, 93, MSB. A work on Islam.

Sahib Durai Hameed of Galle, *Gnana Pen Kummi*, Galle, 1892, IOL. A work on women.

Habib Muhammad ibn Naina Muhammad, Haji Alim Sahib, *Gnanadipa Samkaram*, Colombo, 1893, 34, IOL. A tract on the doctrines of Islam.

Syed Peer Muhammad Alim Haji Sha Khadir, *Nakashékavalikiyamat Almadimahasha Allatu Iruthi Teerpu Nalin Patam*, Madras, 1893, MSB. A work on the Last Judgment.

Syed Lebbai Alim Sahib, *Vatti Vilakku*, Madras, 1894, 32, MSB. A work against interest.

Khatib Muhammad Yasin Sahib, *Larurul Muslimin*, Madras, 1897, 88, MSB. A work for Muslims for use in daily life.

Meideeno Iyer R.R., *Mukamathiyarkalukana Vyasangal, Mudal Varisai, Thozhugai*, Madras, 1897, 28, MSB. A work on praying.

Nayina Marakkayar S., *Sorka Malai*, Chidambaram, 1897, 15, MSB. A work on Paradise according to Islam.

Turab Muhammad Hussain, *Tozhugai Ranjita Alankaram*, Madras, 1897, 1st part, 48, MSB; Madras, 1897, 2nd part, 1897, 72, MSB. A work on praying.

Valai Bawa Sahib, Pettai Amur, *Tozhugai Sirappu*, Madras, 1897, 31, MSB. A work on the greatness of prayer.

Abd al Kadir, Moulana Moulavi, Sahib Alim of Tinnevely Pettai, *Iman*

Unmai Islam Nanmai (*Hakikat al Islam*), Madras, 1898, 174, IOL. A treatise on the principles of Islam.

Abdul Wahab (publ.), *Makripathul Avkathu*, Madras, 1898, 29, MSB. A work determining the prayer time.

Muhyi al Din Maluk Mudaliyar, Kottaru, the younger (Tambi Naniyar Sahib), *Meygnana Vilakkam*, Madras, 1898, ii, 104, IOL. A poem on Islamic doctrine, with some verses by other writers, edited by Naniyar Saiyid Taba Lebbai and K.M. Karuppaiya Pavalar.

Pavul Aiyar, *Islam Markam*, Madras, 1898, 226, MSB. A work on Islamic principles, translated from English.

Seiku Aptul Katiru, *Imanunmai Iculatanmai Ennum Hakikathul Islam*, Madras, 1898, MSB. A work on Islam.

Muhammad Meeran, *Nasihatunnissa Ennum Tokaiyar Upadesam*, Tirunelveli, 1899, 64, MP. Advice to women.

Muhammad Hamsa Lebbai, Kuruvithurai, *Kappar Chindu*, Madras, 1899, 3, MSB. On Prayers.

Sheik Abdul Khadar Alim Sahib S., *Ahkhamul Islam*, Madras, 1899, 70, MP, MSB. A work on the precepts and the faith of Islam.

Valai Haji Abdul Vahab Sahib (ed.), *Faraz Nama and Munajat Nama*, Ambur, 1899, 16, MP. A work consisting of religious precepts, hymns and prayers for the followers of Islam.

Valai Abdul Vahab Sahib, *Paralu Nama and Munajattu Nama*, Madras, 1899, 24, MP. Rules for divine service with some prayers and hymns.

Abdul Wahab Sahib, *Manap Pen Kummi*, Madras, 1900, 14, MSB. Duties of single women.

Saiyed Abdul Nabi Sahib, *Maksamal Iman Vazhi Islam*, Madras, 1900, 80, MP. A work on the Islamic faith.

Shaik Mohidin Khader Miran Khadiri Yuljisti Kalipa Sahib Marakkayar, *Meygnana Sakaram*, Madras, 1900, 96, MP. 'The Sea of True Knowledge' is the title of this poem of instructive verses for Muslims.

Abdul Wahab ibn Muhammad Hadi, al Aturi, *Asrar al Salavat, ala Khair-ul-Bariyat*, Madras, 1901, xxiv, 424, IOL; see also MP, 1901. On prayers for Muslims.

Muhammad Ibrahim ibn Adb al Ghani, Melvisharam, Kadaikkara, *Talkin Fi Muhummut al Din li Aulad al Muslimin*, Madras, 1901, xxiv, 70, IOL. An elementary handbook of Muslim doctrine, edited by Kann Ahmad Makhdum Muhammad.

Muhyi al Din Sultan Pillai, *Irshad al Ibad*, Madras, 1901, viii, 152, IOL. A treatise on Islamic faith.

Sam Shihab al Din ibn Sulaiman, Kayalpattinam, *Mazhar al Ahkam*

(*Tozhugai Malai*), Madras, 1901, Pt. 1, ii, 78, IOL. A series of poems summarising various heads of Muslim doctrine, the first being titled, *Tozhugai Malai.*

Samu Nayina Labbai Halim, *Malukarul Ahkam Tolukai Malai,* etc., Madras, 1901, 84, MP, MSB. A work on worship and praying.

Moulana Moulvi Muhammad Musa Sahib, *Tozhupavarkalukku Nalmarayam*, Madras, 1902, 16, MP. A work meant for worshippers.

Mohammad Ibrahim Sahib, *Tanbihul Anam,* Madras, 1903, 216 MSB. On prayers, death, etc.

Muhiuddin Sultan Pillai Alim Sahib, *Nasihattul Islam Shafiyiyya*, Madras, 1903, 70, MP. A work on Islam.

Subramanya Aiyar, R., *Mahommedan Law*, Madras, 1903, 2, 118, IOL, ANIL. Compiled and translated from English works.

Moulvi Shaik Miran Muhiyiddin Hajiyar, *Ahkamul Islam Shapiyiyya*, Madras, 1904, 25, MP. A work on Islam.

Muhammad Ibrahim ibn Abdal Ghani, *Ahkamul Hitayat Aamalil Pavayitah*, Madras, 1904, 58, IOL. The tenets of Islam rendered in popular verses.

Muhammad Ibrahim ibn Abdal Ghani, *Talkin pi Muhimmatut Din li Avulathul Muslimeen*, Madras, 1904, 86, IOL. An Islamic catechism.

Muhammad Qasin ibn Aliyar Labbai, *Umdattul Islam*, Madras, 1904, 8, 334, IOL. An exposition of the basic dogmas of Islam in question and answer forms.

Abdul Hamid A.K., *Ahkamussiyam*, Vellore, 1905, 48, MP. A work on fasts and feasts of the Muslims.

Mohideen Rautar O.C.P., *Tiruuran Unmai Vilakkam*, Tirunelveli, 1905, 45, MP. A work on Islam.

Muhammad Kamal al Din, *Ahkam al Siyam*, Vellore, 1905, 48, i, IOL. A treatise on fasts.

Muhammad Ziauddin Sahib, *Risalathuthan Bin*, Madras, 1905, 18, MSB. On Islamic ethics.

Shah al Hamid ibn M.A., *Mifthahussalah fee Cilahinnikkah*, Madras, 1905, iv, 200, IOL; Madras, 1915, a.e., IOL. A work on Muslim marriage.

Ibn Oran Muhyidhin, Maulavi, *Ahkamul Islam Sapiyiyya*, Madras, 1906, 20, IOL. A manual of Islamic ritual according to the Shafi rite.

Muhammad Ibrahim ibn Abd al Ghani, Melvisharam, Kadaikkara, *Nasihat al Anam fi Hidayat al Islam*, Madras, 1906, 70, IOL; see also MP. A work on the tenets of Islam including texts in Arabic and Hindustani, in verse and prose, showing the proper conduct of pilgrims to Mecca.

Muhammad ibn Muhammad, al Ghazzali, *Kimiya i Sa'adat,* Madras, 1906, 7, 300, MP, IOL. A treatise on Islamic philosophy, originally written by al Ghazzali in Persian and translated into Tamil from a Hindustani version by Nellikuppam Abd al Rahman.

Muhammad Ibrahim Sahib A., *Maranavilakkam Manataittulakkam,* Vellore, 1906, 34, MP. A work on death and what becomes of the soul after death.

Muhammad Jainul Ghouse, *Tirumana Valttu,* Cuddalore, 1906, 15, MP. Marriage songs or benedictions.

Muhyi al din ibn Muhammad, Kottari, *Tuhfat al Ahbab,* Madras, 1906, viii, 232, 55, IOL. A manual of prayers and of the religious exercises customary on the occasion of the Prophet's nativity, followed by two tracts in Arabic.

Qadir Muhyidhin Mastan, *Purana Meygnana Pokkisha Tiravukol,* Madras, 1906, 88, IOL. Songs on Islamic doctrine.

Abd al Qadir Lebbai (Kamil Wali Daikka), Sheikh, *Pannirandu Malai,* Rangoon, 1907, 40, IOL. Twelve poems on Islamic religion and ethics from Abd al Qadir's *Shariattu Malai,* preceded by a metrical Munajattu by the editor, Virasaram A. Shaikh Muhammad.

Shahul Hamid Lebbai, M.A., *Jawahirul Pavayit,* Madras, 1907, 14, 480, IOL. A treatise on the efficacy of prayers particularly in diminishing disease.

Abdul Rahman Sahib (trans.), *Kimiyaye Sa'adat, 2nd vol., Rukunu-mu-Amlattu,* Nellikuppam, 1908, 8, 332, MP. Rules of Muslim law of conduct.

Shah ul Hamid ibn Aidarus (ed.), *Naskh ul Hadith wa Fath ul Majid,* Madras, 1908, 12, 576, IOL. A treatise upon the traditions of Islam and their authority in doctrine and conduct.

Shahul/Hamid Labbai, *Majmu-us-Salavat,* Madras, 1908, 4, 170, MP. A collection of Muslim prayers.

Shahul Hamid Labbai, *Nashulhadid Vapathul Majid,* Madras, 1908, 8, 576, MP. Muslim rules of conduct and law as derived from the scriptures and tradition.

Shaik Abdul Khadir Labbay, *Yasyedy,* Madras, 1908, 16, MP. Prayer formula to be repeated on special occasions with a view to obtain relief from trouble, pain, etc.

Abdul Hamid M., *Tirumanavaltu,* Porto Novo, 1909, 15, MP. Benedictory stanzas invoking divine blessings on the occasion of the marriage of Nakuda Muhammad Naina Marakkayar.

Alla Pichai Ravuttar M.A. (ed.), *Hatihi Surat Yasin,* Colombo, 1909, 24,

MP. Some prayers in Arabic, printed in Tamil, with two Tamil stanzas and a few brief notes in Tamil.

Muhammad Abd al Salam ibn Muhammad Muhyi al Din, *Meygnana Vija Vidai*, Colombo, 1909, xvi, 124, IOL. An Islamic catechism.

Muhammad Abdul Kaliq Sahib, *Iman Ennum Manga Manivilakku*, Madura, 1909, 8, MP. A work on the unfading light of faith. A tract exhorting persons not to be worldly but to endeavour to follow the Islamic path of virtue.

Shahul Hamitu Leppai, M.A., *Miputtahussalah Pi Yilahinnikah*, Madras, 1909, 20, RMRL. A work on marriage.

Tanga Kasim, *Deiva Bhakti Viveka Vilakkam*, Salem, 1909, 3, 58, MP. Hundred stanzas inculcating the great value of godliness.

Moulvi Shaik Miran Muhiyaddin Alim, *Livavul Islam*, Madras, 1910, I, 4, 126, MP. A work dealing with the greatness of Islam.

Muhammad Ismakil Alim Sahib, *Raunakul Islam*, Valanadu (Tanjore), 1910, 2, 52, MP. Lessons on the teaching of Islam.

Rasul Bivi Ammal, *Gnanamitha Sagaram*, Tenkasi, 1910, 12, 115, MP. Stanzas in different metres bearing upon the teachings of Islam.

Abdul Kader Sahib (Shakir Moulana), *Siratulmustakim*, Vaniyambadi, 1911, 64, MP. A catechism on the principles of Islam.

Abdul Wahab Sahib V., *Gosha Nama*, Ambur, 1911, 1, 29, MP. Lays down in verse the rules to be observed by Muslim women in respect to purdah.

Abdul Wahab Sahib V., *Lukman Nama Saadattu Nama*, Ambur, 1911, 30, MP. Contains in verse the Muslim saint Lukman's advice to his son, and a number of moral precepts culled from the Quran.

Abdur Rahman Sahib (trans.), *Kimiyaye Saadat-Rukunu Muhvikattu* (*vol. 3*), Nellikuppam, 1911, 2, 3, 1, 392, MP. On Muslim rules of conduct and law in Tamil.

Ahmad Sahib Kamil, *Amirtha Vilakkam*, Tinnevely, 1911, 15, MP. Forty stanzas on the religious importance of *Kalima*.

Ahmad Sahib Kamil, *Arulananda Pukazh*, Tinnevely, 1911, Part I, 7, 72, MP. A work in verse devoted to the teaching of Islam and theology.

Fakir Muhammad Sahib A.K., *Tozhugai Mudaliya Padhangal*, Tiruppapuliyur, 1911, 26, MP. Songs in the popular style embodying certain tenets of Muslim theology and religion.

Miran Muhyi ul Din, Sheikh, *Muhamaddiya Mahattuvam*, Madras, 1911, 197, IOL. A book establishing the sacredness of the Quran and the religious importance of prayers and rituals.

Muhammad ibn Muhammad, al Ghazzali, *Mi'raj ul Arifin fi Tarjumathi*

Minhajil Abidin, Madras, 1911, 8, 506, IOL. A Tamil version of Ghazzali's *Minkaj ul Abidin*, an Arabic guide to the religious life for Muslims, transcribed in Tamil characters by Kalai Hasan Ali from a Tamil translation in Arabic script by Shah Muhammad Ziya ul Din Kadiri, from a Hindustani version by Muhammad Mahdi.

Abdur Rahman Sahib M., *Kimiyaye sa adat Rukunu Munjiyattu*, Nellikuppam, 1912, 2, 4, 447, MP. On Muslim rules of conduct and law.

Khatib P.M. Shahul Hamid Labbai, *Kairattul Jamal Pinaba Irrijal*, Tinnevely, 1912, 1, MP. A chart noting down the auspicious days in the year.

Maimun Bibi, *Munajattu*, Tinnevely, 1912, 7, MP. Verses exhorting people to be ever prepared for death by leading a pious life and being free from sin.

Muhammad Abdul Rahman Labbai, T., *Ahkam al Salah fi Ahkam al Nikah*, Madras, 1912, 18, 153, IOL. An exposition of Islamic rules on marriage.

Saiyid Muhammad Shamsuddin Sahib, *Rattibu Mustaba Viyathul Jistiyya*, Madras, 1912, 1, 31, MP. Details regarding offering of individual personal prayers to God, together with some verses in praise of Prophet Mohammad and some saints.

Shah Muhammad Ziyauddin Sahib (ed.), *Akhbarul Parayilu*, Madras, 1912, 10, 756, MP. On the Muslim law of inheritance.

Shah Muhammad Ziya ul Din bin Muhammad Madar Sahib (compiler), *Periya Muhammadiya la Ennum Akbar ul Fara'iz*, Madras, 1912, 10, 756, IOL. A treatise on the Muslim law of inheritance; a translation of the *Fara'iz ul Kadiriyah*, compiled together with material from other sources.

Sheikh Muhammad Madina Sahib, *Meygnana Suyanjothi*, Kottar, Travancore, 1912, 5, 36, MP. A collection of 216 stanzas expounding the tenets of Muslim theology and religion.

Ibrahim Sahib (Moulvi K. Muhammad), *Ahsanun Najat*, Melvisharam, 1913, 7, 204, MP. A poem inculcating many Islamic morals and religious lessons.

Hasan Ali Pulavar K. (ed.), *Miputtahas Supuhani Taruju Matti Majmu al Sultani*, Madras, 1913, 4, 2, 294, MP, IOL. Deals with essential Islamic doctrines related to prayers, pilgrimage, and other religious practices.

Hasan Ali Pulavar, Kalai, *Pancha Rattinat Talattu*, Madras, 1913, 24, IOL;

see also MP, 1913. The basic tenets of Islam expressed in the form of cradle songs.

Muhammad Ibrahim Lebbai, *Kipayattus Dalilun, Hikkayattis Salihis*, Madras, 1913, 322, IOL. A treatise on Islamic theology and ritual.

Pir Muhammad Tarkalai, *Maaripattu Malai*, Madras, 1913, 231, IOL. A metrical treatise on Islamic culture, with the commentary of Nayina Muhammad Pavalar.

Pir Muhammad Sahib, *Meygnana Sakaram*, Madras, 1913, 40, MP. Deals with the unity of God.

Abdul Khadar Sahib E., *Kuyavarai Neekum Iman Thuvakkum*, Nellikuppam, 1914, 8, MP. A pamphlet describing the various causes that constitute infidelity according to Islamic rules and the success of getting over its defilement.

Muhammad Abd ul Kadir Zain ul-Din, Shahan Shah Alim Sahib, Tenkasi, *Vedagnana Tiravukol*, Tenkasi, 1914, 232, IOL; see also MP, 1914. A series of works in verse dealing with Muslim mysticism and religion, based on the writings of Imam Ghazalli and Rumi.

Muhammad Ibrahim Lebbai S., *Kibayattus Salihin, Hikkayattis Salihin*, Madras, 1914, 2, 322, MP. Describes and explains certain Islamic practices.

Sadattu Pir Muhammad Sahib, *Kalima Vilakkam Saliya Muzhakam*, Vaniyambadi, 1914, 47, MP. Explains the unity of God and gives the fundamental principles of Islam.

Shaik Muhammad Abdul Khadir Sainuddin Shahan Shah Alim Sahib, *Manimuthu Malai*, Tenkasi, 1914, second edition, revised, 58, MP. A garland of stanzas dealing with the nature and scope of Islamic faith.

Shaji Muhammad Bawa Sahib A.P., *Allavudaiya Payankaram*, Koothanalur, 1914, 14, MP. Explains the doctrine of hell as expounded by the Prophet Mohammad.

Sheikh Muhammad Pavalar V.A., *Tozhugai Amru Malai*, Adiyakkamangalam, 1914, 35, MP. A garland of 100 stanzas instructing Muslims to follow closely the teachings of the Quran and other sacred books of Muslims.

Abd al Wahhab ibn Muhammad Hadi, V., *Kilid i Danish Ennum Buddhiyin. Tiravukol*, Tiruvarur, 1915, Pt. I, iv, ii, 95, IOL; see also MP, 1915. A work on the moral and spiritual teaching of Islam.

Cinnappa Ravuttar, *Siriya Parulu Malai*, Madras, 1915, 8, MP. States in the form of easy songs certain Islamic rules and practices.

Makhdum Attari, *Larurul Islam Hanafiya*, Ravanasamudram, Kadayam

Post, 1915, 64, MP; see also IOl. Rules and details relating to many religious practices and observances of Islam.

Muhammad Ibrahim Sahib, *Marana Vilakkam*, Madras, 1915, 36, MP. Songs in the ballad style explaining the uncertainty of human life and the inevitability of death.

Mustafa Labbai S.M., *Islamiya Marga Sattam*, Madras, 1915, 72, MP. Explains the fundamental principles of Islam.

Mustafa Labbai S.M. (publ.), *Misbahussalah Bi Taulihinnikah*, Madras, 1915, first edition, 222, MP. Gives rules regulating marriages; also contains discourses on various sexual topics.

Muhyi ul Din, N. Miran, al-Aidarusi al Kadiri, of Jaffna, *Sanmarga Laghu Bodha Vina Vidai*, Jaffna, Madras, 1915, 18, i, 172, IOL. An elementary catechism of the principles of Islam.

Nur Muhammad Sahib K.A., *Islam Mudar Pada Puthagam*, Ilayangudi, 1915, 8, MP. Gives briefly the essential principles of Islam, intended for the use of school children.

Allapiccai Pulavar, *Salavattu Pattu*, Madras, 1916, 94, MP. Prayer songs for the use of the Muslims.

Khadar Pasha Sahib, *Thozhugai Cirappu*, Kumbakonam, 1916, 15, MP. Songs embodying the essential teachings of Islam for the use of Muslim youngsters.

Mahan Muhammat Napi Avarkalin Upateca Ratnam, Madras, 1916, 128, RMRL. A work on Prophet Mohammad's teachings.

Mappilai Labbai Adam Sahib, *Mandiravaralarum Adan Mandiramum*, Melapalayam, 1916, 2nd revised edition, 12, MP. Gives certain religious instructions to be followed in certain cases of cholera and plague attacks.

Mohidin Sultan Alim Sahib, *Islamiya Marga Sattam*, Madras, 1916, 74, MP. Contains rules and laws relating to various Islamic religious practices.

Muhammad Ibrahim, *Marana Vilakkam Manathaittulakkum*, Trichinopoly, 1916, 36, MP; see also MP, 1917, 1920. Popular songs from the Islamic standpoint, pointing out the uncertainty of human existence and the inevitability of death.

Muhammad Ibrahim Ravuttar M., *Sarihatin Darbar*, Pallapatti, 1916, 8, MP. Ballad songs condemning the practice of taking interest on money loans, from the Islamic standpoint.

Muhammad Ibrahim Sahib, *Ahkamunissa Udan Akto Pattimaye Johra*, Vaniyambadi, 1916, 24, MP. Gives the Islamic rules regulating the marriage of women and the story of the marriage of the daughter of the Prophet.

Muhammad Seyinul Ghouse S., *Tirumanavazhthal*, Cuddalore, 1916, 12, MP. Benedictory songs relating to a Muslim marriage.

Naina Muhammad Sahib M.S., *Sajrussappani Varshaipa an Irddikapil Kipa*, Madras, 1916, 20, MP. Treatise on the vicious habit of backbiting condemned by Islam.

Saiyid Muhammad Sahib A.S.M., *Bidattin Vilakkam Tozhugaiyirunukam*, Sattur, 1916, 34, MP. A pamphlet pointing out from the Islamic point of view, the spiritual value of worshipping God and the harmfulness of forming irreligious habits.

Shaik Sulaimanul Khadiri Sahib, *Tangapattu Malai Shiba Malai*, Madras, 1916, 40, MP. Songs and stanzas in the popular style on different Muslim ethical and religious themes.

Shahul Hamid Sahibu Kadiri, Sheik, *Juturimalaiyum Musipattu Vilakkal Munajattum*, Madras, 1916, 38, MP. A wreath of spells and prayers against evils for Muslims.

Sultan Muhammad Sahib, *Din Vilakka Kummi*, Madura, 1916, 24, MP. Kummi songs giving an exposition on the essential teachings of Islam.

Abdul Karim K., *Istihar*, Dindigul, 1917, 11, MP; see also MP, 1918, 1920. A work containing directions for animal sacrifice during *Bakrid.*

Haji Muhammad Abdullah Labbai, *Karpamalaiyum Nasihattunniraivum*, Madras, 1917, 62, MP. A work containing a description of the formation of the human child, prayer to be uttered during travail and general advice to women.

Haji Khadar Muhiyuddin Sahib, *Ulamakkalin Sankaiyum Vatti Vilakku Kummiyum*, Pallapatti, 1918, 10, MP. A tract expressing the doubts of the ulema and Kummi songs against taking interest for money lent.

Hazrata Moulvi Haji Sheiku Miran Muhyi ul Din, *Ahkamul Islam Hanafiyya, Shafiyya*, Madras, 1917, 4 parts, IOL; see also Madras, 1917, 38, 52, MP. Principles of Muslim religious and legal doctrines according to the Hanafi and Shafi schools, etc.

Mastan Sahib, Abd al Kadir, Kunangudi, *Gnana Puthaiyal Arabi Mujajattu* Tarjuma, Madras, 1917, 104, IOL, MP. Arabic metrical prayers for each day of the week with Tamil prose translations, edited by Muhammad Lebbai.

Muhammad Musa Sahib, *Marana Vilakkam*, Madras, 1917, 36, MP. A work stating the necessity of daily prayers. It also contains a number of moral issues.

Muhammad Pir, Kutb ul Alam, *Ma'rifat Malai*, Madras, 1917, i, 232,

IOL; see also MP, 1917. 611 verses on Islamic doctrine, with a prose interpretation by M.A. Neyina Muhammad Pavalar.

Nayina Muhammad A.P., *Vasiyattin Bodhanai*, Madras, 1917, 2nd revised edition, 8, MP. A work on the teachings of the Prophet and Islam.

Nayina Muhammad Pavalar, M.A., *Ceiyatt' Ennum Ponn Anya Malai*, Madras, 1917, 121, IOL. An exposition of the tenets of Islam.

Nu'man ibn Thabit (Abu Hanifah), *Fikhul Akparin Tarjuma* (*Al Fikh al Akbar*), Madras, 1917, 56, IOL. Principles of Islam, translated by Sheiku Miran Muhyi al Din from the original Arabic; the book also contains Abu Hanifah's *Ka'sidah*, an Arabic poem in praise of Prophet Mohammad in Tamil script, with Tamil translation by Sheiku Miran Muhyi al Din, a life of Abu Hanifah in Tamil by the latter and an elegy on him in Arabic and Tamil.

Shaik Miran Muhiuddin Sahib, *Islattin Mahimai*, Madras, 1917, 40, MP. A work on the greatness of Islam.

Shaik Muhammad Alim Sahib Kadir, *Tapavulvapa*, Madras, 1917, 21, MP. A collection of prayers for Muslims.

Abdul Halim Khadiri, *Gnana Agandelivu Kummi*, Madras, 1918, 16, MP. Kummi songs on the wisdom of the purified mind, with other similar songs from a Muslim standpoint.

Ahmad ibn Muhammad, *Navina Vasaka Tirattu*, Kumbakonam, 1918, 40, IOL; see also MP, 1918. A religious tract on the greatness of Islam.

Akamatu Makutimavulana, Muhammatu Pakurtin Caypavargal, *Mucippattuvilakkal Munajattu*, Devakottai, 1918, 3rd edition, 24; see also RMRL. Prayers against obstacles.

Madar Sahib Alim, *Parulu Malai*, Pallapatti, 1918, 38, MP. Verses on certain important principles and rules of Islam.

Muhammad Abdul Kalik Sahib, *Nalvazhi Vilakkam*, Madura, 1918, 12, MP. A pamphlet on certain essential principles of Islam.

Muhammad Ibrahim Sahib M.K., *Gosha Alankaram*, Negapatam, 1918, 16, MP. A work in support of purdah among Muslims.

Muhammad Ibrahim Sahib M.K., *Sariattu Darbar*, Pallapatti, 1918, 2nd edition, 9, MP. Popular songs condemning the practice of lending money for interest by Muslims.

Siniyava Ravuttar S.A., *Valinadai Lavani*, Sivaganga, 1918, 20, MP. Pilgrim songs in the Lavani-style description of certain Muslim festivals.

Hussain Muhammad Pulavar S.V., *Irularai Deepamum Alankara Deepamum*, Pallapatti, 1919, 22, MP. Ballads pointing out the evils arising out of the various immoral pursuits.

Abdul Hamid O.M., *Tirumana Vazhthum Tozhamar Vazhthum*,

Chidambaram, 1920, 2, MP. Wedding songs related to the marriage of one Sahib Marakkayar.

Muhammad Ali K.P. and Muhammad Sultan Sahib K.A., *Vinvazhiakatru Dinvazhi Chindu*, Tiruppur, 1920, 38, MP. An Islamic ballad on the avoidance of illusory ways.

Muhammad M.S.M., *Pariksa Husaini*, Madras, 1920, 32, MP; see also IOL, 1920. Devoted to certain teachings of Islam.

D: The Quran and the Hadith

Abd al Kadir, Pettai Amur, son of Amur Valaibava, *Jawahirul Atis*, Madras, 1875, 150, IOL; see also MP, 1874. A selection of Hadiths rendered in Tamil.

Minna Nooruddin Pulavar, *Ponnariya Malai*, Madras, 1882, 452, 98, MSB. Translation into Tamil of Nabi's words.

Seiku Mukamattu, Tirunaraiyur, *Iratna Vilasam Nasihataulasum*, Madras, 1884, 152, MSB; Madras, 1885, a.e., 156, MSB. Prophet's words.

Sulaiman ibn Muhammad al Sailani, *Rahimat al Mannan*, Colombo, 1897, 112, IOL. Surah 78–114 with a translation into Tamil by Sulaiman.

Quran, Madras, 1897, 20, MSB.

Shah ul Hamid Lebbai, M.A., *Nas Kulkaritin Valpath ul Majitu*, Madras, 1908, 12, 576, IOL. A treatise on Hadith.

Alla Pichai Ravuttar, *Hathibi Surat Yasin*, Madurai, 1909, 24, MSB. A work on *Surah Yasin* of the Quran.

Qadir Muhyi al Din P.V. (compiled by), *Quran Sharif Tamizh Tafsir*, Madras, 1913, 244, IOL. A Tamil commentary on parts of the Quran with the Arabic text and Tamil translation of certain passages. The main text in Tamil is printed.

Shah ul Hamid Lebbai (ed.), *Surattu Yasin* (*Surah XXXVI*), Madras, 1913, 30, IOL, MP; 2nd edition, Madras, 1917, 26, IOL. Arabic text in Tamil characters, followed by Arabic prayers, also in Tamil script, with instructions for the performance of funeral rites and a Tamil translation of one prayer.

P.V. Kadir Muhyi al din bin Muhammad Ibrahim, *Quran Sharippu Tamizh Tafsir*, Madras, 1913, viii, 40, viii, 191, IOL. Section XXX of the Quran (*Juz'amma*) with the Surahs in reversed order, preceded by Surah I, with Tamil interlineary translation, followed by Surahs lxxvii–ixxx with Tamil commentary.

A. Muhammad Tahir Sahib (trans.), *Parisutta Vedamakiya Quran Sharippu*, Vazhuthur, Tanjore, 1915, Pt. 1, iv, 21, IOL. A Tamil rendering of the first chapter of the Quran.

Ahmad ibn Abd Ullah, *Lubab ul Akhbar*, Madras, 1915, 276, IOL. Arabic traditions of the Prophet with Tamil exposition; translated from the original Arabic of Ahmad ibn Abd Ullah by Muhammad Ibrahim Sahib, along with *Tazhkiyat ul Khavatir*, by Adam Sheikh.

Hazrat Moulvi Haji Sheiku Miran Mohideen Sahibu, *Ya Sin Surattin Tarjumah*, Madras, 1917, 26, IOL. An exposition of the *Surat Yasin*, followed by an Arabic prayer thereupon in Tamil script with Tamil translation.

Abdul Hameed Baqavi, A.K., *Tarjamat al-Quran bi-Altaf al-Bayan*, Trichinopoly, 1929, 2nd edition, IOL. A Tamil translation styled *Altaf al-Bayan* and exposition by A.K. Abdul Hameed Baqavi. The previous edition (1926) is without the Arabic text. This translation constitutes the first part.

Moulvi S.S. Muhammad Abdul Kader Sahib Baqavi, Uthamapalayam, *Bayan al Quran*, Koothanallur, 1934, 424, IOL. First 8 surahs of the Quran, the last being incomplete.

Moulvi S.S. Muhammad Abdul Qadir, *Tafsir al-Hamit fi Tafsir al-Quran al-Majid*, Madras, 1940, 4, 738, BNP. Surahs 5 to 9 of the Quran: Arabic text with translation and detailed commentary in Tamil.

Abdul Hameed Baqavi, A.K. (trans.), *Tarjumatul Quran* (2 volumes), Madras, 1948, vol. 1, 10, 40, 181, 247–1, EFEO; Madras, 1950, vol. 2, 8, 732–245, EFEO. A Tamil translation of the Quran with Arabic script.

E: Other Religious, Mystical and Devotional Works

Mastan Sahib, Kunankuti Abd al Qadir, *Tirupadat Tirattu*, Madras, 1847, 234, IOL; Madras, 1860, a.e., 180, IOL; Madras, 1870, a.e., 182, IOL; Madras, 1873, a.e., 182, IOL; see also 1882, BNP. Religious songs.

Mastan Sahib, Kunankuti, *Mastan Sagibu Avarkal Padal*, 1849, See Supplement to the Catalogue of the Library of the Honourable East India Company, London, 1851. Religious songs.

Caravanaperumal Aiyar, T., *Mastane Sahibu Peril Nan Mani Malai*, 1860, s. 1, 35, IOL. Devotional verses by a Brahmin in praise of a Muslim saint.

Vanna Kalanjiya Pulavar, Madurai Meesal, *Rajanayagam*, Madras, 1860 (copy in the private holdings of Janab 'Hasan', Madras). A religious work.

Mastan Sahib, Kunankuti, *Tiruppatarrirattu*, Madras, 1864, 182, RMRL; Madras, 1872, a.e., 182, RMRL; Madras, 1876, a.e., 182, RMRL; Madras, 1893, a.e., 182, RMRL; Madras, 1899, a.e., 182, RMRL; Madras, 1902, a.e., 182, RMRL; Madras, 1905, a.e., 1, 82, RMRL. A mystical work.

Bageer Mahomed Pulavar, *Gnanamani Malai*, Madras, 1870, 84, MP. Verses in praise of Allah.

Ali Pulavar, son of Shaikh Abu Bakr, *Mikurasu Malai*, Madras, 1872, 124, IOL. Religious poem.

Abd al Qadir Nayinar Lebbai, Kayalpattinam, *Munajathukal*, Madras, 1873, 42, IOL; see also MP, 1873.

Mahomed Pulavar M., *Palappadal Tirattu*, Madras, 1873, 208, MP. A work in praise of Islam.

Pir Muhammad Shaikh, *Titaru Malai*, Madras, 1873, 32, IOL; Madras, 1889, a.e., MSB. A work on religious truth.

Abd al Qadir Nayinar Lebbai, Kayalpattinam, *Pannirantu Malai* (*Adapu Malai, Arivu Malai, Usudu Malai, Kakeekathu Malai, Cariattu Malai, Cittru Malai, Kakothu Malai, Tarikattu Malai, Tikru Malai, Taukitu Malai, Makaripattu Malai, Bayanuddin Malai, Pikru Malai*), Madras, 1874, 40, IOL. Religious poems.

Abd al Qadir Ravuttar, *Ataikkala Malai*, Madras, 1874, 24, IOL. A religious poem.

Abdul Qadir, *Akayat Nama*, Madras, 1874, 6, MSB. A religious work.

Kader Mugaideen Pulavar, *Patham*, Madras, 1874, MSB. In praise of Allah.

Kattanai Seikoli Sahib, *Munajattu*, Madras, 1874, 14, IOL, MSB. Prayers to God.

Makhdum Muhammad Pulavar (ed.), *Pala Patal Tirattu*. Madras, 1874, 204, IOL. Anthology of Islamic poetry.

Muhammad Lebbai, *Meygnana Kirtannankal*, Tirunelveli, 1874, 37, MSB. Mystical songs.

Muhammad Lebbai, Kayalpattinam, *Meygnana Aarumaikkarana Malai*, Madras, 1874, 36, IOL. Devotional songs.

Nayinar Lebbai Aali Pulavar, *Mellicai Vannam*, Madras, 1874, MSB. A religious work.

Pir Muhammad Tarkalai, *Gnana Ratna Kuravanji*, Madras, 1874, 8, MP, IOL. A religious dialogue.

Samu Nayina, Kayalpattinam, *Napimarkal Kondundakiya Munajat*, Madras, 1874, 60, MSB. A religious work in Ammanai style.

Samu Nayina, Kayalpattinam, *Kuru An Kurathai Kondundakiya Munajat*, Madras, 1874, 48, MSB. A religious work.

Sheikibrahim Sahib Pulavar, *Arun Manimalai* (*Munajat*), Madras, 1874, 7, MSB. A religious work.

Uthumanayinar Pulavar, *Vannam* (*Munajat-Yanai Viruttam, Vannankal, Patankal*), Madras, 1874, MSB. Religious poems.

Vanna Kalanjiya Pulavar and Sinkakavi Pulavar, *Padham*, Madras, 1874, 6, MSB. A religious work.

Pirumukamattu Cakipu, Tarkalai, *Gnanamanimalai*, Madras, 1875, 34, RMRL; Madras, 1878, a.e., MSB. A mystical work.

Yusuf Lebbai and Nayina Muhammad Pulavar (eds.), *Cakapultinan, Imanputaiya Panarkal*, Madras, 1875, 208, IOL. Religious poems adapted from Arabic sources.

Abd al Qadir Naynar Lebbai, Kayalpattinam, *Sorkka Niti*, Madras, 1876, 20, IOL; Madras, 1878, a.e., 20, IOL. A religious poem; it also contains the poem titled, *Ataikkala Malai*, by Kilakkarai Abd al Qadir Pulavar and another poem titled, *Enneye Cintu*, by Marikkayar Pulavar.

Ahmad Maraikkayar Pulavar, *Nuru Nama*, Madras, 1877, 20, IOL. Devotional verses.

Muhammad Hussain Pulavar, *Taukitu Malai*, Madras, 1877, 20, IOL. A devotional poem; it also contains two similar poems by other authors.

Syed Muhammad Marabal, *Nuru Nama*, Madras, 1877, 20, MSB. A religious work.

Ali Marakkayar, *Munajattu*, Madras, 1878, MSB. Prayers to Allah.

Alli Marakkayar, son of Mira Lebbai, *Pirabantak Kottu*, Madras, 1878, 28, IOL. Religious poems, prayers to God.

Nabi—Peril Patikangal, Madras, 1878, 96, IOL. A collection of devotional songs by various authors.

Saikuti Saib, *Munajittu*, Madras, 1878, 12, MP. A work in praise of God.

Sheikh Tambi Pulavar, K.P., *Karanamalai*, Madras, 1878, 184, IOL. A devotional song sequence.

Katar Mukaiyatin Ravuttar, *Katavulartuti*, Vellore, 1879, 8, 64, RMRL. A devotional song.

Makutu Muhammatup Pulavar, *Ihtu Paracamayakolarippatikam*, Konnur, 1879, 16, RMRL. A religious work.

Mastan Sahib, *Mastan Padal*, Madras, 1879, 182, MP. Religious verses.

Sam Shihab al Din ibn Sulaiman, Kayalpattinam, *Salat al Arkan Malai*, Madras, 1879, 138, IOL. Devotional song.

Shaik Abdul Khadar, *Maharabat-ul-Lain* (*Muharapathullakeen*) (*Kadiya Malai, Katham Malai, Munajattu*), Madras, 1879, 42, MP; see also MSB, 1880. A religious work in a mixture of Arabic and Tamil.

Aidurusu Nayina Pulavar, *Aidurusu Nayinar Patar Tirattu*, Madras, 1880, MSB. Religious songs.

Seikabdul Qadir, *Hidayatinnicai*, Madras, 1880, 63, MSB. A religious work.

Seikabdul Qadir, Tenkasi, *Munajattu*, Madras, 1880, 7, MSB. Religious songs.

Mukamattu Abdul Khader, *Munajat*, Madras, 1881, 24, MSB. Religious work in praise of the followers of Islam.

Peeru Mukamattu Sahib, *Ananta Kalippu*, Madras, 1881, MSB. A work in praise of God.

Peer Muhammad, Tarkala, *Gnana Pukazhchi* (*Gnanananda Kazhi, Muchudar Pathiyangal, Gnana Andadi*), Tanjore, 1881, 573, MSB. Prayers to God, mystical in nature.

Seiku Tambi, Kottaru, *Gnanananda Kazhi*, Tanjore, 1881, MSB. A mystical work.

Seikaptul Kadir, Kayalpattinam, *Katham Malai*, Madras, 1881, 25, MSB. A religious work.

Shaik Mansuru Labbay Sahib S.S., *Gnana Pukazhchi*, Madras, 1881, 160, MP. A religious work.

Madar Sahib Pulavar, Ayyampettai, *Munajattu*, Madras, 1882, 27, MSB. Prayers to God.

Mukamattu Muthu Ravuttar, *Istakupar*, Coimbatore, 1882, MSB. A work translated from Arabic.

Uthumanayinar Pulavar, *Salavatup* (*Kappar Paatu, Unjar Paatu, Kummi Paatu, Talattu, Thozhi Paatu*), Madras, 1882, MSB; Madras, 1883, a.e., MSB; Madras, 1888, a.e., MSB.

Ceykupir Mukammatu, *Titarumalai*, Madras, 1883, 36, RMRL. A religious poem.

Katiru Mukiyittin, *Kummi Paatu*, Madras, 1883, MSB; Madras, 1888, a.e., MSB. A religious song.

Mahomed Ibrahim Sahib, *Velatti Masala Vilakkam*, Madras, 1883, 220, MP; see also MSB 1882. A religious work.

Muhammad Lebbai Alim Aji Saib, *Vellati Masala Marumozhi Vilakkam*, Madras, 1884, 196, MP. A religious work.

Kannakumadu Mohadin Mahmed Pulavar, *Palapadattirettu*, Madras, 1885, 424, MP. A collection of Tamil verses.

Katiru Muhiyittin Cakipu, Vellore, *Pancattinavolivattam*, Kayalpattinam, 1885, 84, RMRL. A religious work.

Katirmukaiyatin Pulavar, *Nasihattul Muminin Malai*, Madras, 1885, 10, 312, RMRL. A religious work.

Sheik Habib Mahomed Ahaji Alim Sahib, *Gnanodaya Dipa Alankaram*, Coimbatore, 1886, 56, MP. A religious tract of writings.

Kannakumadu Makhudum Mukamattu Pulavar, *Ya Seyeedi Maulidu*, Madras, 1887, 22, MSB. A Munajat work.

Sayed Mohiadin Pulavar and Sheikul Ahmadi Pulavar, *Navanita Punjam*, Madras, 1888, 176, MP. A religious poem.

Sheik Mahomed Labbai Alim, *Hidayat ul-Musalmin*, Madras, 1888, 20, MP. A religious work.

Sheik Muhammad Labbai Alim, *Kifayat-ul-Anam*, Madras, 1888, 64, MP. A religious work.

Sheik Mukamattu Yucupu, *Shamsulman*, Madras, 1888, 300, MSB. A devotional work.

Kadar Naina Labbay N.V., *Titarau Malai*, Madras, 1889, 36, MP. Sacred verses on beatitude and the way to attain it.

Kalaiyatta Ravuttar, *Manoranjita Alankaram*, Pondicherry, 1890, 32, INALCO; see also same author, *Karikal*, 1899, 40, INALCO. A religious work.

Cavattamaraikkayariyar, A., *Makkakhovai*, Nahapatnam, 1891, iv, 99(1), RMRL. Songs related to Makka.

Khader Muthaitin Pulavar T.A., *Nasihatul Muminin Malai* (*Meygnana Keertanai, Innicai, Hakkan Peril Thuthi, etc.*), Madras, 1891, 330, MP, MSB. Various songs especially for children.

Sheiku Mukiyittin Labbay, *Jem Kootu Malai*, Madras, 1891, 50, MP, MSB. A religious work.

Hamid Sahibdurai of Galle, *Griacca Pen Kummi*, Galle, 1892, 14, IOL. Religious songs for Muslim women, edited by K.V. Muhammad Muhyi al Din.

Kadar Mohidin O.P., *Nitineri Ananta Kalippu*, Madras, 1893, 12, MP. Sacred songs and lyrics of an instructive kind.

Muhammad Kannu, Perumal Durai Vaidyam, A., *Ashura Karana Kummi Chindu*, Colombo, 1893, 18, IOL. A religious song for the *Ashura* festival.

Piccaiyipurahim Pulavar, A.K., *Tirumatinat Tantati*, Tiricirapuram, 1893, 6, 56 (1), RMRL. A religion poem.

Sultan Muhyi al Din, Tiruvangadu, M.K., *Pavani Alankaram*, Colombo, 1893, 8, IOL. Songs for religious processions.

Nuh Lebbai Alim Sahib, *Veda Puranam*, Madras, 1894, 922, MSB. Mystical work.

Piccaiyipurahim Pulvar A.K., *Pirapantakkottu*, Madras, 1894, 2, 94, RMRL. A religious work.

Seyeedu Mukamattu Makhdum, *Tirupadap Pustakam*, Coimbatore, 1894, 27, MSB. A religious work.

Aptul Katir Cayupu, Valai Bawa Cayupu Kumarar, *Kipayattalmuminin*, Madras, 1895, 32, RMRL. A religious work.

Mappilai Aptulkatirumaraikkayar, *Nanmanimalai*, Rangoon, 1896, 3, 14, RMRL. A religious work.

Muhammad Miran Mastan ibn Lukman Rauttar, *Gnanaratinakaram*, Madras, 1896, xii, 59, IOL; see also RMRL. Religious poems, edited by Kann Ahmad Makhdum Muhammad.

Muhammad Sultan ibn Ahmad Umar Maraikkayar, *Padananda Malai*, Penang, 1896, 51, IOL. Religious poems.

Peer Muhammad Sahib, *Tiru Meygnana Sara Nul*, Madras, 1896, 16, MSB; see also 1910, RMRL. A mystical work.

Pirumukamattu Cakipu, Tarkalai, *Gnanarattinakkuravanci*, Madras, 1897, 8, RMRL; Madras, 1903, a.e., 8, RMRL; Madras, 1905, a.e., RMRL; Madras, 1907, a.e., 8, RMRL; Madras, 1915, a.e., 7, RMRL. A mystical work.

Shah al-Hamid Hasan Ali Pulavar, Sirudaiyarpuram (Kanda Pulavar) and others, *Sangita Chintamani*, Madras, 1897, iv, i, 176, IOL. A collection of religious lyrics, edited by Kann Ahmad Makhdum Muhammad.

Turab Muhammad Husain Ibn Ismail, *Tozhugai Rayita Alankaram*, Dindigul, 1897, Two parts, IOL. Religious lyrics, edited by Muhammad Mir Jawad.

Karuppaiya Pavalar, Kottampati, M. (ed.), *Meygnana Vilakkam*, 1898, IOL. A mystical work.

Muhyi al din Maluk Mudaliyar, Kottaru, the elder (Naniyar Sahib Vali Allah), karuppaiya Pavalar, Kottampatti, M., etc., *Meygnana Tirupadat Tirattu and Tiru Kottattu Kalambakam*, Madras, 1898, ii, xvi, ii, 383, 39, IOL, MSB. Religious poems, edited by Karuppaiya Pavalar and Naniyar Sahib Taha Lebbai.

Peeru Mukamattu, Tarkalai, *Meygnana Tirupadat Tirattu*, Madras, 1898, 935, MSB. A religious work.

Sheiku Tambi Gnaniyar, *Meygnana Vilakkam*, Madras, 1898, 101, MSB. A religious work.

Abdul Wahabu, *Munajat Nama*, Madras, 1899, MSB. A religious work.

Kalauyatta Ravuttar, *Manoranjida Alankaram*, Karikal, 1899, 40, INALCO. A religious work.

Pirumukamattu Cakipu, Tarkalai, *Anantakalippu*, Madras, 1899, 8, RMRL. A religous work.

Muhiyuddin Sahib, *Munajattu*, Tirunelveli, 1900, 8, MP. A religious work.

Rahim Khan Sahib B., *Tirumakkap Pallu*, Tuticorin, 1900, 68, MP. Lyrics on Mecca.

Aliya Ravuttar, *Payahampar Avatara Palavannac Cindu*, Madras, 1901, ANIL. A religious poem.

Kannakumadu Makudu Muhammadu Pulavar (ed.), *Gnanaratna Sagara Matariyya*, Madras, 1901, 160, MP. A religious work.

Muhammad Qadir Vava Ravuttar, S.K., *Salavattu Satakam*, Tirunelveli, 1901, 24, MP. A religious work.

Muhammad Sultan ibn Ahmad Umar Maraikkayar, *Ananda Kirtannai*, Penang, 1901, 6, ii, 88, IOL. Religious lyrics.

Saiyid Muhiuddin Sultan Pillai Alim Sahib, *Irusatul Ibat*, Madras, 1901, 152, MP. A religious work, translated from Arabic.

Shahul Hamid Pulavar, *Ananta Sahityam*, Madras, 1901, 152, MP. A religious work.

Sheik Duman Labbai and Sheik Paséru Labbai, *Gnanodya Punjam*, Madras, 1901, 152, MP. A religious work.

Makhdum Muhammad ibn Pir Muhammad, Kayalpattinam, *Madhura Vakya Kirtana Ranjitam*, Madras, 1902, xxvi, 186, IOL. Religious lyrics, edited by Kann Ahmad Makhdum Muhammad.

Nooru Muhammad Sahib, *Gnanamani Malai*, Madras, 1902, ANIL. A devotional work.

Pakkirkkanip Pulavar T.C., *Penmatiyinalankaram*, Madras, 1902, 30, RMRL. A religious work.

Palli Uduman Labbai Kalipa Sahib, *Meygnana Sikamani*, Madras, 1902, 120, MP. A religious work in the name of Rahman, etc.

Abdul Majid M.K.A., *Asarak Kovai*, Madras, 1903, 174, MP. A religious work.

Abdul Rahman Sahib (trans.), *Mihakkul Matahib*, Madras, 1903, 146, MP. Translated from Hindi.

Ghulam Qadir Navalar, *Pulavar Arruppatai*, Madurai, 1903, 27, IOL. A poem, with commentary.

Muhammad Hamsa Labbai, *Meygnana Ratnavalankara Kirtannam*, Madras, 1903, 88, MP. A religious work.

Muhammad Ibrahim Sahib K., *Tanbihul Anam bin Tuhappattu Avam*, Madras, 1903, 216, MP. A religious work.

Muhammad Nuruddin, *Palapada Tirattu*, Madras, 1903, ANIL. Religious songs.

Khadir Muhiyidin Mastan Sahib alias Muhiyidin Pichai, *Paripurna Meygnana Dipa Sankirttanam*, Madras, 1904, 174, MP. A religious work.

Muhammd Ibrahim Sahib K., *Ahkamul Hidayah fi Amalil Pavayitah*, Madras, 1904, 60, MP. A religious work.

Muhammad Ibrahim Sahib K., *Talkin bi Muhimma Tuttin li Avulatul Muslimin*, Madras, 1904, 88, 2nd edition, MP. A religious work.

Muhammad Kasim Lebbai Alim A., *Umdattul Islam*, Madras, 1904, 356, MP. A religious work.

Mastan Sahib, Abd al Kadir, Munangudi, *Tiru Padat Tirattu Mulamum, pathavurai Mudaliyavum*, Madras, 1905, 2, i, i, 444, xiv, IOL. Religious poems with commentary by Kanchipuram Ramasami Nayudu, edited by Muhammad Pavalar, M.A. Neyina of Chevval, Tirunelveli.

Abdul Vahab Sahib, *Risalat-Tuttan-Bih*, Madras, 1905, 22, MP. A religious work.

Abdul Hamid, *Alankara Valinadai Cindu*, Chidambaram, 1905, 16, MP. An elegant song of a Muslim pilgrim.

Mastan Sahib, *Tirupattar Tirattu*, Madras, 1905, 444, 14, IOL. Religious poems, edited with commentary by M.K. Ramasami Nayakar.

Khadir Muhiuddin Mastan Sahib, Eral, *Purana Meygnana Pokkisha Tiravukol*, Madras, 1906, 2, 88, MP. A complete key to the spiritual knowledge.

Muhammad Jan Labbai Alim, *Nurul Jan*, Madras, 1906, ANIL. A religious work.

Muhamattu Leppai, Alim Cakipu, *Malaiyampasaiyilulla Meygnana Arumaikkarana Malai Kirttanankal*, Madras, 1906, 55, RMRL. A religious work.

Abd al Hamid, A.L.M., *Hamitiyya Sankirta Kirtannam*, Colombo, 1908, Pt. 1, 24, IOL. Religious songs.

Abd al Mazid Ibn Abd al Karim, M.K.A., *Kirtanna Majid*, Colombo, 1907, Part II, 16, IOL. Religious lyrics.

Abd al Qadir Lebbai called Kamil Wali Deikka, *Pannirentu Malai*, Rangoon, 1907, 40, IOL. Ethical and Religious poems, edited by Muhammad Virasaram A. Shaikh; it is preceded by a Munajat by the editor.

Muhammad Pir, *Tiru Meygnana Sara Nul*, 1907, IOL. 30 verses of divination from the breath.

Faqir Madar, *Muhammata Haripa Malai*, Colombo, 1908, 235, IOl. Devotional Poem.

Khadir Muhiyuddin Mastan Sahib, *Sampoorna Gnana Samarasa Kirtannam*, Eralmanagaram, 1908, 8, MP. Three songs in praise of God and truth.

Mastan Sahib Abd al Kadir, Kunangudi, *Mastan Sahib Avargal Padal*, Madras, 1908, ii, 14, 451, IOL. Religious poems with paraphrase and commentary by M. Vadivelu Mudaliyar.

Muhammad Nooruddin, Cuddalore, *Karanak Katchi*, Chidambaram, 1908, 14, MSB. In praise of God.

Pappu Tasan, V.S., *Cinkara Varinataik Patankal*, Tiruvarur, 1908, 30. Religious songs.

Abd al Qadir, O.M.S. Sultan, *Tilana Sankirtam*, Rangoon, 1909, 13, IOL. Religious verses.

Muhammad Abdulla Labbai Alim, *Kirttanaranjittam*, Ayyampet, 1909, 7, 76, MP. Muslim songs.

Tarika Qasim M., *Teyvenpakti Viveka Vilakkam*, Salem, 1909, 58, IOL. Religious poem.

Abdul Khader Sahib, K. Vaniyambadi, *Shakirin Nuthana Arichuvadi*, Vaniyambadi, 1910, 18, MSB. Moral Munajats.

Habibu Rahman (trans.), *Mihakul Madahib*, Madras, 1910, ANIL. A religious work by Ibrahim translated into Tamil.

Rasul Bibi Ammal, *Gnanamrita Cakaram*, Tenkasi, 1910, 127, IOL. Religious poems.

Abdul Rahman, Nellikuppam, *Tuhfatul Hind-Inthiyavuku Kanikai*, Madras, 1911, 2nd edition, ANIL. A work of religious nature.

Akumatu Cakipu Kamil, *Arulanandappukazh*, Tirunelveli, 1911, V (1), RMRL. A religious work.

Alauddin Anbiul Kadri A.M., *Tuaya Murad*, Vaniyambadi, 1912, 16, MP. Contains a number of Arabic-Tamil general passages invoking the mercy of God.

Kalai Hasan Ali Pulavar, *Mihnajul Aripin Minhajil Abidin*, Madras, 1911, 506, IOL. It was written originally by Imam Ghazalli.

Maraikkayar, Sahib, *Mahpupu Parapatak Kirttanam*, Singapore, 1911, 168, IOL. Devotional songs.

Muhammad Lebbai and Muhyi al din Pulavar, K.G., *Nutana Vicittirak Kirttanaikal*, Colombo, 1911, 42, IOL. Religious songs.

Muhyithin Pulavar, *Jamiul Arupar Alankarec Cintu*, Colombo, 1911, 8, IOL. Devotional verses.

Sahib Maraikkayar ibn Ahmad Lebbai Karaikkal, Amuta Kavi, *Mahbubu Parapatha Kirthanam*, Singapore, 1911, 28, 168, IOL. Muslim hymns and odes, edited by Nagur Muhyi ul Din Abd al Kadir.

Iramaccantira Ravuttar, Na. Ra.Rama, *Manippattu Manipancakam Natcattiramanimalai*, Madras, 1912, 12, RMRL. A religious work.

Iramaccantira Ravuttar, Na.Ra.Rama, *Manittacakam*, Madras, 1912, 16, RMRL. A religious work.

Muhammad Abd al Qadir ibn Malik Muhammad, *Aryai Ayul Nanratta Malai*, Colombo, 1912, 12, IOL. Devotional verses.

Muhammad Pulavar, Kilakarai, *Kirtanna Malai*, Madras, 1912, 24, IOL. Devotional songs.

Shah Muhammad Ziauddin Sahib Khadir, *Periya Muhamadiya La Ennum Akparul Parayilu*, Madras, 1912, ANIL. A work on Islamic law.

Shamuna Lebbai, *Irushad Nama*, Madras, 1912, 28, (copy in my possession). A religious work in verse form.

Fakir Mastan V.S., *Vazhinatai Cintu*, Nagore, 1913, 16, MP. Pilgrim songs describing a journey to Singapore to witness a Muslim festival.

Muhamad Ibrahim ibn Abd al Ghani K., *Ahsamunajat*, Madras, 1913, 204, IOL. Religious verses.

Abu Bakr Ravuttar Pulavar, *Arunnantak Kirtannai*, Tenkasi, 1914, 49, IOL; see also MP, 1914. Devotional songs describing the greatness of Islam.

Muhammad Pavalar, V.A., *Tozhugai Amru Malai*, Tiruvarur, 1914, 35, IOL. Religious verses.

Muhammatu Ipurahim Cakip, *Tanpihul Anam*, Madras, 1914, 244, RMRL. A religious work.

Shaik Muhammad Abd al Qadir Zainuddin Shahansha Alim Sahib, *Veta Gnana Tiravukol*, Tenkasi, 1914, 239, IOL. Islamic philosophical and religious poems.

Abdul Wahab V.M., Kuttanallur, *Kilidedanish Ennum Puthiyin Tiravukol, Part I*, Tiruvarur, 1915, 95, MP. A religious work.

Ahmad ibn al Kasim, al Bukhari al Andalusi (al-Hariri), *Subhan Maulid Tarjuma*, Madras, 1915, 64, IOL. Muslim devotional verses from Ahmad bin Kasim's, *Maulid Sharaf al-anam*, in Arabic, transliterated into Tamil script, with a Tamil translation of the same and of the illustrative tales (*Hikayat*) by K. Muhammad Ghaus (Kutti Lebbai).

The whole piece transliterated into Tamil script by Habib Mahmud Lebbai.

Hasan Mohiuddin Alim Sahib, *Meygnana Amrita Sangita Kirtannai*. Eravadi, 1916, 40, MP. A collection of devotional songs relating to Islam.

Hasan Mohiuddin Sahib, *Sinkara Cintu*, Chingleput, 1916, 7, MP. Ballad songs descriptive of the Muharram festival.

Iramaccantira Ravuttar, Na.Ra.Rama, *Tutimanimalai*, Konakar, 1916, 2, 8, RMRL. A religious song.

Mastan Sahib Kunankuti, *Tirupattar Tirattu*, Madras, 1916, viii, 444, xiv, IOL; see also RMRL. Religious songs, edited with a commentary by Ramasami Nayakar and M.A. Nayina Muhammad Pavalar.

Muhammad Shah ibn Muhyi al Din (Mastan Sahib), Tenkasi, *Meygnana Vikasita Kirtannai*, Madras, 1916, 8, 95, IOL. Devotional lyrics, edited by K. Hasan Ali Pulavar.

Muhammad Sain Pulavar Khadar Mohiuddin Udumanayinnar Pulavar, *Dauhidumalaiym Karanakummiyum Padamum, Salavattupattum Padamum*, Madras, 1916, 20, MP. A collection of popular religious songs.

Ramasami Nayudu K. (ed.), *Mastan Sahibu Tirupadat Tirattu*, Madras, 1916, 461, MP. A collection of the devotional and ethical songs of Mastan Sahib.

Turab Muhammad Husain, *Tozhugai Ranjita Alankaram*, Madras, 1916, 32, (copy in my possession). Verses on prayer and worship.

Faqir Labbai, *Tanca Rattina Malai*, Madras, 1917, 44, IOL. Devotional verses.

Khadar Muhiyuddin Raguttar, *Kappal Pattu*, Chidambaram, 1918, 8, MP. The boat song of popular Islamic interest.

Makhdum Muhammad Pulavar (ed.), *Pala Patar Tirattu*, Madras, 1917, 400, IOL; see also MP, 1917, Collection of religious poems by different authors.

Mastan Sahib, *Anantakalippu*, Madras, 1917, 16, MP., A religious and moral poem.

Muhyi al din Abd al Qadir, M.A., *Yucupiyya Malai*, Negapatam, 1918, 16, IOL. Devotional verses.

Sikkandar Ravuttar, *Gnanarasa Temmanku*, Tuticorin, 1918, 4, MP. Songs in Temmanku style, containing the essence of wisdom, from the Muslim standpoint.

Siniyakil Ravuttar, C.A., *Cinkaravazhi Natai Lavani*, Ilayangudi, 1918, 20, IOL. Pilgrim songs describing Islamic festivals.

Abbas Ravuttar, *Palavarna Cintu*, Palghat, 1919, 18, MP. Devotional songs in different styles.

Mastan Sahib, *Meygnana Kanmani*, Ramnad, 1919, 7, MP. Devotional and moral verses.

Sheik Miran Mohiyidin, *Pikahul Akparin Tarjuma*, Islamiya Puthagasalai, 1919, ANIL. A religious work.

Muhammad Amir Sahib, *Meygnana Potham*, Madras, 1920, 22, MP. Moral verses.

Pir Muhammad, M., *Pamancari*, Trichinopoly, 1920, 63, IOL; see also MP, 1920. Popular songs.

Pirmuhamatu Cahibu, *Maharipattumalai*, Madras, 1920, 106, RMRL. A religious work.

Qadir Muhyi al din Pulavar, *Nasihattul Muminin Malai*, Madras, 1920, 2nd revised edition, 321, MP; see also IOL, 1920. Religious poem.

F: Stories, Novels, Dramas, and Maxims

P. Gnanaprakasa Mudaliyar (trans.), *The Arabian Nights Entertainment*, Madras, 1825, 12 volumes, IOL. English and Tamil versions in parallel columns.

P. Sinkarapalavendran Pillai (ed.), *Arabi Kathai*, 1845, s.l.c., 304, IOL. Tales from the *Arabian Nights*.

P. Sinkarapalavendran Pillai (ed.), *Paricuk Kathaikal*, Madras, 1850, 70, IOL. Opening stories only as given in a work called the Persian Wasti.

Riza Husain Khan (trans.), *Vivekacakaram*, Madras, 1854, 178, IOL. A didactic tale translated from the Persian.

A. Annasami Mudaliar (trans.), *Arabi Kathai*, Madras, 1856, vol. I, 488, IOL. Tales from the *Arabian Nights*.

Muhammad Mastan (trans.), *Viveka Vilakkam*, Madras, 1869, 43, IOL; Madras, 1870, a.e., IOL, MP. Wise sayings of prophets, kings and sages from the Persian *Tarikh-i-Guzidah* and other works; compiled and translated into Urdu by Ghulam Ali ibn Muhammad Amin al Din, Arugadu and thence rendered into Tamil.

Vanna Kalanjia Pulavar, *Theen Vilakkam*, Madras, 1869, 296, MP. The story of a battle fought between a Muslim from Medina and Vikrama Pandya of Madura and the triumph of the former.

Vanna Kalanjiya Pulavar, *Alibadusha Natakam*, Madras, 1870, 168, MSB; Madras, 1873, 168, MP; Madras, 1874, a.e., 168, MP; Madras, 1876, a.e., 168, MP; Madras, 1880, a.e., 164, MP. A dramatic sequence.

P.V. Muhammad Ibrahim (trans.), *Vikkiramathitan Kathai*, Madras, 1871, 410, IOL. A prose rendering of a Hindu story.

Ceytakkati Pulavar, *Ceytakkati Nondi Natakam*, Madras, 1873, 20, IOL; see also MP, 1873. A dramatic song sequence on an Islamic theme, edited by Abd al Karim and others.

Abdul Khader Sayubu, *Mucaliman Konte Karanam*, Madras, 1874, 12, IOL; see MP, a.e., 1875; see IOL, a.e., 1877. A tale from Islamic tradition.

Pulukkiyavutaiya Kissa, Yunucu Napiutaiya Kissa, Madras, 1874, 59, IOL; a.e., 1875, IOL. Two Muslim traditional tales.

Abdullah ben Abdilqadir (trans.), *De Pandja-Tandaran Tamilsche Omwerking Van Hit Indische Fabelboek*, Leiden, 1875, 148, INALCO. Translation of Hindu fables, edited by Van der Turck.

Hussain Khan, *Viveka Sakaram*, Madras, 1875, 167, MP; Madras, 1883, re-edition, MSB. A Tamil version of certain Persian stories.

Muhammad Kadir, *Thuthi Nama Ennum Kilikathai*, Madras, 1875, 112, IOL; 1883, a.e., IOL. A collection of tales from Persian.

Abdulla Sahib, *MalukuMulukin Pataippor*, Madras, 1876, 80, MP. A story of Maluku's battle with a giant.

Annasami Mudaliyar A., *Arabi Kathai*, Madras, 1876, re-edition, vol. I, 488; vol. II, pp. 466, IOL. Tales from the *Arabian Nights*.

Narayanaswami Mudali (publ.), *Arabik Kathaikal, Thokuthi 1*, Madras, 1876, 5th edition, 488, MSB. Tales from the *Arabian Nights*.

Mohamed Pulavar, *Saridu Malai*, Madras, 1876, 20, MP; see also IOL, 1876. A Tamil poem based on the legend of King Sarid.

Muhammad Sahib, *Nur Masala*, Madras, 1876, 60, MP; see also Madras, 1877, 79, IOL; Madras, 1878, a.e., 70, MP. A poem about a princess who refused to marry anyone who would not answer her hundred questions.

Abdul Khader Saib, *Satugnanikal Charitram*, Madras, 1877, 500, MP. A translation from a well-known Urdu book, *Char Dervish*.

Muhammad Ibrahim Sahib P.V., *Chardarvish Kathai*, Madras, 1877, 276, MP, MSB; 1881, a.e., MP, MSB. Story of four fakirs, adapted from Persian.

Muhammad Ismail (trans.), *Arayash Mahapil Ennum Hattim Taiyutaiya Kissa*, Madras, 1877, 425, IOL; see also MP, 1877. A rendering of the Urdu version of the Persian tale by Haider Baksh Haidari.

Seiku Yusupu or Mahomed Ibrahim Sahib, *Tajjal Nama* (*Narpattadaiyalangal*). Madras, 1877, 15, MP; Madras, 1878, MSB; Madras, 1882, MSB. The story of Tajjal.

Muhammad Ibrahim, *Abbasu Natakam*, Madras, 1878, 112, MP; see 1884, IOL. The story of the adventures of Prince Abbas.

Sheik Esop Labbay, *Riyalul Kikkam*, Madras, 1879, 102, MP. An account of the Tartar prince who reigned over the Khorasan.

Abdul Qadir, Pettai Amur, *Maluku Muluku Rajan Kathai*, Madras, 1880, 78, MSB, MP. The story of Muluku in Ammanai style.

Arumuga Mudaliar K.V., *Arabik Kathai—Part I*, Madras. 1880, 488, MSB. Tales from the *Arabian Nights*.

Arumuga Mudaliar K.V., *Arabik Kathai—Part II*, Madras, 1880, 468, MSB. Tales from the *Arabian Nights*.

Arumuga Mudaliar K.V., *Arabik Kathai—Part III*, Madras, 1880, 247, MSB. Tales from the *Arabian Nights*.

Singara Palavendiran Pillai, *Anubandha Arabik Kathai*, Madras, 1880, 185, MSB. Tales from the *Arabian Nights*.

Nambuthazhai Sinnavapu, *Thaiyar Sultan Natakam*, Konnur, 1881, (republished in 1990 by Muhammad Ali S.M.) see biblio. A dramatic sequence.

Abdul Kadar, *Zaitoun Kissa*, Madras, 1882, 72, MP. The story of Zaitoun, a princess of Iran, won by Mohammad Anif, one of Ali's sons.

Aliyar Pulavar, *Pururava Chakravarti Kathai*, Madras, 1887, 80, MP. A story of Pururuva Chakravarti.

Manikka Mudaliar P., *The Arabian Nights Entertainment*, Madras, 1887, 1568, MP. A complete edition of the *Arabian Nights* in Tamil.

Arabi Kathai, Madras, 1888, 3 volumes, IOL. A translation of the *Arabian Nights Entertainment*, based upon the edition published by Sokkalinga Mudaliyar and revised by Arumuga Desikar.

Arumuga Desigar (ed.), *Arabi Kathai*, Madras, 1888, vol. I, 503; vol. II, 476; vol. III, 251; IOL. Sokkalinga Mudaliar's version of the *Arabian Nights*.

Sokkalinga Mudaliyar K.V., *Arabi Kathai*, Madras, 1888, vol. II, 625; vol. II, 593; vol. III, 314; IOL. A translation of the *Arabian Nights*, with additions by P. Mannika Mudaliar.

Mohamed Abdulla, *Hussan Bé*, Madras, 1890, 2nd edition, MP. A religious story.

Raja Hussain Khan, *Viveka Sakaram*, Madras, 1890, 183, MP. Fiction, instructive stories.

Kanakkumadu Makudu Mukamattup Pulavar, *Upakara Sanjivi*, Madras, 1891, 535, MP. This story is also known as *Hatim Kissa*.

Muhammad Nizam Muhyi al Din Muhammad, Baburajapuram, *Nidhi*

Vinodha Kathai, Colombo, 1893, i, 38, IOL. Moral stories edited by Uthman Lebbai.

Aptur Katir Cayupu, Valai Bawa Cayupu Kumarar, *Pushpalilavati Kathai, Atipuri*, Madras, 1894, 160, RMRL. A story of Pushpalilavati.

Kadir Sahib S.P.S.K., Penang, *Hasya Manjari*, Penang, 1898, 17, IOL. Nine humorous tales.

Alikutti Musaliar M., *Char Darvish Akparul Munis*, Madras, 1901, 256, MP. Fiction.

Muammad Nayina Marakkayar, *Lal Gauher Natakam*, Madras, 1901, 110; republished in 1990 by Dr Muhammad Ali S.M. (see biblio).

Muhammad Nizam Muhyi al Din Muhammad, Baburajapuram, *Nidhi Sara Manjari*, Madras, 1901, 67, IOL. Moral stories.

Muhammad Tambi ibn Zain al Din (trans.), *Mano Ranjitha Tirattu*, Madras, 1901, 52, 16, IOL. A series of tales, translated from the Hindustani version of the *Hikayat i Latif*, a Persian storybook.

Muhammad Ibrahim Sahib, *Muhammad Anipukissa, Jainularbuhisa*, Madras, 1902, 54, MP. A story of Mohammad Anippu.

Daud Shaikh and Muhammad Shams al Din (trans.), *Navanitagnanan Gnana Suntari Ennum Naupal Gnanak Gnanak Suntar Charitram*, Madras, 1903, vol. I, 464, illus., IOL. A tale said to be translated from the Persian.

Mukamattu Ipurahim Cakipu, P.V., *Periya Vikkiramatittan Katai*, Madras, 1904, a.e., 7, 484, RMRL. Vikkiramatittan story.

Nagur Sinnavappu Marikkayar Talavay, M. (trans.), *Hurmuz kathai*, Singapore, 1904, 2, 2, 279, IOL. A tale translated from Hindustani.

Sinnavappu Marakkayar M. Talavay, Nagore, *Amin pi Charitram*, Madras, 1904, 156, 122, IOL. A novel said to be translated from a work by Mr George.

Sinkarapalavendran Pillai P. (ed.), *Padika Thakuntha Pakka Kathai*, Madras, 1905, xxiv–xxxii, 144, IOL; see also MP, 1906. A rendering of *Arabian Nights*.

Pakir Mohideen (trans.), *Pulukkiyavutaiya Kissavum, Yunus Napiutaiya Kissavum*, Madras, 1906, pp. 53, EFEO. Stories rendered from Arabic into Tamil.

Ghulam Ali M. (trans.), *Imam Jafar Sajah Kissa, Hajarat Amirul Muminin Maula Mushlikusha Kissa*, Trichinopoly, 1907, 16, MP. Two Muslim stories translated from Hindustani into Tamil.

Muhammad Nizam al Din, *Maha Vikata Vinoda Kalanjiyam*, Madras, 1907, 184, IOL. A collection of funny stories and anecdotes.

Ahamed Ghani Marakkayar, Nagur, K., *Jurji Zaidan* (*Ghassan Kannigai*

Charitram), Singapore, 1908, i, 183, IOL. Translated from Zaidan's *Fatah Ghassan* and recast into literary style by Talaway M. Sinnavappu Maraikkayar.

Nagur Sinnavappu Marakkayar, Talavay, M., *Arpuda Vallai Kathai*, Singapore, 1908, IOL. A romance.

Daud Shah B., *Sandrakasan Samarthiyangal, Darbhanga Dasi*, Madras, 1910, 42, MP. A tale of adventure.

Malkhanali V.A. (trans.), *Paithal Mukttisin Yudha Charitram*, Madras, 1910, Pt. 1, 165, IOL. A rendering of an Urdu historical novel dealing with the wars of the crusade and the conversion of a Christian lady and her marriage to a Muslim.

Moulavi Mir Zahir ul Din (trans.), *Gulistan Ennum Pungavanam*, Madras, 1910, 2, 212, IOL. A translation of Sa'di's *Gulistan*, a collection of Persian stories and moral dicta.

Moulvi Muhammad Abdur Rahman Sahib, *Gultasta-e-Shabir*, Madras, 1910, 22, MP. Contains miscellaneous poems.

Shaikh Daud bin Khatib Amin Sahib and Muhammad Shams ul Din bin Khatib Amin Sahib (trans.), *Amir Hamzah Jang or Dastan-i-Amir Hamzah*, Madras, 1910–15, 5 Parts, (Part I, 4, 385; Part II, 410; Part III, 416; Part IV, 403; Part V, 245), IOL. An anonymous romance on the life of Hamzah, uncle of Muhammad, originally written in Persian and translated from the Hindustani version into Tamil.

Husain ibn Ahmad ul Kabir (jalal-ul-Din) Bukhari, *Jahangasht Arpudam*, Madras, 1911, viii, 84, IOL. A book of travels and adventures, originally written in Persian under the title *Musafir Namah i Makhdum i Jahaniyan Jahangasht* and thence translated into Tamil by Muhyi ul Din Khan Sahib (Jamal ul Din) of Tinnevelly and edited by Kalai Hasan Ali Pulavar. It describes the travels of Saiyid Jalaluddin of Turkestan, named Jahangast (globetrotter).

Muhammad Abd Allah Lebbai, *Khadijavukkum Kallanukkum Nadantha Kissa*, Madras, 1911, 56, IOL. A Mulsim traditional tale adopted from an Arabic source.

Muhyidhin Khan (trans.), *J'ihaz Kapttarputan*, Madras, 1911, 86, IOL. A rendering of the Persian book of travel *Musafir Namah*.

Daud Shah N.B., *pandithai Mesmerisa*, Madras, 1912, 214, IOL. A novel relating the adventures of an English lady and her marvellous band of sailors.

Muhammad Abdussalam Alim Mastan Sahib, *Madarniti Manaduvalliyam*,

Trichinopoly, 1914, 11, MP. A collection of 160 moral couplets in popular style, apostrophising the mind as one's own better half.

Aptul Katir Cayupu, Valai Bawa Cayupu Kumarar, *Kulepakavali Kissa Enru Vazankukinra Pushpalilavatikatai*, Madras, 1915, 160, RMRL. A story of Pushpalilavati.

Engman's Indian Series, *Muhammadiya Kathaikal*, Madras, 1915, 60, IOL; see also RMRL. A school reader (tales).

Hakim Shaik Dawood Sahib & Hakim Mohammad Shamsuddin Sahib, *Amir Hamza Jang*, Madras, 1915, 245, IOL. A story.

Mustafa Labbai S.M., *Apunawaz Vikata Kalanjiyam*, Madras, 1915, 55, MP. A collection of funny Islamic stories.

Nayina Muhammad Pavalar, M.A., *Abu Nawaz Vikata Kalanjiyam*, Madras, 1915, 55, IOL. Amorous stories based on the tales of the Baghdad poet, Abu Nawaz.

Sinkarapalavendran Pillai P. (ed.), *Parisukhathaikal*, Madras, 1915, 704, IOL. Tales from the *Arabian Nights*.

Hakim Muhammad Ismail (trans.), *Hattim Taiyudaiya Kissa*, Madras, 1916, 5th edition, 462, MP. Relates the story of an Arabian king called Hatim Tai and his great self-sacrificing charities.

Ismayl Alim Sahib Muhammad, *Sam Unraliyallagu Angudaiya Kissa*, Madras, 1916, 48, MP; see also MSB, 1889. The story of a disciple of the Prophet; contains also some prayer songs.

Muhammad Ismail Sahib (trans.), *Arayish Mahapil Ennum Hattim Taiyutaiya Kissa*, Madras, 1916, 5th edition, viii, 454, IOL. A rendering of the Urdu version of the Persian tale by Haider Baksh Haidari; the story of Hathim Tai, prince of Yemen.

Singarapalavendran Pillai P. (ed.), *Aayirathoru Nalil Solliya Parisu Kathaikal*, Madras, 1916, 704, IOL. A version of the *Arabian Nights*.

Yusuf Labbai (V.M. Muhammad), *Mankathai Vacanam*, Madras, 1917, 40, MP. The story of the deer in prose.

Khadar Muhiyuddin Raguttar, *Nankumantri Kummi Pattu*, Chidambaram, 1918, 8, MP. Kummi songs on the story of four ministers.

G: Medicine

Mahomed Abdulla Sahib, *Unani Vaidya Dhatu Vridhi Bodini*, Madras, 1887, 347, MP. A medical work on the Muslim method of improving one's blood.

Sheik Abdul Khadar Sahib T.P., *Agastyar Purana Kavyam*, Madras, 1888,

166, MP. A poem of 1000 stanzas ascribed to the sage Agastyar, treatise on the Yoga philosophy.

Hakim Syed Ibrahim, *Medical Form*, Madras, 1889, 2, MP. This is a Tamil version of a *Medical Form*.

Muhammatu Aptulla Cayapu, Pa. Hakkim, *Yunani Vaittiya Taruttiya Virutta Potini, Nankam Pakam*, Madras, 1890, 120, RMRL; Madras, 1890, 2nd edition, 120, RMRL. A Unani medical work.

Muhammad Abd Allah, son of Baburajapuram Bawa Sahib, *Yunani Vaidya Dhatu Vriddhi Bodhini*, Madras, 1893, vol. ii, xv–xxx, 636, IOL; see also MP. A medical work based on the Unani system of medicines for strengthening the semen.

Muhammad Abd Allah P., *Taruttiya Virtti Potini*, Madras, 1893, Pt. II, 30, 602, IOL. A Unani medical manual.

Muhammad Abdullah P., *Yunani Vaithiya Dhatu Virutti Pothini*, Madras, 1894, 240, MSB. A Unani medical work for stregthening the semen.

Muhammad Nizam Muhyi al Din ibn Muhammad, Baburajapuram, *Kutumba Samrakshani*, Madras, 1896, xxiv, 410, vi, IOL. A treatise on social hygiene and morals.

Muhammad Abd Allah, son of Baburajapuram Bawa Sahib, *Prameha Nivarana Bodhini*, Madras, 1897, xx, 232, IOL. A Unani treatise on the cure of gonorrhoea.

Abdulla Sahib, *Plague Chikitsa Potini*, Madras, 1898, 171, MSB. A Unani work on precautions against plague.

Mahomed Abdulla Sahib, B., *Siraavaka Nivaarana Pothini*, Madras, 1898, 232, MSB. On venereal diseases, according to the Unani system.

Hakim B. Mahomed Abdulla Sahib, *Raja Vaidya Makutam* (*Yamaka Venba*), Madras, 1899, 76, MP. A rare poetical work on medicine by Téraiyar, an ancient Tamil physician.

Hakim B. Mahomed Abdulla Sahib, *Raja Vaidya Makutam or Selections from Téraiyar's Yamaka Venba*, Madras, 1899, 395, MP. This is a fully annotated edition.

Abd Allah ibn Abd al Karim, Bangalore, *Aandror Anubhoga Kaivalya Vaidya Sangraham*, Bangalore, 1900, 4, viii, 88, IOL. A treatise on the medical art, chiefly in verse, arranged for singing by A. Amrita Vachaka Dasar and edited by T. Ratna Sami Pillai.

Muhammatu Aptulla Cayapu, Pa. Hakkim, *Nayanaroka Nivarana Potini*, Madras, 1900, 2nd part, 478, RMRL. A Unani work.

Ceyyutu Aptur Rahiman Cakipu, Hakkim, *Yunani Patarttakunavilakka Caracankirakam*, Madras, 1902, 272, RMRL. A Unani work.

Hakim Shaik Davud Sahib and Hakim Shamsudeen Sahib (brothers), *Vaidyamirta Bodhini, Part I*, Madras, 1902, 80, MP. A medical work.

Akkim Aptulla Cayupu, Akkim Aptulkarim Cayupu Kumarar, *Anrorkala Larulicceyta Yunani Anupokavaittiya Caracankirakam*. Madras, 1906, viii, 87, RMRL. A Unani work.

Muhammad Abd Allah B., *Anubhoga Vaittiya Navanitam*, Madras, 1906, Pt. I, xxiv, 239; Pt. II, 11, 202; Pt. III, 24, 253; IOL; see also MP, 1907. A Unani medical manual on the preparation of medicines.

Muhammad Abd Allah, B., *Kadukka Prabhava Bodhini*, Madras, 1906, 48, 2, MP. A work on the efficacy of the Indian gall-nut used for medical purposes.

Muhammad Abd Allah, B., *Visha Bedi Nivarani*, Madras, 1906, 74, MP; Madras, 1917, 3rd edition, 84, EFEO. Remedy for cholera.

Nijamukiyittin Cakipu Muhamattu, Hakkim, *Kuttumpasamrakshani*, Madras, 1906, 2nd edition, 420, 6, RMRL; see also EFEO. A book on family hygiene, discipline, morality, etc.

Habilukarathipu Kosu Muhammad Usain Alim Sahib, *Jananukula Manjari*, Chidambaram, 1907, 36. On treatment of disease, especially of pregnant women.

Muhammad Abd Allah, son of Baburajapuram Bawa Sahib, *Ilakka Saumya Sagaram*, Madras, 1907, vol. I, 4, 17, 108; vol. II, 6, 2, 177; vol. III, 2, 2, 177; vol. IV, 2, 2, 167, MP; see also IOL. A metrical handbook of medicine in 8 parts ascribed to the legendary Agastyar, with prose commentary.

Muhammad Abd Allah Sahib, B. (ed.), *Agastiyar Pallu*, Madras, 1907, 17, 237, IOL. A metrical treatise on medicine in 226 paragraphs ascribed to Agastyar.

Muhammad Abdus Salam Sahib, *Iracavata Manjari*, Madras, 1909, 18, 152, IOL; see also MP, 1909. A treatise on the preparation of medicines.

Muhammad Abd Allah, P., *Taruttiya Virutti Bodhini*, Madras, 1910, Pt. 1, 72, 396; Pt. 2, 60, 672; Pt. 4, 24, 215, IOL. A manual of medicine.

Muhammad Abdulla Sahib, Hakim B., *Anubhoga Vaidya Navaneetam, Part 6*, Madras, 1911, 14, 228. MP. A handbook containing instructions for the preparation and use of certain medicines.

Abdus Salam A.M., *Irasavatha Manjarai*, Madras, 1912, second edition, 10, 159, MP. A work on alchemy, with explanations for the preparation of certain medicines.

Muhammad Abd Allah, P. (ed.), *Vikata Tirattu*, Madras, 1912, Pt. 1, 20,

242; Pt. 2, 16, 228, IOL. A metrical treatise on medicine, edited with commentary.

Muhammad Abdulla Sahib Hakim B., *Anubhoga Vaidya Navaneetam, Part 7,* Madras, 1912, 8, 4, 216, MP. A handbook containing instructions for the preparation and use of certain medicines.

Muhammad Ibrahim ibn Hasan Labbai, T.A., *Najathul Anim Fi Nailil Maram,* Madras, 1912, 10, 1, 34, 5, 680, MP, IOL. A treatise on medicine, biology and mineralogy, from classical Arabic sources.

Muhammad Abd Allah, P. (ed.), *Mesmerisa Paatankal,* Madras, 1913, 24, 104, 26, IOL. A treatise on mesmerism.

Muhammad Abdulla Sahib Hakim B., *Yunani Suksma Cikitsa Bodhini.* Madras, 1913–15, Pt. 1, 33, 179; Pt. 2, 38, 218; Pt. 3, 11, 213, IOL. A Unani medical manual on the treatment of diseases.

Muhammad Abd Allah, P., *Anubhoga Vaittiya Navanitam,* Madras, 1914, vol. I, 20, 200; vol. II, 11, 202; vol. III, 20, 252; vol. IV, 20, 228; vol. V, 111, 231; vol. VI, 18, 228; vol. VII, 11, 116; vol. VIII, 11, 216, IOL; Madras, 1917, 2nd edition, MP.

Muhammad Abd Ullah, son of Baburajapuram Bawa Sahib (ed.), *Vallarai Prabhava Bodhini,* Madras, 1914, 12, 96, IOL, RMRL; 1915, a.e., IOL. An account of the medicinal virtues of 'Vallara', according to the Unani system.

Muhammatu Aptulla Cayapu, Pa. Hakkim, *Katukhayp Pirapava Potini,* Madras, 1914, 3rd edition, 118, RMRL. An account of the virtues of some medicines.

Muhammad Abd Allah, *Stri Vaittiya Bodhini,* Madras, 1915, Pt. 1, 24m 240; Pt. 2, 24, 312, IOL. Deals with symptoms, diagnoses and treatment of women's diseases according to the Unani system.

Muhammad Abd Allah, *Taruttiya Virutti Bodhini,* Madras, 1915, 42, 116, IOL (Part 4, 230, MP; previous parts not received for registration). A Unani medical manual for preparing certain medicines.

Muhammad Abd Allah, Hakim B., *Anubhoga Vaittiya Navanitam,* Madras, 1915, IOL (Part 9, 208; Part 10, 241, MP). Contains directions for preparing common medicines found to be of value in relation to various diseases, according to the Unani system.

Muhammad Abd Allah Sahib H.B., *Cikitsa Bodini,* Madras, 1915, Part III, 215, MP. Describes the symptoms of various diseases and their remedies; also deals with the preparation of various medicines.

Muhammad Abd Ullah, son of Baburajapuram Bawa Sahib (ed.), *Sadha Slokam Ennum Vaidya Satakam,* Madras, 1915, 24, 144, IOL. Hundred verses on Unani medicine, with glossaries, notes, etc.

Muhammatu Aptulla Cayapu, Pa.Hakkim, *Yunani Pala Vaittiya Potini*, Madras, 1916, 36, 288, RMRL. A Unani work.

Muhammad Abdulla Sahib Pa., *Visha Petti Nivarani*, Madras, 1917, 3rd edition, 84, IOL. A medical work.

Yakub, *Sunnam 300*, E.R. Gurusami Konar, Madura, 1917, 56, MP. The 300 powders; a work on indigenous medicine.

Yakub, *Vaidiya Cintamani*, E.R. Gurusami Konar, Madura, 1918, 112, MP. The 750 gems of medicine.

Yakub, *Vaiddiya Sustiram*, E.R. Gurusami Konar, Madura, 1917, 40, MP. A work on indigenous medicine.

Yakub, *Lokasenduram*, E.R. Gurusami Konar, Madura, 1918, 58, MP. 300 metallic oxides; a pamphlet on indigenous medicinal preparation.

Abdus Salam A.M. (ed.), *Suyanubhava Vaiddiya Cintamani*, Madras, 1919, 96, MP. A work describing the preparation of various medicines according to the indigenous system.

H: Lithographic Works in Arabic or Tamil Characters

Yusuf, son of Qadir Ahmad Shaik, *Jawahir al-Yaqin fi Tibzin Aqa'id al-Din*, Madras, 1862, 462, lith., IOL. An Islamic religious work.

Fath al-Majid fi Hadith al-Nabi al Hamid, Bombay, 1878, 592, 64, lith., IOL. An Islamic devotional treatise.

Muhammad Yusuf al Hanafi, *Sint al Silyan*, Madras, 1879, 570, lith., IOL. A Hanefite educational trust.

Habib Muhammad, al Bakri al Kahiri, *Al Futuhat al Rahmaniyat*, 1879–84, lith., IOL. A book in Arabic and Tamil, written in Arabic script, with an interlineary translation and commentary.

Ahmad Ibn Ahmad, al Sharji al Zabidi, *Al-Fawa'id fi al-Salat Wa'l-Awa'id*, Bombay, 1810, xviii, 446, lith., IOL. A work on prayers and pious charms, etc.

Muhammad Yusuf ibn Kadir Ahmad, Ammapattanam, *Al Durar al Hasan, Amabitini*, Madras, 1880, vol. I, xiv, 1011, 5, lith., IOL. A Muslim law book in Arabic characters, according to the Hanafi school.

Moulvi Mohammad Usuff Saib, *Simitus Sibyan*, Madras, 1881, 576, MP; Madras, 1884, a.e., 416, MP. Prayer book.

Futuhat al Rahmaniyah fi Tafsir Kalam al Rabbaniyah fi Tafsir Kalam al Rabanniyah, Bombay, 1882, 626, lith., IOL. The text of the Quran with Tamil interlined commentary.

Habib Muhammad, Al Bakri Al Kahiri, *Tanbih al Anam*, Bombay, 1882, iv, 132, lith., IOL. A book in Arabic characters on the interpretation of dreams.

Nuh ibn Abd al Kadir, al Kahiri, *Al-Durar fi Hikayat al-Ghuran or Kisas al Auliya,* Bombay, 1882, 331, lith., IOL. A collection of anecdotes of Muslim saints.

Shaik Muhammad Yusuf Labbay Alim, *Jawahirul Yaldun*, Madras, 1884, 2nd edition, 496, MP. A prose tract.

Sheik Muhammad Yusuf Labbay Alim, *Javahir Nofisa*, Madras, 1884, 330, lith., MP. A religious tract.

Abdul Khadar, title unknown, Madras, 1885, 40, lith., MP. Arabic traditions with translations in a mixed dialect of Arabic and Tamil.

Abd al Kadir ibn Madar, *Futuhat-al-Salam*, Bombay, 1890, viii, 604, 32, lith., IOL. A compendium of Muslim law.

Habib Muhammad, al Bakri al Kahiri, *Bushra al-Karim*, Bombay, 1890, iv, 137, lith., IOL. A work on the interpretations of dreams and the mystic virtues of the Quran.

Hfiz Mahomed Ibrahim, *Fattal Mannan*, Madras, 1890, 218, lith., MP; see also IOL, 1890. A work on the tenets of Islam.

Mahomed Alim Sahib, *Umdatur Sibian*, Madras, 1891, 288, lith, MP. An Arabic work with vernacular aids on the principles of Islam.

Muhammad Kassim ibn Siddik Labbai, *Kitab al-Hisab*, Kandy, 1891, 15, lith., IOL. Elementary arithmetic.

Muhammad Kassim ibn Siddik Labbai, *Turfat al-Mahin*, Kandy, 1891, 112, 1, lith., IOL. A shorter grammar of the Arabic language.

Muhammad Kassim ibn Siddik Labbai, *Usul al-Kira'at al-Arabiyat*, Kandy, 1891, 2 parts, lith., IOL. An elementary Arabic reading book.

Muhammad Sahib ibn Habib Muhammad, *Miftah al Rahman*, Madras, 1891, 88, 31, lith., IOL. A treatise on Muslim eschatology.

Muhammad Tamim ibn Muhammad, *Umdat al Sibyan*, Madras, 1891, viii, 288, 66, lith., IOL. A manual of Muslim religious instruction according to the Shafi school.

Sayed Mahomed Alim Sahib, *Mufta-hur-Rahman*, Madras, 1891, 88, lith., MP. A description of the world in the light of religion, translated from a standard Arabic work.

Muhammad Nizamuddin Sahib, *Nur Namah*, Madras, 1892, 114, lith., MP. A work naming the attributes of God and showing how the Prophet was inspired with knowledge and light.

Sheik Tamim Sahib, *Zarurul Musalmin*, Madras, 1892, 64, lith., MP. A work explaining the simple principles and doctrines of Islam.

Tamin Ibn Sultan, *Tuhfat al Ahbab*, Madras, 1892, 64, lith., IOL. A manual of religious instruction for Muslims.

Ahmad ibn Muhammad Hasan, al Matabatani, *Durrat al ma Fakhir*, Colombo, 1893, 64, lith., IOL. A compendium of religious instruction.

Nuh ibn Abd al Kadir, al Kahiri, *Tuhfat al Kiram*, Bombay, 1893, vols. 2, 3, lith., IOL. A treatise on Muslim ethics.

Muhammad Ghauth al-Madrasi, *Nath al Jawahir fi Manaqil al Sayyid Abd Qadir al Jilani*, Madras, 1896, 319, lith., IOL. A religious work translated by Muhammad Madinah Kottari.

Muhammad ibn Abi Bakr ibn Rashid, al Baghdadi, *Al Witriyah*, Bombay, 1896, 688, 88, 2, lith., IOL. A poem in praise of the Prophet, etc.

Muhammad Kassim Abu Siddik Labbai, *Al-Hidayat al Kasimiyat*, Kandy, 1896, xiii, 242, lith., IOL. A grammar of the Arabic language in Tamil.

Bandah (Abd al Wahab), *Kasa'id i bandah*, Madras, 1897, 32, lith., IOL. A series of Muslim religious poems.

Muhammad ibn Ahmad, al Kadiri, *Fath-al-Daiyan*, Bombay, 1898, 2 parts, lith., IOL. A manual of religious instruction, etc.

Muhammad Ismail ibn Muhammad Madinah, *Hidayat al-Salikin*, Madras, 1898, xxxii, 478, lith., IOL; see also MP, MSB, 1899. Biographies of the principal teachers of the Shazili order followed by a manual on ascetism.

Muhammad Ibrahim Sahib, *Talkin-bi-Muhimma-Tuttinvi-Avulatul-Muslimin*, Madras, 1901, 92, printed and lith., MP. A religious work.

Sam Shihab al-Din ibn Sulaiman, Kayalpattinam, *Mazhal-al-Ahkam*, Madras, 1901, vii, 160, lith., IOL. A religious work.

Abd al Kadir ibn Muhammad Muhyi al din, al Kadiri, *Fath al Samad*, Madras, 1902, 336, lith., IOL. The story of the learned slave girl Tawaddud and her examination of the Ulema before the Caliph Harun al Rashid.

Mahomed Abdul Rahman, *Taytul Rahman*, Madras, 1902, 272, lith., MP. A religious work.

Moulvi Mahomed Tamim M., *Uni-ya-tul-Atfal*, Madras, 1902, 56, lith., MP. A religious work.

Moulvi Muhammad Hussain A., *Salaatul Musafir*, Madras, 1902, 128, lith., MP. A religious work.

Muhammad Abd al Rahman ibn Kadir Miran, *Ta'yid al Rahman*, Madras, 1902, viii, 272, lith., IOL. A manual of the art of reciting from the Quran.

Nuh ibn Abd al Kadir, al Kahiri, *Fath al-Samad*, Bombay, 1902, 90, lith.,

IOL. A treatise on the names of the companions who fell in the battle of Badr and Uhrid and their use for devotional purposes, etc.

Nuh ibn Abd al Kadir, al Kahiri, *Nafahat al Anbar*, Bombay, 1902, vi, 398, lith., IOL. Life of the Sufi saint, Abu al Hasan al Shazili, etc.

Saiyid Amad Sahib (ed.), *Ahkam*, Madras, 1902, 160, lith., MP. A religious work.

Shah al Hamid ibn Aidarus, *Miftah al Salah*, Madras, 1902, viii, 240, lith., IOL. A treatise on marriage and sexual intercourse.

Muhammad Abu Bakr Alim Sahib, *Umdattul Musalli*, Madras, 1903, 64, lith., MP. A religious work.

Shahul Hamid Labbai M.A., *Mif-Thakus-Salah-fi-Sahin Nikah*, Madras, 1903, 63, lith., MP; see also IOL, 1903. A work on marriage.

Ahmad ibn Abd Allah, *Labab al-Akhbar*, Madras, 1904, 10, 132, lith., IOL. A collection of 400 traditions or sayings of the Prophet in Arabic, with a Tamil translation.

Jamal Muhieddin Sahib, *Tuhfat-ul-Atfal le Tahaffuz-e-Lubdat-ul-Amal*, Madras, 1904, 48, lith., MP. A work on the doctrines of the Hanafi sect.

Minhat-ul-Atfal Le Tahaffuze-e-Zubdat ul-Amal, Madras, 1904, 48, lith., MP; see also IOL, 1904. A work on the Shafi sect.

Moulvi Shaik Abdul Khadir Alim Sahib S., *Manahil-ul-Mannan-fi-Mathalib-ul-It Khan*, Madras, 1904, 492, lith. and printed, MP; see also IOL, 1904. A religious work.

Muhammad Abd al Kadir ibn Adam, Téralanduri called Kader Sahib, *Shams-ul-Marifat*, Madras, 1904–1905, x, 184, lith., IOL; see also MP, 1905. A manual of scholastic theology.

Muhammad Ibrahim Sahib K., *Talkin-fi-Muhimmthud-din li-Avala-dil Muslimin*, Madras, 1904, 136, lith., MP; see also IOL, 1904. A catechism of religious instruction for Muslim children.

Muhammad Sultan Alim Sahib, *Sharajatul Anbia*, Madras, 1904, 1, lith., MP. A religious work.

Abdur Raheem Sahib Labbai, *Wihadat un Nabi*, Madras, 1905, 18, lith., MP. Contains the history of the birth of the Prophet in verse.

Moulvi Tambi Mamuna Labbai, *Nizam-ul-Aka-id*, Madras, 1905, 80, lith., MP; see also IOL, 1905. A religious work.

Muhammad Abd al Kadir ibn Adam, Téralanduri called Kadir Sahib, *Sair-al-Salikin*, Madras, 1905–06, xvi, 168, 72, lith., IOL. A manual of religious discipline, with some prayers and talismanic diagrams for religious purposes.

Shah al Hamid ibn Aidarus, *Fawa'id al-Koran*, Madras, 1905–06, 544, lith., IOL; see also MP, 1906 and IOL, 1906. A treatise on the use of Quranic texts, prayers, pious formulae and mystic diagrams, for talismanic purposes.

Mohiuddin Abdul Khadar Sahib Marakkayar, *Dajjal Nama*, Madras, 1906, 32, lith., MP; Madras, 1908, 32, 2nd edition, lith., MP; see also IOL. An account of Dajjal, a powerful person expected to come from the east, before the world comes to an end, persuading people to follow him.

Muhammad Abdul Rahman T., *Ababul Akhyar fi Thurjumati Libabil Akhbar*, Madras, 1906, 136, lith., MP. The holy speeches of the Prophet.

Muhammad Abu Bakr Hanafi, *Haikal-us-Saba*, Madras, 1906, 24, lith., MP. A collection of seven benedictory formulas pronouncing blessing upon the Prophet and His descendants.

Muhammad Inayat Ahmad, *A Manual of the Muhammedan Law of inheritance*, Madras, 1906, xvi, 176, viii, lith., IOL; see also IOL, 1907. Translated from Hindustani into Tamil by Muhammad Abdul Rahman.

Muhammad Sharafuddin (ed.), *Umdattunissa*, Kolimalaimailyilpatti, south Arcot, 1906, 88, lith., MP; see also IOL. Muslim commandments to women, edited with Tamil commentary.

Ahmed Ibrahim M.S., *Tibbul Akbar*, Nagore, 1907, 24, lith., MP; see also IOL, 1907. Islamic purificatory ceremonies.

Haji Muhammad Abdulla (publ.), *Ilm-un-Nissa*, Madras, 1907, 32, lith., MP. A work on Islamic marriages.

Moulvi Abdul Rahman Sahib, *Sirathul Islam Sirathunnajat*, Nellikuppam, 1907, 72, lith., MP. A work on religious doctrines.

Moulvi Muhammad Abdul Khadir alias Khadir Sahib, *Mujma-ul-Asrar fu Salat-il-Abrar*, Tiralandur, Tanjore dist., 1907, 408, lith., MP; see also IOL. A selection of prayers in Arabic with the Tamil translation.

Moulvi Muhammad Abdul Rahman Sahib (ed.), *Ilmul Parayiz*, Madras, 1907, 200, lith., MP. Muslim law, moral and religious.

Muhammad Abd ul Kadir ibn Adam, Teralanduri, called Kadir Sahib, *Majma'ul-Asrar fi Salat il-Abrar*, Madras, 1907, viii, 400, lith., IOL. Rules for ceremonial purifications and prayers for Muslims.

Majma-ul-Munajat, Madras, 1907, 16, lith., MP. Contains supplications to God to be addressed after offering prayers.

Abdul Aziz (publ.), *Yasidi Mala*, Madras, 1908, 16, lith., MP. A short collection of Arabic poems in praise of the Prophet and the ministers of Islam; contains also prayer formulae for the aversion of calamity.

Ghulam Dastagir Sahib, *Muhimmat-us-Sibyan fi Mazhab-e-Abi Hanifatin Nuhman*, Madras, 1908, 64, lith., MP. Contains rules regarding offering of prayers to God five times a day.

Haji Sheik Muhieddin, *Aria-ul-Arsh*, Madras, 1908, 16, lith., MP. Invocations or blessings upon the Prophet and his descendants.

Mana Abdul Rahaman Sahib and Nagoor Miran Sahib, *Thodu Vodai Hanafi*, Madras, 1908, 32, lith., MP. A short treatise on Hanafism.

Majma-ul-Moonajall, Madras, 1908, 16, lith., MP. Prayer formula.

Moulvi Ahasanuddin, *Mufeedul Anam*, Madras, 1908, 140, lith., MP. A work on dreams.

Moulvi Muhammad Tamim, *Farayaz-ul-Muslamina Shafai'ah*, Madras, 1908, 32, lith., MP. A work on Islamic doctrines.

Moulvi Muhammad Tamim, *Milad Nama*, Madras, 1908, 48, lith., MP. A work on the important events that took place at the time of the birth of the Prophet.

Muhammad Abdu Rahman Labbai (trans.), *Vasatlul Mirdolti Turzooma-i-Dalanial-Klyralt*, Madras, 1908, 400, lith., MP. Formulae of salutations and blessings.

Muhammad Abdu Rahman Sahib (ed.), *Eilmunissa*, Madras, 1908, 32, lith., MP. A work on the etiquette to be observed on the occasion of the nuptial ceremony among Muslims.

Muhammad Abdul Rahman (ibn kadir Miran) Sahib Labbai, T., *Al-Jawahir ul-Khamsat ul-Kabirat*, Madras, 1908, 536, lith., IOL; see also MP, 1908. A work dealing with aspects of natural history, erotics, diseases, excellence of the Quran and the talismanic virtues of the *Asma ul Husna* and other names.

Muhammad Abdur Rahman Sahib T., *Ahakam i Salah fi Ahakam i Nikah*, Madras, 1908, 296, lith., MP. Scriptural commands on marriage and notes on omens and astrological disposition of planets.

Muhammad Asanuddin (ed.), *Vafath-ul-Rasool*, Lalpet, 1908, 24, lith., MP. A short account of the circumstances relating to the death of the Prophet.

Muhammad Fazlullah Sahib, *Unjal Nama*, Madras, 1908, 16, lith., MP. Songs in praise of the Prophet and some saints.

Muhammad Fazlullah Sahib, *Yasin Tafsir*, Madras, 1908, 32, lith., MP. Short notes on *Sura-i-Yasin*, a chapter of the Quran.

Muhammad Fazlullah Sahib Labbay, *Yasin Faida*, Madras, 1908, 32, lith., MP. A work on the benefits to be derived from reading the *Sura-i-Yasin*, a chapter of the Quran.

Muhammad ibn Sulaiman, al-Jazuli, *Dala'il ul-Khairat*, Madras, 1908, xvi,

400, lith., IOL. A Muslim prayer book in Arabic, with an interlinear Tamil translation and a marginal Tamil commentary, etc.

Muhammad Mohiuddin Sahib, *Nabiulla Malay and Rasool Malay*, Madras, 1908, 36, lith., MP. Poems in praise of the Prophet and the saints.

Muhammad Sulaiman Sahib (ed.), *Dakka-i-Akkas*, Madras, 1908, 32, lith., MP. A prayer formula intended to seek protection from epidemic diseases.

Muhammad Sulaiman Sahib, *Khasia-i-Ramzan*, Madras, 1908, 32, lith., MP. A work on the holiness of the month of Ramzan.

Muhammad Sulaiman Sahib, *Rathib-i-Jalalia*, Madras, 1908, 32, lith., MP. Certain poems in praise of the Prophet together with some select prayers addressed to saints.

Muhammad Sulaiman Sahib (publ.), *Tolai Fathaha*, Colombo, 1908, 48, lith., MP. A short collection of Arabic prayers for securing wealth and prosperity, in verse and with Tamil translation.

Muhammad Sulaiman Sahib, *Thodu Vodai Hanafi*, Madras, 1908, 32, lith., MP. A work on prayers according to the Hanafi rites.

Muhammad Sulaiman Sahib, *Thodu Vodai Shafi*, Madras, 1908, 32, lith., MP. A work on prayers according to the Shafi law.

Muhammad Sulaiman Sahib, *Thofatul Vildun ul Sibian*, Madras, 1908, 32, lith., MP. A short treatise of the orthography of the Arabic characters and on the appropriate manner of reading the Quran.

Muhammad Sulaiman Sahib T.M.S., *Majmu-e-Dua-e-Gani-ul-Arash*, Colombo, 1908, 96, lith., MP. Devotional passages and prayers.

Muhammad Tamim Sahib, *Minhul Gaffon*, Madras, 1908, 48, lith., MP. A work on the benefits to be derived from the systematic offering of Islamic prayers; also contains translations of a few selected passages from the Quran.

Muhammad Yakub al Ansari, *Mufid al Ameen*, Madras, 1908, 140, lith., IOL. A religious work.

Muhammad Yakub Sahib, *Eilmunissa*, Madras, 1908, 32, lith., MP. A work on the etiquette to be observed on the occasion of the nuptial ceremony among Muslims.

Muhammad Yakub Sahib, *Yakutba*, Madras, 1908, 20, lith., MP. A work in praise of Mahs-ul-Subbani, a holy man.

Muktasar e-Mouhabat-ul-Sibyan, Madras, 1908, 40, lith., MP. A work on the Shafi sect and the Islamic doctrines.

Muktasar-e-Mouhabat-ul-Wildan, Madras, 1908, 40, lith., MP. A work on the Hanafi sect and its doctrines.

Nina Labbay H., *Hakeekathul Malay*, Madras, 1908, 128, lith., MP. Poems on the theology of the Sufis.

Tsodi Amar, Madras, 1908, 64, lith., MP. A work on the merit of punctual attendance of prayers.

Saiyid Muhammad Sahib, *Thala Fathia*, Madras, 1908, 48, lith., MP. A short account of the family and life of the Prophet.

Shah ul Hamid ibn Aidarus (ed.), *Naskh ul Hadith wa-Fath ul Majid*, Madras, 1908, 12, 576, lith., IOL. A treatise on the tradition of Islam and its authority in doctrine and conduct.

Shahul Hamid Lebbai M.A., *Qissah Bibi Maryam*, Madras, 1908, 88, lith., IOL. An account of the Virgin Mary.

Abd al Qadir ibn Madar Shaik, *Fath al-Rahman fi Tafsir al Koran*, Madras, 1909, 141, lith., IOL. An interpretation of the *Surah al-Fatiha*.

Abdul Aziz Sahib (publ.), *Vallati Qissa-Vallati Masla*, Ambur, 1909, 16, lith., MP. A dialogue on the unity of God.

Appa Pillai, Abdul Aziz Sahib, *Sakrat Nama*, Madras, 1909, 20, lith., MP. A work on death and its fears.

Chowdri Chownakutti Badruddin Sahib, *Qissa-e-Maryam*, Vaniyambadi, 1909, 48, lith., MP. A story of Mary.

Chowdara Chowra Kutti Badruddin, *Qissa-e-Maryam*, Ambur, 1909, 48, lith., MP. The story of Mary.

Inayat-Namh fi Tandih Nur-Namah, Madras, 1909, 144, lith., IOL. A Muslim theological treatise.

Moona, Moona, Saiyid Ibrahim, *Faiz ul-Majid-Fe-Manaqib-us-Saiyid-us-Sultan Ibrahim*. Madras, 1909, 96, lith., MP. A work in praise of Saint Ibrahim.

Mowlana Abdul Rahman bin Ismail, *Al-Maizathul Khutba-fi-Tarjamathul Khutba*, Madras, 1909, 492, lith., MP. Friday sermons delivered in mosques in praise of the Prophet and his successors, in Arabic together with their translation in Tamil.

Muhammad Abdul Aziz (publ.), *At-Tarjamatu-ya-Kuthba*, Madras, 1909, 24, lith., MP. A poem in praise of the Prophet.

Muhammad Abdul Aziz (publ.), *Takka-Faruzur-Malah*, Madras, 1909, 16, lith., MP. A work on the principles of Islam in verse.

Muhammad Abdu Rahman (publ.), *Talai-Mudi-Erakkana-Qissa*, Madras, 1909, 2nd edition, 16, lith., MP. The story relating to the shaving of the head of the Prophet.

Muhammad Abdur Rahman, *Firdous-ul-Asfia Fi Qasas-il-Auliya*, Madras, 1909, 688, lith., MP; see also IOL, 1909. A work in praise of holy

Muhammad Ghouse Labbai, *Movahibul Makkiya Majmaul Favayed*, Madras, 1909, 900, lith., MP; see also IOL, 1909. The book contains two parts. The first part gives the life of the Prophet and an account of his successors; the second part is an Arabic poem, with a Tamil translation on the life of Muslim saints.

Muhammad Kamaluddin bin Abd ul Kadir, Jildukkara (ed.), *Olivu Nama*, Pallapatti, 1909, 152, lith., MP; see also IOL, 1909, A brief account of the life of the Prophet.

Muhammad Sulaiman Sahib T.M.S., *Talim-Nama and Tarjuma-e-Hindustani*, Colombo, 1909, 288, lith., MP. A religious work.

Munshi Abdu Muhammad Ibrahim (publ.), *Vallati Masla*, Vaniyambadi, 1909, 24, lith., MP. A dialogue on the oneness of God.

Shahabuddin-Sam-Naina, *Tokai Malai*, Madras, 1909, 24, lith., MP. Poems describing the value of learning and setting forth the standard of social and moral excellence according to the precepts of the Prophet.

Shahul Hamid (publ.), *Majmuo-ul-Salath-ala Khyrul-Bariath*, Madras, 1909, 288, lith., MP. The first part contains a religious catechism relating to the offering of prayers; the second part contains a few select benedictions to be read on different ceremonial occasions.

Shahul Hamid, *Al-Favued ul-Asna-Fe-Thayamath-e-Asma-il Husna*, Madras, 1909, 120, lith., MP. A work in praise of the 99 names of God.

Shahul Hamid *Ash-Shaja-Rat-ul-Muhammaddiya Fe-Sirat-ul-Ahmadiyya*, Madras, 1909, 476, lith., MP; see also IOL, 1909. An account of the life of the Prophet.

Shahul Hamid (publ.), *Enayeth-Namah Fe-Thouzih-e Noor Nama*, Madras, 1909, 144, lith., MP. A work on the Oneness of God and in praise of the Prophet.

Shahul Hamid, *Tabir ul Monam*, Madras, 1909, 222, lith., MP; see also IOL, 1909. A work on dreams and astrology.

Abdul Aziz Sahib (Appa Pillai), *Bustami Mas-ala*, Ambur, 1909–10, 16, lith., MP. Gives an account of a supposed religious discussion between a Christian missionary and a Muslim saint.

Abdul Khadir Sahib, *Sakrath Nama*, Madras, 1910, 32, lith., MP. Poems describing the critical condition of the soul at the time of death, intended to encourage non-attachment, devotion to God and resignation to His will.

Abu Bakr ibn Muhyi-ul-Din ibn Ali, al-Umani, *Al-Barakin ul-Aliyyah*, Madras, 1910, 46, lith., IOL; see also MP, 1910. The manners and customs of a Muslim sect known as Shazliah in southern India.

Arba in Hadith, Madras, 1910, 48, lith., IOL. A translation of 40 Hadiths with explanations.

Moulvi Abdul Qadir Sahib (ed.), *Hilqatul Niswan fi Hiftah-ul-Jinan*, Tiralandur, Mayavaram Taluk, 1910, 92, lith., MP. A summary of the creed of Islam.

Moulvi Khadir Ahmad, *Tohafattul Tullab*, Cuddalore, 1910, 96, lith., MP. A booklet on etymology in Arabic grammar.

Muhammad Abdur Rahman, T. (publ.), *Pen Putti Malai*, Madras, 1910, 36, lith., MP. A work on the respect and regard due to women.

Muhamad Hussain Sahib, *Thowheed Malai*, Madras, 1910, 32, lith., MP. Stanzas in proof of the Unity of God.

Muhammad Ibrahim, *Ketab-ul-Fouth, Fe, Bayan-ul-Houth*, Vellore, 1910, 48, lith., MP. A poem on death and its fears.

Muhammad Ibrahim, *Pallu-Muthu-Malla*, Vellore, 1910, 36, lith., MP. An exposition in verse of the worthiness and the value of Islam.

Muhammad Jaffer Sahib, *Muzeluh-Tul-Shirk*, Melvisharam, 1910, 144, lith., MP. A work on how to abstain from sin.

Naina Muhammad Sahib (annotated by), *Yasin Tafsir*, Madras, 1910, 32, lith., MP. A commentary on the *Surah-e-Yasin*, the last chapter of the 22nd *parah* or part of the Quran.

Saiyid Muhammad Alim Sahib, *Peria Manhibatussibyanul Hanafi*, Madras, 1910, 128, second edition, lith., MP. A translation of 5 *kalimas* and of some sayings of the Prophet Mohammad.

Sha Muhammad Ziauddin Sahib, *Marajul Arifin fi Tarjumayah Minkajul Abidin*, Madras, 1910, 460, lith., MP. Gives the moral and religious principles needed for the attainment of salvation.

Shahabuddin-Sam-Naina, *Adabo Malai*, Madras, 1910, 176, lith., MP; see also IOL, 1910. A book on morality.

Shaik Abdul Khadir, *Fath a-Hur-Rahman-fi-Tafsirul Koran*, Madras, 1910, 32, lith., MP. An interpretation of the *Sura-i-Fatiha*, which is a preface to the Quran.

Shahabuddin-Sam-Naina, *Peer Sahib Ammal Hadiss*, Madras, 1910, 68, lith., MP; see also IOL, 1910. A short biography in verse of a woman saint, Peer Sahib Ammal.

Shahul Hamid (publ.), *Almunafa-ul-Atham, fi-Tafsir-e-Um*, Madras, 1910, 120, lith., MP. The literal translation of a portion of the Quran, with a commentary and marginal notes.

Shahul Hameed Labbai M.A., *Kissa e Yusuf Malai Alai Kissalam*, Madras, 1910, 200, lith., MP; see also IOL, 1910. An account of the life of Patriarch Joseph.

Shahul Hameed Labbai M.A., *Matalibush Shurfa fi Manakibul Khulfa*, Madras, 1910, 120, lith., MP; see also IOL, 1910. Gives a brief account of the lives of Prophet Mohammad's disciples and descendants.

Shahul Hameed Labbai M.A., *Tarjumah Arbayin Hadis Mayah Nasihat Namah*, Madras, 1910, 48, lith., MP. Comments on forty of the sayings of the Prophet Mohammad with suitable advice.

Shahul Hameed Labbai M.A., *Thaluhai Adavu Shafiyah*, Madras, 1910, 44, lith., MP. Rules to be observed during the conduct of daily prayers.

Abdul Aziz Sahib (Appa Pillai), *Vallatti Mas-ala*, Ambur, 1910–11, 20, lith., MP. The story of a slave girl who was able to answer some difficult religious questions put to her by Muslim priests.

Abdul Aziz Sahib (Appa Pillai), *Vallatti Mas-ala*, Ambur, 1910–11, 12, 20, lith., MP. Gives in fuller detail the same story as above.

Hajji Jilani Fakir bin Manna Muhammad (trans.), *Kuran—Kalam-ul-A'la*, Madras, 1911, 184, lith., IOL. Surat 46 to the end, forming the last five sections with a Tamil interlinear translation.

Muhammad Muhyi ul-Din ibn Muhammad Muhyi ul-Din, al-Shangamani, *Munirat ul-Nizam*, Madras, 1911, 264, 172, 380, 4, lith., IOL. An account in Tamil of the early Muslim conquests in Syria, Asia Minor, compiled chiefly from the *Futuh ul-Sham* of Muhammad ibn Umar al-Wahidi. With Arabic translation.

Naina Muhammad Sahib (commentator), *Tafsir Surat Ya-sin*, Madras, 1911, 32, lith., IOL. Being Surah XXXVI; with Tamil interpretation and commentary.

Naina Muhammad Sahib, *Jawahirul Masiyil*, Viracalam, Ramnad district, 1910–11, 1, 204, lith., MP; see also IOL, 1912. An authoritative exposition of the rules and principles to be ordinarily observed by Muslims.

Abdul Wahab Sahib, Amur Valai, *Lukman Nama Maya Sa Adat Nama*, Ambur, 1911, 20, lith., MP; see also IOL, 1911. A work on ethics.

Al Ghazzali, *Hi Raj al-Arifin fi Tarjumal Minhaj al-Abidin*, Madras, 1911, 460, lith., IOL. A religious work rendered from the Arabic.

Fakir Madar, *Muhyi-ul-din Malai*, Madras, 1911, 136, lith., IOL; see also MP, 1911. A series of poems celebrating the life and work of the Muslim theologian, Abd ul Kadir Jilani.

Hajji Jilani Fakir bin Manna Muhammad (trans.), *Kuran, Kalam-ul-ala*, Madras, 1911, 184, iv, lith., IOL. A work on Surat 46 to the end, forming the last five sections, with a Tamil interlinear translation.

Kader Muhiuddin Pulavar, *Purshana Tettidum Puvaiyargal Parashugal*

Pattidum Pangu, Madras, 1911, 80, lith., MP. A book of religious and moral advice to women.

Muhammad Abdur Rahman Sahib (publ.), *Minhatul Atfal*, Madras, 1911, 56, lith., MP. Lays down the rules to be observed in connection with prayers and fasts.

Muhammad Abdur Rahman Sahib (publ.), *Thohfatul Atfal*, Madras, 1911, 56, lith., MP. Lays down the rules for prayers and fasts.

Muhammad Abdus Salam Shaik, *Meygnana Talattu*, Madras, 1911, 8, lith., MP. Cradle songs of a religious and didactic character.

Muhammad Husain Labbai (Khanj), *Javahirummunazzarnat fi Silke Kalima Ti-n-Nafiat*, Cuddalore O.T., 1911, 340, lith., MP. A philosophical tract dealing with the unity of God.

Muhammad Hussain Pulavar, *Penbuthi Mala*, Madras, 1911, 36, lith., MP; see also IOL, 1911. Advice to Muslim women.

Muhammad Ibrahim Sahib, *Bustanum Ahkam fi Zikra Kissata Ibrahim bin-a-Adham*, Madras, 1911, 232, lith., MP; see also IOL, 1911. A sketch of the life of Ibrahim bin-a-Adham.

Muhammad Labbai, *Alkan Zil Afkham fi Manikabal Ghousul Aazam*, Madras, 1911, 616, lith., MP. Describes the miracles said to have been performed by Ghousul Aazam.

Muhammad Tambi, *Izamul Favayid Finizamil Akayid*, Perambur, 1911, fifth edition, 72, lith., MP. Treats of the unity of God and certain other Islamic principles.

Naina Muhammad Sahib (commentator), Madras, 1911, 32, lith., IOL. It is a work on Surah xxxvi with Tamil interpretation and commentary.

Saiyid Haji Jailani, *Kalamul Aala Tarjuma-a-Khamsa Juz*, Madras, 1911, 184, 1, lith., MP. A reprint of the last five parts of the Quran with an Arabic-Tamil translation thereof.

Shahul Hamid ibn Aidarus (ed.), *Rauzat ul-Asfiya fi Kisas li- Anbiya*, Madras, 1911, 12, 2 vols., 332, 444, lith., IOL; see also MP, 1911. Muslim accounts of the patriarchs and Prophets.

Shahul Hamid Labbai M.A., *Hikayat Latifa*, Madras, 1911, 96, lith., MP; see also IOL, 1911. A collection of short, interesting stories translated from Persian.

Shakul Hamid Labbai, M.A., *Kaziyarukkum Kallanukum Nadanda Kissa*, Madras, 1911, 56, lith., MP. An interesting story of a Kazi and a robber.

Sham Naina Labbai Aalim Sahib, *Irshad Nama*, Madras, 1911, 56, lith., MP. Treatise of the religious value and importance of prayers.

Abdul Ghafur Sahib, *Aan Faralu Ennum Palan Faralu*, Ambur, 1912, 43, lith., MP. Contains songs in praise of the Prophet Mohammad and other Prophets, poems describing death, the Day of Judgment, etc., and an account of a miracle performed by the Prophet.

Abdul Wahab Sahib, *Gosha Nama*, Ambur, 1912, 20, lith., MP; see also IOL, 1912. On purdah.

Dastagir Pasha, *Tavaddud Vallatti Mas-ala Mukhtasarun*, Madras, 1912, 32, lith., MP. A statement of a religious discussion bearing on Islam, said to have taken place between a slave girl and four learned men.

Faqir Madar, *Raja Manimalai*, Madras, 1912, 416, lith., IOL, see also MP, 1911–12. Contains an account of the lives of the Prophet Mohammad, his descendants and his four immediate disciplies.

Makhdum Pulavar, *Majmu Namah*, Madras, 1912, 40, lith., MP. A miscellaneous collection of varied songs on varied subjects.

Muhammadavil Karkari (ed.), *Assalahul Akbar Lide e Rihul Ahmar*, Melapalayam, 1912, 32, lith., MP. Arabic passages invoking the mercy of God, with meaning in Arabic-Tamil.

Muhammad Ibrahim ibn Saiyid Muhammad (trans.), *Majmu, Miftah-ul-Sulhani*, Madras, 1912, iv, 276, lith., IOL. A catechism of Muslim doctrine with regard to religious practice.

Muhammad Ibrahim Sahib, *Miftahussabhani Tarjumah-a-Majmaussultani*, Madras, 1912, 3, 276, lith., MP. Lays down the Islamic rules to be observed in offering prayers, giving alms, going on pilgrimage to Mecca, etc.

Muhyi ul-Din Abd ul-Kadir ibn Muhammad Nayinar Maraikkar, *Jawahir ul-Hadis*, Madras, 1912, 300, 20, lith., IOL. Discourses on some traditions of the Prophet.

Saiyid Muhammad, *Bisharatus Salakin*, Colombo, 1912, 16, lith., MP. Expains the significance of Bismillah and other similar religious terms.

Shahul Hamid M.A., *Kissa-e-Bibi Marayam*, Madras, 1912, 87, lith., MP. An account of the life of Bibi Marayam.

Shaik Ahmad Alim Sahib, *Ahkamul Haj-o-Umrah*, Madras, 1912, 124, 12, lith., MP. Lays down the rules of praying in Haj.

Muhiuddin Abdul Kadir, *Jawahirul Hadis Amaruf Bahzawajir-e-Sharif*, Madras, 1912–14, 300, lith., MP; see also IOL. An authoritative exposition of the sayings of Prophet Mohammad, with stories illustrating them.

Abdul Nahab Sahib, *Arab Tamil Kaadah*, Madras, 1913, 18, lith., MP. A primer in Arabic-Tamil.

Kamaluddin Sahib (Jildu Kara), *Abu Shahmah Kissahmayah Izwat Nayah Kissah, Part I*, Madras, 1913, 64, lith., MP. The story of Abu Shahma, who, in accordance to Islamic law, was beaten to death on a charge of adultery.

Kamaluddin Sahib (Jildu Kara), *Hidayat Namah fi Bajani Nur Namah, Part I,* Madras, 1913, 64, lith., MP. Deals with the relation between God and Prophet Mohammad and with the significance and value of following Islamic religious rules closely.

Muhammad Ibrahim Lebbai, *Majmuatul Avorad,* Madras, 1913, 104, lith., MP. Benedictory stanzas in Arabic to be recited by Muslims on auspicious occasions.

Muhammad Ibrahim Sahib K., *Ahsanul Najat, Part I,* Melvisharam, 1913, 56, lith., MP. A book explaining in detail the sayings of Prophet Mohammad.

Muhammad Ibrahim Sahib K., *Nasihatuzzavajain,* Madras, 1913, 132, lith., MP. Gives in detail, guidance for women in their social and religious duties.

Muhyi al din Abdal Qadir ibn Muhammad Nayinar, *Jawahir al-Hadith,* Madras, 1913, 300, 20, lith., IOL. An exposition of the Hadith.

Pir Muhammad Sahib, *Bismil Kuram,* Madras, 1913, 96, lith., MP. Verses in Arabic-Tamil dealing with the unity of God.

Pir Muhammad Sahib, *Meygnana Sakaram,* Madras, 1913, 40, lith., MP. A work dealing with the unity of God.

Shah Muhammad Ziya ul Din Kadiri (trans.), *Rahima,* Madras, 1913, 48, lith., IOL. Being Sa'di's *Karima* or *Pand Namah,* an ethical poem in Persian, with Tamil interlinear translation and notes.

Shaik Abdul Kader K., *Mokhta Sarul Imanvo Nasihatul Islam,* Madras, 1913, 20, lith., MP. Lays down the fundamental principles of Islam and gives certain religious instructiions.

Ibrahim Sahib (P. Muhammad), *Riyaz-e-Kadir Mayah Gulsar Namah,* Ambur, 1913–14, 60, lith., MP. Contains stanzas in different metres in praise of the Prophet Mohammad and Ghousul Azam, one of his descendants and the description of a miracle said to have been performed by the Prophet's daughter.

Kamaluddin Sahib (Jildu Kara), *Hidayat namah fi Bayan-e-Nur Namah Mayah Elm Namah fi Bayan-e-Adali Namah, Part 2,* Pallapatti, 1913–14, 112, lith., MP. Deals with the relation between God and Prophet Mohammad and with the significance and value of closely following Islamic religious rules.

Munnavar, *Nuru Masalah,* Ambur, 1913–14, 148, lith., MP. Gives hundred important religious rules to be observed by every Muslim.

Abd al Qadir Nayinar Lebbai, Kayarpattinam, *Pannirentu Malai*, Madras, 1914, 71, lith., IOL. Muslim religious poems.

Ibrahim Muhammad, *Tupparavana Bivi Maryam Kissa*, Madras, 1914, 44, lith., MP. An account of Mary.

Muhammad Ghouse Sahib, *Jawahirul Khamsah*, Madras, 1914, 344, lith., MP. On Muslim theology and religion.

Muhammad Hamzah Labbai, *Meygnana Rattina Alankara Kirttanai*, Madras, 1914, 144, lith., IOL. Islamic devotional verses.

Muhammad Ibrahim Sahib (trans.), *Takviyatul Asfiya fi Tazkiratil Ayolia*, Madras, 1914, 104, lith., MP; see also IOL, 1914. Contains the biographical sketches of the lives of saints, Imam Jaffarusadikh and five others.

Pir Muhammad Sahib, *Abu Shah Malai*, Madras, 1914, 92, lith., MP. Gives, in verse, the story of Abu Shahma, who was found guilty of adultery and was stoned to death according to the Islamic law.

Sheik Abdul Kadir Labba, *Pannirendu Malai*, Madras, 1914, 72, lith., MP. A book on Islamic belief concerning the Godhead.

Shaik Abdul Kader Sahib, *Futahul Fatah Fikhulasati Ahkamuunikah*, Madras, 1914, 300, lith., MP; see also IOl, 1914. Gives the religious duties to be observed during marriages.

Abdul Ghafur Sahib, *Ain Pural Palan Pural*, Madras, 1915, 40, lith., MP; see also IOL, 1915. Verses describing the different stages through which a soul has to pass after death, according to Islamic ideas.

Adam Shaikh, *Tazhkiyat-ul-Khavatir*, Madras, 1915, 276, lith., IOL. Arabic traditions of the Prophet with Tamil exposition, translated by Muhammad Ibrahim Sahib.

Muhammad al Kancavi, Kwajah P. *Mana'ih al-Qudsiyah fi Siyar Khulafa al-Chistiyah*, Madras, 1915, 52, lith., IOL. A work on the lives of the disciples of Muin-al-din Chisti.

Muhammad Hamzah Labbai, *Meygnana Rattina Alankara Kiratannai*, Madras, 1915, 414, lith., MP; see also IOL, 1914. Verses dealing with the mysticism associated with Islam.

Muhammad Hamzah Labbai, *Tala Fatihah*, Madras, 1915, 40, lith., MP. Gives out the method of offering prayers to the souls of all the Prophets in general and to those of Prophet Mohammad and his descendants in particular.

Saiyid Muhammad S.M., *Bidayatul Hidayah*, Madras, 1915, 224, lith., MP; see also IOL, 1915. Deals with the significance and value of closely following the Islamic religious principles with a detailed description of observing them.

Shah Muhammad Diya al din Qadiri (trans.), *Rahima fi Tarjummal Karima*, Madras, 1915, 48, lith., IOL. A rendering of the *Pand Namah*, together with its Persian text.

Husain, Khajah Muhammad, *Durarunnizam fi Jamuyul Ashar-i-Val Ahkamil Ezam*, Cuddalore O.T., 1916, 272, lith., MP. Contains long odes in Arabic-Tamil written in praise of Prophet Mohammad and certain principles of Islam essential for the offering of prayers.

Makhdum Muhammad ibn Makhdum Pillai, Kann Ahmad, *Rasul Ghaul*, Madras, 1916, Part I, 340, Part II, 328, lith., MP; see also IOL, 1916. Describes the incidents that took place during the lifetime of the Prophet.

Maulana Sahib Labbai Alim (trans.), *Dalayilul Khairat-vo-Shavarikul Anwar*, Madras, 1916, 16, lith., MP. A collection of devotional passages in Arabic with their meanings in Arabic-Tamil.

Miran Pulavar Saiyid, *Papparatiyar Ammanai*, Madras, 1916, 48, lith., MP. Verse describing the heroism of Ali and his marriage with Zeitoun.

Muhammad Husain ibn Ahmad, Kwajah, *Durar-al-Nizam fi Jami il-Ash'ar wa'l-Ahkam il-Izam*, Cuddalore, (Madras, printed) 1916, lith., 272, xii. Muslim devotional poems and doctrinal discourses.

Muhammad Ibrahim Sahib, *Tazkiyatul Khavatir fi Tarju Matiz Zavajir*, Madras, 1916, 276, lith., MP. Contains explanations of some of the sayings of the Prophet.

Muhammad Sahib (P. Khaja), *Hadiyatul Rabbulmatin fi Manakilish Shaiki Mayiniddin*, Big Conjeevaram, 1916, 112, lith., MP; see also IOL, 1916. Gives a full account of the life and career of Khajah Moiniddin Chisti of Ajmer.

Muhammad Sahib (P. Khaja), *Mana Ihulkudsiah fi Seyarie Khulfayichistiyah*, Big Conjeevaram 1916, 52, lith., MP. Gives short sketches of the lives of all disciples of Khajah Moinuddin Chisti.

Muhammad Sahib (P. Khaja), *Tuhfatul Aliyil Mabrid fi Fazayilil Shaikh Masud Usmanal Mahmud*, Big Conjeevaram, 1916, 24, lith., MP; see also IOL, 1916. A short sketch of the life of Saiyid Masud (saint).

Saiyid Muhammad Alim, *Babus Salat*, Madras, 1916, 52, lith., MP. Gives rules and regulations for the offering of Islamic prayers.

Saiyid Muhammad Alim Sahib (ed.), *Minhatul Atfal fi Talimulaamal*, Madras, 1916, 52, lith., MP. Expounds the fundamental principles of Islam for the guidance of the beginners.

Shahul Hamid Labbai M.A. (compl.), *Hidayatul Atfal*, Madras, 1916, 16, lith., MP. Expounds some of the divine commands to be learnt by heart by every young Muslim.

Shahul Hamid Labbai M.A., *Rasul Ghaul,* Madras, 1916, Part II, 340, lith., MP. Describes the incidents that took place during the lifetime of Prophet Mohammad.

Shaik Abdul Kadir Alim Sahib, *Fatahul Mutta al fi Hadiyatul Atfal,* Madras, 1916, 120, lith., MP. Explains the fundamental principles of Islam, together with a correct reading (intonations) of the Quran and some Arabic passages for recitation in trouble.

Abdul Kadir Sahib, *Kissah-i-Zaitun,* Madras, 1916–17, 80, lith., MP. The life and career of Muhammad Hanuf, the son of Ali bi Zaitun.

Abdulla Sahib Muhammad, *Karpa Mala,* Madras, 1917, 48, lith., MP. Lullaby songs describing the essential principles of Islam.

Muhammad Hussain ibn Ahmad K., *Durar al-Niran fi Jami-al-Ash'ar,* Madras, 1917, 272, lith., IOL. An Islamic devotional poem in praise of the Prophet, with some notes on prayer rituals.

Muhammad K.S., *Hadyata Mala,* Madras, 1917, 8, lith., MP. A didactic poem.

Muhammad K.S., *Mohibatus Sibian,* Madras, 1917, 160, lith., MP. A work on the fundamentals of Islam.

Muhammad K.S. *Muhiuddin Mala,* Madras, 1917, 8, lith., MP. A garland of verses in praise of Muhiuddin.

Muhammad K.S., *Rabibattu Jalaliyah,* Madras, 1917, 16, lith., MP. A handbook for the daily practice of *Jalaliyah.*

Muhammad Sahib Khaja P., *Faizus Salam Siratul Khizar Alaikis-Salam,* Madras, 1917, 80, lith., MP; see also IOL, 1917.

Muhammad Sahib Khaja, *Gulshan-i-Kasaidi,* Madras, 1917, 20, lith., MP. Poems in praise of the Prophet and some of His saints.

Abul Barkat (ed.), *Tulakai Namah,* Madras, 1918, 64, lith., MP. The prayer book containing the fundamentals of Islam.

Haji Muhammad (Singapore Moulvi), *Attufatus Samadiyah fi Tarjin Mat-i-Alfazul Arabiyah,* Madras, 1918, 464, lith., MP. The presentation of *Samadiyah* being the translation of Arabic words in an Arabic dictionary with meanings in Arabic-Tamil.

Muhammad Burhanuddin ibn Yusuf, Moulvi (trans.), *Tafsirul Kuran bi Ahsan-al-Burhan,* Parampet, 1918, 202, lith., MP; see also IOL, 1918. A commentary on a portion of the Quran.

Sharfuddin Abdul Mazahir Sahib, *Alkavalua Savab fi Tabhik-i-Masalatul Hijab,* Madras, 1918, 42, lith., MP. A work proving the necessity of veil in Islam.

Saiyid Muhammad, *Minhatul Atfal,* Madras, 1918, 56, lith., MP. An exposition of certain sayings of the Prophet.

Abdul Ghafur Sahib, *Vayat Paruz*, Madras, 1919, 16, lith., MP. A book on the Oneness of God.

Ibrahim Sahib Muhammad, *Kitabul Favut fi Bayanul Mavut*, Madras, 1919, 48, lith., MP. A work on after-life.

Muhammad Ibrahim, Rayavellur, *Kitab al-Fout fi Bayan al-Mout*, Madras, 1919, 48, lith., IOL; Pallapatti, 1920, a.e., 36, IOL. An Islamic poem on after-life.

Saiyid Muhammad Abdur Rahman Sahib, *Majmaul-Munajat*, Madras, 1919, 16, lith., MP. A collection of prayers invoking the mercy of God.

Shahul Hamid Labbai M.A., *Mizan ul Akyaz fi Tarjuma Tai-Mizan-ul-Ajuaz*, Madras, 1919, 96, lith., MP. Arabic grammar.

Ibrahim Khadar Muhammad, *Char Kursi*, Madras, 1920, 26, lith., MP. A genealogy of the Prophet, with instructions on how to follow him with prayers and fasts.

Ibrahim Khadar Muhammad, *Khasayia-i-Khadar*, Madras, 1920, 16, lith., MP. Poems in praise of the Prophet and His descendants.

Ibrahim Khadar Muhammad, *Unjal Nama*, Madras, 1920, 16, lith., MP. A collection of lullaby songs.

Ibrahim Sahib Khadir (Munsi Mohammad), *Majmu i-Koil Padam Ma-il Yadam Par Dal Padam Najmunissa*, Madras, 1920, 16, lith., MP. Songs sung on occasions of marriage, etc.

Jaffer Alim Maulana Muhammad, *Muhimmat Uddin*, Madras, 1920, 32, lith., MP. A rendering from certain verses of the Quran.

Muhammd Khatir (Ahmad bin), *Talimul Atfal fi Taqim-ul Akwal*, Tirunelveli, 1920, 36, lith., MP. An Arabic-Tamil primer.

I: Controversial Works by Muslims and Christians

Islamanavanum Kiristtuvanavanum Piracastiram, Tranquebar, 1803, 46, IOL. A Christian missionary tract containig a dialogue between a Muslim and a Christian.

Daniel B., *Sama Vadam*, Jaffna, 1844, 2nd edition, 12, IOL. A dialogue between a Christian and a follower of Prophet Mohammad.

Punari Mudaliyar (trans.), *Karuna Malai*, Jaffna, 1844, 3rd edition, 20, IOL. A translation of the life of Abdool Messee (formerly called Shaikh Sahib, a convert from Islam and an agent of the Church Missionary Society, 1776–1827), as published in one of the quarterly papers of the Church Missionary Society (viz. no. ixii, Midsummer, 1831).

Author unknown, *A Treatise on Mahomedanism*, Madras, 1871, 90, MP. A tract exposing the defects of the Muslim religion.

Muhammad Ismail, son of Mira Sahib, *Masputtul Iman Ennum Rattu Vahapiyar Mata Kantanai*, Madras, 1876, 258, IOL. A controversial Islamic religious treatise said to have been compiled from Urdu sources.

Khader Hussain Dr., *Mukamattu Marka Makuthuva Singaram*, Madras, 1883, 160, MP, MSB. A work in defence of Islam against Christian criticisms.

Saidu Umar Navalar, *Parasakti Akaval*, Madras, 1885, 8, MP. Stanzas in praise of Sakti.

Asan Sahib, *Kristu Marga Vilakkam*, Salem, 1892, 16, MP. A Muslim tract turning down the religious system of Christ in reply to a Christian tract criticising the religion of the Prophet.

Saidu Mukamattu Annaviyar, *Makabharata Ammanai*, Tanjore, 1892, 1st part, MSB. A religious work.

Muhammad Sulaiman Lebbai, Jaffna, *Charu bandham Eka Padarthovama Tarka Nirakaranam*, Jaffna, 1895, 8, IOL. Two controversial essays on the interpretation of a passage in the *Futuh al Sahm* and on some verses published in the same connection.

Abdur Rahman, *Tuhfatul Hindu*, Madras, 1896, 1st part, MSB. It demonstrates some defects of Hinduism. It contains the translation by a Hindu guru, Anantaram, a convert to Islam.

Javadu Pulavar, *Kodumallur Subramaniyar Padikam*, Madras, 1896, MSB. A work on God Subramanya.

Mukamattu Icumayil Cakipu, Mera Cakipu Kumarar, *Maspattul Imanennum Rattuvahapiyarmata Kantanai*, Madras, 1896, 4, 4, 258, 4, RMRL. A work on Wahabism.

Abdul Rahman Sahib, *Kristuvarkal Islamikal Sambashanai*, Madras, 1903, 22, MP. Conversation between Christians and Muslims.

Abdil Khadir Rowtar M.K.M., *Pamban Balasubramaniya Swami Kovil Kumbabhisheka Valinadai Cindu*, Madras, 1904, 20, MP. A Hindu religious work by a Muslim.

Muhyi al Din ibn Hamid Muhyi al Din, K.M. of Nagur, *Alim al Fasikin Jahul al Muskarkhin*, Colombo, Madras, 1906, 8, IOL; Kulasekaranpatnam, 1910, 2nd edition, 8, MP. Verses deriding certain worthless pretenders to learning, who interpret the Quran wrongly.

Muhammad Shamsuddin Sahib P.V.M., *Kiristu Mata Tiriyekattuva Maruppu*, Madras, 1907, 2, 36, MP. A Muslim tract against Christian doctrine.

Muhamaddappa Sahib, *Hindu Muhammadiya Makotsava Sabha Ranjani*,

Tenkasi, 1907, 16, MP. Account in song and verse celebrating the Hindu and Muslim festival at Tenkasi.

Shaikh Tambi Pavalar, Kottaru, Fakir Miran, *Ettu Criminal Case* (*Ellarkum Parkkattakunta Ettu Kiriminal Kes*), Madras, 1907, viii, 263, IOL, see also RMRL; Madras, 1917, 2nd edition, 312, RMRL; see also MP, 1907. Episodes from the *Ramayana* and *Mahabharata* represented as criminal cases, with trial and punishment.

Ceykutampip Pavalar, K.P., *Tevalokak Kiriminalkes*, Madras, 1908, 2nd edition, RMRL. A controversial work.

Katarmukaiyatin Ravuttar, N., *Pazanimanakaram Tevasttanam Cinnamavuttan Tintukkullil Kompanaiyal Manta Kuppucami Cettiyar Alankaram, Mutal Pakam.* Madras, 1908, 8, RMR. A work related to a certain Cettiyar.

Katarmukaiyatin Ravuttar, N., *Koyammatur Vazinataic Nutanamettu Cantanattevan Temmanku, Irantampakam*, Madras, 1908, 8, RMRL; Madras, 1911, a.e., RMRL; Madras, 1913, a.e., RMRL. A religious song.

Muhammad Jiyauddin Sahib Kadari Alvaiza, *Iyesu Kiristavarkal Pirappu*, Madras, 1908, 16, MP. A work on the birth of Christ.

Sheikh Tampi Pulavar, K.P., *Vetanta Vivakarak Kiriminal Case*, Madras, 1908, 8, 254, IOL; see also MP, 1908. Vedanta philosophy in the form of a law court report.

Abdul Khadir Ravuttar M.K.M., *Karpu*, Sotukudi, 1909, 2, 33, MP. A lecture on feminine chastity from the Muslim and Hindu standpoints.

Ahmad Ibrahim Alim Sahib, *Mottu Seykai Ottum Yeeti*, Tuticorin, 1909, 8, MP. A refutation of the heretical teachings of a Shaik.

Khadir Muhaiyadin Ravuttar N., *Palani Antavar Valinadai Chindu*, Dharapuram, 1909, 8, MP. Songs to be sung by the pilgrims on their way to Palani temple.

Khadir Muhaiyadin Ravuttar N., *Palanai Antavar Valinatai Chindu*, Dharapuram, 1909, Part I, 26, Part II, 16, MP. Songs to be sung by pilgrims on their way to the Palani temple.

Madar Shah Rauttar ibn Jamal Shah of Ambagarampalaiyam, *Sulakkal Mariyamman Ammanai*, Pollachi, 1909, 11, IOL. Stanzas in popular metre in praise of Goddess Mariyamman of Sulakkal.

Muhammad Ziya al Din, S., *Kataksamulla Napi*, Madras, 199, 107, IOL; see also MP, 1909. A Muslim missionary tract attacking Christianity.

Katarmukaitin Ravuttar, R.M., *Surulistalamiruntu Virapanti Mariyamman Kovilvarai Valinatai Alankaracintu*, Madurai, 1910, 12, RMRL, MP.

Pilgrim songs on the way to the temple of Goddess Virapandi Mariamman from Surulisthalam.

Khadar Ibrahim S., *Tanjainagar Mariyamman Vazhinadai Alankaram*, Trichinopoly, 1910, 7, MP. Pilgrim songs to be sung on the way to the temple of Goddess Mariyamman of Tanjore.

Miran Muhyi al Din, Sheikh, *Livavul Islam*, Madras, 1910, Pt. I, 126, IOL. A refutation of Christian criticisms of Islam.

Muhyiddin Fakir L.M., *Kottavi Gnana Maruppu*, Negapatam, 1910, 2, 22, MP. A controversial pamphlet on the teachings of Islam its being a criticism of another pamphlet named *Jivaratna Jagajothi Malai*.

Shahul Hamid Alim, *Jivaratna Jagajotimalai Kandanam*, Negapatam, 1910, 27, MP. A pamphlet controverting the teachings contained in the '*Jivaratna Jagajothi Malai*' of Muhammad Muhiuddin of Muthupet.

Abdul Sahib, *Tirukkalar Kumbabhishekakummi*, Tirukkalar, 1911, 7, MP. Pilgrim songs descriptive of the Kumbabhisheka or temple consecration ceremony conducted at Tirukkalar.

Abulkhair Ahmed Ibrahim, *Albur Hanul Jamil*, Negapatam, 1911, 15, 39, 1, MP. A reply to the criticism advanced against a Muslim religious pamphlet, *Tanbihuttalihin*.

Katirukani Pulavar, *Panja Varalatru Viḷakkam*, Madras, 1911, 34 (copy in my possession). A work on *Panja* traditions.

Muhammad Hussain Sahib A., *Deepa Tharisana Vazhinadai Patham*, Nellikupam, 1911, 5, MP. Pilgrim songs sung on the way from Pondicherry to the Saiva shrine of Tiruvannamalai.

Muttu Marakkayar M., *Kimiya Urai Marukhumtheruvikharivippu*, Topputhurai, 1911, 8, MP. A pamphlet on life after death, according to Islam, in reply to a criticism made by the Christians.

Katiraracana Maraikkayar, *Kiristu Mata Qihai*, Madras, 1912, X, 255, IOL. A Muslim polemical treatise attacking Christianity.

Khadar Ibrahim S. and Nagaiya Nayakar S.K., *Kulumayamman Tiruvila Valinadai Singaramum, Padikamum*, Trichinopoly, 1912, 7, MP. Songs in the Kummi style, recited by a pilgrim to his beloved on their way to the temple of Kulamayi, worshipped at Puttur.

Mahomedsa Ravuttar P., *Sembaiyamel Padikam Mudaliyenna*, Vriddachalam, 1912, 13, MP. Stanzas and songs in praise of the deities worshipped at Mudinaimanagaram.

Muhammad Kasim of Amritsar, *Bisharat Fatimah Ennum Miss Keat Charittiram*, Penang, 1912, ii, 64, IOL. The story of two English converts to Islam, Mr Joseph and Miss Keat and their happy marriage;

translated from the original Urdu by Talavai M. Sinnavappu Marakkayar.

Abdul Khader Sahib E., *Kurana Baibila,* Nellikuppam, 1913, 23, MP. A controversial publication seeking to prove that the sayings in the Holy Bible are incongruous and false and that Jesus is not the son of God

Adam Sahib Pulavar T., *Adhisaya Vella Cindu*, Marupalayam, south Arcot, 1913, 7, MP. Dance songs descriptive of the sacred river Kavery in flood.

Khadar Ibrahim S. and Nagappa Nayakar S.K., *Alankara Cindu,* Trichy, 1913, 7, MP. Songs in Kummi style in praise of Goddess Kulamayi, worshipped at Trichy.

Moideen Fakir C.M., *Mathabhimanam*, Adiramapatnam, 1913, 16, MP. A pamphlet that sets forth the religious importance of reading the Quran and criticises a remark by the Hon'ble Ahmad Tambi Marakkayar to the effect that the study of Quran should be only secondary to the study of English.

Miran Muhyi al Din, Sheikh, *Livavul Islam*, Madras, 1914, Pt. I, 120, IOL. A refutation of Christian criticisms of Islam.

Muhammad Ibrahim Sahib K., *Pasharattul Muminin* (*Mayah*) *Tanbihul Jahilin*, Melvisharam, 1914, 20, MP. A controversial pamphlet in reply to an unfavourable criticism on a work titled, *Ahasanunajat*.

Muhyi ul din ibn Monna Muhammad Kadiri Shuttari, Shaikh Miran, *Liva ul Islam* (*Puthagam*), Madras, 1914, vol. I, viii, 190, IOL, MP. Contains refutations of various hostile arguments against Islam, specially by Christian critics.

Abd al Qadir, K.M., *Intu Markamum Islam Markamum*, Tinnevely, 1915, 20, IOL. A reading of an English pamphlet on the similarities in the beliefs between Islam and Hinduism.

Muhammad Ibrahim Sahib, M.A. of Kilvelur, *Sri Avarai Ananda Swamigal Tottira pa Malai*, Tiruvarur, 1915, 13, IOL. Four poems in praise of a Saiva guru known as Avaraiyananda Swami.

Abdul Karim Sahib M., *Valaiyar Cindu*, Trichinopoly, 1916, 7, MP. Songs in the popular balled style, descriptive of the sports of God Subramanya as worshipped at Tiruchendur.

Kutbuddin R., *Vina Vilakkam*, Kuttur, 1916, 7, MP. Contains certain unfavourable criticisms on the writings of one A. Muhammad Tahir of Valuttur.

Muhammad Tahir Sahib A., *Kodiya Idi Minnal*, Valuthur, 1916, 40, MP. A Muslim controversial pamphlet replying to certain arguments contained in another pamphlet of a similar nature.

Shahul Hamid Alim Sahib, *Munnir*, Pattukota, 1916, 4, MP. A Muslim controversial pamphlet written in reply to another pamphlet criticising a publication of the author.

Shahul Hamid Alim Sahib, *Vachiradangam*, Pattukota, 1916, 4, MP. A religious pamphlet written in reply to another controversial pamphlet criticising a publication of the author.

Khadar Ibrahim S., *Drama Kalaka Chindu*, Trichinopoly, 1917, 7, MP. Ballad songs on a riot in a theatre in Trichinopoly.

Mohiuddin Sahib V.K.M., *Parikkal Tiruvizha Vazhinadai Cindu*, Parikkal, 1917, 7, MP. Pilgrim songs in praise of a Visnu shrine.

Shaik Miran Muhiuddin Sahib A.S.M., *Livavul Islam Puthagam*, Madras, 1917, 40, MP. A controversial work in refutation of various arguments urged against Islam.

Sheikh Tampi Pulavar, K.P., Kottaru, *Devalokak Kiriminal Case*, Madras, 268, 4th revised edition, MP. Criminal case of the celestial regions—therein are discussed, the righteousness of certain actions attributed to great personages in the Hindu epics and *puranas* in the form of imaginary trials before courts of law in the Devaloka.

Sheikh Tampi Pulavar, K.P., Kottaru, *Vetanta Vivakarak Kiriminal Case*, Madras, 1917, re-edition, 8, 313, IOL. Vedanta philosophy in the form of a law court report.

Abdul Khadiri Ravuttar M.K.M., *Ilakkiyankandatharku Ilakkanamıyambel*, Madura, 1918, 15, MP. Grammatical justification of (apparently ungrammatical) expressions: A controversial pamphlet.

Abd al Majid, P.G., *Atmat Tiravukol*, Trichinopoly, 1919, 32, MP; see also IOL, 1919. A Vedantist philosophical treatise in the form of a court case.

Madar Shah Rauttar ibn Jamal Shah of Ambarampalaiyam, *Sulakkal Mariyamman Ammanai, Kummi and Karana Chindu*, Pollachi, 1919, 18, IOL; see also MP, 1919. Poems on the cult of the Goddess Mariamman at Sulakkal, Pollachi taluk, Coimbatore district, edited by N.A. Siva Suryan Pillai.

Moidin Fakir L.M., *Condemnation of the Hon'ble Mr Yakub Hasan Sahib's Muslim Marriage Registration Bill*, Tanjore, 1919, 11, MP. A controversial work.

Muhammad Nainar (publ.), *Or Narpothanai*, Paramakudi, 1919, 15, MP. A controversial tract condemning certain statements said to have been made by Mr A.M. Muhammad Ayyuduns Sahib, President of a Muslim Society at Abhiramam, Ramnad district.

Nur Muhyi Dhin, V.M.K., *Or Cankarimaniyin Poli Narpotimaikku*

Maruppu, Madura, 1919, 13, IOL; see also MP, 1919. A Muslim controversial pamphlet.

Amjat Ibrahim Sahib K.A., *Gulsare Jannat*, Manargudi, 1920, 8, MP. A controversial tract relating to certain Islamic practices.

Muhammad Ayinuddin M.J., *Valaiyar Chindu*, Palghat, 1920, 8, MP. The ballad of the bangle in praise of Sri Subramanya Swami and his consort.

Sami Nayudu M., *Inbarasa Alankaram*, Palghat, 1920, 6, MP. Amusing popular songs on the story of a Brahmin girl said to have been given up to a Muslim by her own father.

Secretary, Muslim Sangam, Natchiyarkoil (publ.), *Muslim Sanga Mudarkamalam*, Madras, 1920, 212, MP; ANIL. A work containing a number of controversial subjects; a collection of 20 leaflets.

Katar Mukaitin Mastan, N., *Paktarkalukku Mutti Kotukkum Pazani Antavar Malai*, Pazani, 2 vols., 15, 15, RMRL. A work related to Pazani Antavar.

Secretary, Muslim Sangam, Natchiarkovil, *Muslim Sanga Marukamalam* (*Another Lotus Blossom of the Muslim Sabha*), Natchiarkovil, 1921, 206, IOL. A collection of leaflets on Muslim religious matters.

J: Secular and Other Works

Shah Ali Sayyid (ed.), *Civil Satta Puttakam*, Madras, 1850, vol. I, 213; Madras, 1854, vol. II, 244, IOL. A Tamil version of the civil law in force in the Madras Presidency.

Santulala, Salemkottai, *Tamizh Muhamattiya Nerivilakka Vokkabileri*, Madras, 1874, 61, IOL, RMRL. A brief Tamil-Urdu vocabulary.

Muhammad Ghouse, A.C., *Intustani-Tamizh Vokkabileri*, Rangoon, 1876, 72, 49, 24, IOL. An Urdu-Tamil vocabulary.

Muhamattu Kautu, A.C., *Parma Tamizh Okkapileri*, Madras, 1876, 72, RMRL. A Burmese Tamil vocabulary.

Ghouse Khan Sayupu, *Intustan-Tamizh Vokkabileri*, Madras, 1880, 31, MP, MSB. An Urdu-Tamil vocabulary.

Mukamattu Labbai, Kutavati, *Muthu Sevu Kanakku*, Palayamkottai, 1881, 16, MP, MSB; Madras, 1887, a.e., 12, MP. A work on how to handle pearls.

Muhammad Ghouse A.C., *Intustani-Tamizh Vokkabileri*, Rangoon, 1882, 72, 64, 24, IOL. A combined Urdu-Tamil, Burmese-Tamil, English-Tamil vocabulary, all these languages being represented in Tamil characters.

Kadar Sahib Pulavar V.S., *Valinadai Singara Padam*, Madras, 1883, 18, MP. An account in verse of a journey to Cuddalore.

Muhammad Ghouse A.C., *Intustani Tamizh Vokkabileri*, Rangoon, 1885, 78, 72, 25, IOL. Urdu-Tamil, Burmese-Tamil and English-Tamil vocabularies; the foreign words all being represented in Tamil characters.

Cevatta Marikkayar, Nakur K.A.V., *Malakhap Piravecattirattu*, Madras, 1886, 4, 6, 38, RMRL. Some songs on a journey to Malacca.

Kulam Katiru Navalar, *Maturaikkovai*, Madras, 1888, 77, RMRL. A poem.

Muhammadu ali Lebbai Alim, Syed Muhammad Lebbai Alim and Muhammadu Pulavar, *Makuthathu Sakathathennum Seethévithanathin Pokkisham*, Madras, 1888, 156, EFEO.

Mumakattu Mukamattu, *Muthu Chevu Kanakku*, Madras, 1888, 2nd edition, 12. A book describing the methods to find the weight of pearls for the Labbais who are greatly in this trade.

Mir Abbas, *Firing exercises for Martini-Henry Rifle*, Trichinopoly, 1888, 64, MP. A Hindustani book printed in Tamil characters for the use of Tamil Muslims.

Syed Abbas, *Payaring Exercise*, Trichinopoly, 1888, MSB. A manual on firing.

Syed Abbas and Mir Abbas, *Firing Exercise*, Trichinopoly, 1888, MSB. A work on how to shoot, meant for the Sepoys.

Kader Mohideen Ravuttar, T.A., *Ainutru Irupathaintu Raathal Konda kandi Vaipaadu*, Madras, 1890, 108, MSB. For the use of businessmen.

Mir Abbas Ali, *Tamizh-Hindustani Sor kalanjiyam*, Madras, 1890, 32, MSB. A Tamil-Hindustani vocabulary book.

Cakiputtambi, Kayarpattinam Muhamattu Leppai, *Muttalavukanitam, Part I*, Madras, 1890, 152, RMRL, MP. A book of tables of weights of pearls for the use of dealers.

Samuna Labbai, *Tarala Nayagam*, Madras, 1890, 16, MSB. A book on the weight and the quality of pearls for the use of Labbais.

Shamsuddin Saib, *A Wonderful Magic Prudent Computation* (*Vinoda Vichitra Jala Yukti Kanakku*), Madras, 1890, 16, MP; see also MSB, 1891. Arithmetical riddles and puzzles with solutions.

Mahamatu Sikandar Sayubu, M., *Maatantira Kooli Vaippadu*, Madras, 1891, 6, MSB. Tables for the use of Labbais.

Yusuf ibn Muhammad Muhyi al Din Maraikkayar, Nagapattinam, *Vanikakanitam*, Madras, 1891, i, 99, 4, IOL. A work on arithmetic for the use of Labbai traders.

Muhammad Kassim ibn Siddik Lebbai, *Tamizh Mudar Puttakam*, Colombo, 1892, 70, IOL. A Tamil primer.

Sheik Muhammad Labbai Alim Sahib, *Vatti Vilakku*, Madras, 1894, 32, MSB. A book on interest.

Muhammadu Mastan, *Tirumanapavani*, Madras, 1895, 94, EFEO. Marriage procession.

Muhamattu Nijamuhaiyitin Cakipu, Pappurajapuram Muhamattu Cahibu Kumarar, *Kutumpasamrakshani*, Madras, 1896, 24, 410, 6, RMRL; Madras, 1906, 2nd edition, EFEO; Madras, 1913, 3rd edition, 420, RMRL. A general work for children, women and everyone.

Muhammad Kassim ibn Siddik Lebbai, *Asrar al Alam*, Colombo, 1897, ii, 4, 200, IOL. A popular work on science.

Hakim Muhammad Nizammudin Sahib, *Nitisara Manjari*, Madras, 1900, 72, MP. Fiction.

Hakim Muhammad Nizamuddin Sahib, *Niti Vinoda Kathai*, Madras, 1900, 82, MP. Fiction.

Muhammad Nizam Muhyi al Din ibn Muhammad, Baburajapuram, *Mahajala Rahasya Vilakkam*, Madras, 1901, 2, 105, IOL. A work on the art of jugglery and optical illusions.

Yusuf Rauttar ibn Madar Sahib, *Manjai-Kollai*, Rangoon, 1901, 98, IOL. Ready reckoner (in English, Burmese, and Gujarati) containing reduction of weights, edited by Broker M. Essoof Rawther, etc.

Akpar Patusa, *Pulavunul Ennum Intiya Camaiyal Castiram*, Madras, 1903, 64, RMRL; Madras, 1908, a.e., 68, RMRL. A work on Indian cuisine.

Muhammad Jamaluddin Sahib K., *Valtu Padigam and Kalyana Kirtannam*, Madras, 1903, 12, MP. Marriage songs.

Siria Ratna Kavirayar, *Pulavar Attupadai*, Madura, 1903, 30, MP. A poetical work.

Siria Ratna Pulavar, *Pulavar Attupadai, Mulamum Uraiyum*, Madura, 1903, 38, MP. A poetical work with commentary by Gulam Kadir.

Muhammad Abd Allah Hakim Sahib B., *Arapu Tamizh Akaratai*, Madras, 1905, 144, IOL; see also MP, 1905–06. An Arabic-Tamil dictionary (incomplete).

Papucakipu V.S., *Jekan Mokana Cinkara Javalivarna Mettu*, Madras, 1905, V(1-), RMRL; Madras, 1906, a.e., V(1-), RMRL; Madras, 1908, a.e., V(1-), RMRL; Madras, 1912, a.e., V(1-), RMRL; Madras, 1919, a.e., V(1-), RMR. A work on music.

Abdul Khadir Ravuttar, M.K.M. *Madurai Tamizh Sanga Maniyam*, Madras, 1907, 2, 15, 2, 34, MP. An account of the Madurai Tamil Sangam in verse.

Muhammad Nizam Muhyi al Din Muhammad, Baburajapuram, *Maha Vikata Vinoda Kalanjiyam*, Madras, 1907, 184, IOL. A fund of witticisms and sportive sayings.

Muhammad Shariff O.E., *Manakanakku, Mudar Pakam*, Ambur, 1907, 99, MP, Arithmetic.

Shah ul Hamid ibn Aidarus (ed.), *Jawahirul Favaith*, Madras, 1907, 14, ii, 480, IOL. A series of essays on the 100 names of God, their mystic efficacy and talismanic applications, curiosities of natural history and outlines of physiology, medicine, and pharmacopaeia (pp. 57–80 and 105–120 are lithographed).

Shaik Abdul Khadir M.K., *Chandirakalamalai*, Sandarpettai, Tirunelveli, 1907, 16, MP. A poetical tract adressed to a woman.

Muhammad Ghouse Pavalar and Ghouse Muhammad Hussain Alim, *Jananukula Manjeri*, Cuddalore, 1908, 4, 36, MP. A pamphlet containing instructions regarding certain omens, astrological phenomena, magic, medicine, etc.

Muhammad Nuruddin T., *Karanak Katchi*, Cuddalore, 1908, 14, MP. A short description of a vision.

Abdul Khadir Ravuttar M.K.M., *Caramakavimanjari*, Sotukudi, 1909, 4, MP. Memorial stanzas in honour of P. Chidambaram Chetti of Madura.

Davud Shah Sahib, Naraiyur, B., *Hipnatism Ennum Manovasyatattuvam*, Madras, 1909, 8, 1, 188, MP. A work on hypnotism.

Davud Shah Sahib N.B., *The Text Examiner*, Madras, 1909, 96, MP. It contains exhaustive questions on the Tamil text for 1909 for the Matriculation Exam of the University of Madras, with full and concise answers.

Syed Muhammad Abdul Khadir Sahib, *Pudiya Civil Procedure Code Section-Kalum, Criminal Procedure Code Section–Kalin Surukkamum*, Madura, 1909, 47, MP. Abstract of the sections in the new Civil and Criminal procedure codes, the Indian Penal Code, etc.

Abdul Khadir Ravuttar M.K.M., *Nel Ikai*, Madras, 1910, 3, 33, MP. A work containing a paper on paddy and its cultivation and an essay on the giving of gifts.

Janiya Sahib K., *Salem Plague Chindu*, Salem, 1910, 8, MP. Songs of lament on the outbreak of plague in Salem town.

Khadir Ibrahim Ravuttar S., *Yanai Jivanamsa Kes*, Trichinopoly, 1910, 8, MP. A poem in popular ballad style describing a case for maintenance said to have been filed by an intelligent elephant before a judge at Mauritius.

Khadar Muhaiyaddin Ravuttar N., *Plague Charittiram*, Dharapuram, 1910, 7, MP. Songs about the outbreak of plague.

Madarsa Ravuttar J., *Ulakaccara Cindu*, Ambarapalayam, 1910, 8, MP. Songs about the ways of the world.

Nur Ismail Sahib S., *Dharmakhadal*, Madura, 1910, 15, MP. A metrical exhortation to live a righteous life.

Cinnakalai Ravuttar M., *Velayudan Chettiar Vinoda Alankaram*, Madura, 1911, 8, MP. Songs said to have been recited by an eyewitness regarding the tragic murder of one Velayudan Chetti of Pudur.

Daud Shah Sahib N.B. (Tavutsa Na.Pa), *Hypnotism Ennum Manovasya Tattuvam*, Madras, 1911, Part II, 4, 1, 325, MP; see also RMRL. A book on hypnotism.

Hassan Bava Ravuttar A.M., *Meenvettai Kummi*, Madras, 1911, 16, MP. Songs in Kummi style descriptive of the ways and pleasures of angling.

Nur Ismail Sahib S., *Gita Rasa Javalikal*, Trichinopoly, 1911, 14, MP. Amorous songs in praise of one Krishnavijaya Bhucendran, Zamindar of Marungapuri in Trichinopoly district.

Daud Shah N.B., *Pantitai Mesmerisa* (*Manovasya Tattuvam, 3rd part*), Madras, 1912, 2, 1, 214, IOL. A work on mesmerism.

Khadar Ali, Madras, 1912, 16, MP. Two stories pointing out the evils of ingratitude and disobedience.

Muhammad Abdu Karim Mastan Sahib, *Annamalai Chettiar Alankola Chindu*, Kayatar, 1912, Part I, 7, Part II, 7, MP. Lament songs in Kummi metre, describing how one Annamalai Chettiar of Kalugumalai committed suicide.

Muhammad Abdul Kader (ed.), *Madurasamanbaul Ula*, Kuttanallur, 1912, 46, MP. The annual report of the Madrasa-e-Manbaul Ula.

Muhammad Ibrahim ibn Hasan Lebbai, T.A., Mudukulatturi, *Najat ul Anam fi Nailil Maram*, Singapore, Madras, 1912, 54, ii, 5, 684, IOL. A treatise on Muslim lore concerning medicine, physics, magic, theology, and religious practices.

Abdulla Sahib P., *Perumazhai Cindu*, Nellikuppam, 1913, 7, MP. Ballad songs descriptive of the havoc caused by the floods in south Arcot district.

Muhammad Abdulla Sahib, Hakim B. (ed.), *Mesmerisa Patangal*, Madras, 1913, 1, 16, 4, 104, MP. Lessons in mesmerism.

Muhammad Sharif Sahib E., *Mana Kanaku*, Ambur, 1913, 2, 29, MP. Short mental arithmetic.

Tahir Sahib A. Muhammad, *Mesmerism*, Madras, 1913, 2, 95, MP.

Instructions for the practice of mesmerism with the help of illustrative charts.

Tavutsa Na.Pa., *Cuvasamé Uyir*, Madras, 1913, 136, RMRL. A work on breath.

Abdul Latif Sahib, Sowcar, *Sukshnaga Nitam*, Melvisharam, 1914, 45, MP. An easy method for arithmetical calculations.

Bawa Sahib T.V., *Beedi Cindu*, Salem, 1914, 7, MP. Ballad songs describing the *beedi* (a kind of patented Indian cigarette).

Daud Shah N.B. (Tavutsa Na.Pa.), *Personal Magnetism* (*Parama Rahasyam*), Madras, 1914, 166, MP; see also RMRL. A series of lessons giving hints on the practice of personal magnetism.

Daud Shah N.B., *Suvsamai Uyir*, Madras, 1914, 140, MP. A short treatise giving instruction for controlling the breath and practising yoga.

Husain Sahib, *Vipareetha Cindu*, Chidambaram, 1914, Part I, 8; Part II, 11; Part III (*Vadivulankara Cindu*), 7, MP. Ballad songs descriptive of the recent flood disaster near Chidambaram.

Uduman Aliyar Sahib S.P., *Eksuns Istandu Yavun Bukku*, Ranipet, 1914, 74, MP. Ready reckoner for determining the value of articles ranging in weight from one pound to ten thousand pounds at different rates.

Haji Usman Labbai (publ.), *Dalilul Ha Sanabi Ahvali Jalilul Kairat*, Trichinopoly, 1915, 24, MP. A report of the proceedings of the working of a Muslim school at Mailampatti.

Muhammad Mirin Sahib M.P.V., *Arubattu Naladi Pukazhasiriya Virutham*, Madras, 1915, 7, MP. A collection of stanzas in praise of Venkataswami Devar, Zamindar of Uttamanur.

Rajagopalachariar, *Rahima*, Madras, 1915, ANIL. A work by a Hindu.

Shahul Hamid Labbai M.A., *Muhammad Second Reader*, Madras, 1915, 84, MP. A Muslim school book.

Abdul Hamid D.M., *Parithapa Cindu*, Chidambaram, 1916, 7, MP. Ballad songs descriptive of the loss of lives and property caused by a cyclone in south India.

Abdullah Sahib N., *Repairing Report*, Chidambaram, 1916, 8, MP. Gives a report of the receipts and expenditure relating to the repair of a tank at Kuttanallur in the Mannargudi taluk.

Khadar Ibrahim S., *Mayirpidi Sandai*, Madras, 1916, 7, MP. Ballad songs descriptive of the strained feelings said to exist between a mother-in-law and her daughter-in-law in Indian households.

Shahul Hamid Labbai M.A., *A Tamil Muhammedan Infant Primer*, Madras, 1916, 30, MP.

Abd al Salam A.M., *Kaitozhil Castiram*, Madras, 1916–18, Pt. I, 120;

Pt. II, 120, IOL. A manual explaining the preparation of various medicines and articles of handiwork.

Aptur Rahim, *Rajacevaiyum Intiyavum, Allatu Kanam Mistar Aptur Rahimin Maruppurai,* Madras, 1917, xiv, 320, RMRL; see also MP, 1917. A work by Justice Abdur Rahim.

Pir Muhammad Sahib and Subbaiya Nayuda, V., *Payilvan Tirudan Paatu, Part I,* Kumbakonam, 1917, 17, MP. The story of a thief who endeavours to elope with a damsel.

Cinnappa Ravuttar, *Karanappurappattu,* Pallapatti, 1918, 4, MP. The song of the somersaulting pigeon.

Haji Ahmad Sahib K.S., *Madurasa Kuttanallur,* Mannargudi, 1918, 18, MP. Report of receipts and expenditure of a Muslim school at Kuttanallur.

Muhammad Ibrahim ibn Hasan Labbai, T.A., *Al-Tuhfah al-Samadiyah fi Tarjumat al-Ayar al-Arabiyah,* Madras, 1918, vol. I, 424, 8, IOL. An Arabic-Tamil dictionary, with the Tamil in Arabic characters.

Samsuddin Rowther K.M., *Kalvipayirchi,* Petai, 1918, 2, MP. A pamphlet on the value of the promotion of education among Muslim youth.

Shaik Miran Sahib (publ.), *Hidayatunnisvaran Silavu Kanakku,* Madura, 1918, 11, MP. The account of receipts and expenditures of a Muslim Girls' school at Sakkimangalam.

Abd al Salam A.M., *Kaitozhil Castiram,* Madras, 1919, re-edition, Pt. I, 120, IOL; see also MP, 1919. A manual explaining the preparation of various medicines and articles of handiwork.

Abdul Rahman Sahib (publ.), *Madarasa Manbaull Ula,* Tanjore, 1919, 49, MP. Report on the working of an Arabic madarasa at Kuttanallur.

Muhammad Ayuddusin Sahib A., *Rules of the Manfa-ul-Kairath Muslim Dharma Sabha, Abdhiramam,* Madura, 1919, 38, MP.

Muhammad Ibrahim Sahib M.K., *Puthumaicindalankaram,* Pallapatti, 1919, 10, MP. A ballad describing the havoc caused by a fever.

Muhammad Sherif (ed.), *Rules of the Muslim Balija Sabha, Natham, Madura,* Madura, 1919, 8, MP.

Muttu Ravutar, *Alankara Chindu,* Paramakudi, 1919, 18, MP. Ballad songs on the Muslim Badminton Team.

Secretary, Anjuman Rahmat (publ.), *Anjumane Rahmat Arikkai Pattiram,* Madura, 1919, 22, MP. Annual Report of the Anjumane Rahmat of Madura.

Ahmad Tambi Marakkayar, *Satta abaiyil Ettu Varusha Vélai,* Madras, 1920, 84, MP. Rendered from English; related to Legislative Assembly work.

Jannaba Sahib T.M., *Podiyin Perumai*, Trichinopoly, 1920, 6, MP. A work on the excellence of snuff manufactured by one T.S.R. Subramanya Pillai of Trichinopoly.

Khadar Muhaiyaddin Ravuttar R.M., *Viparitha Plagaue Chindu*, Periyakulam, 1920, 8, MP. A ballad on the terrible outbreak of plague in certain places of Madura district.

Mohitin Cayapu, T.N.B., *Appiyacak Kaittozil Potini*, Tancavur, 1920, III, 110, RMRL, MP. A manual on hand-work.

Muhaiyaddin Abdul Khadar A.N.V., *Pulaiyan Pattu*, Madura, 1920, 8, MP. The song of the *Pulaiyan* (depressed class) resenting the ill-treatment accorded to them.

Muhammad Mira Rowther A.M.C., *Singarakkummi*, Madura, 1920, 36, MP. Five Kummi songs descritive of a choultry built at Vallalnagar by one Arunachala Chetti.

APPENDIX II

Tamil Muslim Books Included in John Murdoch's Catalogue of Tamil Printed Books

Seykaptulkatir Pulavar, *Adaikkala Malai*. Prayers, praise of the Prophet, etc.: 26.*

Seyyitapupakkar Pulavar, *Apayesitulpustami*. About a Muslim saint who is said to have converted 1,000 fathers and 50,000 laymen: 18.

Vannaparimala Pulavar, *Ayiramasala*. About creation, heaven, hell, etc.: 173.

Seyyitapupakkar Pulavar, *Ipulisu Nama*. Prophet Muhammad converses with Satan on various subjects. Future punishments described, with various hells: 47.

Aptulkatar Sayapu, *Iratna Mukammatu Karana Sarittiram*. History of the Prophet: 72.

Mastan Sayubu, *Kiristumata Kandana Vassira Tandam*. Prose. The author lived at Trichinopoly where he often disputed with missionaries and catechists. He professes to have written this work after careful examination of the Bible. Among the points treated are the following: (i) Christ is man, not God as Christians assert. (ii) The Bible is not the Word of God. (iii) Christians are wrong in asserting that Jesus

*Numbers indicate the page number in Murdoch's text.

Christ came to this world to suffer and die for the sins of men, etc.: 140.

Aptulkatar Sayapu, *Karana Valtu.* In praise of the Prophet: 6.

Mastan Sayapu, *Mastan Sayapu Padal.* This work is published by Hindus as they consider Mastan Sayapu Padal as one of their *rishis.* The book is an imitation of the poems of Tayumanavar. It consists of Sufi philosophy and is interspersed with praise of the Prophet. The language is purer than the other Muslim works. It had a large circulation among Hindus: 42.

Savatu Pulavar, *Mukiyittinandavar Pillai Tamizh.* Poem on saint Mukiyitin: 42.

Kavikalansiya Pulavar, *Napiyavatara Ammanai.* History of the Prophet in verse: 24.

Makutum Mukmmatu Pulavar, *Nakur Patikam.* In praise of the Muslim saint of Nagore: 8.

Seyyitakumatu Maraikkayar, *Nuru Nama.* In praise of the Prophet: 24.

Saiyitapupakkar Pulavar, *Gnana Kummi.* In praise of t he Prophet, Hassan, Hussain, etc.: 26.

Takarpir Mukammatu Sayupu, *Gnana Ratna Kuravanji.* Man-woman dialogue about creation, God, prayer, etc.: 10.

Minnanuruttin Pulavar, *Osiyattu or Ponnariyamalai.* The fight of the Prophet, his victories, etc.: 48.

Valaipapa Sayapu, *Parasu Vilakkam.* About religious beliefs and practices: 48.

Kontalakan Pulavar, *Palulun Sukapai Malai.* On Prophet Mohammad's successors: 48.

Aptulkatar Sayapu, *Sakkarattu Nama.* In praise of the Prophet: 38.

Seykaptulkatiru Leppai Alim, *Sariattu Malai.* In praise of the Prophet, his kin, etc.: 28.

Saitapupakkar Pulavar, *Sira Kirttanam.* A history of the Prophet: 520.

Jamaluttin Pulavar, *Sukapulliman.* A Muslim guide to heaven: 23.

Utumanayinar Leppai Alim, *Taymakal Yesal.* A dialogue between a mother and her daughter about the Prophet: 23.

Anonymous, *Taymakal Yesal.* A dialogue between a mother and her daughter about a Muslim saint: 8.

Kasim Pulavar, *Tiruppukal.* In praise of the Prophet: 78.

Nayina Mukammatu Pulavar, *Tinilai Tankappattu.* Sufi philosophy: 32.

Tolukaiyadavu. A translation from Arabic. Prose account of Islamic creed, prayers, etc. Portions of the work are in Arabic with explanations in Tamil: 45.

Mukammatu Pulavar, *Unjarppattu*: 10.

Mukammatusain Pulavar, *Penputti Malai*. Advice to women: 22.

Makammater Pulavar, *Alipattusha Kappiyam*. History of the King and his sons: 43.

Seytakkati Pulavar, *Apushakama Malai*. About a king and his two sons: 61.

Aliyar Pulavar, *Intirayan Padaippor*. Tale in two parts about battles, etc.: 50.

Aliyar Pulavar, *Ipuniyantan Padaippor*. About a battle with a giant of Khorasan: 66.

Aiyasami Mutaliyar, *Kunangudinater Patirruppatanti*. Poem by a Hindu in praise of Mastan Sahib: 16.

Mukammatu Pulavar, *Saritu Malai*. Tale of a king: 23.

Kungumusu Pulavar, *Saiyitattu Padaippor*. About a king of Arabia to whose assistance the Prophet sent an army: 62.

Malukkumutali Pulavar, *Vaittiya Satakam*. Medical work containing 101 stanzas: 28.

Pulavunul. On cookery. Translated from the Persian.

Rev. P.P. Schaffter, *History of Mahomet*. 1856: 344.

Muhyi al Din Husain ibn Zin al Abidin, *Viveka Sakaram*. Translated from the Persian by Riza Husain Khan of Tinnevely, 1858.

Bibliography

INDIA OFFICE LIBRARY AND RECORDS, LONDON

Madras proceedings:
Madras Govrnor's Reports
Public Department
Madras Ministry Affairs

NATIONAL ARCHIVES OF INDIA, NEW DELHI

Home Department Files: Public, Political
Rajagopalachari Papers

NEHRU MEMORIAL MUSEUM AND LIBRARY, NEW DELHI

A.S. Venu Papers

TAMIL NADU ARCHIVES, MADRAS

Department Records: Public, Home, Education
Under-Secretary's Secret Files
Fortnightly Reports, Madras
Native Newspaper Reports, Madras

LIBRARIES

India Office Library and Records, London
SOAS Library, London
Madras University Library
Commemara Library, Madras
Maraimalai Adigal Library, Madras
Seethakathi Trust Library, Madras

Tamil Nadu Archives Library, Madras
Rosa Muthiah Research Library, Madras
Anjuman Nusrathul Islam Library, Kottakuppam

TAMIL NEWSPAPERS AND PERIODICALS

Al Kalam (Muslim)
Al Islam (Muslim)
Dar-ul-Islam (Muslim)
Dravida Nadu (Dravidian)
Dravidan (Dravidian)
Hafizatul Islam (Muslim)
Kudiarasu (Dravidian)
Muslim Murasu (Muslim)
Sanmarka Sanku (Muslim), *Karikal*
Santhi Vikatan (Muslim)
Shah Jehan (Muslim)
Swadesamitran (Nationalist)
Tattuva Islam (Muslim)
Taj-al-Islam (Muslim)
Viduthalai (Dravidian newspaper)

ENGLISH NEWSPAPERS

Deccan Times (Muslim)
The Hindu (Nationalist)
Madras Mail (Loyalist)
Mail (Loyalist)
Sunday Observer (Dravidian)
Revolt (Dravidian)

LIST OF PERSONS INTERVIWED

Raza Khan, Mohammad, ex-Madras Muslim League leader, journalist.
K.M. Sheriff, Tamil Muslim poet, writer and nationalist.
Mohammad Yousuf Kokan, Chennai, educationist, writer.
K. Veeramani, General Secretary of the Dravida Kazhagam.
A.K. Rifaye, writer, President of *Isha-at-ul-Islam*.
A.K.A. Abdus Samad, editor of *Manivilakku*, former President, Tamil Nadu Muslim League.
Moulvi Abdul Latif, former general secretary, Tamilnadu Muslim League.
Capt. Ameer Ali, Chennai, educationist.

Syed Mohammad 'Hasan', Tamil Muslim scholar.
S.M.M. Mohamadali, Professor, writer.
Janab Jainulabidin, Kottakuppam.
M.M. Husain, Kazi of Pondichery.
A.M. Ali, Karikal, Tamil Muslim journalist.
A.M. Yousuf, editor of *Marumalarchi*.

CATALOGUES AND ENCYCLOPAEDIAS

Barnett, L.D., Pope, G.U. *A Catalogue of the Tamil Books in the Library of the British Museum*. London, 1909.

Barnett, L.D. *A Supplementary Catalogue of the Tamil Books in the Library of the British Museum*. London, 1931. *Catalogue of the Library of the Madras Government Museum*. Madras, 1894.

Gaur, Albertine. *Second Supplementary Catalogue of Tamil Books in the British Library*. London, 1980.

Kani, R.P.M. *Islamiya Ilakiyak Karuvulum* (Tamil) (contains a Catalogue) Madras, 1963.

Mohamedali, S.M.M. *Meygnana Sindhu* (Tamil) (contains a Catalogue), Madras, 1990.

Murdoch, John. comp. *Classified Catalogue of Tamil Printed Books with Introductory Notes*. Madras, 1865.

Taylor, William, Rev. *A Catalogue Raisonné of Oriental Manuscripts in the Government Library*. Vol. I, II, III. Madras, 1862.

Madras State Bibliography.

Islamiyat Tamizh Ilakkiangal Nurpattiyal (Tamil). Kilakkarai, 1990.

Islamiyat Tamizh Ilakkiya Katturai Kovai (Tamil). Tiruchirappalli, 1978.

Encyclopaedie de l'Islam. Tome VI. Leiden, 1986.

The Encyclopaedia of Islam. Vol. III. Leiden, 1971.

First Encyclopaedia of Islam, 1913–1936. Vol. III. Leiden, 1987.

The New Encyclopaedia Britannica. Vol. 26. Chicago, 1990.

The New Encyclopaedia Brittanica. Vol. 2. London, 1998.

The Cambridge Encyclopaedia of China. New Edition. Cambridge, 1991: 340.

BOOKS

Abdul, Karim M. *Islaamum Tamizhum* (Tamil), 2nd edition. Madras, 1985.

Ahmad, Imtiaz. Ed. *Caste and Social Stratification Among Muslims in India*. New Delhi, 1973.

——. Ed. *Famiy, Marriage and Kinship among Muslims in India.* New Delhi, 1976.

——. Ed. *Ritual and Religion among Muslims in India.* New Delhi, 1981.

Ahmad, Rafiuddin. *The Bengal Muslims, 1871–1906: A Quest for Identity.* Delhi, 1981.

Aiyangar, S. Krishnaswami. *South India and Her Muhammadan Invaders.* New Delhi, 1921.

Ali, S. Husain. *Social Stratification in Kampong Bagan: A Study of Class, Status, Conflict and Mobility in a Rural Malay Community.* Singapore, 1964.

Allapichai, A.M. *Just a Peep into the Muslim Mind.* Madras, n.d.

Ameer, Capt. Ali. *Vallal Seethakathiyin Vazhvum Kaalamum* (Tamil). Madras, 1983.

Arasaratnam, S. *Merchants, Companies and Commerce on the Coromandel Coast, 1650–1740.* Delhi, 1986, 114–115.

Arnold, T.W. *The Preaching of Islam.* Reprint. Lahore, 1965.

Arunachalam, M. *An Introduction to the History of Tamil Literature.* Tiruchitrambalam, 1974.

Arunachalam, S. *The History of the Pearl Fishery of the Tamil Coast.* Annamalainagar, 1952.

Aziz, Ahmad. *Studies in Islamic Culture in the Indian Environment.* Oxford, 1964.

——. *An Intellectual History of Islam in India.* Edinburgh, 1969.

Aziz, E.M.E. *Ilankaiyil Islam* (Tamil). Jaffna, 1963.

Badger, G.P. Ed. *Travels of Ludovico di Varthema, A.D. 1503 to 1508.* New York, 1964.

Balagna, Josée. *L'imprimerie Arabe en occident (XVIe, XVIIe et XVIIIe siècles).* Paris, 1984.

Baljon, J.M.S. *The Reforms and Religious Ideas of Sir Sayyid Ahmad Khan.* Leiden, 1949.

Bannerji, B.N. *Religious Conversions in India.* New Delhi, 1982.

Bouchon, G. *Les Musulmas du Kerala à l'époque de la Découverte Portuguaise.* Geneve, 1973.

——. *Regent of the Sea: Cannanore's Response to Portuguese Expansion, 1507–1528.* Delhi, 1988.

Baqavi, A.K., Abdul Hameed. *Iyarkkai Matham* (Tamil). Tiruchy, 1930.

——. *Tarjumatul Quran* (Tamil). 6th edition, Madras, 1986.

Bayly, Susan. *Saints, Goddesses and Kings: Muslims and Christians in South Indian Society 1700–1900.* Cambridge, 1989.

Brass, Paul. *Language, Religion and Politics.* Cambridge, 1974.

Briggs, John. Trans. *History of the Rise of Mahomedan Power in India Till the Year A.D. 1612*. Vol. I. Reprint. Calcutta, 1966.

Bristow, Robert. *Cochin Saga*. London, 1959.

Carter, T.F. *The Invention of Printing in China and its Spread Westwards*. New York, 1925.

Chand, Tara. *Influence of Islam on Indian Culture*. Allahabad, 1963.

Chitty, Simon Casie. *The Tamil Plutarch*. Jaffna, 1859.

Dahmen, Pierrre. Ed. *Robert de Nobili: L'Apotre des Brames, Première Apologie, 1610*. Vol. III. Paris, 1931.

Dames, M.L. Ed. and Trans. *The Book of Duarte Barbosa*. Vol. 2. London, 1921.

Delacroix, S. Ed. *Histoire Universelle des Missions Catholiques- Les Missions Modernes*. Vol. II. Paris, 1957.

Demeerseman, A. *La Lithographie Arabe et Tunisienne*. Tunis, 1954.

——. *L'Imprimerie en Orient et au Maghreb: Une Etape Décisive de la Culture et de la Psychologie*. Tunis, 1954.

Devie, M. Trans. *Les Merveilles de l'Inde*. Paris, n.d.

Diehl, K.S. *Early Indian Imprints*. New York, 1964.

Dikshitar, Ramachandra, V.R. *The Cilapatikaram*. Madras, 1978.

Dumont, Louis. *A South Indian Sub-caste: Social organisation and Religion of the Pramalai Kallar*. Delhi, 1986.

——. *Homo Hierarchicus*. Rev. ed. Delhi, 1988.

——. *La Civilisation Indienne et Nous*. Paris, 1975.

Duverdier, Gérald. *L'Apparition de l'Imprimerie à Madras et sa Disparition à Pondichèry*.

Eisenstein, Elizabeth I. *La Révolution de l'imprimé dans l'Europe des Premiers Temps Modernes*. Paris, 1991.

Elliot, H.M. *The History of India as Told by its Own Historians*. Edited by Dowson. Vol. I, II. Allahabad, n.d.

Fatimi, S.Q. *Islam Comes to Malayasia*. Singapore, 1963.

Graham, William A. *Beyond the Written Word, Oral Aspects of Scripture in the History of Religion*. Cambridge, 1987.

Geertz, Clifford. Ed. *Old Societies and New States: The Quest for Modernity in Asia and Africa*. New York, London, 1963.

——. *Islam Observed: Religious Development in Morocco and Indonesia*. 1968.

Gupta, Ashin Das and M.N. Pearson. Eds. *India and the Indian Occean, 1500–1800*. Calcutta, 1987.

Hameed, K.P.S. *Ilakkiya Pezhai*. Madras, 1966.

Hardy, Peter. *The Muslims of British India*. Cambridge, 1972.

Hasan, Mushirul. *National and Communal Politics in India, 1916–1928.* Delhi, 1979.

Hourani, George. *Arab Sea-faring in the Indian Ocean in Ancient and Early Medieval Times.* New Jersey, 1951.

Huntingford, G.W.B. Ed. and Trans. *The Periplus of the Erythraen Sea.* London, 1980.

Husain, Mahdi. Trans. *The Rehla of Ibn Battuta.* Baroda, 1976.

Issawi, Charles. Trans. *An Arab Philosophy of History: Selections from the Prologomena of Ibn Khaldun of Tunis (1332–1406).* 2nd edition, London, 1955.

Irschick, Eugene. *Politics and Social Conflict in South India: The Non-Brahman Movement and Tamil Separatism, 1916–1929.* Berkeley, 1969.

Jackson, Peter. *The Delhi Sultanate: A Political and Military History.* Cambridge, 1999.

Kanakasabhai, V. *The Tamils Eighteen Hundred Years Ago.* Madras, 1904.

Kani, R.P.M. *Islamiya Ilakiyak Karuvulum.* Madras, 1963.

Karim, Abdul M. *Sirapurana Thiranaivu* (Tamil). Madras, 1980.

Kesavan, B.S. *History of Printing and Publishing in India: South Indian Origins of Printing and its Efflorescense in Bengal.* New Delhi, 1985.

Khaldun, Ibn. *The Muqaddimah: An Introduction to History.* 3 vols. Princeton, New Jersey, 1958.

Madan, T.N. Ed. *Muslim Communities of South Asia.* New Delhi, 1995.

Madani, Arignar. *Pothu Marai Ethu? Kurala? Kurana?.* 2nd edition, 1st edition, 1968. Dindigul, 1974.

Major, R.H. Ed. *India in the 15th Century.* New York, n.d.

Malamoud, Charles. Trans. *Ahkanase Nikitine: Le Voyage au delà des Trois Mers.* Paris, 1982.

Mangaiyarkarasai. *Varalaru Kanda Vaikom Veerar* (Tamil). Madras, 1980.

Mathew, K.S. *Portuguese Trade with India in the 16th Century.* New Delhi, 1983.

Metcalf, Barbara. *Islamic Revival in British India: Deoband, 1860–1900.* Princeton, New Jersey, 1982.

Meile, Pierre. 'Les yavanas dans l'Inde Tamoule'. *Mélanges Asiatiques.* Paris, 1940–41.

Meuwese, C. *L'Inde du Bouddha Vue par les Pélerins Chinois Sous la Dynastie Tang.* Paris, 1961.

Miller, Roland. *Mappila Muslims of Kerala.* Madras, 1976.

Mines, Mattison. *Muslim Merchants: The Economic Behaviour of an Indian Muslim Community.* New Delhi, 1972.

More, J.B.P. *The Political Evalution of Muslims in Tamil Nadu and Madras, 1930–1947.* Hyderabad, 1997.

Morelet, Arthur. Translated from Portuguese. *Journal de Voyage de Vasco da Gama.* Lyon, MDCCCLXIV.

Muhammad Ali, S.M. Ed. *Meygnana Sindhu* (Tamil), Madras, 1900.

Muhammad Ali, S.M. Publ. *Lal Gauher Natakam.* Reprint. Madras, 1990.

Muhammad Ali, S.M. *Thaiyar Sultan Natakam.* Reprint. Madras, 1990.

Mujeeb, M. *The Indian Muslims.* London, 1967.

Nainar, S.M.M. *Bahar-i-Azam Jahi, Ghulam Abdul Qadir Nazir.* Islamic series, No. 11. Madras University, Madras, 1950.

Mustafa, Manavai. *Tamizhil Islamiya Meygnana Ilakkiyangal* (Tamil). Madras, 1980.

——. *Tamizhil Islamiya Ilakkiya Vadivangal* (Tamil). Madras, 1986.

Nambiar, O.K. *The Kunjalis: Admirals of Calicut.* Bombay, 1963.

Narasimhan, C.R. *Rajagopalachari: A Biography.* London, 1993.

Navalar, Arumuka. Ed. *Periya Puranam by Cekkilar.* Madras, 1884.

Nayinar Muhammad, C., P.M. Mansoor, V.M.A. Noor Maideen. *Islamiya Tamizh Nul Attavanai.* Tiruchirappalli, 1978.

Pedersen, Johannes. *The Arabic Book.* Translated by Geoffrey French, Princeton, New Jersey, 1984.

Periyar, E.V.R. *Ina Izhivu Ozhiya Islamay Nanmarunthu* (Tamil). Erode, 1947.

Pillai, M.S. Purnalingam. *Islam Founder and Islamic Poets.* Tirunelveli, 1942.

Pires, Tomé. *The Sumo Oriental.* Liechenstein, 1967.

Priolkar, A.K. *The Printing Press in India.* Bombay, 1958.

Rahim, M.R.M. Abdul. *Islamiya Kalai Kalanjiyam.* 3 vols. Madras, 1976.

Rajamanickam, S. *Vanakkam* (Tamil). Tuticorin, 1963.

Rakuman, Dr. Abdul, Dr. Muhammad Ali Jinnah. *Islamiyat Tamizh Ilakkiyangal, Nur Pattiyal* (Tamil). Kilakorai, 1990.

Rasool, Janab. *Parda Engai?* (Tamil). Dindigul, n.d.

——. *Seerazhiya Cinemavai Paarunkal.* Dindigul, n.d.

Reinaud, M. Ed. and trans. *Relation des Voyages Faits par les Arabes et les Persans dans l'Inde et à la Chine dans le IXe Siècle de l'ère Chrétienne.* 1st ed. Paris, 1845. 2nd ed. Osnabruck, 1988.

Reiniche, M.L. *Tirouvannamalai, Un Lieu Saint Sivaite du Sud de l'Inde.* Vol. 4, Paris, 1989.

ricci, Aldo Trans. *The Travels of Marco Polo.* London, 1950.

Rifaye, A.K. *Tamizhakathil Islamiyar Varularu* (Tamil). Tenkasi, 1988.

——. *Samuthaya Neerotathil Sangamam.* Tenkasi, 1987.

——. *Kavmin Kavalar*. Tenkasi, 1983.

——. *Kayithe Millath Pesukiraar*. Tirunelveli, 1983.

Rosny, Léon de. *La Bibliothèque Tamoule de M. Ariel de Pondichèry*. Paris, 1866.

Rowlandson, M.J. *Tohfut-ul-Mujahideen*. London, 1833.

Ryan, N.J. *A History of Malaysia and Singapore*. Kuala Lumpur, 1976.

Saali, J.M. *Islamiyat Tamizh Kaaviyangal*. Madras, 1978.

——. *Tamizhakathu Tarkakal*. Madras, 1981.

Sachau, Edward. *Alberuni's India. An Account of the Religion, Philosophy, Literature, Geography, Chronology, Astronomy, Customs, Laws and Astrology of India about A.D. 1030*. Vol. I and II. New Delhi, 1983.

Sami, A.M. *Tamizhil Islamiya Ithazhkal* (Tamil). Madras, 1994.

Sadiq, Muhammad. *A History of Urdu Literature*. 2nd edition, Delhi, 1984.

Sastri, S.M. Ed. *McCrindle's Ancient India as Described by Ptolemy*. Calcutta, 1927.

Sayubu, Marakkayar. *Mastan Sahib Waliullah Varalaru Pezhai*. Madras, 1981.

Sheriff, K.M. *Vallal Sethakathiyin Varalaru*. (Tamil). Madras, 1988.

Sha, P. Daud (Dawood). *Aariyarkku Oru Vedigundu* (Tamil). Madras, 1927.

Shu'ayb, Takya. *Arabic, Arwi and Persian in Sarandib and Tamil Nadu*. Madras, 1993.

Sourdel, Dominique. *L'Islam*. Paris, 1981.

Spate, O.H.K., A.T.A. Learmouth, B.H. Farmer. *India, Pakistan and Ceylon, The Regions*. London, 1960.

Subramanyam, S. *Improvising Empire: Portuguese Trade and Settlement in the Bay of Bengal, 1500–1700*. Delhi, 1990.

Sulaiman, S.M., M.M. Ismail. *Islam, Indian Religions and Tamil Culture*. Madras, 1977.

Tara Chand. *Influence of Islam on Indian Culture*. Allahabad, 1954.

Thani Nayagam, S. *A Reference Guide to Tamil Studies*. Kuala Lumpur, 1966.

Thomas, P. *Christians and Christianity in India and Pakistan*. London, 1954.

Thurston, Edgar. *Castes and Tribes of Southern India*. Vols. II, IV, V, VI. Madras, 1909.

Troll, W. Christian. Ed. *Islam in India: Studies and Commentaries*. Vol. 1, 1985. Vol. 2, New Delhi, 1982.

——. *Sayyid Ahmad Khan: A Reinterpretation of Muslim Theology*. New Delhi, 1978.

Toderini. *De la Littérature des Turcs*. 3 vols. Paris, 1789.

Venkataramannaya. *The Early Muslim Expansion in South India*. Madras, 1942.

Veeramani, K. Ed. *Periyar Kalanjiyam*. 4 vols. 2nd edition, Madras.

Uvais, Dr Muhammad. *Islam Valartha Tamizh* (Tamil). Madras, 1984.

Uvais, Muhammad, M., P.M. Ajmal Khan. *Islamiyat Tamizh Ilakkiya Varalaru* (Tamil). Vol. 1. Madurai, 1986.

Uvais, Muhammad, M. *Islamiyat Tamizh Ilakkiya Varalaru* (Tamil). Vol. 2. Madurai, 1990.

Uvais, Muhammad, M. *Islamiyat Tamizh Ilakkiya Varalaru* (Tamil). Vol. 3. Madurai, 1994.

Uvais, Dr. M.M. *Tamizh Ilakkiya Arabu Sol Akarathi*. 1983.

Uwise, M.M. *Muslim Contribution to Tamil Literature*. Madras, 1990.

Venkataramanya, N. *Early Muslim Expansion in South India*. Madras, 1942.

Washbrook, D.A. *The Emergence of Provincial Politics: The Madras Presidency, 1870–1920*. Cambridge, 1976.

Weber, Jacques. *Les Etablissements Français en Inde au XIXe Siècle (1816–1914)*, Paris, 1988.

Weber, Max. *The Religion of India: The Sociology of Hinduism and Buddhism*. Glencoe, Illinois, 1958.

Yule, Colonel. Ed. and trans. *The Book of Marco Polo*. Vol. 1, 2. London, 1903.

Zubaid, Ahmad. *The Contribution of Indo-Pakistan to Arabic Literature*. Reprint. Lahore, 1968.

Zvelebil, K.V. *A History of Indian Literature*. Vol. X. Tamil Literature, Nederland, 1974.

ARTICLES

Arasaratnam, S. 'A Note on Periathamby Marakkayar'. *Tamil Culture, Journal of the Academy of Tamil Culture*. XI, no. 1. (1964).

Aubin, Jean. 'Les princes d'Ormuz du XIIIe au XVe siècle'. *Journal Asiatique*. 241 (1953): 77–138.

Birge, Kingsley. 'The Printing of Books in Turkey in the 18th century'. *The Moslem World*. XXXIII (1943): 292–294.

Bjerrum, H. 'The Tamil Moslems of South India'. *The Moslem World*. 10 (1920): 172–175.

Bouchon, G., D. Lombard. 'India and the Indian ocean in the Fifteenth Century'. In *India and Indian Ocean, 1500–1800.* Ed. Ashin Das Gupta, M.N. Pearson, Oxford, 1987.

Carter, T.F. 'Islam as a Barrier to Printing'. *The Moslem World.* XXXIII (1943): 213–216.

Diehl, K.S. 'The Printing Press-An Agent of Strength'. *Journal of Tamil Studies.* 2, Part II (October 1970) II: 1–13.

D'Souza, Victor. 'Status Groups among Moplahs on the South-west Coast of India', In *Caste and Social Stratification among Muslims in India.* Ed. Imtiaz Ahmad. Delhi, 1978, 45–60.

Duverdier, Gérald. 'L'Apparition de l'Imprimerie à Madras et sa Disparition à Pondichèry'. *Sonderdruck Aus Dem Gutenberg.* Jahrbuch, 1976.

Elliot, Walter. 'The Edifice formerly known as the Chinese or Jaina Pagoda at Nagapatnam'. *Indian Antiquary.* VII: 2247.

Gaborieau, Marc. 'Life Cycle Ceremonies of Converted Muslims in Nepal and Northern India'. Yohannan Friedman. *Islam in Asia.* (Jerusalem) 1 (1984): 241–262.

Karashima, Noburu. 'Trade Relations between South India and China During the 13th and 14th Centuries'. *Journal of East-West Maritime Relations.* 1, 2 (1989): 9–81.

Lombard, Denys and G. Bouchon. 'India and the Indian Ocean in the 15th Century'. In *India and the Indian Ocean, 1500–1800.* Ed. Das Gupta, Ashin, Pearson. Oxford, 1987.

Mcpherson, K. 'The Social Background and Politics of the Muslims of Tamilnadu, 1901–1937'. *IESHR.* VI (December, 1969): 381–402.

McGilvray, Dennis, B. 'Arabs, Moors and Muslims: Sri Lankan Muslim ethnicity in regional perspective'. In *Contributions to Indian Sociology.* 32, 2 (1998): 435–483.

Mines, Mattison. 'Islamisation and Muslim Ethnicity in South India'. *Man.* 10, no. 3 (1975).

——. 'Social Stratification among Muslim Tamils in Tamilnadu'. In *Caste and Social Stratification among Muslims in India.* Ed. Imtiaz Ahmad (Delhi, 1978): 61–71.

More, J.B.P. 'Some Maritim Aspects of the Indian Ocean Region'. *Indian Ocean and Cultural Interaction.* (*A.D. 1400–1800*). Ed. K.S. Mathew, Pondicherry, 1996.

——. 'The Marakkayar Muslims of Karikal, South India'. *Journal of Islamic Studies* (Oxford) 2, 1 (1991): 25–44.

——. 'Musim Evolution and Conversions in Karikal, South India'. *Islam and Christian-Muslim Relations* (Birmingham) 4, 1 (June 1993): 65–82.

——. 'A Tamil Muslim Sufi'. In *Islam and Christian-Muslim Relations.* 10, 1 (1999) 15–21.

Ner, Marcel. 'Les Musulmans de l'Indochine Française'. *Bulletin d'Ecole Française d'Extrême Orient.* XLI (1941): 151–200.

Ray, Haraprasad. 'Indian Settlements in China—An Exploration of the Phenomenon of Indian Diaspora from A.D. 1015 (The Chola period) to 1487 (End of Cheghua Reign in China)'. In *Indian Ocean and Cultural Interaction (A.D. 1400–1800).* Ed. K.S. Mathew, (Pondicherry, 1996): 52–81.

Rahim, M. Abdul. 'Islam in Negapatam'. *Bulletin of the Institute of Traditional Cultures.* (July–December, 1974): 85–99.

Rajamanickam, S. 'Padre Henrique Henriques, The Father of the Tamil Press'. Paper presented at the Second Tamil International Seminar, 1968.

Robinson, Francis. 'Islam and Muslim Separatism'. In *Political Identity in South Asia.* Eds. David Taylor and Malcolm Yapp. London (1979): 78–112.

——. 'Islam and Muslim Society in South Asia'. *Contributions to Indian Sociology.* 7, 2 (1983): 185–203.

——. 'Technology and Religious Change: Islam and the Impact of Print'. *Modern Asian Studies.* 27(1) (1993): 229–251.

Schulman, David. 'Muslim Popular Literature in Tamil: The Tamirmancari Malai'. *Islam in Asia.* Ed. Y. Freiedman, Colo, 1 (1984): 174–207.

Syed, S. 'Urdu Journalism in Tamil Nadu from 1840 to 1850'. *Annals of Oriental Research.* XXVII, Parts I and II.

Uwise, M.M. 'Muslim Literary Forms in Tamil Literature', paper presented at the Second International Seminar of Tamil Studies. 1968.

Vinson, Julien. 'La Domination Musulmane dans le sud de l'Inde'. *Revue du Monde Musulman.* 23 (1913): 199–204.

——. 'Les Musulmans du sud de l'Inde'. *Revue du Monde Musulman.* 2, 6 (1907): 199–204.

——. 'Un Journal Musulman en Langue Tamoule'. *Revue du Monde Musulman.* 1, 4: 622–23.

Wright, Theodore. 'The Muslim League of South India Since Independence: A Study in Minority Group Political Strategies'. *The American Political Science Review.* LX (3 September 1966): 579–99.

MISCELLANEOUS

Census of India 1931. Vol. XIV, Madras, 1932.

Muslim Sangha Mudarkamalam (A collection of 20 leaflets) Natchiarkovil, 1919, 205.

Muslim Sangha Marukamalam. (a collection of leaflets), Natchiarkovil, 1921, 206.

Qadianikalin Tavarana Kolkaikal. Madras, 1935.

More, J.B.P., Review of Susan Bayly's *Saints, Goddesses and Kings: Muslims and Christians in South Indian Society, 1700–1900*. In *Contributions to Indian Sociology*. New Delhi, 28, 1994.

——. Review of C.R. Narasimhan's *Rajagopalachari, A Biography*. *Journal of South Asian Studies*. Australia, XIX, 2, December 1996.

Mcpherson, K. 'The Political Development of Urdu and Tamil- Speaking Muslims of the Madras Presidency, 1901–1937', M.A. dissertation, University of Western Australia, 1968.

Rahim, M. Abdul. 'The Muslims of Tamil Nadu 1801–1900 A.D.', Ph.d. dissertation, Madras University, 1980.

Souvenir—*Islamiya Tamizh Aarayichi Maanadu Nikazhchi Kovai*. (Tamil). Tiruchirappalli, 1973.

Index

T

X

Y

Z